ALPHA 92

ALPHA 92

Current Research in Literacy: Literacy Strategies in the Community Movement

Edited by

Jean-Paul Hautecoeur

ALPHA 92
Prepared by the
Unesco Institute for Education

with the assistance of the
Direction de la formation générale des adultes (DFGA)
and of the Direction des Communications of the
Ministry of Education of Quebec

and the National Literacy Secretariat of the Department
of Multiculturalism and Citizenship of Canada

Cover photograph
"Les balles rouges de l'espace"
by André Mathieu, sculptor

ISBN 92 820 1061 9

Unesco Institute for Education
Feldbrunnenstrasse 58
W-2000 Hamburg 13
Germany

Printed by
Robert Seemann · Bramfelder Strasse 55
W-2000 Hamburg 60 · Tel. 040/61 89 46

TABLE OF CONTENTS

INTRODUCTION

Jean-Paul Hautecoeur

International Literacy Year, 1990, marked for many not a renewal of the mandate in the "fight against illiteracy", but rather the end of an affair. At least the end of an uncomplicated affair. It was during this time that the simplified phenomenon, known as "functional illiteracy", was formulated, and during which all kinds of offensive, healing or preventive measures were taken.

Fortunately, the situation has become more complex. Allegedly, the idea of illiteracy has been transformed into a many-sided issue with conflicting, expansive or regressive trends. It cannot be measured as is done for road accidents, or even for scholastic failures, nor do we know who has the most appropriate skills for treating it. In some countries, the various literacy initiatives have been channelled into regular adult education programs. In others, on the contrary, the area of activities has considerably expanded to include many different participants.

To understand the changes that have occurred in these recent international developments, a closer examination of popular movements in different regions was required. Popular associations had been responsible for the first initiatives in the literacy movement. They are still involved with practically the whole spectrum of current initiatives. This document focuses on the experiences of the popular movement, which started with a local event, simple in the beginning.

In 1980, at Val Morin, Quebec, the first international seminar on popular literacy was also the occasion of the first publication of *Alpha: ALPHA 80*. In 1991, in Namur, Belgium, a seminar brought together all the authors of *ALPHA 92*, under the common theme of the popular movement in literacy. Apart from the continuity of publication and the similarity of the theme, the two seminars were completely different events.

In 1980, militant volunteers gathered together to create a strong, committed movement, in an unoccupied and almost uncharted territory[1]. Ten years later, International Literacy Year demonstrated how much the theme of literacy had "caught on" in many industrialized countries, especially in North America. Literacy has become a "dominant" ideological theme, crystallizer of social consensus, adopted by numerous and various organizations, and yet it has also already become commonplace. In several countries, it has been replaced by concerns that are closer to the economic market and employment, or has been integrated into the vast educational market.

After the climax of International Literacy Year - which not only enabled the work of literacy organizations to be recognized, but also revealed the current dominant trends, better identified the fringe elements and better indicated the crises - where was the independent literacy movement? Can it continue to be referred to as a specific movement, in the singular? What experimental and defining part is the literacy movement now playing? What places and what roles are being fulfilled by popular associations in different national contexts? What are they now saying about literacy? Which other players are they associated with, or would they like to be teamed up with? Why and for whom are they working? With what means and to what end?.

These questions are the main focus of *ALPHA 92*, under the generic heading *"Literacy Strategies in the Community Movement"*. Around fifteen different popular associations participated in the realization of the publication - from Belgium, Quebec, the United Kingdom, France, Germany, Portugal and Spain - according to a process of program-based research, conducted locally by those who design the strategies, who test them out, who live them in all senses of the term.

Until now, the publications of the *ALPHA* collection had been put together from a distance, without the authors having the opportunity to meet. This time, we had the chance to get together for several days to share texts, to discuss experiences, to address the main local, regional and national issues. We also tried to find ways of maximizing the benefits of this meeting, the publication and the international network[2], under whose auspices this publication falls. (The last chapter gives an account of the seminar at Namur. A separate report will also be published in the series *UIE Reports* of the Unesco Institute for Education).

The experience of meeting, during the production of a group project such as this, proved to be a learning experience on several accounts. The table of contents takes on new aspects: real people; a retrospective dialogue on the manuscript; exchanges which lead to a synthesis; bilateral, multilateral projects; long-lasting collaborative understandings; the search for more effective ways of distributing the publication; the considerable support that the international meeting gives to the hosts in the region; and the large network of partners that had to be established to realize the event.

In total, around thirty organizations actively collaborated in this global process of program-based research. The table of contents was multinational; the entire process became international, first of all, owing to the welcoming of the project by the Unesco Institute in Hamburg, and then through a new network of collaborators who give another dimension to that which we have called a "popular movement" for literacy.

Another important event occurred following the seminar at Namur: the UNESCO international seminar on literacy in industrialized countries, in December 1991, in Hamburg. This seminar aimed at evaluating the changes brought about since 1986 (date of the previous seminar), so as better to identify the major trends of today and the main research questions to be studied in the years to come[3]. Some of the main themes pointed out during this seminar were also at the heart of the concerns at Namur. It would be worthwhile to mention them briefly, because they define the international, sociopolitical context, which influences the focus of groups today.

First main observation: the meaning of the notion of literacy has changed considerably. It is used more and more in the plural form ("literacies"), so as better to incorporate and emphasize the diversity of linguistic and cultural practices between countries, and also within individual countries. Two major simplifications are to be deplored, because they have played down the older, more humanist and critical vision, which regards literacy as a fundamental endeavour of justice and social equality: the economic simplification, which tends to use literacy for technical ends in improving information processing skills in the economic sector, and the pedagogical simplification; this tends to create an independent sector of education, separate from social practices and cultural exchange, which provide individuals with a local and living sense of literacy.

Furthermore, the socially constructed myth of mass illiteracy, creator of a rising class of illiterates, is rejected in favour of a positive understanding of the differences in cultural practices and of the skills of individuals, and also in favour of pluralistic initiatives in education, which emphasize the concepts of equal exchange, participation, cultural pluralism and human rights.

The second observation concerns policies. The field of literacy has become fragmented. The players, the organizations, and the sectors of activity, which are involved in the literacy movement and curriculums, are now numerous, diversified, in competition with each other - and sometimes in conflict. Two main trends militate against a general desire for collaboration between all the players: on one hand, the state control of curriculum, which leads to a uniform program, but one of universal accessibility; on the other hand, the privatization of the educational market, which results in subjecting literacy, first and foremost, to the calculation of profit. The two trends are not necessarily incompatible. It does occur, in fact, that government and private enterprise are sometimes joined in the same activity of ideological and economic monopolization of the new market.

In such cases, the quality of services is questionable; the working conditions of professionals do not improve or even worsen; the participation of those who use the services (also referred to as "clients") takes on a negative image in the form of constraints, or even of compulsory enrolment and of penalties for withdrawal; volunteer organizations are marginalized, often with no other option but to integrate into the government-run program, to compete according to the rules of the market place, to subcontract or even to close down.

New kinds of contracts are required between all the players in the literacy movement and governments, in the context of new cultural policies. These policies will have the role of preserving pluralism, the participation of all the players, the quality of services, the equality of working conditions, and especially the role of small, local associations in this continuous testing ground of education; and also of community action and cultural creativity, which are what literacy is all about.

The final observation concerns the *ALPHA* collection in particular. Regarding the area of current research to be carried out and supported, the seminar at Hamburg pointed out that, while institutional research for planning purposes above all has been commissioned and supported as well as costly, large-scale statistical surveys

- local research in literacy practice (program-based, participatory) is also important.

The seminar has also indicated the importance of conducting descriptive and comprehensive research on the daily practices of exchange and communication within different social groups in diversified contexts, as well as on the different literacy initiatives for which appropriate evaluation strategies should be perfected.

Reflecting the activity of this international meeting, and also the interactive current reality of the new multicultural Europe, the seminar in Hamburg has recommended that East/West and North/South co-operation be developed in terms of research, publishing and distribution, to serve national policies as well as local literacy organizations.

Following these reports on the present international context and the expressed willingness to take more effective action, *ALPHA 92* highlights the relevancy of the issues, according to orientations that do not always reflect the main trends and principal ideologies that determine national policies. Yes, the educational market has absorbed many literacy organizations. Yes, education policies have institutionalized and universalized (not everywhere!) the basic education services for adults. Yes, certain governments have relied heavily on popular movements, sometimes improving working conditions, but also increasing the financial burden. Is there still a place, and a justification, in the field of literacy (which varies from narrow to complex), for independent, non-profit organizations that are non-professionally licensed, and moreover, politically active?

Through detailed documentation on local experiences with literacy, *ALPHA 92* seeks to answer this question, which some have already dismissed as being anachronistic and outdated. Most of these initiatives are experiments, led by committed and motivated professionals - in collaboration with local players - who are seeking institutional or private support which guarantees the independence required for experiment.

Here is an important role that justifies long-term support of popular associations: participatory research, based on the local context and literacy methods that help individuals and communities to break out of "unequal exchange". Generally speaking, it is in terms of interaction in networks or circuits of exchange (economic, cultural, social, symbolic) that the right conditions for true literacy can be created. Joelle Dugailly expressed the same idea as follows:

"We are illiterate, we become illiterate, we remain illiterate, in spite of literacy classes, because we are not an integral part of the circuits of participation, of communication and of cultural and social, political and economic expression"[4]. Yet, these conditions can only come about through the creation of an experimental situation that deviates from the routine practices of education. Having the means is essential.

Another irreplaceable role, which is practically unavoidable for groups integrated into a community, area or neighbourhood, is to provide absolutely essential services: to respond to emergencies - above all in the areas of communication, representation and liaison. Linguistic training and job placement programs do not meet "social" survival needs, while the scope of exclusion is widening in all countries. Above and beyond training programs, and everywhere else - except in the limited area of formalized learning - there is a great need for reaching out to usually "non-aligned" groups. Yet, these services are relegated to voluntary operations or delegated to very short-term, temporary employment programs. These services are destined to the same fate as the people they are supposed to serve: exclusion.

A third equally unavoidable role of groups confronted with exclusion on a daily basis (which stand out owing to the obstacles created by illiteracy, under-qualification, technological inferiority) is the political expression of the voiceless. This role, which is indispensable in the practice of participatory democracy, especially in this case - where intolerable and desperate living conditions call for magic solutions - presupposes the support of popular education, whose goal is to facilitate the fundamental possibilities of democratic dialogue (a noble ideal for literacy!). It also involves the creation of new legitimate areas of expression and negotiation, which are difficult to acquire in the prevailing power set-up. This opening to political participation outside the party structure is a major role played by these groups, which work in the subtle area of participation, where many bridges have been torn down.

Symbolic exchange, or cultural/intercultural interaction through the various means of speech, writing, the body, images, music and other technological media, has been especially rejected from the difficult field of "functional" literacy. By creating a new class of "illiterates", the written code and the usefulness of textual practices have also been too much stressed. Popular associations work on the fringes of strictly understood literacy, in a different way, not with "illiterates", but with those excluded from all sides, ("allographs", as Hélène Blais uniquely calls them[5]). Nor do they teach writing, but help to express that which is most profound, heartrending, desirable, in an individual way and in a collective history, by finding the right code, and by creating much sought after opportunities[6]. This cultural/intercultural role of literacy is played almost exclusively by the small and medium-sized associations, but it is rarely recognized and supported as a role of literacy.

The goal of this document is to increase awareness of current research into the popular movement, as pointed out in the main roles that have been mentioned. Apart from the authors and their associations, the following organizations helped in producing this document: the Literacy Service of the Quebec Department of Education, the Communications Branch of the same department, the Coordination Lire et écrire of the Belgian French Community, the Affaires internationales of the Belgian French Community, the Coordination Lire et écrire in Namur, the Fondation Roi Baudouin, the National Literacy Secretariat of the Canadian government, the Service of Continuing Education of the Spanish Department of Education, and the Unesco Institute for Education.

ALPHA 92 is part of the program-based research plan of the Unesco Institute for Education on literacy strategies in industrialized countries. This volume is also part of the publication of the *ALPHA-Literacy Research* collection, co-published by the Quebec Department of Education and the Unesco Institute in the original French version, with translation into English and Spanish. The entire research is part of the work program of the International Network of Literacy Specialists, coordinated by the Unesco Institute for Education in Hamburg.

Notes

1. Hautecoeur, Jean-Paul. 1980. *Alpha 80 - Compte-rendu du Séminaire sur l'alphabétisation populaire*. Montreal: Quebec Department of Education.

8

2. The International Network of Literacy Specialists, coordinated by the Unesco Institute for Education, provides the framework for the research on literacy strategies in industrialized countries.

3. *The Future of Literacy and The Literacy of the Future: Report of the Seminar on Adult Literacy in Industrialized Countries, UIE, Hamburg, 4-7 December 1991.* UIE Reports 9. 1992. Hamburg: Unesco Institute for Education.

4. Dugailly, Joelle. 1991. De l'Alpha ... à l'Omega. La pratique du chef-d'oeuvre en formation d'adultes. Brussels (Unpublished).

5. Blais, Hélène. 1992. Sur les chemins allographes. Pour une vision renouvelée de l'analphabétisme et de l'alphabétisation. Montreal (Unpublished).

6. Gatti, Armand. 1992. Mon théâtre, mes films, qu'est-ce que c'est? *Le Monde diplomatique*, February; Bellet, Alain. 1991. La riposte des exclus. *Le Monde diplomatique*, December.

ILLITERACY
DIRECTION? ACTION? RESULTS?

Jean-Paul Hautecoeur
Unesco Institute for Education
Hamburg, Germany

International Literacy Year was an attempt to renew efforts in the battle against illiteracy throughout the world. In both the Northern and the Southern hemispheres, the problem and the battle are similar although the fight is much more intense in the South.

The same word could be used to describe the phenomenon in both hemispheres although in the North we add an adjective with a technical connotation: "functional" illiteracy (the French use a different term - "*illettrisme*" - a term not used in Belgium or in Quebec). The difference between North and South is simply one of degree or place in the historic "continuum" of the long journey from the primitive (or infant) state of illiteracy to the developed (or adult) state of universal and functional literacy.

The purpose of this paper is to simplify the issue of literacy in industrialized countries. This is a *multi-faceted* issue because it involves very different national contexts; it is *complex* because it involves conflicting social and ideological facts; it is a *changing* issue but it cannot simply be described as a movement of linear evolution on a single historical path.

The issue will be presented in a very general way. What do we mean by illiteracy - functional or dysfunctional - in industrialized countries? What type of action is taken in fighting what is called the "battle against illiteracy"? What are the visible effects and results of the battle, more in terms of meaningful social change than in terms of individual learning?

Illiteracy in Industrialized Countries

The use of the term is very different depending upon the professional group using it, depending upon national "traditions" and depending upon your standpoint. Here is a preliminary list:

1. *Illiteracy - no education or low levels of education*

The criteria which determine the degree and frequency of illiteracy in a region or a country are: school attendance, length of schooling and educational mobility. These criteria are valid for both adults and children. Standards for promotion set by the school system have the value of an initiation rite. The only variable is the level of difficulty, which is constantly increasing: the minimum level was 4 or 5 years, the equivalent of the primary level; it now tends to 9 to 12 years, equivalent to the end of secondary school, where standards have also increased.

In North America, it is still common to equate total illiteracy with a low level of education at the primary level and functional illiteracy with a low level of education at the secondary level.

Thus, in Quebec, the national adult literacy program is superimposed on the basic training program for young people and is supposed to achieve the same objective: a secondary school diploma[1].

In Portugal where illiteracy still often means no schooling, the adult literacy program's minimum aim is a primary school diploma.

2. *"Illettrisme" - mediocre or inadequate ability to read*

The French have split the concept of illiteracy, which, after a century of obligatory schooling, was deemed inappropriate or unsuitable. It is now applied only to the immigrant population. *"Illettrisme"*, the term used to describe French nationals who have attended school, has taken on the meaning of the official definition inspired by the expression used by the *Association française pour la lecture* (AFL): it means mediocre reading ability measured in terms of speed.

Attending school clearly does not make all students good readers. The unfortunate result is that of the one in six adults who do not make use of the written word (are non-readers), approximately half cannot read. This technical meaning given by the French to the concept of *"illettrisme"* has also produced the substitute concept of eliminating illiteracy: *"lecturisation"*[2].

3. *Functional Illiteracy - ineffective use of the written word in practical aspects of daily life*

What then are the basic skills deemed necessary to be able to "function" in American society today? This expandable group of basic skills includes the practical ability to solve ordinary problems of daily life which require basic use of the written word in the national language but also some familiarity with the cultural context of the problems posed, the way in which they are presented, etc. It is a measure of the ability to adapt to situations which are considered to be typical of life in that country, rather than abstract linguistic ability or linguistic ability applied in a very narrow context, such as at school or the workplace.

According to the criteria of minimal ability, an individual may have gone to school, be perfectly literate and even be considered well-read in the original cultural context, but be considered functionally illiterate within North American society. As we have seen, this usage embraces a socio-semiotic register which is much broader than the linguistic or even academic register. It is estimated that between one adult out of three and one adult out of five respectively is functionally illiterate in Canada and the United States[3].

4. *Residual Illiteracy - deficiency, handicap, maladjustment*

The vast range of pathological problems is fertile ground for the concept of illiteracy, especially among professionals in the fields of rehabilitation, re-education, and compensatory education, etc. This "clinical" use of complete or functional illiteracy is particularly prevalent in Northern Europe as well as in Germany and Austria and is common wherever literacy has been developed as a speciality in adult education programs. It is also evident in "special" branches of the normal school system where many educators retrained in adult literacy got their training.

In this sense, illiteracy is a residual rather than a generalized difficulty, a group of individual technical problems to be dealt with in a specialized environment. The fact that such problems are found among adults justifies making prevention a priority, identifying and dealing with these problems as early as possible. Hence developments in the "battle against *'illettrisme'"* in certain psychiatric institutions, in the theoretical and clinical side of cognitive psychology, in pre-school and extra-curricular activities[4].

5. *Illiteracy - characteristic of certain cultural, national or immigrant minorities*

Although illiteracy may be considered abnormal in the indigenous population, it may be accepted as a recurring, majority and "normal" fact for some linguistic minorities whose mother tongue is essentially oral and is considered foreign in that country. Illiteracy is an ethnocentric attribute projected onto cultural minorities who form the local element of the Third World, who are "ghettoized", and are not well-received in national institutions, where they have positions on the domestic staff only or are poorly integrated in the dominant society because of contradictions in a situation involving bilingualism, etc.

Examples are the Gypsies in Europe, North Africans in France, Haitians in Quebec, Francophones in Canada outside Quebec, Amerindians, etc. The ostensible denial of difference is a permanent condition of intercultural conflicts, which are often solved by acculturation, assimilation - what is known as inevitable integration, at the risk of exclusion.

Linguistic relegation of such minorities to an oral and private mother tongue, which is a symbol of their illiteracy in the receiving society ("receiving society" is meant as a benevolent term), may lead to different methods of refusing to become literate in the dominant language, or a vague desire to become literate as a way of showing resistance to the mother tongue, renewed demands for rights, services, allocated jobs, etc.[5]

6. *Illiteracy - being under-qualified or down-graded in a given work situation*

The relationship between linguistic competence and the job market is especially obvious in periods of structural unemployment: this has been the case in most industrialized countries for the past decade. The growth of basic training programs whose aim is vocational reintegration corresponds to technological transformations that affect most industrial sectors as well as to new requirements for professional qualifications[6].

The direct relationship between competence and employability and productivity is, however, only one aspect of the major issue of training. It has often been said that the demand for unskilled labour (or what is described pejoratively as illiterate) was greater in the growing service sector than the demand, in equivalent positions, for a better educated national labour force which demands higher salaries, better social benefits, more mobility, etc.

Basic training programs, upgrading programs, vocational training and retraining have, in many countries, become a requirement before one can receive unemployment benefits or social assistance, or before one can qualify, not directly on the job market but as employable by agencies dealing with under-employment. Eliminating illiteracy has become a new formula for time management for the unemployed: that is a realistic description given by many literacy professionals.

7. *Illiteracy - cultural aspects of poverty, a symbol of more or less generalized exclusion*

The international association ATD-Quart-Monde, and many others, have for a long time associated illiteracy with serious poverty. The association is very negative about the "rags and tatters" sub-culture of the "fourth world", a culture whose "trademark" is the cast-offs accepted for the sake of survival or out of resistance to radical exclusion.

The fourth world has grown considerably in industrialized societies over the past twenty years: "the new poor", young people and old people excluded in larger numbers from the networks of socio-economic exchange, excluded from traditional communities; immigrants in urban centres or in ghettoized suburbs who are not even members of the proletariat; immigrants' children who are headed toward delinquency because of their refusal to be socialized in a monocultural society.

In this context, illiteracy takes on a symbolic rather than objective value: it really means having an identity outside social conventions rather than a linguistic deficiency or handicap. It symbolizes forced marginality, exclusion from social, cultural, economic and political networks.

Socio-cultural intervention in these areas is many-faceted and must be adapted to priorities. Language learning and basic training are often considered secondary while other services are considered essential. The approach used in a literacy program is not the same as the approach used in a formal education program: literacy programs are a type of cultural activity aimed at enabling people to express an identity, to claim and receive recognized basic rights and to organize their own survival. In the vocabulary of public services this is known as "social integration"[7].

8. *Secondary Illiteracy - generalized effect of mass culture on "silent majorities"*

This last meaning, in a list which is far from complete, may be seen as semantic abuse or it can be taken seriously. It supposes a careful analysis of the market of cultural products, communication infrastructures, public and private production and broadcasting policies, private means of consuming these messages, etc. It refers to the masses who watch the same television program at the same time in the same country, under the stimulus of tobacco, alcohol and subliminal advertising. It refers to a mechanical, obedient type of literacy, gratefully received, unintended by the broadcaster, non-selective, non-critical. It also refers to universal education through stereotypical programs which reach derelict environments, workers who are discouraged and depressed, and it refers to conflicts which are either suppressed or silenced, whose youthful participants are also the most avid consumers of television.

Today a clear example of this type of dying "literacy" is particularly evident in what was communist Europe. In the West, only a minority of intellectuals see it this way and are concerned about it. Can this type of analysis only be explained as a view of secondary literacy accepted by a few cliques, as was formerly the case for the small number of people who were educated? The question deserves to be examined.[8]

***

Therefore, it is difficult to talk about illiteracy in the singular. Reducing it to a universal phenomenon is a mythical function or a militant strategy. Using statistics to prove the point can also amount to political demagoguery or journalistic mis-information.

Illiteracy is essentially a social theory: a set of ideological facts. What is important is to know who created the theory rather than whom it applies to, and why the theory was developed by a particular group. What is the theory good for, and whom does it serve?

The reason why we have traced this path is to show that social definitions or their uses are varied, that they can be contradictory and antagonistic. Another study might analyze how groups and their various theories converge on certain occasions, how they can come together to create a consensual litany for the purpose of a particular celebration such as International Literacy Year.[9]

What many of these theories have in common is the coercive function of their convictions. The ability to convince others that the problem is serious and that something must be done about it; the ability in particular to convince those who are illiterate that they must recognize the fact. That is the main ideological reason for efforts at eliminating illiteracy: to convince the individual that he is what you say he is, and then to transform him from victim to beneficiary.

In order to understand the recent phenomenon of illiteracy in the professional, journalistic and political discourse of industrialized countries, it is useful to change camps. To see how the problem is perceived from the other side, to see whether "the problem" is being talked about and what is being said about it[10]. Variations of cultural practices, representations and values are much greater than those between one professional group and another. Illiteracy is denied. The means and methods of communicating by the usual networks are effective. Individuals generally know how to deal with written communications. It is rare for an individual to seek the benefit of a training program. To quote a literacy professional who obviously knows his public well: "The majority of illiterate people do not attach much importance to our efforts . . . To put it crudely, "the illiterate" do not want to become literate. That is not their aim, it is ours.[11]

Finally, in this complex but unequal game of multiple and antagonistic interactions, illiterates are simply a small minority of those who realize that that is what they are in other peoples' eyes. These people have found a raison d'être in a negative, internalized identity. There are such people. They are the voluntary specimens of illiteracy and they tell their story to journalists. Their main function is to convince others. They play a crucial role in demonstrating the necessity and benefits of eliminating illiteracy[12].

Actions Undertaken in the "Battle against Illiteracy"

Globally, we are dealing with an area of activity which has been increasing over the past twenty years in the United States for example, and for a decade in most European countries.

There is remarkable enthusiasm for *mobilizing* campaigns to fight against illiteracy. There are many associations which have invested in this work. In North America, in the UK, in Ireland, in Belgium and in France, such associations are still doing most of the work to eliminate illiteracy by providing either volunteers or grants. In addition to established organizations whose sole purpose is the elimination of illiteracy, powerful new lobbies have appeared which do not have a particularly charitable vocation: for example, libraries, the book and paper industry, the press, business organizations, humanist, nationalist, cultural movements involved in the field of education and trade unions. These groups act directly by offering services to the public; they are especially active in providing information, mobilizing, making people aware, putting pressure on public authorities, supporting organizations on the front line.

Many countries regard the elimination of illiteracy as a *national priority*. They are investing more and more resources and public services in this field. Commitments vary from country to country:

- legislation creating a special sector to deal with illiteracy or basic education in the field of adult education (e.g. the Netherlands, Portugal, Germany, Quebec)[13];

- in the form of grants to provincial authorities or to non-governmental organizations supported by public information campaigns, mobilization, recruitment (e.g. the United States, Canada, the UK)[14];

- in the form of training programs, varying according to economic and social circumstances, and depending upon the policies of the parties in power; these programs are generally administered by non-governmental organizations on a contractual basis (e.g. France and the French Community in Belgium)[15];

- reinforcement of activities designed to prevent illiteracy in the field of special or compensatory education, in school and in the community, at the pre-school level, alternating with periods of employment, etc. (e.g. Sweden, Denmark, but also to varying degrees in the other countries)[16]

The consequence or corollary of these developments in voluntary societies and by the public authorities is clearly a significant increase in the area of *training*. What we are seeing is the professionalization of an activity which originally was basically voluntary and militant. We are witnessing a structure developing around jobs in this field, knowledge of the area, training of the teachers, etc. University and private research in this sector is expanding. Witness the number of theses written on the subject, or the increase in the number of bibliographical references.

Two contrary movements can be observed. On the one hand, as a result of the many different interventions, the field has expanded, the market has opened up and there has been interdisciplinary investment. On the other hand, the field has become more closed and is subject to professional regulation and incorporation into the clearly defined sector of education. In some countries one or the other tendency prevails; in others, the two compete with one another.

There has been an increase in activity and an increase in the *public involved*, but also the catchment area has expanded. Literacy, basic training, upgrading, social and professional integration now affect "clients" of all ages whose socio-professional status varies - employed or unemployed, free or institutionalized (psychiatric institutions, prisons, various types of homes, etc.), handicapped or non-handicapped, homophones and allophones, primary and even post-secondary levels. (In Quebec, for example, a literacy journal - Literacy across the Curriculum - is published by a college for an audience of pre-university students).

The image is that of a professional field which enjoys a particularly strong boost and which has shown steady growth since its inception. One might expect that the amount of money spent in this area would reflect this growth. But it is universally true that that is certainly not the case. Rather, the pattern has been to decrease funds for basic training, to redirect funds into training programs which are clearly more "effective", more in tune with the job market. Even where basic training has been institutionalized, professionalization has usually meant that the job has a *precarious status* rather than creating equality with working conditions of educators working in the regular and adult education sectors. With a few exceptions (the Netherlands?), professionals working in the field of literacy have not, despite the growth in the field, had their status reevaluated. In many countries, most basic activities are still community-based and are totally or partially voluntary. And where the private sector is involved in training, its priorities follow the demands of the job market, and national policies lead to selective, technical training. Thus socio-cultural intervention is abandoned as being pointless.

A typology of the principal approaches to literacy in Europe and in North America would identify the various tendencies as follows:

- the traditional *Anglo-Saxon* approach - *individual assistance* given by volunteers in the context of a local organization or in the very structured context of a national or international organization. This approach may be either independent or integrated into a public adult education system;

- the *school* approach, whose learning objectives are the same as those of schools, and which tends to be organized in "harmony" with the regular stream of national education. Adult education may be different, especially in theory and because of its "adult education" practices. However, structurally, it operates within the system of education, and it obeys that system's basic standards and guidelines (e.g. Quebec);

- the *ABE* approach (Adult Basic Education), a pragmatic model of basic education, relatively autonomous as compared to the regular school system, able to provide all basic adult education of an "academic", civic, professional, practical, physical, etc. nature. In such a flexible context (which may become a national program, e.g. in the Netherlands), the linguistic and cultural concept of literacy is included in the multi-faceted concept of basic skills;

- the *socio-professional integration/reintegration* approach is defined by its objectives rather than by an administrative framework or course content. Its basic purpose is access to employment. This is a multi-faceted approach to training which may be the responsibility of a variety of public sectors (social, economic, manpower) rather than the educational system. This can mean (especially in France) considerable expansion in community-based and private sector training;

- the *popular education/community action* or socio-cultural approach, also known as the holistic approach, of integrated development and, in its most political version, the awareness approach. This means various local efforts by associations whose objectives are defined in terms of the individuals concerned. Literacy belongs to the linguistic and cultural register and is closely related to the personal and social history of the group and the neighbourhood. The aim is to understand that history and to relate it in order to improve it or change it;

- the *cultural/intercultural* approach consists of acting on the material, organizational and imaginary context of a locality, region, or social group rather than educating individuals directly: by creativity, cultural productions, improving communication networks, libraries, presenting demands or political lobbying, developing cultural industries, etc. In different cultural and linguistic environments, these activities may consist of creating an intercultural environment or demanding rights and the means of achieving those rights.

The new multi-ethnic urban environments in industrialized countries require, sometimes urgently, that theories and practices pertaining to the elimination of illiteracy be expanded. This may involve radical changes in national cultural traditions:

- the *preventive, or extra-curricular, or inter-generational* approach. The significant aspect of this approach is its international tendency to remove literacy programs from the professional sectors of more or less formal training and put them in a social context, in a setting where children learn - or should learn - to speak, to read, to communicate, to use books, tools and sources of information, etc. This system is organized on the periphery of the school system - parents' school, homework school - but also farther and farther away - store-front libraries, activities in day care centres in underprivileged areas, ecological or historical community projects involving both young and old, etc.;

- there is still the entire sector of *special education*, for example the hearing impaired, the visually impaired, learning disabled, emotionally disturbed. In some countries, this sector is integrated into broadly based literacy programs. It may even be the dominant factor and may therefore contribute to giving a medical and rather "clinical" meaning to literacy, new ground for the activities of psychotherapists.

In conclusion, the variety of efforts at eliminating illiteracy are still largely experimental. University departments and research centres which are interested in this field and devote themselves entirely to it, are multiplying and diversifying. However, symbolically and economically, literacy professionals have not, in actual fact, risen in status.

Literacy has become a little banal. It has lost some of its power to attract and mobilize people. Politically, the issue of illiteracy now attracts new conservative groups rather than left-wing groups. It may help mobilize resistance to the erosion of values, our heritage, and the national language, more than it helps in the battle against poverty or in intercultural needs. The focus is no longer, or very little, on international development activities. People in literacy circles are becoming more and more cynical and saying that the point of institutionalization is mainly to "better integrate people in their marginality" and to monitor the dangers of exclusion as inexpensively as possible[17].

Results

Clearly what we must do is to gear down. Each type of program has its own objectives which justify being evaluated separately. But also, an evaluation of the results, even in a general way, of literacy activities presumes that it is possible to specify the relevant providers: planners and decision-makers from the public services, political staff, training professionals, community movements; and the target public: victims or beneficiaries of the services offered, depending on how they are analyzed.

The issue also implies that their other functions, or social purposes, should be questioned. These will be seen to have clear meaning if we know the history and the context from which they emerged. Schematically, and perhaps with provocative nuances, it can be said that the results of literacy measures according to the principal theoretical objectives, are, *if not nil, then frankly mediocre.* Officially, literacy advocates and their organizations show results which are "presentable". However, if we apply methodical observation and post-operational self-criticism, we will get the following type of testimony:

> Despite all our pedagogical strategies and efforts, literacy remains a problem with little likelihood of a solution. No young person has left the "Boîte à lettres" knowing how to read and write properly.[18]

> Clearly there has been some success from literacy activities. But, frankly, success has been marginal and these efforts do not get at the root of the problem.[19]

From the "learner's" point of view, despite positive and even enthusiastic reactions to the friendly atmosphere in many literacy centres, we must face the fact that *the learner's basic expectations are very different from the objectives set by the services.* They do not express themselves in terms of education, language or integration but rather in terms of participation, communication, relationships and human sentiments or in terms of social rights, the right to work or the right to housing, etc. Linguistic demands are usually just an excuse, a tactic to get on a par with those providing services which may be useful in other ways; or even the simple answer to an offer which has the legitimacy of knowledge, the power of definition. Thus a formal teaching service which is therapeutic and "professional" may actually *exclude most learners* - a general observation which is recognized by many of these organizations.

There is a radical incompatibility between provision and demand for literacy. Demand is simply prescribed by the provision, and the principal effect is to obscure the reality of that demand. There is no historical demand for literacy on the part of the illiterate, a fact which is difficult to grasp positively. The demand has been created by people who do not see themselves as literate, educated, included or integrated, but as social workers, educators or trainers. These socio-professional identities have been built on an artificial negation. When? why? and how? would be the subject of another very interesting study[20].

Thus one of the most obvious results of the literacy campaigns and literacy tools has been to *create a new class of citizens* who have been declared incompetent, who feel badly about themselves, etc., but who are salvageable, educable, retrainable. The sociologists, the statisticians, the journalists have proven and measured the existence of this. Their estimates are on the upgrade.

Is this a new class or a new label for the poor and the excluded? A class supposes a classification. And it is not unimportant that a class should express itself in cultural terms rather than in economic terms. There is no other immediate solution to socio-professional downgrading, to temporary and long-term unemployment. The only solution is educational, cultural ideological action. Its function is to shame the victim personally by his own incompetence; persuade him that his disqualification is not his destiny and that the solution is within his grasp; integrate him into a network of services which communicate with other networks while awaiting a temporary solution; in short, *occupy the excluded in a positive way to block and neutralize revolt.*[21]

The strategy is not new. Literacy campaigns have appeared where it has become necessary to manage large numbers more effectively by persuasion rather than by force. This is done by linguistic unification, a broad brush offensive which is technical, technological, ideological and political in nature[22]. If we examine literacy campaigns from a sociological point of view, it becomes clear that such efforts must be unified: to speak of literacy campaigns, in the plural, at the same time and in the same social (or national) space amounts to provocation! Therefore intercultural ideas/actions are not looked on favourably if they demand differences and plurality when management strategies are unitary[23].

More than one observer has expressed surprise that literacy campaigns are necessary in industrialized countries. For a long time there has been linguistic peace, aside from some "regional conflicts" (Canada and Belgium for example). And universal schooling has long since been achieved. There are still some isolated cultural minorities who are poorly integrated although they are in the process of becoming settled. So why are there so many people who are illiterate (between 10 and 40% of adult national populations), and what is the point of efforts to mount new literacy campaigns?

Education and cultural action, having replaced the Church in these functions, have enormous powers of consensus and enormous potential for effectiveness. How were these new illiterates created? There is no lack of explanations: rise in the standards of qualifications, skills declared inadequate, inadequate schools, mass culture, personal difficulties and handicaps, etc. Because of the serious social crises which affect all industrialized countries today, the old strategy of cultural and moral mobilization has been reactivated. A placebo would be just as effective.

We should look for results not in the activities of literacy campaigns but in *the ideological effects of literacy campaigns*. Same danger, same battle. Literacy campaigns are largely motivated by a generous and virtuous consensus. That is its most important function[24].

As has already been pointed out, the other logical result is a *remarkable growth in the professional sector of basic training*. This has been particularly welcome in countries where money and jobs in the field of education have decreased. It has been a good thing for much of the community movement when responsibility for these activities has been transferred from volunteers to sub-contractors and even sometimes to private enterprise. It has provided prolonged if not permanent retraining for many social, socio-cultural and socio-political workers demobilized during the heyday of liberalism.

Growth, but also *research and experimentation* in local activities and organizations are more effective because institutional objectives have been transformed into objectives renegotiated locally, redefined and taken over again by more organic networks of communication and solidarity. The field of literacy is also fertile ground for *experiments in participatory democracy* at a local, multicultural level. As we have seen, literacy professionals still have a precarious, marginal and heterogeneous status as compared to organizations made up of social, educational and cultural activists. And although the available resources sometimes tend to become institutionalized so that "specifications" are more tightly controlled, there are still many unresolved issues - there is room to manoeuvre between technical control and anthropological adventure in the game of language and in the game of languages[25].

However, from the point of view of literacy organizations, the picture is not all rosy. Organizations which jumped on the bandwagon of national policies and programs, especially with training programs in education and employment, have benefited from the growth. On the other hand, *popular organizations involved in education*, independent community action groups and socio-cultural action groups, *have been marginalized*. In certain national contexts where all public monies are devoted to basic training programs, such organizations have had no choice in the shorter term but to integrate or shut down[26].

Should the general fact that the individuals targeted do not respond, or give up when they have just responded out of suffering or poverty, be considered a negative result? The answer must be yes when the effect of such failures is *reinforcing campaigns of recruitment, using coercive measures to register people*, making attendance obligatory (as at school, military service, or even religious functions), imposing *negative sanctions* such as reducing or withdrawing social assistance if the individual is absent or quits. When programs have been created, when public resources have been invested and when there is a consensus about the necessity of being literate, failing to respond may become an offence[27].

Illiteracy is neither a neutral nor a stable condition. If it is not treated - some claim that the solution is simple and universally available - there is a risk of delinquency. In the United States, it is common to describe illiterates as "a population at risk" (title of a report by President Reagan: "A Nation at Risk"). To use an historical analogy: "Working Class, Dangerous Class" was an expression used more than a century ago in Europe. In Canada, it is also often said that the highest rate of illiteracy in our population is found in the prison population and that, therefore, illiteracy creates criminals.

To conclude on a less strident note, we must also recognize that the domestication of illiteracy, as Paulo Freire said, has fertilized its antithesis (or its parasites, to be less dualistic, or in other words, more monistic), *cultural experimentation in the fertile field of language*. Aside from the training market, there are writing workshops, local newspapers, productions and publications in the local language and history, poetry contests, opportunities for correspondence and international exchanges, "free" community radio where the illegal may become a public message, adventures in collective writing presented as theatre to recreate the equivalent of the mysteries of the Middle Ages. Popular culture has gained a little space for production, expansion and legitimacy replacing programs in continuing education. Foreign cultures have also been able to gain a little elbow-room, without folklore masks or a special permit[28].

Less visible, less spectacular, but no less active has been the work of the community movement in organizing, coordinating, liaising, representing, and in making demands for autonomy, representation and effectiveness. It is certainly important to have brought about "political" changes at the local and regional levels in the relations between "passive" populations and public authorities[29]. And so, how and to what extent has the advent of national literacy campaigns helped to transform communications by developing alternative networks? To what extent have literacy campaigns for public salvation also generated, thanks to the reappropriation of some funds and the means of communication by those designated as victims, their own antidote - literacy campaigns of resistance?[30] One of the most interesting questions to explore.

Notes

1. Hautecoeur, Jean-Paul. 1990. Literacy Policy in Quebec - a Historical Overview. In J.-P. Hautecoeur, ed. *Alpha 90: Current Research in Literacy (31-52)*. Montreal: Quebec Ministry of Education; Hamburg: Unesco Institute for Education.

2. Espérandieu, V.; Lion, A. and Bénichou, J.P. 1984. *Des illettrés en France*. Paris: La documentation française.
   Vélis, Jean-Pierre. 1988 *La France illettrée*. Paris: Seuil.

3. See, for example, Kosol, Jonathan. 1985. *Illiterate America*. New York: Anchor/Doubleday.

4. Kamper, G. and Rübsamen, H. 1990. Illiterates and Literacy Training: The Federal Republic of Germany has its Share. In J.-P. Hautecoeur, ed. *Alpha 90: Current Research in Literacy* (269-326). Montreal: Quebec Ministry of Education; Hamburg: Unesco Institute for Education.

5. Wagner, Serge. 1990. Literacy and the Assimilation of Minorities: The Case of Francophones in Canada. In J.-P. Hautecoeur, ed. *Alpha 90: Current Research in Literacy* (53-80). Montreal: Quebec Ministry of Education; Hamburg: Unesco Institute for Education.

6. Sticht, T. and Mikulecky, L. 1984. *Job-related Basic Skills. Cases and Conclusions*. Columbus, OH: Ohio State University, Columbus Center for Research in Vocational Education.

7. Fox, M. and Baker, G. 1990. Adult Illiteracy in the United States: Rhetoric, Recipes and Reality. In J.-P. Hautecoeur, ed. *Alpha 90: Current Research in Literacy* (81-112). Montreal: Quebec Ministry of Education; Hamburg: Unesco Institute for Education.

8. Enzensberger, H.M. 1987. In Praise of the Illiterate. *Adult Education and Development* 8.
    Cf. the work of Richard Hoggart.

9. Hautecoeur, Jean-Paul. 1990. L'analphabétisme des pays industrialisés: du mythe à la reconstruction des faits. Hamburg: Unesco Institute for Education, unpublished.

10. Street, Brian. 1984. *Literacy in Theory and Practice*. Cambridge: Cambridge University Press.

11. Arrijs, Omer. 1992. This volume.

12. Hautecocur, Jean-Paul. 1986. *Anonymus-Autoportaits*. Montreal: Ed. Saint Martin.

13. Hammink, Kees. 1990. *Functional Illiteracy and Basic Education in the Netherlands*. Hamburg: Unesco Institute for Education.

14. National Literacy Secretariat. 1990. *Partners in Literacy: National Literacy Program*. Ottawa: Multiculturalism and Citizenship.

15. Goffinet, S. and Van Damme, D. 1990. *Functional Illiteracy in Belgium*. Hamburg: Unesco Institute for Education.

16. Commission of the European Communities. 1988. *Report on the Fight against Illiteracy*. Brussels: DG for Employment, Social Affairs and Education.

17. Arrijs, Omer. 1992. This volume.

18. Roy, Sylvie. 1992. This volume.

19. Arrijs, Omer. 1992. This volume.

20. Hautecoeur, Jean-Paul. 1990. Generous Supply, Flagging Demand: The Current Paradox of Literacy. In J.-P. Hautecoeur, ed. *Alpha 90: Current Research in Literacy* (113-132). Montreal: Quebec Ministry of Education; Hamburg: Unesco Institute for Education.

21. Hautecoeur, Jean-Paul. 1988. Poids et mesures de l'analphabétisme au Québec. In J.-P. Hautecoeur, ed. *Alpha 88: Recherches en alphabétisation.* Montreal: Quebec Ministry of Education.

22. Goody, Jack. 1986. *La logique de l'écriture.* Paris: Armand Colin.

23. Hautecoeur, Jean-Paul. 1986. Langue, école, culture et analphabétisme. In J.-P. Hautecoeur, ed. *Alpha 86: Recherches en alphabétisation.* Montreal: Quebec Ministry of Education.

24. Havelock, Eric. 1986. *The Muse Learns to Write.* New Haven CT: Yale University Press.

25. Boucher, R. and Lefebvre. 1984. L'alphabétisation avant la lettre. In J.-P. Hautecoeur, ed. *Alpha 84: Recherches en alphabétisation.* Montreal: Quebec Ministry of Education.

26. Hautecoeur, Jean-Paul. 1991. Le mouvement d'alphabétisation populaire au Québec. *Revue d'action sociale* 3.

27. See Note 12.

28. See, for example, Azzimonti, Francesco. 1992. This volume.

29. Chapotte, A. and David, F. 1992. This Volume.

30. Wagner, S. and Grenier, P. 1991. *Analphabétisme de minorité et alphabétisation d'affirmation nationale.* Toronto: Ministry of Education.

BASIC EDUCATION AND
PERSONAL DEVELOPMENT STRATEGIES

Pierre Georis
Centre d'information et
d'éducation populaire, Brussels, Belgium

This paper presents a report on a series of pilot projects conducted in Wallonia (Belgium) on job integration for disadvantaged groups.

The conclusions drawn in a variety of papers on the subject of associations and literacy as a social phenomenon outside Belgium are cumulative: there are many striking similarities in the projects themselves and the problems experienced. Although the project on which this paper is based is geographically specific, there appears to be a common thread running through the actual situations discussed here.

One postulate is essential to the argument which follows: the vision guiding any advances made in the geographic area in which the project was conducted must be a positive vision. Although this statement may seem naive, it is justified for the area in question.

Wallonia, my home state, is a land of old industries and large companies, of grinding work which destroyed our parents' health, and killed a good many of them. Social conflict has frequently been extremely harsh, and the recession has hit very hard: a number of regions are real disaster areas. For years Walloons have been experiencing company closures. In the past 20 years, all discussion of domestic matters has had one focus: the recession. From all the discussion, the causes of the situation have gradually emerged and, as a result, tentative suggestions for ways to get out of it. The unhappy consequence of all the discussion, and its underlying connotation of decline, is that the Walloons now have a very negative image of themselves and their future.

Although discussions of recession have certainly not disappeared, there has been a gradual upsurge in discussion of (re)development. This is quite a radical change in viewpoint, the consequences of which are still far from clear. But if it is true that troop morale is decisive to victory, talking about and hearing about development is obviously more stimulating than hearing about recession and the notion of worker resistance.

The hypothesis underlying this paper may be stated in the following terms: *new forms of social assistance (including literacy) must be based in part on economic development.*

Formulated in these terms, the hypothesis leads us directly to the subject of employment-training integration.

Near Consensus on the Importance of Training

One outstanding feature of recession management throughout the 1980s has been the permanence of the training-employment debate. The key word in the debate has incontestably been "integration", usually qualified as both social and vocational. Literacy is at the heart of the debate, the terms of which are summarized in the following paragraphs.

The near consensus is essentially based on statistical fact: overall, the probability of being chronically unemployed is inversely proportional to level of education. Although this is an accepted fact, an employment policy which is strictly a training policy must be judged in the light of comments made by a number of observers[1]. In any event it is erroneous to believe in the existence of an automatic link between training and employment.

Of course a teenager who drops out of school and gets a job as a labourer has few prospects, especially if that teenager is a woman. But is unemployment due here to low level of education, massive cutbacks in blue-collar jobs, or to the fact that blue-collar jobs are held mainly by adults and become available only in dribs and drabs as the adults who hold them retire? If the teenager is a woman, is it due to the fact that blue-collar jobs are held almost exclusively by men? Or is it because the teenager has the bad luck to belong to a very large age group? These are only a few of the possibilities.

Conducting an analysis of unemployment inevitably instils prudence because of the large number of interlocking factors involved. Furthermore, although it is true that additional training gives additional protection against unemployment, it does not follow that the unemployment problem can be solved exclusively by training: raising the level of education of each individual does not create a single new job (with teachers perhaps the only, and marginal, exception). In fact the effect is essentially an increase in individual competitiveness: where the total number of jobs remains unchanged, the more competitive individual replaces the less competitive one.

The training-job link is not automatic. This statement has several corollaries.

- On the average, fifteen years after entering the labour force, not more than one worker in two still practises the trade for which he or she was trained[2].

- The initial proposals can be countered by the observation that, in fact, never throughout history has the average level of education been as high as it is today.

From this observation, a proposal exactly contrary to the usual one may be made: unemployment is currently such a serious problem because people have too much education (and unrealistically high expectations of the job market).   This reverse argument, which we definitely do not support, has (because of its provocative aspect) heuristic importance: it demonstrates the error of conducting social analysis based on a simple cause/effect relationship.

- An unshakeable commitment to making "job" the automatic result of "training" can easily lead right up against a blank wall.

Employers would have to be asked to define the jobs of the future and the training prerequisites for those jobs, a difficult task in the medium term.

Although initiatives of this sort have been tried, results have been positive only in the very short term. Employers are able to say that they expect to hire when a position opens up, but they have no time to wait until a specific individual trains for a job, perhaps for three years. They have no idea what jobs will be open in five or ten years. If we wish to plan education in relation to the requirements of the economy, this is the scale that has to be considered. In practical terms, the task is impossible. The only option remaining is to go with the current and provide instruction in new technologies. The individual's only option is to collect as broad a range as possible of diplomas and certificates, just in case.

In other words, although there is a link (from the individual viewpoint) between education and employment, an employment policy based solely on training would produce nothing more than a number of "communicating vessel" phenomena in the job market.

If the training-job link is valid at the micro-economic level (that of the individual), it is considerably more difficult to justify at the macro-economic level. This does not necessarily mean that an increase in the level of education is without macro-economic impact. On the contrary, it is virtually a condition of remaining in the technology race. The simple fact is however that, at the macro-economic level, the training-job link is not automatic: education does not automatically create jobs for all the unemployed.

The Primary Objective of Training Job Seekers is Social and Vocational Integration

Integration is always qualified as both social and vocational. The reasons for this should be examined: if the double qualification is justified, its value as a postulate is greater. At the very least, the following relationships are justified:

- Having a job means taking part in production. It also means having an income and being a consumer. Integration as a producer entails integration as a consumer.

- A job has a whole series of additional functions indispensable to psychological balance. A job imposes a time structure, a rhythm of life, on the individual. It provides the setting for social contacts outside the family and facilitates meaningful dialogue between individuals. It links the individual to projects and goals that transcend the personal (i.e. exceed individual goals). It defines the individual's social status and identity. It imposes action[3].

A job performs so many functions simultaneously that it seems difficult to imagine how a household can be considered socially integrated unless at least one of its members is professionally integrated.

We are however in an evolving society, one in which the points of reference are changing. The possibility that all the functions of a job can be performed by some means other than a job cannot be discounted. However this may be, the lack of any practical alternative requires our support for the following statement: in today's world, vocational integration is the best form of social integration.

Exclusion is the result of many causes (e.g. problems related to employment, education, income, family), which interact with and impact on one another.

Ideally, it would be possible to consider all aspects at once. When faced with poverty, each intervener is a little like a photographer asked to take one (and only one) typical view of the main square in an old town. The photographer has a number of options: take a picture from each street leading into the square; try to fit the church and the town hall into one picture; photograph only the facade of the town hall, or a single detail of the façade; rent a helicopter and take an aerial view. Although each photograph presents an accurate view, whichever one is selected some aspects of the square are necessarily left out.

Faced with poverty, we are like that photographer: we must select one point of view. When interveners talk about social and vocational integration, it is a bit like locking the focus on "job". Two related aspects (education and income) are caught in the frame; everything else remains outside.

This is the angle from which this paper is written.

The Path to Integration

Our society has a specific conception of what it considers the ideal path to integration: when an individual completes basic schooling, he or she finds a job and occupies a position in the hierarchy, corresponding to the level of education reached in the educational hierarchy. It is as if society were made up of two boxes. Vocational integration designates the individual's path from one box to the other.

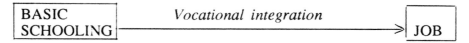

One result of recession is the ever-widening gap between the number of regular job seekers and existing demand. This gap creates a variety of other phenomena: the young school-leaver does not find a regular job quickly; the individual who loses a job does not easily find another. A third box (known as *vocational transition*) appears between the other two. This third box is neither school nor job: an individual may take a casual job for a few months; take a course lasting a few weeks; collect unemployment insurance; have a part-time job that, if all goes well, will turn into a full-time one; or work part-time and take a course part-time. *Vocational transition is anything that is not a regular job but leaves room for the possibility that all doors leading to a regular job are not locked.* The situation is not limited to initial integration (integration on leaving school), but is repeated many times over the life of an individual[4].

The above definition of vocational transition allows for the possibility that some doors may be locked. This means that the diagram requires a fourth box (exclusion) to include all individuals who are unsuccessful in getting a job by any path, either direct (basic schooling to job) or indirect (vocational transition).

In my opinion (although there is no unanimity on this point), the exclusion box represents, not a homogeneous population, but three populations.

a) The group commonly known as the hard-core poor, formerly known as the sub-proletariat and today often called the fourth world. Unlike the classic proletariat, the sub-proletariat has never become integrated into production except on a short-term, temporary basis. This has two effects: low income (poverty) and non-integration into the collective defence structures of salaried individuals.

b) Many young people find themselves in the exclusion box, although their parents may (or may have) held productive jobs. The group consists largely of secondary school dropouts. In earlier times they would have been able to find labourers' jobs somewhere; today they are largely unprovided for. Because they are not eligible for unemployment benefits, their situation is extremely difficult if they are not on good terms with their parents.

c) The third group is made up of individuals sliding from vocational transition toward exclusion. These people are not eligible for unemployment benefits or have been unemployed for such a long time that it is unrealistic to continue considering their status as transitional.

These observations indicate that the exclusion box is culturally non-homogeneous, even though all the situations involved may be defined economically: the fourth world culture is not the same as the culture of a young person who has never worked or of someone who formerly held a regular job. The second and third situations are those experienced by what is often called the new poor. It is very important that this be understood before any action is taken: a series of measures may be effective for some of the excluded, but totally ineffective for the others.

This development suggests two goals for action.

a) Assistance to children and families, especially at the community level (e.g. after-school classes, creative expression centres, shop-front libraries), to avoid the slide from basic schooling toward exclusion.

b) Assistance to the under-educated who are again unemployed:

- by highly effective management of the vocational transition phase to provide them with job access; or

- for individuals who have fallen into the exclusion box, by taking the measures required for them to break out of its confines and at least move up to the vocational transition box (or even move directly into a job)[5].

The Popular Education Experience

As we have seen, a job is not the only reason for education. There is justification for making a distinction between the objectives of education and the objectives of employment. An education policy strives to find a delicate balance between individual fulfilment and training in everything required for community living: training as such (there really are things that have to be learned), and more purely educational aspects that enable the individual to be a citizen, understand his or her society and play an active part in it. This means that teaching is primarily philosophical and ethical in nature, before becoming a scientific project. There is no getting away from a debate on values. (What must be taught? What is the ideal status of the student or trainee on completion of the program?)

Generally speaking, it is safe to say that all our experience in the community association movement points to the conclusion that *democratic ethical values must be affirmed.* There must be a defined minimum level of education: education is a *right* which must be the same for everyone. Those who have not reached that level in school must be given the opportunity to do so at some later date. This right to education is considered to be comprehensive, i.e. affecting the whole person. This viewpoint is diametrically opposed to that underlying the type of project which, since it considers an assembly line worker who repeats a single motion for eight hours to be integrated, merely trains individuals in weekly reiterating one particular operation. Our educational objectives are far broader than this kind of training and have an entirely different focus[6].

The common aims referred to in the preceding paragraph are those underlying what is known as popular education (sometimes called lifelong education). The framework is ideal for literacy programs. Because the concept, although valuable, is relatively unknown, a brief explanation is in order. We go on to demonstrate that literacy has a further strategic function in a regional policy aimed at vocational integration of disadvantaged individuals and, more generally, in the collective definition of a new development policy.

The concept of popular education covers a broad spectrum of educational and collective experience at the community level and is based on ethical values. Its characteristics are the following:

a) At the outset, there is an ethical principle, which must be clearly stated. The labour movement works actively to counteract the fatalism which allows the lower levels of society to be exploited and excluded from active citizenship (and from the possibility of taking part in public decision-making).

b) The battle may be waged in many ways, all of which can complement one another (e.g. legislative action by a political party, public statement by a pressure group). Popular education is a type of action aimed directly at the community as such. Because of this, it is different from the action of a political party or a pressure group (e.g. an association which regularly speaks for consumers on the basis of the results of surveys conducted by technicians, but does not organize consumer groups). If a pressure group does take action on popular education, that action will give public expression to the opinions gathered by actually working with community groups.

c) While the popular education experience is educational or pedagogical, it is also a kind of collective action. Its main feature is the refusal of predetermined content, i.e. content defined exclusively by persons other than the interested parties themselves. The first step is to admit that the individual knows and understands his or her own experience. The individual faces specific problems in a specific situation: he or she is not likely to embark on an education program without some assurance of finding solutions to these problems. Popular education operates at a number of levels. Understanding often takes a very long time, and requires a knowledge of the environment (e.g. company, neighbourhood, hospital); familiarity with the actual problems faced by the people; formulation of a possible solution to these problems; making sure that supply is compatible with demand; and possible adjustments.

Within a company, popular education may be concerned with serious safety problems. In a public housing project, the starting point may be the rent charged. In a neighbourhood, it could be installing a traffic light in front of the school. When dealing with unemployed, unqualified young people, the point could be income earned in a workshop program.

The problems that people have are usually experienced at the individual level. One feature of popular education is the implementation of a collective response, involving the bringing together of people experiencing the same problems.

d) The action taken by popular education movements is not of course confined to catching the eye, even if progress is made when instant solidarity is created among individuals who do not automatically think in collective terms.

In some cases, over-concentration on the "appeal" aspect can result in a corporatist type of action. The challenge here is to respect the ethical principles underlying community education. It is also possible to become involved in actions of solidarity for the benefit of others without seeking an immediate benefit at the personal level. The requirement here is that the individuals involved perceive the society in which they live as a medium in which to define and build a development project, one in which they can play an active role (as citizens of their society). Although a project of this kind exceeds individual abilities, it should have a place for everyone.

This aspect of popular education work is usually linked to more structured education projects, although the contractual aspect is still a factor (adjustments can be made depending on supply)[7].

Popular education strategy entails working to consolidate successful overtures with broader education or solidarity action aimed at a variety of groups; it also entails creating points of contact for the different groups. It is an enormous undertaking.

Within a trade union, fighting social duality and creating solidarity entails interacting with workers to encourage them to broaden the scope of their demands beyond the purely corporatist, a course of action which can lead to even greater exclusion.

It is also true that self-defence is the best defence. In many situations, it is the action of a special interest group that has forced the hand of the majority (if women had not organized into groups, the workers' movement would have had less incentive for supporting their anti-discrimination stand). The best possible development for the fourth world is the assumption of responsibility for its claims by labour movement organizations. This kind of assumption of responsibility requires regular stimulation by the actions of the "fourth world" groups themselves.

Finally, it is absolutely essential that common ground be found. A broad range of experience indicates that this can be done. In Belgium, for example, starting from the particular problem of gas and electricity service to clients in arrears being cut off in the winter, consolidated action by social assistance recipients, social workers and gas and electricity workers has produced results. In Wallonia anti-poverty forums operate on essentially the same principle. Each instance of solidarity represents a highpoint, even if these are only sporadic.

Literacy programs are linked to popular education in that they are designed for the general public, approach a problem collectively rather than individually and are not restricted to purely mechanical learning methods. The very existence of such groups constitutes an impressive challenge to the body social and tears down a whole series of walls between groups which have rarely interacted with one another in the past (e.g. social assistance, continuing education, various government representatives, even representatives of business)[8].

Literacy is an Indispensable Piece of a Complex Puzzle or How to Define Literacy within a Development Strategy

In recent years, a number of training programs have been set up for unemployed workers. Changes have occurred in steps, with each new program grafted onto, rather than replacing, the earlier programs. This has produced a high degree of complexity, but this is not necessarily a problem if the programs are complementary rather than competitive.

It is not unlikely that a similar step-by-step evolution has occurred in other industrialized countries:

1) At a time when unemployment was not a very serious problem, the procedure was to use public job training services for the unemployed to adjust the skills of job-seekers to the job supply. The program's success contributed to spreading the idea that sound training is the key to a good job (or training guarantees a job). The training-job link became a firm tenet of public opinion.

2) The second step occurred at the onset of the recession. The unemployed, convinced that training is an automatic passport to a job, applied in large numbers for the shrinking number of training places available. Vocational training services gradually raised entrance requirements, admitted only the cream of potential workers, and of course maintained a high placement rate for their trainees. All the others, and there were many of them, were not eligible for any training program. This led private popular education associations to set up groups referred to (in the Francophone culture) as "mise à niveau des connaissances" [personal development]. The courses offered included mathematics, mother tongue and introduction to current and social affairs, starting from the everyday concerns and experience of the participating adults. Generally speaking it is this type of movement which provided the impetus for more recent literacy programs.

3) At about the same time there appeared a broad variety of customized training projects. These involved training groups of five to ten individuals specifically for the creation of a small business. The aim was to provide solutions (essentially through personal development) for individuals whose skills level proved inadequate because the job-training link was not sufficiently direct. However it is extremely difficult to create employment in settings which, by definition, have no capital to inject. It must be admitted that the relatively few successes of this type of

venture are all the more remarkable considering the large number of failures.

4) However all such programs require that beneficiaries voluntarily seek training. A large proportion of the most disadvantaged, many of them not even eligible for unemployment benefits, are not interested in education. They are interested in an income sufficient to feed themselves, and would like to get it by doing something more fulfilling than standing in line in a welfare office. For any pedagogical action to be even remotely success-ful with this group, the education must have the appearance of work rather than training and it must provide an income. This is the hypothesis underlying the many on-the-job training programs set up in Wallonia beginning in 1984. These programs go by a number of names (e.g. vocational training company, integrated development action, intermediate company, production school); project objectives and methods can also vary. It is not our intention to discuss the matter in any detail here. The thing to remember is that the great majority of on-the-job training[9] projects, regardless of their differences, are based on the same pedagogical hypothesis. Although it is not unusual for such projects to include literacy under their umbrellas, they are not by definition literacy projects.

An observation: as time goes on, there are many indications that interest in job integration is steadily growing. This can be observed in different ways:

- Creation of jobs fully financed by the economic activity of various workshops (mainly in the construction industry, occasionally in cleaning).

- More systematic search for a foothold in an economic activity: contacting companies to encourage them to hire young people; negotiating to set up training programs to meet the real needs of companies (e.g. a supermarket chain may agree to cooperate in training butchers, who are subsequently hired in the various branches).

- Study of channels to find areas of potential development suitable to the placement of poorly qualified individuals. For example, everyone knows that many young people are fascinated by things mechanical. This knowledge could lead to a decision to set up a workshop for building and repairing bicycles and motorcycles. However this is an industry in which job development is highly random. Conversely, most forecasts, taking into account the ageing of our populations, with an increase in the incidence of handicaps and the cultural fact that an increasing number of individuals want to remain independent as long as possible, suggest a promising future in wheeled vehicles for the handicapped. There are positions to be occupied, negotiations to be undertaken to link up a workshop and a corporation to facilitate conversion of the bicycle/motorcycle workshop.

- A willingness, at any rate, to help interested individuals break out of the exclusion round by giving them the opportunity to enrol in other training programs where they can earn recognized diplomas or certificates that make them better qualified for the job market.

If this type of initiative is to succeed, it is important to avoid making ghettos of our training programs for the disadvantaged. They must be part of a broader program, if possible at the sub-regional level, with the contacts such consolidation implies. In short, the following points should be stressed:

a) Recognize the need for four distinct types of adult education:

- literacy
- on-the-job training for the highly disadvantaged
- personal development
- customized training (related to specific vocational qualifications or creation of economic activities)

b) Promote joint action by the four above types with the aim of decentralization and maximum effectiveness: avoid duplication, work together to fill gaps, giving inhabitants of rural areas the benefit of adapted opportunities (one problem could be that literacy groups are organized only in cities).

c) Work on coordinating the four program types to ensure that the individual is protected from running up against a blank wall, and is able to progress (from literacy to personal development; from personal development to customized training).   It would be extremely disheartening to see an individual, highly motivated by his or her experience (his investment) in a literacy group, miss a training project opportunity because of the lack of a connecting path (e.g. leading to vocational training).

If an education program of this kind is to succeed, the individual must be encouraged to draw up a plan.   The aim is to enable the disadvantaged individual to break out of the ghetto, instead of being condemned to marginal structures for marginal people.   There is the possibility of earning a real, recognized and certified qualification, or designing a detailed project and finding the assistance required to make it happen.   It is not impossible for the plan to lead to the creation of new community services jointly run by a number of organizations (e.g. an agency to support the creation of economic activity).

Who Will Run this Development Project?   Or: The Relationships between the Community Associations, Public Services and Government

Relationships between community associations, public services and government are sometimes (if not often) difficult. The main sources of tension deserve some consideration. It is not enough to envisage a development strategy: if it is to be implemented, someone has to run it. This is the rationale for defining the roles of the different groups. So many projects grind to a halt because of conflict among the organizations responsible.

The sources of tension

Voluntary community associations (i.e. non-governmental organizations) play a conspicuous role in literacy programs in a number of industrialized countries.

In some countries, the fight against illiteracy only began in earnest when such associations revealed the truth about a problem rarely directly tackled by government or public service. Generally speaking, the scenario is the same everywhere: associations get together and decide to deal with the problem themselves, with few resources. If things go well, after a few years government (national, regional or local) recognizes the seriousness of the problem and, in the ideal situation, passes some kind of literacy legislation, most commonly implemented through grants and assignment of personnel (whose status is usually tenuous) to recognized associations. In some ways, this method means recognizing that community associations can provide the population with useful services that complement traditional public services. The legislation makes hopes run high; and often a whole series of new associations spring up in its wake.

In spite of the progress made, however, the situation of sponsoring associations remains fragile, as if government can never quite go all the way in recognizing the usefulness of the services which they provide.

Even more serious, this is often followed by criticism of associations for non adherence to the rules and, in more serious cases, withdrawal of entire pockets of public monies. The most seriously affected victims are association employees.

The problem has two facets. The first is related to the shortage of public monies, a problem frequently addressed by reducing government expenditure. Activities delegated to non-governmental agencies, especially if they are not supported by a powerful lobby, are an easy target. In the overall scheme of things, the literacy association lobby wields little power.

Government financial problems also have an impact on a variety of public services (e.g. education and vocational training for the unemployed). This is where the second facet of the problem arises: as things get tighter in the schools and vocational training institutions, public services and public service unions tend to view community associations as competitors that siphon off the public monies to which they are entitled. It is as if, from the moment a problem not dealt with by public services is taken on by publicly funded associations, the public services sit up and take notice. Associations are strongly criticized in the hope of obtaining their funding to upgrade public service operations. A government trying to save money often feels justified by these disputes to make cutbacks in association funding.

There is no doubt that, when problems are revealed, there is always disagreement on responsibility for solving it. Should the means to do so be given to existing associations, or should associations be considered so many cuckoos in the public service nest?

It is extremely difficult to give a definitive answer on the respective roles of associations and public services. The debate will undoubtedly heat up even more in most countries in the coming years, particularly those countries where the government is in serious financial difficulty. For the time being, the best that can be suggested is concerted action at the local level aimed at formulating a kind of social pact that would more clearly define the complementary roles of the various participants and allow for cooperation on new joint projects[10]. The associations have at least two cards to play when local social pacts are being drafted, both of which justify their continued presence. Primarily, associations should be (and are capable of being) lessons in democracy. In addition, they have a legitimate interest in economic development.

The close ties between community associations and democracy

These can be described in a few words, as solid arguments have been put forward elsewhere[11].

Community associations have at least implicit links to democracy.

1) *The association plays a part in the cultural development of individuals.* Associations give individuals real experience in social action: it is through associations that individuals become active citizens, through self-expression and by learning negotiating, planning and action skills. In an association, the individual becomes more than a mere consumer of goods and services; the association gives an active dimension to citizenship. It provides a kind of proof that cultural development, rather than being restricted to a minority, is universal in scope. Although

associations have no monopoly on popular education activities, at the very least the association spirit serves as a facilitator.

2) *Many associations are involved in the fight against life's inequalities.* Countless associations were created by a few individuals as a protest against inequality and injustice. Literacy programs, community after-school classes, neighbourhood associations, creativity centres - all are products of solidarity. The accomplishments of each succeeding decade and each succeeding generation are worthy of admiration and a source of hope for the future.

3) *Furthermore, associations do have links to political democracy.* The concept of political democracy is difficult to define. Strictly speaking, it is the doctrine which states that sovereignty should belong to all citizens as a group. Implementing the principle entails two problems: on the one hand, it is obviously impossible to involve everyone, all the time, in all decision making; on the other hand, the mechanism for temporary delegation of decision-making powers to elected representatives has terrible flaws - how many democratically elected politicians end up behaving like despots from another age! However, caricature is not our aim: representative democracy is, happily, more than that. In spite of the temptations that plague our elected representatives, the press and other pressure groups (in spite of *their* respective imperfections) exercise at least something of a counterbalance: generally speaking, there are limits to what elected representatives can get away with at any given time.

If one takes a closer look at such practices, associations are seen to play a crucial role. They are strategically situated: they demonstrably refute the premise that active citizenship is confined to voting and that citizens should otherwise remain totally passive. They have a mediation function and can transmit concerns regarding elected representatives. The concept of citizenship is at the heart of the close links between the spirit of the association movement and the spirit of popular education.

Associations have a legitimate interest in economic development

In short: development potential in a region does not ensure implementation of that development. The effects of legislation are not automatic.

On the contrary: concrete results depend on local organization of grassroots development opportunities. Potential is never realized unless individuals take the initiative. Taking the initiative is the responsibility of the individual: it is acquired behaviour and improves with practice. It is within associations that individuals learn this behaviour.

How to make an implicit argument explicit

The aim of the preceding paragraphs is to demonstrate that literacy programs, as long as they are not operated as an isolated service, can be a vital aspect of a personal development strategy.

Two premises underlie this strategy:

- Within a region, education programs are like the pieces of a puzzle, which together form the whole picture. Negotiation must be based on the concept of a path. (Is it possible to have integration-oriented training paths for individuals? How can complementarity be achieved?)

- All other things being equal, there is nothing wrong with setting oneself job-integration objectives. However it has been stressed that there is no automatic, unequivocal training-job connection. The objective of a training program should not be merely to meet company requirements. On the contrary, the primary goal is educating the population, i.e. individuals able to understand what goes on around them, to get along in the world, to design projects and negotiate with others to ensure their implementation.

The strategy promoted in this paper is fully consistent with the philosophy of popular education. This in no way implies that community associations should not, as part of the process, seek a more stable position, considering the invaluable services they provide. For the time being, what we are proposing is negotiation of "local social pacts" on joint management of personal development projects by associations and public services.

If this can be made to work in a region, the success would offer a real solution to those involved in the heated theoretical debate on the duality of society.

Over the past ten years, the dual society concept has been debated long and hard in many countries. Many observers have pointed out the steadily widening gap between the two main divisions of society: the group in which economic activity is strong, workers are protected and income is high; and the marginal group made up of relatively unprotected workers in marginal industries. Obviously a division of this kind is unacceptable. This is a macro-social fact.

Commenting on the various measures taken to solve the problem (e.g. on-the-job training), some of the same observers consider that such measures only strengthen social duality by developing small marginal markets for marginal people.

Although at the macro-social level the dual society concept is helpful in defining a real problem, at the micro-social level it loses its usefulness and becomes an ineffectual facile slogan, an empty bit of sociological jargon. What argument can a social worker use to refute a vague, undefined, categorical accusation of creating a dual society? Social workers who follow traditional methods are criticized; those who try something new are stigmatized. The social worker is thus left with nothing to say, no course of action possible: doomed to fail.

There are a number of responses to this apparent dilemma:

a) The dual society that some people seem to have recently discovered is nothing new. What else is the fourth world but a dual society which has existed since the industrial revolution?

b) In order to fight social duality, interested parties must join forces, create many instances of solidarity, speak out: collective social action is essential. If all these initiatives (including the food banks which operate in France and Belgium in the winter) provide an opportunity for collective action, they make an effective contribution to social change.

c) Underlying the social duality question is a major theoretical and practical tug-of-war: action theory and action as such must accommodate both the macro-social and micro-social viewpoints.

The personal development concept can help attain this goal. As we have seen, not only is it possible to accommodate even the tiniest of operations under the development strategy umbrella, the internal reasoning underlying most new social assistance practices is strikingly similar to the principles underlying the concept of personal economic development:

- mobilize local resources
- meet local needs
- always keeping in mind the channel concept, i.e. economic complementarity with other local activities

For the moment, all of this is only implicit. What is at stake is making it explicit: if we can define an overall strategy that can accommodate even the smallest operations, we will have the potential for mobilizing under the flag of that strategy a far larger number of participants than are currently involved[12].

Notes

1. See the works of Alaluf, Matéo et al. (Institut de sociologie de l'Université libre de Bruxelles) or those published by the Institut supérieur du travail de l'Université de Louvain-la-Neuve, Belgium (Marvoy, Christian; Charlier, Jean-Emile et al.)

2. Delors, Jacques. 1987. Interview in the weekly *Pourquoi pas?*. Brussels, 11 June.

3. Adapted from Johada, Marie; Lazarsfeld, Paul and Zeisel, Hans. [1933]. *Mariental, the sociography of an unemployed community*. London: Tavistock Publications, reissued 1972.

50

4. See also the journal *Critique régionale, cahiers de sociologie et d'économie régionale,* 1983, No. 9 (Institut de sociologie, Editions de l'Université de Bruxelles);
Alaluf, Matéo and Vanheerswynghels, Adinda. 1988. *Adéquation enseignement - marché de l'emploi.* Brussels: Fondation Roi Baudouin.

5. Cf. Georis, Pierre and Poelman, Myriam. 1988. *Jeunes et exclusion.* Brussels: Fondation Roi Baudouin.

6. Cf. Meirieu, Philippe. 1984. *Itinéraire des pédagogies de groupe.* Lyon: Chroniques sociales. (2 vols, but see esp. vol. 1, pp. 139-188)

7. In Belgium this is the case for training programs given by the Institut supérieur de culture ouvrière in both French and German: ISCO, rue de la Loi 103, 1040 Brussels.

8. Cantinaux, Roger; Creutz, Emile; Georis, Pierre and Liénard, Georges. 1989. *Exclus et non exclus.* Records of the Colloque du Conseil supérieur de l'éducation populaire, Liège, 1 December. Liège: Ministère de la Communauté française.

9. Cf. Georis, Pierre. 1986. *Les Entreprises d'apprentissage professionnel.* Brussels: Fondation Roi Baudouin.
Les Entreprises d'apprentissage professionnel may be contacted at EAP-Consultance, rue Bélliard 23A, 1040 Brussels.
Les Actions intégrées de développement may be contacted at AID, rue de la Loi 103, 1040 Brussels.

10. The EC is working in this vein to define the projects it supports under the umbrella of its 3rd anti-poverty programme (Poverty 3).

11. Fondation Marcel Hicter. 1987. *Des associations.* Brussels: PAC/Vie ouvrière.

12. Cf. Georis, Pierre. 1988. *Namur lutte contre la pauvreté. De l'aide sociale à la pratique économique.* Charleroi: Editions alternatives wallonnes.

BREAKING DOWN BARRIERS:
A LOCAL APPROACH TO ADULT BASIC EDUCATION

Blair Denwette
Maria Walker
Lynn Tett
WABET, Dundee, U.K.

Background to the Project

In the last decade public attention in Great Britain has increasingly focused on the many problems associated with life in our cities, with the issues of urban decline and how to reverse it high on the agenda. In 1988 the Government produced a White Paper, *New Life for Urban Scotland,* which examined these difficult issues and how to tackle them, setting out ten indices by which to identify deprived areas. Whitfield, the site of the project, meets all these indices and is a typical example of the multiple deprivation described in the White Paper.

Whitfield is an extensive housing estate on the northern edge of the Scottish east coast city of Dundee, almost entirely composed of local authority housing owned by Dundee District Council. It has developed a range of severe problems over recent years because of some very poor housing stock (particularly in the deck-access blocks of the Skarne area), a considerable transient population, a lack of jobs locally, the highest level of unemployment in Dundee, and a high rate of dependence on income support and housing benefit. The population has declined and the number of vacant houses has increased dramatically. The whole estate, in fact, has a very poor image.

There are no major industrial or commercial employers located within Whitfield and male unemployment, at 40%, is more than double the rate for the rest of the city. One in six people has been continuously unemployed for more than five years, and those in work are mainly on low incomes. There is a high incidence of poverty, with 73% of the tenants in receipt of housing benefit and an increasing number of single-parent families.

The estate was designed as a pedestrian zone, with vehicles restricted to the main road which circles the periphery of the estate, and to the car parks at entrances to residential blocks. Footpaths criss-cross the large areas of open space separating residential areas from shopping and other facilities: in practice, however, as a result of the distances involved (up to two miles) and poor street lighting at night, the footpaths are not well used. The shopping centre itself is inadequate and run-down, and the pub which is situated there is a constant source of conflict. A number of voluntary groups are active in the area but there is insufficient provision for young people, and the community facilities which do exist at Whitfield High School are little used in the evening because of its isolated location.

The Whitfield Partnership

As a result of Government White Paper, the Whitfield Partnership was set up in June 1988 'to develop and coordinate the implementation of a strategy for the long-term regeneration of Whitfield, in line with the Government's objectives for urban regeneration'. The Partnership comprises representatives of central and local government, national housing, economic and industrial agencies, together with representatives of the local community. It proposes a broad-based strategy rather than a detailed blueprint for the regeneration of Whitfield, and its aim has been to build on the strengths of the area and on the efforts already made to improve it.

Housing and environmental change are an essential part of the regeneration of Whitfield but they cannot progress in isolation: improvements in employment and training and in community facilities are essential features of long-term opportunities in the area. A coordinated and sustained investment programme will be required over the next five to ten years if regeneration is to have lasting success. Needless to say, the challenge this presents is one of considerable magnitude, and not the least part of the task is to motivate the residents of the area behind the strategy. It is here that Adult Basic Education can play a significant role in the regeneration of Whitfield.

Adult Basic Education

If, nationally, one third of the adult population of Great Britain has basic education needs, an area of multiple deprivation like Whitfield, with a population of between 10,000 and 12,000, may be expected to have a considerable need for ABE. In practice, however, most of the areas of social priority in Scotland tend to be under-represented in terms of ABE provision. In 1986, Tayside's Adult Basic Education Unit had virtually no presence in what is the largest deprived area in the Region, and there had been no group provision of ABE offered there for more than three years, one of the major reasons being that there was no demand to justify such a group. It was not that ABE was not available to people in Whitfield, but response to ABE advertising on TV and in the newspapers had never been successful. The situation was, therefore, at odds with statistical expectations.

Traditional ABE practice in Scotland usually involves a two-hour-per-week face-to-face contact with the adult student. The mode of delivery is 1:1, with a volunteer providing the tutoring skills. Depending on funding, there will be some professional support, but this varies greatly across Scotland. Volunteers are used as *cheap* educational labour, but this is a fallacy, as 1:1 tutoring needs a high level of support and training. Similarly, it assumes the student is highly motivated and confident, to at least the degree of *admitting* there is a *problem*, and undertaking a great deal of self-study in his or her free time.

In 1986 a ABE worker based at the Continuing Education Unit in Mitchell Street, Dundee, was given the task of trying to build up a responsive ABE provision in the Whitfield area. The idea was to work towards a strategy that would allow the unit to work with as many people as possible. An explanation of alternative modes of delivery was necessary, not only as an attempt to respond to Whitfield but in the hope of informing a rationalisation of the total provision within Tayside.

The aims of the project were specified as follows:

- to raise the profile of ABE in Whitfield;
- to make ABE more accessible to Whitfield residents;
- to establish local referral points to obviate the need for direct contact with the Mitchell Street base in the process.

A traditional ABE group was not seen as the way forward. It seemed better to work at making the Whitfield area as self-sustaining as possible by using local volunteers and local agencies and by tapping into education already provided. The method used was to talk to professionals and volunteers in the many local agencies, rather than to set up yet another agency. Each of these visits had much the same structure: the intention was to give information about the ABE unit, to find out about the work of the agency, and to emphasize the ABE role of the service which could be useful to the agency and its clients. The hope was to put ABE in the minds of contacts. Reliable and appropriate reaction to needs was seen as a priority and ABE input was not to be restricted only to the unit: it was hoped that the networking process would allow the unit to act in a mediating role.

This initiative had mixed success. Contacts with local people helped to confirm ABE needs and it is probable that these needs would not otherwise have been expressed. To fulfil demand, groups were set up and this extra time commitment took away from the time that was intended for networking. At the outset, professional workers had low opinions of local commitment and these appeared to have been borne out in the initiative over that year. The evidence, however, was not nearly conclusive. While having a worker in situ may have removed some barriers to involvement, commitment and motivation, many others seemed to have been created by workers and agencies themselves.

The ABE response was also heavily marred by unnecessary barriers. Access to local referral points was subject to the problems above and there was pressure to base provision in under-used centres. Many of the recruited volunteers doing their training at the Mitchell Street Centre actually became volunteers there, rather than in Whitfield. In writing his conclusion to the initiative, the worker at the time made some very important observations:

> Given the size and nature of Whitfield's problems, it is easy to conclude that much more time should be spent in ABE work. While ABE groupwork has a limited response, it is better than nothing at all. However, given the apparent reluctance of local residents, the patterns of groupwork would certainly need to be further modified in order to work. It seems that agencies such as ours need to move further towards the community, rather than to expect the community to come to us. In

practice this would mean that we should adapt our work to realities and actual patterns of interest in the area, perhaps by offering groups in places where people already meet, perhaps by integrating what we offer with what people already do, or with what they would like to do. Group provision cannot be the whole answer, because many barriers, including lack of confidence, lack of social skill or lack of hope or knowledge would mean that individuals would not readily come to an ABE group or any other type of group in Whitfield. Other means of access are needed.

Traditional methods did not work in Whitfield because of the factors already mentioned - low motivation, because of the lack of expectation that education is worthwhile; lack of self-confidence; inadequate social and family support; and economic instability. It was clear that an entirely new approach was needed, and when, in October 1988, the Minister for Education in the Scottish Office, Mr. Michael Forsyth, announced that there would be money totalling £30,000 per annum to set up an Open Learning Centre in Scotland for Adult Basic Education, the opportunity to initiate an innovative project was very tempting to Tayside Regional Council's Continuing Education Unit.

The timetable for submission was short, and within a week, Tayside Community Education Service's staff formulated a proposal for an outreach adult basic education base which would be locally accessible, friendly and without stigma. They wished the project to be a collaborative venture between the Region, other voluntary bodies and the local people.

Once the idea was formed, voluntary bodies already working with the Unit were asked to become part of the Trust which submitted the proposals. These voluntary bodies were:

- Dundee Resource Centre for the Unemployed;
- The Aberlour Trust;
- Tayside Community Enterprise Support Team;
- and various community organisation representatives.

The Whitfield Adult Basic Education Trust was formed by these interested voluntary bodies in Whitfield and, in essence, aimed to set up a project which was a voluntary organisation through and through - directors, volunteers and students - all contributing to the new approach to ABE. The area covered by the Project's remit included

not only Whitfield itself, but also the adjacent housing schemes of
Fintry and Mid-Craigie. In formulating the aims of the Whitfield
Adult Basic Education Project, the experiences of the previous
initiative in 1986 were important. Equally important was the feeling
in ABE circles in Scotland that the traditional methods only work in
a limited number of cases. The aims of the Project were as follows:

a) *Adult Basic Education*
   Generally this was to involve short course work over one to two
   days per week, rather than the traditional two hour per week
   model. The main emphasis would be on group work, looking at
   particular skills, e.g., spelling and numeracy in the workplace. It
   was also proposed that there would be issue-based work. The
   Trust hoped to target local families and the unemployed, as well
   as local groups. Because of the interest shown by one of the
   founder members, the Aberlour Trust, particular emphasis was to
   be given to family work, probably in the evenings, to try to
   break the cycle of illiteracy.

b) *Adult educational guidance*
   The Trust proposed a facility for educational guidance with
   regard to opportunities within Tayside. Guidance regarding adult
   education and employment opportunities would also be available
   as the Trust made contact with local providers.

c) *Enterprise education*
   Particular attention would be given to individual enterprise. This
   would involve encouraging abilities and motivation through
   confidence-building and using this to develop competence. It was
   not seen that the Trust would be in competition with other
   enterprise bodies: rather, it would try to develop skills within the
   individual which would make enterprise work possible.

d) *Job seeking*
   The Trust hoped to encourage group tuition for the Scottish
   Vocational Education Council (SCOTVEC) Modules in relevant
   subjects. There would also be opportunities for Computer-assisted
   Learning and Basic Computer Literacy. It was hoped to encourage general confidence- building through group work and
   communications to lead to better job-seeking skills.

The project was submitted for Scottish Office approval and confirmation of a grant of £30,000 per annum was the signal for the work to begin in earnest. Suitable premises had to be found for the Project. The choice facing the Trust comprised: a disused police station; a maisonette with ground-floor entry; and a vacant shop previously used as a launderette. The idea of a shop as a base appealed - it would seem more *business-like* than the usual family centre type of premises. Thus, although it was more expensive than the other alternatives, the shop was thought by all concerned to be the best option. Taking on such a project meant that the Trust had to adopt a more suitable legal status.

WABET had been planned as a Trust, with a constitution not unlike those of many other voluntary organisations, and with representatives from Tayside Regional Council, as well as a membership of local people. When it was decided to lease a shop, however, the initial ideas had to change.

Leasing the shop meant undertaking a contract of 20 years with the property owners, which was out of the question, given the three-year funding of the Project. After correspondence with the property owners, however, a lease of four years was agreed, provided they were dealing with a limited company. Other factors regarding tax and general liability were also prompting the original members to seek limited company status, and the Trust's solicitor was instructed accordingly. This inevitably slowed the pace of work, as the Trust had to wait for the various administrative and legal requirements to be completed.

Meanwhile local consultation began. The Team were very anxious to include local people in both the management and the actual life of the Project. It is true to say that quite extensive opposition was encountered in the beginning, because the Project had obtained funding without any real consultation with the local people. Local activists and Whitfield residents were, not surprisingly, very cynical about yet another professional organisation "parachuting" into the area. There were already very many voluntary organisations, community groups, Urban Aid projects, and government initiatives in Whitfield. The early days of WABET Ltd. also coincided with the early days of the Central Government-funded Whitfield Partnership.

Limited local consultation *had* taken place and this caused many problems in the early weeks. Some local activists felt that the

Project should not be supported, while others thought that, though the way the Project had to be submitted meant little consultation had been possible, now that it had some to Whitfield, it should be given full support. When the situation was explained, however, most local community groups were happy that the Project was coming to Whitfield. A long series of public consultations began, culminating in April, 1989, when the Limited Company was formed, and, after the first few months, the Directors of WABET Ltd. had whole-hearted support from local people, politicians and officials.

As the builders moved in to the former launderette, the Team were determined that it should be a bright attractive place, with no trappings reminiscent of office or school. Even the chairs were re-covered easy chairs, rather than normal office furniture. About this time, it was learned that the Training Agency also intended to sponsor the Learning Shop and a grant of £20,000 was received to purchase new technology equipment. This equipment proved to be one of the best buys, as the computers and word processors attracted many people into the shop who might never otherwise have crossed its threshold.

People were prepared to admit that they were computer illiterate and thereby to do something about their literacy, which would never have happened had that equipment not been available. Certainly a few mistakes were made in the purchase of equipment but nothing too serious. Reflecting on that time, the Directors and workers were extremely busy and tasks had to be allocated and fulfilled very quickly. In many ways, it was a time of team building among these people and the strong bond forged between Directors and Project Coordinator has never yet been broken - though often tested!

Perhaps a few words are necessary about the Directors. At the time of writing there are eight Directors of the Company, two from the local authority, one from an Urban Aid Community Enterprise Support Team, one from the Aberlour Trust and four members of the Whitfield community.

The Project Coordinator's Experience

This section relates the personal experience of Blair Denwette, the Project Co-ordinator, in setting up and developing the Project. To convey the essential element of direct experience, it has been deliberately kept in the first person.

As has been stated earlier, ABE involvement with the peripheral areas of Dundee has never been entirely successful.

Despite some initial reservations on being asked to co-ordinate this Project, I found the prospect both exciting and challenging, because it would allow me to approach ABE from a local base in a developmental way.

Initial contacts were made with local professionals from Tayside's Community Education Service to:

- advise them of what was envisaged, and
- identify a local network of professional organisations and local community-managed projects.

It was during this period that I became aware that communication and collaboration with the local community - both activists and professionals - was not only desirable but essential. The task, therefore, was to involve local people from the outset or within a short period of time.

Our two principal objectives in this preliminary period were:

1. to establish a high profile and a working provision in the area, and
2. to negotiate for premises in the area.

Networking model

My approach to objective (1) involved the recruitment of local and other interested volunteers (tutors and students already committed to ABE) to discuss how best to make these initial contacts. Following detailed discussion among ourselves, we decided on a networking model. In his paper *Adult Education and Community Development - A Network Approach*, Tom Lovett talks of Adult Education as a resource for Community Development and describes a project set up in Liverpool as a network model (see Appendix 1). This approach required considerable training and legwork: but as a method of obtaining and giving information it was to prove very successful.

Initial contacts were made to:

- identify what information we should be giving at this stage;
- establish possible links/areas of collaboration with local organisations;
- identify any immediate provision requirements; and
- obtain information on access to clients/users of the local agencies and services.

Once a clear method of addressing the above had been established within the networking group, a strategy was devised to raise the confidence of group members and train the volunteers in networking.

This training involved responding to the expressed needs of the group, as well as participation in direct face-to-face contact with agencies/organisations in the community. In my capacity as Co-ordinator, and accompanied by the college student on placement, I visited high-priority agencies, giving and receiving the information required. This information was then discussed and appropriately recorded by the group as a whole, prior to any further visits. The initial pair then split up and took responsibility for involving another two group members, thus developing a pyramid structure. This style of development was extended until all group members were actively involved in the exercise.

As a method of recording, the group devised a flow chart that could be easily followed and would display visually the current stage of contact.

It was during this visiting period that many local educational needs emerged which required immediate response; these ranged from people who wanted to brush up on spelling, to those who weren't sure what they wanted but knew it involved study skills. By utilising the expertise of our tutors, and acting on the positive response from local agencies to our requests for space/accommodation and creche provision, we were able to respond to the community demands identified at the outset of the exercise.

It should be noted at this stage that these requests came not only from existing groups, but also from individuals within the community at large.

The use of the networking approach should not be seen as a one-off exercise: we have found that there is a continuing need to affirm and reaffirm our community involvement.

Negotiation for premises

In addition to the development of ABE, the Company, in consultation with the local community, had to negotiate for suitable premises and, as has already been mentioned, settled on a shop as the best option for our purposes. Architectural guidance was sought, and plans were submitted to the local authority, so that the very extensive refurbishment could commence. Our initial idea was that a shop front would provide an easy means of access to informal, locally-based education and guidance.

Many major headaches were encountered during these early stages of the Company's existence. On reflection, however, the constant to-ing and fro-ing to meet with builders, architects, etc. allowed us to get to know local residents and shopkeepers.

The official opening of *The Learning Shop* was held at the beginning of September 1989.

Having a base to work from had many advantages: for example, people could drop in for education as they would drop in to a newsagent for a newspaper, and it provided a constant source of learning opportunities in the heart of the community.

There were, however, disadvantages, in that much of the proactive outreach work had to be curtailed to accommodate staffing and security needs and the day-to-day running of the Learning Shop.

At this stage the staff consisted of the Project Co-ordinator, one full-time and one part-time adult education worker, one part-time clerical support worker, a small number of part-time paid group tutors and volunteers, and by December 1989, further funding had been obtained to appoint another full-time project worker (ABE).

Publicity

The provision and take-up of provision over the months prior to the opening of the Shop had raised our awareness of how we should publicise the work and development of the organisation. Posters and leaflets made little - often no - impact, in that what we were offering would only ever be identified through basic educational needs: e.g. spelling courses, budgeting courses, etc. Local newspaper adverts likewise brought no response.

The lessons learned from this exercise directed us into a dialogical approach to addressing the effects of illiteracy and innumeracy; e.g. a parent unable to help a child with homework, or someone unable to claim benefit because inability to read about, or claim for, the benefits available.

Our main method of publicity has, therefore, been by word of mouth: this has been particularly effective in promoting new technology as a tool for developing and addressing ABE needs.

Constant dialogue with community groups and individuals has also directed us into issue-based learning, incorporating ABE. Issues have ranged from someone requiring help to write a letter regarding a dampness problem, to a group raising community awareness of the culture and history of graffiti. Taking on this type of crisis or issue is a strong motivator for learning.

Drop-in

As I have already said, from a professional point of view the advantages of having the shop as a base are many - people can drop in for education as they would drop in to a newsagent for a newspaper, and it can provide a constant source of learning opportunities in the heart of Whitfield. Before this happy state could be achieved, however, the team needed to work hard, through the networking process, to raise local awareness of the presence of the Learning Shop and the services it could offer the community.

The Project offers a flexible educational provision which is deter-mined by individual learning needs and styles. These individual styles range from a person seeking individual tutoring on a week-by-week basis, to someone utilising the premises for self-directed study work with limited tutor support. In the Appendices to this Chapter are some accounts of individual experiences of the Learning Shop's flexible provision system.

Local co-investigation

The adoption of the networking model opened dialogue with all community organisations and user groups. We needed to develop a strategy to reach those sections of the community which had not been reached through the community organisations. A group of users and workers was formed to further develop a strategy to reach out into the community.

The Co-investigating Group's aims might be summarised as:

- to contact those local people for whom schooling has been an unsuccessful and uninviting experience;

- to enable those people to identify the issues that confront them;

- to assist people to build relevant educational and action programmes, in the light of the issues identified; and

- to help people reflect on their new knowledge and/or action in order to address the issues more creatively or more critically.

These general aims may be said to be a methodological description of the educational process developed by Paulo Freire in his book *Pedagogy of the Oppressed.*

We carried out a co-investigation of the area, utilising local volunteers and technology - a video camera, audio equipment and stills cameras. We approached this task in four stages:

1. Recruitment of volunteers from among individuals already using the service, as well as others interested in this particular approach.

2. Training in the technological aspects of the equipment, as well as how the material produced could be redirected to the community.

3. Discussion of themes and issues identified through audio or visual material.

4. Re-presentation of the material and of themes and issues to the community.

One project undertaken by part of the Co-investigation Group was to photograph local everyday life. The photographers' only remit was that they should identify three key points for each photograph taken, which were:

- What am I taking?
- Why I am taking it?
- Who am I taking it for?

These photographs were then processed, developed and presented to the group as a whole for discussion and analysis of main themes or issues. This method of identification of issues brought about an open and honest dialogue between group members, which raised fundamental questions of moral judgement, discrimination and prejudice, and eventually resulted in greater group solidarity and strength.

One of the issues identified by the group was that, during the summer months, vast numbers of the local population virtually disappeared for the *berry picking*. The agricultural land around Dundee is a famous soft fruit-growing area, and many local people take an casual work picking the fruit in the summer months. The group decided to do a photographic study of this exodus, as well as recording the thoughts, feelings, and difficulties surrounding basic skills in number and written communication; for example, how do I know if I'm being cheated, if I can't understand the difference between kilos and pounds?

On completion of the practical tasks of visiting the berry fields and having the photographs processed and developed, an exhibition was mounted in the Learning Shop window for public viewing and comment. This exercise, along with others of a similar nature, has encouraged many people to address their specific needs in basic skills development.

Mothers' Planning Group

Here is the experience of a tutor using the co-investigation approach with a group:

The *Mothers' Planning Group* are a group of 13 women who meet every fortnight. They initially met informally, and through discussions identified issues concerning their lives.

In the Co-investigation style of work, once we identify the community's issues, we re-direct them to the people. The issues we identified were around children, and the need for a Soft Play Room. It was realised that this was a necessity, particularly for the mothers of children with special needs, who seem to be more isolated.

The first part of the co-investigation was concerned with what we call *secondary information,* which is a research period consisting in the gathering of knowledge about the identified issue. In this way, other similar projects were contacted and visited, including Rainbow House in Mid-Craigie and ALP Edinburgh.

Subsequently a survey was drawn up and people went out into the streets to discuss the issue with the community and gather information. At the same time some questions aimed at parents of children with special needs were sent to several schools, which agreed to send copies to children's parents.

The group regularly discussed the information gathered, and set up a campaign for a Soft Toy Room, drawing posters and inviting new mothers to join the group.

Other issues have been identified, such as health, vandalism, dog fouling, and teenagers' and pensioners' integration into the neighbourhood.

A photo-investigation called *No Place To Go* is currently expanding on one of the identified issues - the lack of facilities in the area.

As the group is progressing in their work, letters are being sent; e.g. to shopkeepers, the local clinic and nursery. New skills are required such as writing letters, spelling and even budgeting for the group's campaign. New ABE courses are being set up in order to provide for such needs.

In this way the co-investigation has struck a balance between action and reflection, and the educational process has been established around issues concerning the community, at the same time as giving its members self-confidence and skills, such as listening and working in groups.

Raising professional awareness

Much of the work of the Project has concentrated on breaking down the stigma and cycle of illiteracy by addressing the effects of inability to read, write and count. This has involved raising not only the community's awareness, but also that of professionals coming to work in the area: for example, social workers, police and the formal education sector. To this end, a seminar was organised to which all professionals from the area were invited. We were greatly encouraged by the number of participants, and also by the level of debate and interest in future collaborative work.

We are currently two years into the Project and now feel that we have an identity with, and within, the local community. Much has been achieved through experimentation. To a great extent, this process is still being worked through, with new ideas emanating from a variety of sources within and without the community. It is essential that we continually assess our work through evaluation and reflection.

In conclusion, I would hope that, by using this process and by continuing to listen to the community, we can create a worthwhile partnership to develop an educational curriculum that is for the community, in the community and, most importantly, developed by the community. This ultimate goal will continue to challenge, inform and direct the work of the Project in the future.

Styles and Methods of Provision

Tutor training

The thinking from the outset of WABET's community involvement has been directed towards an open-ended educational curriculum which would be in the community, for the community and developed by the community. This philosophy has been realised only to a limited extent. A major difficulty has centred around the mystique of education and the skills required to tutor an adult in basic education. When this is coupled with low confidence and self-esteem it has, in many cases, prevented local people from offering their help.

Tutors have, therefore, been recruited from other, more affluent areas of Dundee, a factor which may, unfortunately, create the impression that education can only be facilitated by outsiders.

There are, however, a number of local people who, by addressing their own learning needs, have become confident of their own ability and are taking more responsibility in assisting other learners. For those individuals who have reached this stage, this is a major step, and for the Project workers it has required considerable effort in building trust and developing relationships.

Training for WABET's tutors has been developed in collaboration with Tayside Region's Continuing Education Unit. This has a set eight-session *Induction Programme* looking at attitudes, awareness and skills requirements, such as spelling and early reading.

This induction should equip the volunteer with a base for beginning to work with a student. However, the *real* training starts when a tutor identifies the specific needs of the student/learner. The Project can then respond to these specific training needs.

As the Project has moved away from traditional ABE approaches, it has had to develop an additional groupwork training course for tutors involved in this area. The training is run over six sessions, and covers subjects from group dynamics to consideration of how literacy and numeracy - as related to issues such as budgeting or helping children with homework - can be facilitated through the groupwork process. It is hoped that the success of this training so far will allow greater flexibility in what is already on offer in the Learning Shop.

ABE seeks to identify individual skills and strengths and to build on them. A *holistic* or whole-person approach ensures that literacy and numeracy are only a part of the whole picture. Very often the illiterate person will be sigmatised and marginalised, and will feel he/she has failed and been rejected by society. The Project, through collaborative work in the community, has striven to dispel these myths.

As has already been discussed in the methodology section, the Learning Shop offers a wide range of opportunities which can broadly be described as computer-assisted learning, enterprise education, family education, and adult basic education. Educational guidance is also available, both at the Learning Shop on a drop-in basis and at the end of courses, so that students have the opportunity to think about where they should go next. Because individuals vary in their learning styles, a range of degrees of participation is offered, including one-to-one, group work, self-direction and immediate help with specific problems.

The *drop-in* provision available in the shop is greatly assisted by having the tutor rota system, where a tutor will spend, for example, one regular morning or afternoon per week in the Learning Shop. As well as being *on duty* to deal with immediate requests, the trained volunteers are encouraged to utilise this time and space for personal educational development. The rota system also allows an opportunity for support and supervision and, furthermore, can assist in identifying volunteers' specific training needs (see A Volunteer's Perspective - Appendix 2).

Types of provision offered

In terms of computer-assisted learning, the shop offers a variety of opportunities using the computers as an attraction and as a tool. As well as using computers in one-to-one contacts with students, the shop offers a *Dabblers* group to satisfy casual interest, two groups covering basic computer literacy, and a more advanced group for those who wish to move on from the basic provision. Students can also book time on the computer for self-directed learning. Computers have been used to assist in learning keyboard skills; basic programming; basic wordprocessing skills; use of technology to assist the search for work (CV's, letters of application); pursuit of training opportunities by using the database of learning opportunities contained in *Training Access Points*; and acquiring a basic grounding before going on to study the subject at a higher level in a Further Education College (see An Ex-Student's Perspective - Appendix 3).

There is a steady demand for Enterprise Education relating to the ever-changing face of Whitfield. Since their arrival in the area, the Whitfield Partnership, implementing their social strategy plans, have sought to work with the local community in areas of general concern. This, in turn, has generated demands from individuals who need to write letters or fill in forms, and from treasurers of local committees who require basic book-keeping skills. Provision for groups has been in terms of communication skills courses, which have centred around areas of written and verbal skills as well as written and verbal presentation, and seeking and planning information. These courses have also allowed individual group members to pursue for any further ABE provision they may require.

The establishment of links with other agencies in the area has enabled the Learning Shop to identify specific issues for group work, not always immediately associated with basic education. The demand for book-keeping and secretarial skills from members of local committees has already been mentioned. There were also a number of individual requests to address study skills. With guidance from the Continuing Education Unit, SCOTVEC Modules were developed and are currently being delivered in *Options and Choices*, and *Com-*

munications II. Ways of raising the community's involvement with local schools' adult education provision are also being sought.

Provision is made in several other locations as well as the Learning Shop. St. Matthew's Family Centre, which can provide a creche, hosts the book-keeping group, a return to study group, and a creative writers' group. A fathers' group, men who are bringing up their children alone, meet in the Whitfield Family Centre where, by sharing their experiences, fears, etc., through the group, they are beginning to address what *education* can do for them personally and how this can happen. A mothers' planning group meets in Fintry Church. The group has identified a variety of community issues concerning members' lives, including health, vandalism, integration of teenagers and pensioners, and the lack of facilities in the area, and are acquiring the skills which will help them tackle these issues.

A group have been meting in Mid-Craigie to begin to investigate the needs of the community there at grass-roots level, but this is a new area which has so far been rather unresponsive, and perhaps a different strategy will be needed.

. Family education concentrates on helping parents with the issues they identify, which can range from helping with children's education using computers, to fighting for better facilities in the area for children. Although Open University packs are available, the uptake has been low and their use in groupwork has been limited.

A very interesting development has been the *co-investigation* projects, which have used Freirian methodology to help local people identify and investigate the issues which are important to them. Both the fathers' group and the mothers' planning group began life in this way, and there is also a Whitfield History Project group which began in May 1990 and is continuing. One very interesting co-investigation project was *The Berry Season.* The recordings and photographs taken were made into an album which could be used for de-codification sessions. A similar project concentrated on the graffiti with which the area is plagued, and produced an album of photographs of various graffiti which were discussed with the community.

Problems

A number of factors which work against consistent student/tutor meetings, including difficulty in contacting students by telephone, and social, economic and personal factors which may inhibit the take-up of provision after the first contact with staff were identified, and a new referral system was introduced in August 1990. This procedure utilises the rota of experienced volunteers who can attend immediately to interested individuals and thus work to achieve a first positive feedback. Working within a social strategy area with serious financial problems and inadequate childcare provision, in addition to problems of low expectations, has major implications for educationalists. Much of the team's work and pro-activity has therefore involved looking at ways of providing childcare facilities and alleviating financial restrictions through collaborative work with other local organisations.

It became apparent early in the Project that there could be a danger of providing a drop-in social environment. This, no doubt, had a lot to do with the shop's informal, relaxed and open atmosphere and approaches to adult education. For this reason a number of ground rules had to be set for project users, to achieve a balance between education and socialisation.

All the provision made by WABET has come about as a result of a real dialogue between the workers and the local community about their issues. This is why it has succeeded.

Main Lessons Learned from the Project

What has been learned from the Project which will enable WABET to provide more appropriate basic education for its students and help funding bodies to understand what they can expect?

The first lesson is the time it takes to get anything off the ground, particularly in areas of deprivation. Funding bodies must not expect quick results from a project such as this which, of its very nature, is a long-term undertaking. Time is necessary to gain the trust of the local community, who are naturally suspicious of professionals. The latter are often perceived by locals as *do-gooders* who will shortly leave the area again without having made any impact, a perception for which the professionals themselves are frequently to blame.

Arising from this point is the further lesson that, if you listen to and work with the community, a worthwhile partnership can be created that will, to quote Blair Denwette, result in: "an educational curriculum that is for the community, in the community and developed by the community."

Listening to the community, building up networks and negotiating a curriculum takes resources, especially staff time, and money. Another lesson learned from Project is that adequate funding is necessary, both for the staffing of the shop and the continuation of the vital networking and outreach activities. There is an unfortunate tendency in official circles to expect first class results on the cheap, but genuine and lasting achievements in this field are only possible if adequate funding is available. People will not drop into a shop to *buy* education. They need to know what is on offer, and the mechanisms to disseminate the information required must be there, and must be paid for.

In terms of publicity, the Project has clearly illustrated that advertising courses is a totally ineffective strategy, whereas talking to key activists, local groups, local leaders and key professionals, can be effective. Posters and leaflets have little immediate effect, but word-of-mouth, through satisfied students, tutors and volunteers, has proved to be the most effective way of involving local people.

An important lesson in terms of the curriculum is that in many social priority areas, basic education must be approached obliquely. Very few people are willing to seek help with basic literacy skills, but many are attracted by the opportunity to learn basic technological skills such as word processing. The objective in both cases is the same - to give people the opportunity to improve their basic communication skills -but the means must be attractive to the users of the service. Flexibility and a willingness to adapt ABE practice to suit changing perceptions of educational need are essential; otherwise, of course, the service will not be used.

The image of the Project is crucial, both in terms of the availability of new technology and in terms of its purpose. WABET was clear that it had an educational purpose, and so all students worked to achieve negotiated learning outcomes, covering a short time period, and which were re-negotiated as necessary. This meant that no student was dropping into the shop just because it provided a warm, comfortable environment.

Since the Project is the only one of its kind in Scotland, it has created a high degree of interest from organisations throughout the country. There were times when visits from interested parties seemed almost to take over from the actual work of the Learning Shop. The interest shown, and the questions raised with regard to our styles and methods of work have allowed us to challenge and assess our work and philosophy continually.

In terms of learning opportunities, WABET has provided a bridge between informal and formal learning opportunities, by enabling students to take the first step back to learning, but then offering opportunities for them to move on. It should not be forgotten that, to adults unaccustomed to participation in this field, the perceived image of further education and the effort involved in pursuing a course of study can be as intimidating as they are attractive. Educational guidance was played a crucial role in enabling people who have taken their first step back into education to clarify what they want to do and where they could move on to. The provision of guidance facilities in the Learning Shop and to the student groups has been a vital method of ensuring that individuals are informed about the choices and options open to them.

A final lesson is the value of the Project in terms of human resource development. We have already spoken of the blurring of the tutor/student distinction and the value to anyone who embarks on a learning programme of the increase in self-confidence. Each person who takes part in such a programme has a multiplier function, in terms of the benefit to that individual's family, the wider community, and the economy as a whole. Since each student is likely to have a direct effect on at least three other people (children, partner, parents, friends), the long-term benefit to the community is immeasurable. Community regeneration of any kind is impossible without the whole-hearted support and participation of the people. Motivate the individual and you will be well on the way to achieving your goal.

APPENDIX 1

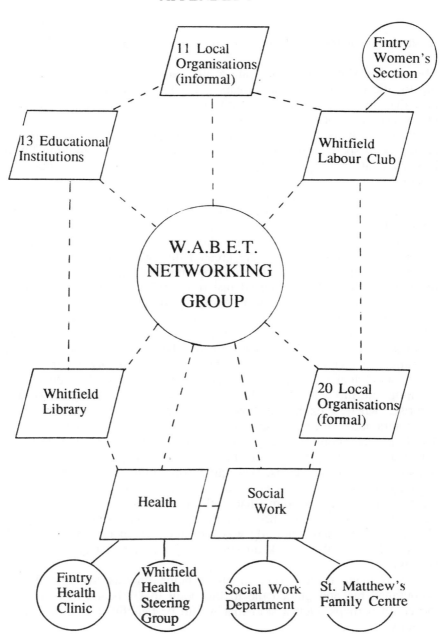

APPENDIX 2

A Volunteer's Perspective: Volunteer Tutor Training

My name is Maureen Smith. I am a 39 year old housewife who, discovering for the first time in many years that I had only myself to think about now that my son had left home and my husband was working abroad, had no excuses for not doing the things that I wanted to do.

I had not worked for approximately ten years, most of my working life having been spent in the secretarial field. When I began looking for work I discovered very quickly that I had no experience of modern office machinery; i.e. word processors, computers, fax machines, etc.

I made enquiries into further education and in doing this heard about Voluntary Work for the first time. I telephoned Brian Maddox at Mitchell Street who invited me along for an informal chat. I have to say that I had not even realised there was such a thing as Adult Basic Education. I had heard of the problems that were created through illiteracy via the media, i.e. newspapers and television programmes, but it was not until I sat listening to Brian that I realised just how difficult it was for people who cannot read and write to cope in everyday situations.

Brian gave me some literature to read and also gave me the names of other people who might be able to help me. One of the names he passed on to me was that of Blair Denwette of The Learning Shop at Whitfield. I arranged a meeting with Blair. That was back in December, 1990 and since then I feel that I have learned so much. I applied to do my Tutor Training, but the next course did not start until 15th January, 1991. To my surprise, when I explained how little experience I had, especially in computers and word processors, Blair suggested I spend some time within The Learning Shop, generally helping out where I could. I have to say it was very easy to yes, but the reality of attending The Learning Shop, ignorant of its basic needs, was quite something else. However, on the morning of Monday, 3rd December, 1990 I duly arrived at Whitfield. By the time I left at 5.00 p.m. that night I felt, for the first time in many years, that I had accomplished something. I had been shown round by very kind and helpful staff. Nothing was too much for them. I am one of these people who will always ask questions, and I found that there was always an answer.

I was made to feel very much at home on this my first day; they encouraged me and guided me to the point that I began to realise that I too could perhaps learn a skill that would be beneficial to others in some capacity.

By the end of the first week I had a basic knowledge of computers and word processors. The most important thing for me was the fact that I had been watching and listening to what was going on within the Shop and I was very impressed by the facilities being offered, but even more impressed by the manner in which the staff dealt with the students coming in. Nothing was too much for the staff. Of they themselves could not specifically help, they would not let anyone go empty-handed. They just looked further afield for whatever it was the student was after.

As December was drawing to a close, I was beginning to feel confident in what I was doing and I was looking forward to the official training time in the hope that I too could become a volunteer tutor.

On one occasion when the staff were preparing some work for one of their groups, I asked if I could help and was assisting by doing some photocopying. I was enlarging something and didn't know what it said so obviously I asked. To my surprise it was a greeting in Gaelic. It said *A Merry Xmas and a Happy New Year*. To me it could have been French, German, Arabic - in fact, any foreign language. This was when I realised what it must be like for people who cannot read English. I actually think it would be a very good example for letting people see what it's like not to be able to read.

A few days before the Shop closed for the Christmas break, due to ill health, one of the tutors did not arrive and she had been unable to cancel her appointment with her student. On the student's arrival I was asked if I would like to help. I have to say I was both eager and nervous. However, the student soon put me at my ease and I discovered I was really enjoying myself. I had been listening and watching for a few weeks but it's like everything else - the professionals make it look so easy. I discovered then, and only then, the reason for training.

After the student had left, I asked Audrie Taylor if she would explain something to me. At one point during the session the student had begun to talk to me about herself and I found that this was taking over what we were doing. It was here that I realised I didn't know how to proceed, without hurting the student's feeling.

Audrie said she had been watching me and that I had dealt with it adequately, but as I said above, it was then that I realised that there is more to this than meets the eye.

I would like to finish by saying that I hoped to achieve a level of knowledge that I could pass on to someone else, and that by doing this, hopefully, it would help someone. In trying to achieve this, I have actually gained so much more myself.

I am very grateful for the opportunity Blair has given me, because even if I do not make the grade as a volunteer tutor the past few weeks have not been wasted, as I have really benefited from the experience.

APPENDIX 3

An Ex-Student's Perspective

I was unemployed for 6 months and had no experience in word processing. I was registered at the Whitfield Job Cabin and they referred me to WABET. I attended every Tuesday; then I gained employment and then went during my lunch hour every Wednesday. After about 8 visits to WABET I felt more confident in using the word processor. They were very helpful, taking it one stage at a time, going over things again if I did not understand them.

I feel it is no longer necessary for me to attend as my employer sent me on a full-time word processing course.

I would recommend WABET to anyone who wishes to further their skills.

ILLITERACY –
SOLELY AN EDUCATIONAL PROBLEM?

Ute Jaehn
Arbeitskreis Orientierungs-
und Bildungshilfe, Berlin

Introduction

Functional illiteracy is not only a problem with the written language but always includes a related problem too.

Becoming literate, therefore, is more than solely the acquisition of the written language, it also includes solving the related functional problem.

Every definition leaves something out, because it always deals with only partial aspects – whether it is the UNESCO definition or the above.

In our modern consumer society, in which knowledge and education are also consumed, being able to read and write inevitably has only an inadequate impact on the personal well-being of the person involved.

Theoretically, one could make a distinction and state that

a) inadequate mastery of the written language results in lower self-esteem or
b) defective acquisition of the written language can only result from existing personality defects.

For our problem it is unimportant what came first, it is merely a question of punctuation, i.e. it is arbitrary.

Studies on the origins of functional illiteracy make reference to multifactorial causes. One factor is the family circumstances, though it is more likely in this respect that reference will be made to class-specific circumstances.

Starting from the premises of system theory[1], I would like to direct attention to the family and the relationships of illiterate people and illustrate the value that can be attributed to these factors in the development of learning problems (described using reading and writing problems).

In describing the Arbeitskreis Orientierungs- und Bildungshilfe [Orientation and Education Assistance Study Group], I am attempting to give an abridged, generalized description of the fight against illiteracy.

In section 2, I use three examples of specific cases (selected in accordance with the frequency with which they occur) to discuss in more detail the relationship between reading and writing problems and family structures.

In section 3, I examine the impact on the personalities of illiterate people of their inability to express themselves in the written language to the degree demanded by society.

Section 4 deals with the personalities of those who help illiterate people and attempts to show their compulsions and developmental defects.

Finally, section 5 deals with the impact of acquisition of the written language on the learner and his relationships with other people.

In the concluding section, I attempt to indicate critical aspects of this concept and to discuss possible changes.

1. **Introduction and work of the Orientation and Educational Assistance Study Group, Berlin.**

If adults come to us, the Orientation and Educational Assistance Study Group, their development as functional illiterates has been underway for a long time. We deal with very diverse personalities who are all motivated by – in addition to social circumstances - very personal motives, dreams of what they want from life, disappointments and developments which, in the last analysis, resulted in their not being able to acquire adequate proficiency in the written language.

In order for us to be able to offer each of these personalities concrete assistance on a practical basis, each individual's development and uniqueness has to be looked at, without losing sight of the factors he has in common with other illiterates.

We first attempt to acquire through counselling sessions an initial picture of the background which led the person concerned to decide that he had a reading/writing problem, of his motivation in wanting to change his present condition and of his own assessment of his own knowledge level. This counselling is carried out by the counsellor either one-to-one with the person seeking help or with his spouse, mother, social worker – in brief an important reference person – present.

The reference persons are very important in this counselling process.

This may be illustrated by a small digression into the history of the Orientation and Educational Assistance Study Group. Until 1982/83 (the Orientation and Educational Assistance Study Group had been a non-profit organization since 1977), we always conducted the counselling sessions with the persons concerned alone.

At that date, the organizational division between counselling and instruction that we now have was not yet in place. All staff counselled participants and all gave courses. However, the participants were always counselled by someone other than their own instructor.

The people who had decided to take our program subsequently entered a two-month orientation course. In this orientation course, they then had the opportunity (usually for the first time in their lives) to exchange information with others who had similar problems and to gain insight into their own achievements (which they had previously disparaged) through the achievements of these other persons despite this defect (for example, supporting a family, obtaining a driving licence, having successfully concealed this weakness from friends and acquaintances etc.). This course, which 10–12 people usually took part in and which was given by two instructors, offered the instructors and counsellors an opportunity to compare the participant's own estimate of his level of knowledge with the instructors' assessment.

At the end of the two months, another counselling session was conducted with the participant in which motivation was examined, changes determined and precise goals agreed upon.

At the same time, the participant entered a learning group which usually consisted of 5–6 members and was guided by one or two instructors. Counselling sessions were conducted at intervals of 3–4 weeks.

At some point we were faced with the problem of *drop-outs*. There were various explanations for these. We were astonished to discover that it was precisely those persons, who in our assessment had made good progress and something equivalent to a breakthrough, who dropped out, frequently without notice, without any concluding discussion.

This caused us to take a closer look at the other living conditions of the participants and to analyze more closely the impact of the participant's learning on his direct environment.

The result was the intensification and professionalization of the counselling process (through the continuing education of instructors and counsellors) by establishing the counselling/instruction structure and by including the reference persons in the counselling process.

At present, 7 people (3 graduate psychologists and 4 graduate teachers) work in the pedagogical-psychological field in the Orientation and Educational Assistance Study Group, 2½ in counselling and 4½ in instruction.

We counsel and instruct 80–100 participants for 175 hours per week. As a rule, participants attend a course for 1–3 years. The courses are held twice a week for two hours each time. The first contact is usually by phone and frequently at the urging of third parties (social workers, probation officers, friends, acquaintances, relatives, etc.).

The initial counselling sessions are conducted prior to the arrangement of the orientation phase, the second counselling sessions (examination of the assessment) at the end of two months.

Counselling sessions during a course can be initiated by the instructor, the participant or the counsellor herself. The reasons for this are varied, for example a participant may have a problem in the course which she cannot, however, discuss in class; another may have a problem in regard to her job, or the instructor thinks that a counselling session is called for based on her observations in class. This also applies to therapeutic sessions.

In principle, the participant has two discussion partners, and although the instructors may change, the counsellor will be responsible for the participant until the end of the program.[2]

Instructors discuss course problems in their team. The counsellors exchange information on counselling problems in the counsellor team. Both teams conduct concrete case discussions. The cooperation between the counsellor and instructor starts after the initial counselling session has been conducted, by the counsellor giving the instructor information about and assessments of future participants.

The second exchange takes place after the orientation course: the instructor gives the counsellor her impression of the participant, based on the information provided by the counsellor and the instructor's experience with the participant in the course.

Both then review the target plan.

The *target group* is a very diverse group. Recently, we have seen an increase in people who hardly know the letters of the alphabet. The range extends from illiterates (2–3 letters are recognized), to people with severe writing and reading problems, to people with minor reading and writing problems but who suffer greatly from them and experience an intense feeling of dependence.

Instructor and group

In our view the instructor's main responsibility is to guide the participant towards acceptance of responsibility for his learning process and to work out with him his individual learning strategy. Training the participant in the course to assume responsibility for his learning assumes a simultaneous, successive relinquishment of responsibility (and the willingness to do so) on the part of the instructor. For example, this occurs by the instructor not marking or correcting mistakes in a participant's text but making available to the participant a correct text (for example, the participant's text retyped on a typewriter), allowing him to compare the texts himself and discover his incorrect and correct words in this way.

Two things are achieved with this method. On the one hand, the learner is sensitized to his own sources of error, so that over a longer period of training he is put in a position to recognize crucial spots and, for example, to check them independently using a Duden [Translator: Duden is the tradename of a publisher of dictionaries and other reference works on German spelling, grammar, etc.]. His dependence on a controlling/helping person is decreased, his own ability to assess his work increased.

On the other hand, this method forces the participant to compare individual letters and, therefore, promotes the differentiation of visual perception. In addition, the instructor's request that the participant compare the texts and find incorrectly or correctly written words himself entails a high degree of confidence in his abilities. This is especially important if the participant has low self-esteem.

A precise analysis of the functions of the learning group would go beyond the limits of this essay, but I would like to point out a few essential functions.

In their everyday lives, illiterate people often do not know any other illiterates but only people who do not have any problems with the written language. Consequently, the group is frequently their first exposure to other people who are in the course for the same reason they are.

The image of themselves with which the participants begin the course is often a very negative one marked by assessments like: I cannot do anything, I have not accomplished anything, am stupid, a failure, and so on.

This negative self-image starts to crumble as a result of their meeting other participants in the group who have similar problems. The participant is more likely to recognize that the other participants are not stupid, have achieved something, etc.

The group has very important functions: from breaking down the old negative self-image to developing a positive self-image.

Another essential function is the space which the group makes available to try out new, unusual forms of interaction. The groups contain garrulous people, laconic people and many in between. It is not the instructor's responsibility to bring them all to one level but to see to it that no one is taken advantage of by another. Conflicts arising in the group are brought up by her and worked out together. It is essential that each group participant is included, which can usually only be guaranteed at the beginning by the instructor questioning individuals directly. Basic communication models often have to be learned first (listen, refer to what is being said, etc.).

The inclusion of each individual by the instructor results in a validation of each group member. They come to realize that someone is interested in their opinion.

We frequently observe with female participants in particular that they think they cannot contribute anything important to the group process, that their opinions are uninteresting. In our view, before the need to express oneself in writing can arise, the need to express oneself orally has to be developed and explored. The group offers an outstanding opportunity to do this.

The instructor's responsibilities extend far beyond specific instruction in the written language. Acquisition of the written language encompasses more than the acquisition of instrumental capabilities and skills, it involves a change in the person of the learner and, therefore, a change in his views on life. How far an individual can go in this process depends on many factors, like relationships, work opportunities, environment and his own ability to change.

Counselling

As the above description made clear, the process of acquiring the written language entails more than the acquisition of the subject matter to be learned. It entails a change in one's very personal views, attitudes, assessments and leads to a change in one's perspectives on life.

This can result in severe psychological conflicts. As a result, counselling sessions have very different objectives. With one participant their purpose is to assess the use of the written language in everyday life, the reactions of others to this change, and to define at the same time further minor steps forward.

With others, the function of counselling is to guide them through crises and to support them in mastering these crises. The crises can be triggered by stagnation of the learning process, by great advances in learning, by changes in the everyday life of the person concerned, by their changing the person to whom they are attached, etc. Counselling makes clear more quickly whether the demands on the participant are excessive or too moderate.

The joint target planning of counsellor and instructor in regard to personality and the written language prevents this and makes it more likely that conflicts, antagonisms and refusal, etc. will be recognized and countered.

The methodological basis of the counselling is the holistic view of the person. The methods applied are based on individual psychology and system therapy.

A basic premise of the Orientation and Educational Assistance Study Group is that learning is a life-long process and everyone can learn, he only has to find the conditions under which he learns best and his individual learning tempo.

We are the escorts in this process for one to three years. In order to prevent, if at all possible, that what has been learned is unlearned again, or that the path of independence is left again, we refer in the program we offer the learner to his concrete everyday situation. The *learning program* we offer is as individual as the concerns of the participant. For example, we teach skills, so that one person can accept a retraining course or another program from the employment office, we prepare another for his driving test, we teach basic knowledge so that a third can choose his groceries better, and much more.

For this purpose it is necessary to work together with other organizations in a close *co-operative network.*

These co-operative partners include the most varied counselling and contact offices (drug addiction counselling, women-in-crisis counselling offices, counselling offices for young people, disabled people, foreigners; welfare counselling offices, employment offices, Berlin Neighbourhood Homes, etc.), which refer people to us or to which we refer people. Frequently, people come to us who are lonely and who would like to have more regular contact with other people than we can offer them. In addition, we work with organizations for the handicapped (clinics, homes, residential communes, transit houses), whose clients we counsel and with whose contacts in these organizations we develop a realistic target plan for and with the clients. We also co-operate with public health offices, which counsel people seeking assistance and, for example, also provide therapy, with probation counselling organizations and family assistance offices. These agencies frequently send us clients. Information is exchanged (with the consent of the clients) with these agencies regarding the target plan and the course of the program.

We also co-operate with the organizers and implementers of programs to increase qualifications: either they send people to us or we attempt to send people to them.

In all cases, moreover, information is exchanged on the concrete goals, the planning for them, and whether it was possible to attain them or what prevented their realization.

In the continuing education sector, we refer to the Berlin Volkshochschulen [adult education centres] people who in our opinion are capable of participating in an adult education course (do not therefore require our extensive supervision); they are referred either right after the first counselling session or after they have participated in one of our courses (for varying amounts of time). Where people participate in one of our courses, we usually also offer to supervise them for a further quarter-year while they are taking an adult education course, in order to ensure that each client is well integrated and does not terminate the adult education course as a result of any difficulties.

We also co-operate with other continuing education organizations, such as programs for young people aimed at their making another attempt at secondary school leaving qualifications.

Also, we are in contact with a few regular schools to the extent that once in a while they send us students who are in the top class, so that we can support them in a broader way than would be possible in the special programs in the schools themselves.

Twice a year we conduct an arithmetic course together with the Schöneberg Adult Education Centre (for our clients, too).

In co-operation with the Deutsche Bibliotheksinstitut [German Library Institute], we support (at present, however, specifically only one) libraries in selecting easy-to-read books with the goal of making libraries more accessible for adults who are learning to read.

These are the most important, but not all, of the institutions and agencies with which we co-operate.

The *financing* of the Orientation and Educational Assistance Study Group corresponds to the diversity of its clientèle. Our main source of financing is the uncovered demand financing by the Senatsverwaltung für Schule, Berufsbildung und Sport [Senate Administration for Schools, Vocational Training and Physical Education]. The Bundessozialhilfegesetz [Federal Social Assistance Act] provides other sources of income for which our clients can file individual applications for financing. In addition, there are also special agreements, such as that with the Karl-Bonhoeffer-Nervenklinik [Neurological Clinic], for which we run a course for a group of so-called mentally handicapped people.

2. Reading and Writing Problems as Family Problems

At first glance, the families of people with reading and writing problems are quite varied.

There is the illiterate or the person with writing problems who grew up in a village with 10 siblings, but there is also:

the person   whose sister passed the university matriculation examination;

the person   whose father was an alcoholic;

the person	in whose family violence and abuse occurred;
the person	whose parents are also illiterate;
the person	whose father has a high position in business;
the person	who grew up in a small family;
the person	who grew up in an institution;
the person	whose parents place no value on education;
the person	whose parents placed great value on education;
the person	who attended a special school;
the person	who has a junior high school diploma.

Despite these very different family backgrounds, there are common features which are defined via a defect.

There is the *defect* in competence in the written language and there are the dependent relationships entered into with the assistance of this defect – of course in all possible variations.

We can distinguish several basic patterns.

One basic pattern is that a child grew up in a family in which the parents had no time for their children and the children were forced to occupy themselves. Then the child experiences that a parent has time for it only when it cannot do something.

Stated somewhat briefly: after some time it learns to obtain attention through a defect. In this case, supervision of the homework assigned by the school is often the means. For example, the child experiences that when it cannot solve a problem, its mother sits down beside it and helps it to solve the problem. If it were able to solve the problem alone, the mother would not come. A *failure orientation* is born. Even if the attention given by the mother is very negative (for example linked with beatings), it still represents attention to the child which would not be given otherwise.

Once the pattern is learned, it is used again and again as a means of creating closeness. It becomes a basic pattern of human behaviour for the person concerned.

In his adult relationships, too, he will attempt to create closeness through the fact that he cannot do something, i.e. enter into further dependent relationships.

The idea of remedying this defect by becoming independent and learning to do what one cannot is no longer possible.

<u>Case A:</u>   <u>Nearness – distance – relation</u>

Family background

Parents: Hanna, 50, Erwin, 52, self-employed
Children: Sabine, 22, and Hermann, 28

Client: Sabine, married to Uwe, 29. They have a daughter, Hilde, 5.

Hanna and Erwin both work outside the home, they have a newspaper stand. They are always taken up with work, at home too. Hermann, the brother, was always easy to look after, hardly had any problems at school. He obtained a technical matriculation certificate (electronics). Hermann made few demands on his parents. Sabine always perceived herself as someone who did nothing but take time away from her parents; she also always had the feeling that she received too little affection. For example, she hardly remembers any situations in which her parents played with her. Hermann was responsible for this, but he did not want to always be looking after his little sister. She was not allowed to bring friends home, because her mother thought that they only made work for her.

Sabine started elementary school at 6 years of age, where she attracted attention for her quiet, somewhat subdued personality. She was considered of average intelligence but had problems with spelling from the time she started to learn to read and write. Her intelligence was assessed as good. She completed the regular school attendance requirement and obtained her secondary school leaving qualification. Her parents, in particular her mother, supervised the children's homework, Sabine's too. She remembers that his often involved her crying, but her mother sat beside her for as long as it took to finish her homework. When Sabine was an adult and already had her own apartment, her mother continued to take care of Sabine's written affairs – including even the writing out of a love letter.

This prevented the mother and daughter separating and guaranteed a great intimacy over a long period. Sabine's mother was able to continue to feel responsible for her, and Sabine did not need to assume complete responsibility for herself.

Current living situation

Sabine now has her own family. Her husband is a computer specialist and her daughter is supposed to start school next year.

Her mother and husband now help her to take care of any written matters. Sometimes the two of them argue about whether what the other has done is correct.

After obtaining her secondary school diploma, Sabine became a hairdresser, and she worked as such. She stopped working once her daughter was born. In her own opinion, she has no problems with reading but makes many spelling mistakes when writing independently.

Sabine's motivation to improve her writing skills is found, on the one hand, in the fact that her daughter will soon be starting school and she does not want to look like a "stupid" mother to her daughter. On the other hand, she no longer wants to feel so dependent on her mother and husband, who sometimes make her acutely aware that she needs their help. It can, however, be clearly felt in the counselling session that she is also afraid to take this step.

Her husband and daughter are present during counselling. Her husband emphasizes that he would absolutely like his wife to be able to be more independent so that she no longer needs her mother. In his opinion, his wife and his mother-in-law are together so much for that reason. She would not need a perfect knowledge, because he is there and in any case it would be better if he did his daughter's homework with her.

It was agreed that Sabine should attend the orientation course. A counselling session was scheduled with her alone for two months later. Following this, a discussion might be conducted once again with her husband and her.

Assessment/course

As a girl, Sabine felt rejected by her parents. Neither of them had had much time for her. However, her parents were interested in her keeping up in school. If Sabine had had no problems in school, she would have received no time, or very little, from her mother for homework. In this way, Sabine learned to obtain attention from a person through a defect, specifically not being able to do something.

This attention was not solely positive for Sabine but very often negative, but it was time which her mother devoted to her.

This pattern continued during Sabine's subsequent life. She utilizes her husband for written matters just as she does her mother. However, the negative aspects of this pattern are becoming increasingly intolerable for her: being at the mercy of other people, having to rely on their help and, on the other hand, always being afraid that at some point there will be no one there to help. In addition, there is also her responsibility for her daughter.

Sabine does not know how the future will look for her and intuitively senses the risk she is undergoing in being willing to become more independent.

During the counselling session, I pointed out to her and her husband that their relationship will change if Sabine learns to handle the written language on her own. At the same time, I made clear that there was a good method of controlling this change. This method was learning slowly. If Sabine learned slowly and also made use of what she had learned in her everyday life at a slow pace, she would have an opportunity to check how her husband was reacting and whether she should perhaps stop learning for a while at some point. Also, her husband would have an opportunity to recognize changes in Sabine's behaviour early on and to make possible limits clear through his reaction. This would remove their fears of an unforeseeable future, allowing more planning and control.

It was an arduous path for Sabine, because her mother and husband put a great deal of pressure on her to terminate the reading and writing course when they realized that Sabine would soon no longer have to rely on them. Sabine reacted with strong guilt feelings but succeeded with the support of her instructor, the other group participants and her counsellor. Talks with her mother and husband together were necessary for this purpose, however.

Sabine has succeeded in re-defining her relationship to her husband and her mother. This success has not been attained in other cases, with the result that either the reading and writing course or the relationship was terminated.

Over a two-year period, Sabine improved her ability to write on her own to such an extent that, although she retained a few persistent spelling mistakes, she could live with them without having to turn to others for help.

Another basic pattern is that a child learns to express closeness through identification with one family member, combined with a simultaneous distance from another family member. This pattern is often found in families in which violence prevails. The weak members often exercise solidarity against the violent family member through their supposed weakness.

Case B: Partner substitute

Family background

Father: unskilled worker, alcoholic, 60 years of age
Mother: housewife, cleaning woman, 54
Children: 8 children, Lisa, 38, Kurt, 36, Hans, 35, Klaus, 33, Paula, 30, Anna, 27, Heike, 25, Susanne, 20

Klaus is the index patient. In his case, the family situation resulted in an identity problem.

Klaus always felt very drawn to his mother. He never really understood his father, nor his brothers Hans and Kurt. He got along best with Lisa, he always had to look after Susanne. He started elementary school at 6 years of age. After 2 years he was sent to a special school – he no longer remembers precisely who initiated this. School was no fun, with the exception of sports. He did not like to go to school, was often absent, but was not conspicuous for his behaviour but, if anything, inconspicuous. At home, neither his mother or father looked at his homework. His older siblings did not help him with his homework either, nor did he know whether in fact they had done any themselves. Lisa did not have problems with reading and writing, but he definitely knew that Kurt, Anna and Heike also had problems. His father could read and write. His mother had problems, she too could recognize only a few letters and only write her name. He always felt sorry for his mother, his father often beat her and told her how stupid she was, when he had been drinking. He often beat the children. He often had to protect his mother, but he had probably done too little. At some point she finally separated from him.

Current situation

Klaus is no longer in touch with his father, he visits his mother regularly. He now lives alone.

He can read to some degree, i.e. haltingly, but he can deduce information from a text, copying is no problem, he makes an enormous number of mistakes when writing on his own (turns letters around, omits things, misuse of upper and lowercase) to such an extent that the word cannot be recognized.

Klaus can follow the counselling discussion, has no comprehension problems whatsoever, grasps connections and can present things coherently.

Klaus worked for a long time in construction as a labourer, then became unemployed, and the employment office has now proposed that he do an apprenticeship as a bricklayer.

His poor German was noticed during a preparatory course. If he does not improve his German, he will not pass the course. In everyday life, he avoids reading and writing situations in public. Where such a situation cannot be avoided, it frequently results in his breaking out in a sweat: for example, when he is in the post office filling out a money transfer form. He is afraid that other people will realize from his sweating that there is something not right with him or that the postal clerk will point out to him that he has written something incorrectly.

Assessment/course

At the beginning of the counselling session Klaus was very anxious, reserved – he was sweating and rubbed his hands together.

His mother, to whom even today his attachment is very strong, was of central importance to him during his childhood. It was impossible for him to identify with his father, who was violent and drank. It is not inevitable that children in such families develop reading and writing problems. Many sets of symptoms can be expected.

Education was not a topic in this family and, nevertheless, some of the siblings have no, or few, problems with reading and writing.

How did it happen that Klaus developed problems? I developed the hypothesis that Klaus used his reading and writing problems to try to put himself on the same level with his mother and, therefore, to guarantee her his support. If he were to learn to read and write it would result in problems for the relationship between himself and his mother.

Klaus entered the orientation course, and after two months I invited him and his mother to a discussion.

As we continued to work with Klaus and his mother, it became clear that Klaus' greatest fear was to become like his father. If he were to learn to read and write, it would be as if he were to leave his mother. His mother, on the other hand, was tormented by the fear that it was her fault that Klaus had not learned the written language adequately, because she had always bound him to her. He was her confidant in the family.

The generation boundaries in the family became blurred. Klaus was no longer her son but also a partner substitute for the mother. Even today Klaus was still the child who was most concerned about her and who visited her most frequently. She herself lived very withdrawn. She had no circle of friends of her own, organized her day around when her son visited her. These visits were the high-lights of her life.

Mrs. B. looked depressed during the counselling session. In my opinion, the son could only be helped if the mother succeeded in developing more energy and interest in herself. Only then would she be able to let Klaus live his own life.

During a few individual discussions with the mother over half a year in which she first was able to recount all of her anguish and disappointments (for the first time in her life she confided in someone), we were able to develop a few small goals for her life.

On the one hand, her dependence on the Welfare Office bothered her; on the other, she found it convenient.

She developed the goal of looking for a job for herself as a cleaning woman for a few hours per week so that she would no longer have to rely on welfare. In addition, it became clear that she was interested in handicrafts but did not have the courage and energy on her own to find an appropriate outlet for this interest.

Mrs. B. timidly attended an adult education course in pottery and was surprised by her own skill and her enjoyment of it.

She also found a cleaning job for a few hours a week. However, she could increase these hours later. In the meantime (after 2½ years), Mrs. B. is actively involved with the Grey Panthers and appears well-balanced.

Klaus experienced problems when his mother began to become independent. He was afraid of losing the attachment to her and urged her to stop what she was doing. She was also afraid of losing him. By working with both of them for an extended period, it was possible for him to develop so much confidence in the stability of the relationship between him and his mother that both were able to continue the relationship on a more adult level.

Through increased practice and his great willingness and ability to learn, Klaus has now reached a point where he does not break out in a sweat when faced with having to write in public. He feels considerably more secure and no longer has any problems with reading, either. He still turns letters around and mixes them up when writing however. He began his apprenticeship as a bricklayer and is just about to complete it successfully.

In addition, he met a woman at work, with whom he has had a relationship for some time.

* * *

Another basic pattern is that the child is the link between the parents, i.e. assumes responsibility for holding the family together and for its functioning. This is frequently the case with couples who find their purpose in having a child and who more likely would separate if this wish were not fulfilled.

Right from the beginning the child is exposed to massive emotional demands which are obviously excessive.

On the one hand, it is supposed to be a child one can show off, who will become something; on the other hand, it is supposed to always remain with them, if possible, so that the parents are not faced with dealing emotionally with themselves and their problems. In spite of everything, the parents want the best for their child.

These children have great difficulty in maintaining a distance between themselves and their parents and in establishing limits, because they are threatened by permanent encroachments and demands and have parents who do not respect the boundaries between generations. Often the only way that these children have of establishing limits is through extreme behaviour, because nothing else would be accepted.

Case C: Connection

Family background

Father: bank worker, 58
Mother: housewife, 55
Son: Theo, 18

Theo is considered slightly mentally handicapped and has suffered from neurodermatitis since infancy. He was definitely a child who was wanted by his parents, both parents had great hopes for him and absolutely wanted a son.

The mother is present at the counselling session. The parents have many disappointments regarding Theo. Theo was sent to a special school for the mentally handicapped where he was always very conspicuous on account of his behaviour. For example, he tipped over chairs, always had problems concentrating right from the beginning, played the class clown.

Theo and his father did not get along at all, the father was too disappointed in Theo's lack of progress.

Current situation

Theo sits in the counselling session, making a great effort to appear bored. His mother would like him to learn something because she wonders, "What will become of him when we are no longer there?"

Theo still lives with his parents, in a small room. He knows all the letters of the alphabet but has difficulty in saying them. He can put letters together with a great deal of effort, but does not understand their sense. He can print his first name and last name in capitals. He cannot write his address. We reach agreement in the counselling session that one goal could be his writing his address on his own.

Agreement: Theo will take part in the orientation course. Parallel to this, regular counselling discussions were agreed on, which were supposed to be conducted both with Theo alone and also jointly with his parents.

Assessment/course

Theo was born relatively late. Mr. and Mrs. C had lived without children for a long time. Mrs. C was 37, Mr. C 40. In the course of the counselling program, it became clear that they both saw the goal of their life in raising a son, hoping to gain more closeness in their relationship through him. Prior to Theo's birth, neither of them had very much to say to the other, each of them lived more their own life rather than a joint one. Mr. C's life revolved around his work, Mrs. C was active as a church volunteer. Their hopes were directed towards Theo. Theo was a premature child and had to spend some time in the incubator of the hospital. As an infant he got neurodermatitis. He needed great care right from the beginning. Later new worries appeared: he had no interest in school, preferred to play or later on to go to a disco. Theo grew up very protected. He had no secure private sphere. His neurodermatitis allowed his parents to enter his room at any time of the day or night, because they were worried that he could become worse again and they wanted to prevent him scratching himself till he bled.

On the other hand, he was definitely aware of the opportunities inherent in his position. He had learned that he could strongly influence the emotional state of mind of his parents and made use of this knowledge, too. The parents were very worried about Theo's development and attempted to further him in every conceivable way (his own tutor, etc.). They now had a lot to say to each other and this allowed them to forget that there were problems in their relationship before Theo was born. Theo could not decide anything on his own, even regarding the clothes he wanted to put on. His parents decided what he was to do. His beginning a reading and writing course was also his parents' decision. Right from the beginning he had no real interest in learning. What interested him in the group was the other members; he began discussions with them, told them about himself and his newest favourite cassettes.

In order to protect himself against his parents' control and to establish a necessary distance, he rejected their proposals by proving to them that these did not work. He could simply not concentrate in the course. It was especially difficult for him to keep his parents at a certain distance, allowing him to develop on his own, because he was so eagerly awaited by his parents and especially since they both still looked after him in a loving manner. He could not run the risk of hurting them greatly if he insisted on keeping them more out of his life. Theo received all of their attention, positive as well as negative. He could not fulfil the goal set for him unconsciously by his parents. If he became the son they truly had expected, he would hurt them and have to leave them. Then they would be alone with one another again. Through his disease and the fact that he was a difficult child, he held his parents together.

In the course he made it clear through his lack of interest that he was there because he wanted/had to please his parents. Under these conditions, Theo spoiled any chance he had to learn. The struggle with his parents, over who was to decide things, was being fought out in the arena of learning to read the written language.

I conducted a counselling session with Theo alone during which I presented the problems to him. Theo was relieved by the fact that he was understood. We agreed that I and his instructor should speak to his parents. I reached agreement with Theo that he would take a break of 2 months which he would make use of to draw up a list of priorities, what he liked doing and what he liked doing less (he wanted to make things clear). In addition, I gave him the task of asking himself every day what clothes he would like to put on, to reach a decision on his own and to assert himself against his parents.

In the discussion with his parents, it was very important to us to provide them with feedback in the form of our understanding that they had truly been very concerned about their son. As a result, we exonerated them and Theo. The second important point for us was to make clear to them that for Theo the reading and writing course represented taking the second step before the first. Before taking the course, he had to learn to make decisions on his own and to accept responsibility. At first, both parents reacted with: "He cannot do that, decisions have to be made for him." We negotiated an agreement with them that they did not have to give up all decisions and responsibility to Theo because this would place an excessive burden on him. However, they were to allow him one sphere for which he was responsible but which they could supervise – his clothes. In addition, we clarified with them that Theo was coming to the course out of love for them, but it was still beyond him, and that they should give him a chance to develop his own motivation. Both parents were very relieved by the discussion and wanted to observe the agreements.

Two months later, the father telephoned and reported that Theo still did not want to take a writing course but that things were much quieter at home, Theo appeared more balanced, his wife felt much better and the two of them were confident that Theo would still make something of himself because he was behaving in a much more adult manner.

3. **Personality Development**

The experience of not mastering social conditions which are "taken for granted", or not mastering them adequately, results in a more or less markedly negative self-image.

By adapting one's behaviour in a suitable manner, one attempts to keep this defect from the external world. In society today, anyone who has problems with written language is considered stupid. Very few of those concerned take the offensive and admit that they have a problem. In our experience, a large number are afraid of being revealed as illiterate and, therefore, stupid.

In counselling, we find again and again that the clients tend to blame their laziness or stupidity for their "failure" to learn properly. They are less likely to connect their own problems with other people in their direct environment, like parents or teachers. It is also "popular", however, to identify yourself as dyslexic. Then you are not responsible for the problem, for you cannot be held responsible for a disease, and you can use it to explain future failure.

Consequently, we consider the dyslexic concept, regardless of whether such a disease exists or not, as dangerous, because it renders those concerned passive in the face of their problems with the written language so that they can no longer see that their situation can be changed. We also deal with people whose written work was not evaluated in school because they were so called "dyslexics", i.e. they often have no ability to assess their situation at all in order to make a statement regarding their error frequency. As a result, they have a diffuse picture of their problems.

Fear of revelation is one great fear, another is the fear of failing again, of exposing oneself to the danger of disappointing others again. Another fear is to discover at some point that you are too stupid to learn.

As a result of society's evaluation of him and of the fears he has developed, the illiterate person is forced to develop a distrust of others. Sometimes it takes a long time for him to develop trust in others. We have had cases in the Orientation and Educational Assistance Study Group in which spouses of many years knew nothing about the illiterate person's writing problems. In most cases, however, at least the partners are aware of the problem and are involved in it because they provide support. This mistrust forces illiterates to keep control of every situation, which frequently results in their seeking out old, known situations, and avoiding new ones. This leads to a narrowing of their individual behaviour patterns and, in the last analysis, of their personalities.

As a result of their lack of competence in the written language in an environment oriented towards the written language, illiterates are forced to invent their own orientation systems. For example, a woman who bought food for her cat oriented herself on the different colours of the tins; a man, who had to distribute medication in a clinic, on the colours and geometric shapes of the packages. He did not make a single mistake in 15 years.

Reducing perception and transfer skills to the non-written extends skills in other directions, in the same way, for example, as the hearing of a blind person improves.

Another skill which is well trained as a result of the fact that nothing can be written down is the ability to note and to memorize things. We continually see in the courses, for example, that someone who cannot read can remember a DIN A4 page of material which is read aloud to them and reproduce it word for word. A performance which otherwise only eidetics are capable of.

There are always dependent relationships with literate people because everyone has to fill out at least a form at some point. This implies a feeling of helplessness, of being at the mercy of others as well as a feeling of "power" because you have someone who helps you and give him the opportunity to show that he can do more than you.

This is linked with the fear of being exploited, being taken advantage of.

Where you take the risk of learning, there are often fears that the other person will leave you if you can manage it yourself.

4. The Co-illiterate

Mothers are frequently very close reference persons of illiterates and partners. These reference persons can also be professional helpers, however, like social workers. The basic pattern is that they can always feel better than the illiterate, in this connection their perhaps minor problems with the written language are less likely to be noticed, for example. They are often people who are themselves very insecure, who lack social recognition and who feel morally superior, of greater value, as a result of their partner's illiteracy. They need such a partner because they do not regard themselves as particularly valuable.

Often this is combined with the fear that their friends could discover that they spend time with a "stupid" person, which could lead to conclusions regarding their own person. In addition, there is the fear that their partner may only be with them or remain with them because he needs them. In this case, too, a low self-esteem is found.

If your partner starts a reading and writing course in order to learn – which you yourself may have advised him to do – the fear arises that he could learn to read and write well and then leave you. The helper can only feel better than the illiterate as long as he can still help. Where his help is no longer needed, it can lead to personality breakdowns, like depression, etc. in extreme cases.

Mothers who see their life's work in helping their adult son take care of written matters and, consequently, maintaining his status as a child become afraid of losing the son, who might have only come to visit them when he needed help with written matters.

The helper is dependent on being able to help. If his help is no longer needed, he is forced either to seek new fields in which he can provide help or to change his personality. The struggle will always be directed mainly towards maintaining the existing patterns. Of course, it must be taken into account that the helper does not intend to harm the person he is helping.

5. Changes in Relationships/in Personality

To learn means to change. Where people attend a course they want to change, to alter, something. If possible, however, in such a way that everything else remains as it is. Only a part is to be changed and, if possible, without pain. It is only during the course that the breadth of the changes in their personalities and relationships become clear.

Where an illiterate who, for example, only knows a few letters learns to use these letters in a sensible way, to expand his knowledge and can then write his name without help, this represents a change in his personality and in his partner relationship. He will learn to have more confidence in himself, to try something on his own, no longer to rely on the other person so much. This also means that the other person must be willing to change, to give up something and to risk acquiring a partner who is somehow different. This is a difficult process that requires guidance. In learning part of the written language, the illiterate acquires more than merely that. He learns that he can learn, that he can be independent, that he can have more respect for himself. He also learns, however, that he contributed to his not being able to read and write in the past. He learns that he can influence his situation, can change it.

His first successful learning experience, one which he also considers as such, is a crucial point in his learning history. It is decided at this point whether he trusts himself to enter into more new experiences or whether he or his partner is afraid of changing and he does not want to risk the relationship.

At this point, discussions are necessary with both persons concerned, in which their fears may have to be verbalized with the support of the counsellor, because the one does not believe the other capable of having such fears. The significance of bringing up and discussing these fears and the matter-of-factness with which this is done is an enormous psychological relief for both partners.

Getting involved in the learning process once again means being willing to relinquish old orientation systems with which one always had problems but which have helped one for years and decades. It also means wanting to subject oneself to learning experiences regarding which one cannot know whether they will help one more than the old and result in recognition. Added to this is the fact that all adult illiterates have had negative learning experiences in attempting to learn to read and write.

6. **Summary/Assessment**

There is not only *one* method of teaching people to read and write. Restriction to one method of acquiring the written language (corresponding to the prevailing spirit of the times, either the analysis/synthesis method or, for example, the whole word method) in elementary school definitely contributed to the occurrence of reading and writing problems. The willingness to learn, capability to learn, the learning tempo and the learning opportunities of the individual student had to be disregarded in this case.

This mistake was repeated when the first attempts were made to teach illiterates to read and write in Europe as well as in the first years of the Orientation and Educational Assistance Study Group. At that time, the preferred method was morpheme segmentation[3]. This lost in popularity to the language experience approach[4]. In the meantime, the view has also gained acceptance in the literacy movement that the method used

a) must correspond to the learning level of the participant and
b) must be applicable by him in everyday life.

Application in everyday life involves a change in the learner's attitude. For example, if on the way home from the course a beginner in the literacy program tries to find in his environment the A he has learned, this change in attitude would have been achieved. This change in attitude signifies a change to an active involvement and a farewell to passive suffering. It also signifies assuming responsibility for one's own learning process.

We have counsellors and instructors available to support this process. For us, the convincing aspect of our approach is the opportunities it offers the participants, opportunities which are included in a program offering, on a broad basis, recognition of his developmental steps and the necessary support measures. However, the prerequisite for this is intensive co-operation between the instructors, between the counsellors, and between the counsellors and instructors. It is precisely this that is the difficult aspect of this concept in practice.

The co-operation required, for example to develop small partial goals for the participant's learning process, becomes problematic if there is competition among the instructors or between the counsellors and instructors. The danger exists that this competition will result in doubts and reservations not being expressed, developments not being perceived, one's own assessment being asserted obstinately against one's better judgement. The demands on the skill of the instructors and counsellors who want to work with this method are high.

This co-operation will only succeed if the instructors and counsellors are willing to work on their own learning problems and thus to learn constantly to expand their assessment of their own person. Critical reflection in the instructor or counsellor team[5] also expands viewpoints and is indispensable for a professional program.

As a result of the double opportunity for participants to address problems and of the need for constant skills improvement, such a structured program is an expensive but efficient method. However, it is not necessary to offer such close supervision for all illiterates; many do not need it, but the opportunity should be created for those requiring this assistance.

We do not assume that this approach is the exclusive literacy concept. Rather, greater differentiation is necessary in literacy work than was previously the case, so that the great variations in people with reading and writing problems can be taken into account.

Notes

1. Every action is communication. One cannot not act. Within a system, the actions of an individual affect all members of the system. If one variable in the system changes, then the system has to be redefined.

2. Unless the counsellor establishes that her own learning history prevents her from being able to offer the participant appropriate counselling. Should this be the case, she will transfer the participant to another counsellor.

3. Breaking down words into their smallest meaningful units. Example: Kleid-er-ständ-er.

4. Words, sentences, etc., are developed on the basis of the everyday language experience of participants.

Bibliography

Bateson, G. 1981. *Ökologie des Geistes*. Frankfurt/Main: Suhrkamp.

Bateson, G. 1982. *Geist und Natur*. Frankfurt/Main: Suhrkamp.

Döber-Nauert, M. 1987. *Verursachungsfaktoren des Analphabetismus*. Frankfurt/Main: PAS.

Duss v. Werdt, J. and Welter-Enderlin, R. 1980. *Der Familienmensch*. Stuttgart: Klett.

Ehling, B. et al. 1987. *Über Analphabetismus in der Bundesrepublik Deutschland*. Bonn.

Guntern, G. 1981. Streß und Bewältigungsmechanismen in menschlichen Systemen. *Familiendynamik* 6(2).

Haley, J. 1980. Ansätze zu einer Theorie pathologischer Systeme. In Watzlawich, P. and Weakland, J.H. eds. *Interaktion*. Stuttgart: Huber.

Kamper, G. 1985. *Elementare Fähigkeiten*, Band 1. Berlin: Systemdruck.

Kamper, G. 1987. *Elementare Fähigkeiten*, Band 2. Berlin: Systemdruck.

Kamper, G. 1990. *Analphabetismus trotz Schulbesuch*. Berlin: AOB.

Napier, A. and Whitacker, C.A. 1979. *Tatort Familie*. Köln: Diederichs.

Schneewind, K. et al. 1983. *Eltern und Kinder*. Stuttgart: Kohlhammer.

Selvini-Palazzoli, M. et al. 1972. *Paradoxon und Gruppenparadoxon*. Stuttgart: Klett.

Watzlawich, P. and Weakland, J.H. eds. 1980. *Interaktion*. Stuttgart: Huber.

KNOWING WHERE WE ARE: PARTICIPATORY RESEARCH AND ADULT LITERACY

Mary Hamilton
Roz Ivanic
David Barton
Lancaster University, U.K.

1. Introduction

In this paper we outline the work we are doing in linking research and practice in adult literacy. We explain our aims, how far we think we are achieving them and the main practical principles underlying our approach. We also place our work in the context of other similar efforts and traditions which have contributed to our own ideas.

Although we are based in a university, as members of the Research and Practice in Adult Literacy group (RaPAL) we work closely with experienced practitioners and learners in adult basic education, who are searching for new ways of reflecting on their experiences and acting on the knowledge they have. In drawing together in one place ideas that have come from many, we hope that the paper will be useful to others who are interested in new models of human enquiry: ones which enable us to share power and knowledge with one another and assert the value of firsthand experience as a source of information as real as any of the traditionally privileged "objective" measures.

2. What is Research?

What is research? Is it something you might do in your everyday life? What kind of activities count as research? There are many examples of activities where it is uncertain whether they count as research. Is it research to put together a petition to persuade the local council to instal street lighting? Finding out what makes people come to an adult education group? Finding out what sort of learning opportunities people would like in your local area? Why people put full stops where they do when they write? Asking people how they feel about the local variety of the language they speak? What it was like at school 20 years ago? Finding out whether local schools are interested in setting up parent support groups, and what works and what doesn't? Finding out what students like about the ABE group they belong to? Finding evidence to convince people that dyslexia exists?

Our answer is that all these activities involve research. Research is asking questions, seeing patterns, finding out in some systematic way the information you need to answer the questions. Sometimes research is needed to convince other people of something you already know and includes finding ways of recording the answers and then communicating them to others. (For more examples and a more detailed answer to the question of what is research, see *Research and Practice in Adult Literacy Bulletin* Nos. 9 and 12; Ivanic and Baynham, 1985; Lobley, 1988; Barton and Murphy 1990).

3. **Why Link Research and Practice: The Great Divide**

Traditionally, research has been done by a few experts - governments, journalists, academics. A few people get to ask the questions, most people answer other people's questions. Their own questions go unnoticed and don't even seem to be important. The traditional research model has been called "objective" research, suggesting that it is neutral and therefore nearer to the truth. But it is also "outsider" research - the perspective of someone who does not know how it feels and who doesn't have the same stake in it as those involved. This "outsiderness" has been seen as a virtue. However, it is easy to argue the opposite: that being an outsider is an unacceptable constraint on understanding and acting to change things. It is not an objective, impartial perspective, just a different one; and if not balanced by "insider" views it can be completely one-sided.

As one American practitioner puts it: "Given this framework, ordinary people are rarely considered knowledgeable or capable of knowing about their own reality.....people are research subjects and knowledge about their lives is created and carried away by "experts"." (Gillespie 1989)

The traditional research model has reinforced boundaries and separated researchers from the researched, academics from practitioners, creating a great divide that we stare mistrustfully across. This divide is apparent in practical ways that become obstacles to working together.

Because of our dissatisfaction with the way that traditional research has been carried out, what has been valued and what dismissed and despised as sources of information, and how research is viewed as a result of this set-up, we hoped to be able to encourage a different model within the field of adult literacy. As a field, Adult Basic Education (ABE) in the UK had developed very rapidly with many innovations but few resources. Where they existed, written reports or other records of innovatory projects were often not widely circulated or systematically followed up.

When RaPAL began, research into this field was almost non-existent. After 10 years of experience in ABE in the U.K. many of those involved felt the need for time to reflect and share what had happened. ABE itself has developed in the U.K. with a strong learner-centred philosophy which is at odds with the traditional model of research. This creates both an opportunity and an imperative to do things differently.

4. **Research and Practice in Adult Literacy: What we (and Others) are Doing**

When we began, we had some knowledge of traditions nearest to literacy work. These are traditions of teacher research in schools (Rudduck and Hopkins, 1985; Walker, 1985; Duckworth 1986) of community publishing (Morley and Worpole 1982; Fitzpatrick, 1990), community development (Lovett, Clarke and Kilmurray 1983) of the ideas of Paulo Freire and the notion of popular education that has grown out of his work (Freire, 1985; Kirkwood and Kirkwood 1989; Arnold and Burke, 1983). As we developed our approach we came across other people who seemed to be aiming for the same things, albeit in a different field or with a different emphasis from our own: feminist writers and researchers searching for new ways of documenting women's experience and understandings (Roberts 1981; Spender, 1980; Olson, 1980; Acker, Barry and Esseveld 1983); oral historians (Duffin, 1989); action research within educational or other organizations (The Talk Workshop Group, 1982; Goswami and Stillman, 1987; Reason, 1988) which is usually small-scale, focused on a specific set of circumstances, a problem or innovation and documents change as it happens.

All these traditions lead to a central idea of "participatory research" where those affected by the research are in control of it, and the decisions that shape it (See Hall, 1984; Participatory Research Network, 1982).

We are still finding other strands which connect with us, getting clearer at articulating what we see as the core ideas to our approach, the key principles of a participatory approach to researching literacy. Our own focus has been on finding out how adults make sense of literacy, what they use reading and writing for, and how they learn. However, adult learners of literacy themselves do not necessarily have such a narrow view of how they can use research for their own purposes, and as their voice becomes heard in the research process, so the agenda changes.

RaPAL began with a series of conferences bringing together practitioners and academic researchers. Although our original thought was to generate specific questions for research, we quickly moved onto broader questions of what is meant by research, what counts as research, critiquing the traditional model of research and thinking about who does it and why, who benefits from it. A first step was to form a network, mainly within the U.K., but also making contact with people in other countries who are thinking along the same lines. RaPAL began to publish a regular bulletin paying conscious attention to finding a way of talking about research that is accessible, and providing an outlet for reports and projects that would not have otherwise got into print. The newsletter is edited and published collectively, and the process of doing this itself has strengthened our links and clarified our aims.

Here we we want to describe two other activities through which we are beginning to make new links and to discover the difficulties and rewards of pushing the research and practice approach further. Firstly, we have been organizing workshops on research techniques that involve both learners and teachers in ABE. Secondly, we have been working collaboratively with people learning new forms of writing to research the process and changes they are going through.

5. "Doing Research" Workshops

The first type of activity we want to describe are the "Doing Research" Weekends we have been involved in, one organized by people at the Lee Community Education Centre, London, and the other by people at Bradford and Ilkley Community College in the North of England. The lessons we have learned from the "Doing Research" workshops have been written up in two issues of the RaPAL bulletin and a longer paper (See RaPAL Bulletins, Nos. 9 and 12; McMahon et al 1991). These workshops followed the model of a residential weekend organised by the National Federation of Voluntary Education Schemes NFVES: during this weekend students, tutors and researchers met to choose and plan a joint project which they later carried out together and wrote up (Mace and Moss 1988).

Each meeting had a different focus. The Lee Centre weekend offered sessions on research skills. There were sessions on doing interviews, experiences of dyslexia, what happens in groups, recruiting black tutors, using video, writing questionnaires, using personal stories, writing up and publishing research results.

The Bradford weekend was a mixture of small groups planning their own research projects and people telling about research they had done. The projects that were put together during the weekend were: a video exchange between two groups about how people change as they learn; understanding learning in groups; getting to and staying in classes (a research and publicity project); a history/writing project; producing an investigation pack for groups on "what is literacy?".

As you would expect, many good things came from these workshops (planned and unplanned!) but we also learned from mistakes we made.

It was important that people came in small groups together, not as individual participants. The best combination seemed to be a group of two or three students, together with a tutor they knew well. This gave people the chance to work together beforehand to prepare for the workshop, and often it enabled them to carry on afterwards. It also helped ensure that individual students got support from one another and from tutors during the weekend. We got wiser about the need for such support from meeting to meeting. The ideal would be fully collective planning for the workshop, but this is difficult if participants are spread across the country. The idea of small groups feeding in their views and plans is a first step towards joint organization. It still leaves a lot of responsibility and practical planning for the event in the hands of a small group.

People came to the workshops with different expectations and these were often unclear. It is important to find out early on what people want to get out of the event and to sort out potential confusions. Getting to know one another at first is essential if people are going to relax into learning. Thinking about how this can be done at the very first session such as games and icebreakers is very important. It actually starts before this, from the minute people arrive. At the very beginning it is useful to agree some simple "ground rules" that will help people to ask for and give each other the support that is needed. At Bradford our ground rules were:

1. Appoint a wordwatcher (this is someone who is responsible for asking for explanations of long words, jargon and abbreviations)

2. Appoint someone to take notes

3. Make sure everything is read out

4. Make sure everyone who wants to speak does

5. Make sure everyone understands everything that is discussed

6. If you want to write, ask for help if you need it

Finally, a successful workshop has a flexible structure and allows people time to reflect and understand. While it is important to plan sessions in advance, and some people have to come prepared to organize sessions, it is also necessary to allow for the unexpected. Some needs come to the surface only as the weekend goes on, and it is important to be able to respond to these by rescheduling events and making room for new ones. For the first time in Bradford we had a group from another country - Germany. At first we worried about how this would work, especially how we would deal with translating between different languages. It soon became clear that the presence of this group was an added bonus to the event. Translating between languages helped us all by forcing people to explaining clearly and by slowing us all down enough to give time for everyone to check out their understanding of activities with each other.

6. Research Which Grows out of Learning

A very different sort of activity is where a specific researcher works with learners on a small-scale research project. Roz Ivanic describes two examples of working in this way with learner-writers at Lancaster College of Adult Education. In each case the research grew out of one-to-one teaching, so it fitted naturally into the regular activities of the programme.

Research about punctuation

In this research I talked with ten learner-writers about the drafts of the writing they were doing to put in the college magazine. In ordinary tuition we might not have talked about every single full stop and comma they used, or every single place where a punctuation mark was missed out, but because it was "research" we did. Because it was "research" the learners didn't take my attention to their punctuation as correction or criticism. Rather, we all approached the task with curiosity - trying to figure out why the full stops and commas have to go where they do, and why the writers put them where they did. The writers got the same benefits as they would have done from an ordinary one-to-one tuition session; they learned more about how to use the conventions of punctuation as a result of our discussion.

We tape-recorded the discussions, and I then worked on the recordings, writing down all the explanations everyone gave for their choices of full stop or comma. I divided these into "punctuating by quantity", "punctuating by sound", "punctuating by meaning" and "punctuating by structure", and I counted up the number of times people used different punctuation strategies successfully and unsuccessfully. I found out, for example, that "punctuating by sound" works better for placing commas than for full stops.

I then wrote up the results in two ways. One was a short article for the college magazine, telling everyone - students and tutors -

what we had found out so that it could help them in their future work. The other was a longer article with more detail about linguistics (Ivanic, 1988).

Research about conflict of identity in academic writing

This research grew out of my work as a volunteer for the College, first with John Simpson, then with Denise Roach. They are both students who returned to study in their 20's having left school with no qualifications. In both cases we gradually turned our "tuition" sessions into "research" sessions. The difference between tuition and research was quite subtle. In "tuition" I was suggesting how they could improve their writing; in "research" we were discussing why they wrote what they wrote, how it differed from conventional writing, and what they wanted to do about it. Instead of always talking about how the writing should be done, Denise and John often gave good reasons for keeping it the way it was, and as a result of our discussions, they often had the confidence to stand up for their own ways of writing. I think the main difference was in our relationship. In "tuition" I was the knower, the tutor, the teacher. In "research" we were joint investigators, each bringing different insights to the problem at hand. It seemed that by turning tuition into research we were putting into practice two fundamental principles of ABE: maintaining equality among adults and empowering learners. John and Denise still said that they learnt a lot about academic writing from these sessions, even though the focus was not on learning. That is, they didn't feel they were giving up their time to research for my benefit only.

When John and I had been working in this way for two years, it occurred to us that we might also write about our observations collaboratively. Our first piece was called "Clearing away the debris: learning and researching academic writing". Writing this title was like the whole piece; we both wrote our own version, then we put them together. "Clearing away the debris" was John's image for the way we worked together; "learning and researching academic writing" was my rather drier description of what I thought we were doing. This was published in the RaPAL Bulletin (1988). Since then we have written a much longer article to be published in a book (Ivanic and Simpson, 1991). Meanwhile, Denise and I had begun working together and have also written up our insights collaboratively (Ivanic and Roach, 1990). We think it is particularly important for us to write in a way that other mature students and their tutors can understand. John and Denise keep a constant watch over my writing in this respect!

Research is a natural development for one-to-one teaching and learning situations. Learners and tutors often discuss a piece of writing in order to figure out how to improve it. By keeping records of these discussions they can collect information which may eventually be interesting to other people - in other words, research.

7. Making Changes: How to Link Research and Practice

Paulo Freire pointed out ways in which literacy is a form of power. Literacy that is imposed and learned for other people's purposes helps to enslave them. Literacy that is self-generated and springs from people's own needs to communicate and act on the world is empowering. The same is true of research: it is not neutral but it always serves some purpose. Our business is to see to it that research about literacy serves the learners' purposes. If there is one basic principle to this approach, it is therefore one of sharing power.

Other common themes in the activities described above are the theme of reclaiming voice, breaking silence - allowing perspectives, experiences to be spoken and heard that have not been present in traditional research. Our notion of research includes the outcome. Reflection or finding out should be closely linked to action. Often the focus is on solving problems. Within learning groups, this becomes an insistence that what we are doing when we learn and teach is a form of research, and that it makes no sense to divide these activities into separate worlds.

How then can we share power, amplify voices, connect reflection and action? Here are the core practical steps that we have identified as essential to link research and practice.

Learners guide the goals of research
This is crucial, difficult and of all the links will probably have the most far-reaching effects. We have learned something about how this can be done through our "doing research conferences". We need to invent a new format of "conference" to make it a comfortable forum for people to meet and genuinely exchange knowledge. It means

researchers, teachers, learners all talking to each other, making opportunities to reflect on our different and similar experiences, setting goals, identifying problems together. Funding is essential for this to enable everyone to take part. In the case of both "Doing Research" weekends we had to find money to support students to be there, both travel and living expenses.

Learners share in the process of research as active decision-makers, not as objects of it
This involves agreeing a framework, deciding how the research will be done, and being involved in all stages of it: collecting and recording information, interpreting the results and having a say in what is written up. It entails openly discussing what the research is about and why it is worth doing.

This shared research has some important outcomes that make it better than traditional research. Firstly, the learners find that researching their own learning helps them to understand it and so do it better in future. In this way research feeds into practice. Secondly, learners have a right to the research skills involved: it is empowering in itself to know how to carry out interviews, how to put a questionnaire together and how to organize information into a report that will convince others.

Thirdly, because the learners themselves were involved in the research process their detailed insights, comments, opinions and perceptions are included more centrally than they might have been if they were just the subjects of research. The research results are richer as a result. We described an example of this above in the research on punctuation.

Finally, shared research ensures that different sources of information are included and given equal status: it is built on the assumption that first-hand experience is a valid source of data and an essential complement to outsider sources and understandings.

Learners and researchers write about their research collaboratively
We described an example of this in the research on the conflict of identity adults feel when they return to learning. Collaborative writing is not easy but it is worth it. As well as upholding the general principle of shared credit for shared understanding, it has other benefits for all concerned. Firstly it avoids the problem most researchers have about whether they have represented their "infor-

mants'" views properly. Writing the report collaboratively means that the "informants" have control over what is being said about them. They can ensure there is no breach of privacy, or misrepresentation of their ideas.

Secondly, all participants learn a lot about writing in the process. By sharing the process with a more experienced writer, the students learn things about writing which are impossible to teach by conventional methods. The researcher, stuck in a style of formal, academic writing, learns ways of expressing herself which will be more accessible to other people. This includes making the writing more "speech-like" in various ways, and using more vivid metaphors rather than explanations full of dry, abstract nouns.

It can also solve the problem of acknowledging your sources. In traditional research reports the people who provided the information are usually gratefully acknowledged and then dismissed - often disguised with pseudonyms in the main part of the report. The report is written about adult literacy students, but not written by them. As a result, the "researchers" gain the status of experts and the adult literacy students do not. One way of challenging this is to make sure the learners have their names on the articles and books about them along with tutors and researchers. Involving all research participants in the writing and in conferences where the research is discussed are other ways of giving credit where credit is due: the people who understand adult literacy from the inside are the people credited with knowledge-making about it.

8. Conclusion

Participatory research and action is the logical model for literacy work because of the philosophy behind the teaching and because learning literacy is about creating knowledge (in Freire's words: reading the world); strengthening voices that have been silenced (writing who you are) and telling others what you have discovered (reaching an audience).

RaPAL developed in response to this need but has so far only begun to explore the long path of realising it. Finding links with others working in the same direction has been important to us. We hope this paper will enable others to share this view of the possibilities for future research in literacy and work with us to make changes.

Note

RaPAL, the Research and Practice in Adult Literacy Group, can be contacted at Bolton Royd Centre, Manningham Lane, Bradford BD8 7BB, UK. Our bulletin appears three times a year and back issues are available.

Bibliography

Acker, J. Barry, K. and Esseveld, J. 1983. Objectivity and Truth: Problems in Doing Feminist Research. *Women's Studies International Forum* 6 (4): 423-435.

Arnold, R, and Burke, B. 1983. *A Popular Education Handbook.* Toronto: Participatory Research Group.

Barton, D. and Murphy, S. 1990. Linking Research and Practice: Ten Examples of Adult Literacy Research in Britain. In J.P. Hautecoeur ed. *Alpha 90: Current Research in Literacy* (149-164). Montreal: Quebec Ministry of Education/Hamburg: Unesco Institute for Education.

Baynham, M. and Mace, J. 1986. *Doing Research.* Lee Community Education Centre, Goldsmiths College, University of London, June. (From Lee Community Education Centre, 1 Aislibie Road, London SE12 8QH.)

Duckworth,E. 1986. Teaching As Research. *Harvard Educational Review* 56 (4), November: 481-495.

Duffin, P. 1989. Reminisence: At the Sharp End. *Oral History* 17 (1): 15-21. Special Issue on Health and Caring, Spring.

Fitzpatrick, S. 1990. *Working Around Words: A Report of Editorial Work with two Gatehouse Books.* Manchester: Gatehouse Publishing Project.

Freire, P. 1985. *The Politics of Education.* South Hadley MA: Bergin and Garvey.

Gillespie, M. 1989. Research Within Reach. *Focus on Basics* 2 (2) Spring: 8-9.

Hall, B. 1984. *Participatory Research : Popular Knowledge and Power.* Participatory Research Group, 394 Euclid Ave, Suite 308, Toronto M6G 2S9 Canada.

Hamilton, M. and Barton, D. eds. 1985. *Research and Practice in Adult Literacy.* Papers of the Association for Recurrent Education, Centre for Research into the Education of Adults, Cherry Tree Buildings, University of Nottingham, Nottingham NG7 2RD UK.

Ivanic, R. 1988. *The Logic of Non-standard Punctuation.* Lancaster Papers in Linguistics No. 51. Lancaster: University of Lancaster.

Ivanic, R. and Roach, D. 1990. Academic Writing, Power and Disguise. In Clark et al. eds. *British Studies in Applied Linguistics* 5: Language and Power.

Ivanic, R. and Simpson, J. 1988. Clearing Away The Debris; Learning and Researching Academic Writing. *RaPAL Bulletin* 6: 6-7.

Ivanic, R. and Simpson, J. In press. Who's Who in academic Writing? In Fairclough, N. ed. *Language Awareness: Critical Perspectives.* London: Longman.

Ivanic, R. and Baynham, M. eds. 1985. Research and Practice in Adult Literacy: The London Seminar. *ILEA Language and Literacy Unit Occasional Paper* No.1, September. Southwark College, East Peckham Branch, Asylum Rd, London SE15 2RJ.

Lobley, G. ed. 1988. The Second London Conference on Research and Practice in Adult Literacy: Work in Progress. *ILEA Language and Literacy Unit Occasional Paper* No.4. London: Inner London Education Authority.

Lovett, T. Clarke, C. and Kilmurry, A. 1983. *Adult Education and Community Action.* Beckenham (UK): Croom Helm.

Kirkwood, G. and Kirkwood, C. 1989. *Living Adult Education: Freire in Scotland.* Milton Keynes: Open University Press.

Mace, J. and Moss, W. 1988. *How do People Decide to Join a Literacy Class?* NFVLS 131 Camberwell Road, London SE5 OHF and Lee Community Education Centre, 1 Aislibie Road, London SE12 8QH.

McMahon, M. 1991. The Bradford Doing Research Conference. *Research and Practice in Adult Literacy, Working Paper* No.1.

Morley, D. and Worpole, K. 1982. The Republic of Letters. *Comedia.*

Olson, T. 1980 *Silences.* London: Virago.

Participatory Research Network. 1982. *Participatory Research: An Introduction.* From International Council of Adult Education, 720 Bathurst Street, Suite 308, Toronto, Ontario M5S 2R4. Canada.

Reason, P. ed. 1988. *Human Inquiry In Action: Developments in New Paradigm Research.* Newbury Park CA: Sage.

Roberts, H. 1981. *Doing Feminist Research.* London: Routlege and Kegan Paul.

Rudduck, J. and Hopkins, D. 1985. *Research as a Basis for Teaching: Readings from the work of Lawrence Stenhouse.* London: Heinemann.

Schwab, I. and Stone, J. 1989. *Language, Writing and Publishing.* ILEA Afro-Caribbean Language and Literacy Project Report. London: Inner London Education Authority.

Shor, I. ed. 1987. *Freire for the Classroom: A Sourcebook for Liberatory Teaching.* Upper Montclair NJ: Boynton Cook.

Spender, D. 1980. Learning to Create Our Own Knowledge. *Convergence* 13 (1-2).

Stanley, L. and Wise, S. 1983. *Breaking Out: Feminist Consciousness and Feminist Research.* London: Routledge & Kegan Paul.

Walker, R. 1985. *Doing Research.* London: Methuen.

The Talk Workshop Group. 1982. *Becoming Our Own Experts.* London: The ILEA English Centre.

COMMUNITY DEVELOPMENT PROJECT AMONG THE GYPSIES OF SÃO GREGORIO

Olívia Oliveira, with the
cooperation of Sameiro Nova
and Glória Coelho
Braga, Portugal

1. Introduction

The community development project being carried out in the township of São Gregório, on the outskirts of the city of Braga in northern Portugal, began at the initiative of the Regional Social Security Office as an effort to improve living conditions among the gypsies of São Gregório. The aim is to help them survive without social assistance, to facilitate their integration into Portuguese society, and to set up specific links for mounting a cooperative effort between the Portuguese Red Cross, the Municipal Council of Braga (local government), the School Extension Program (Adult Education Division), the Health Centre, the Employment and Vocational Training Institute, the Manufacturers Association of Minho, and the Sports and Recreation Directorate. Apart from the Social Security Office, the organizations which have played the most important role in this effort are the School Extension Program and the Health Centre.

The idea of the project first arose when the Regional Social Security Office began to notice that the gypsy community of São Gregório was increasingly reliant on its services, becoming the heaviest users of its social benefit programs. However, their growing resort to the Social Security Office did not mean that members of the community knew how to obtain more and better benefits.

Closer examination of the relevant files revealed serious deficiencies at the social, economic and educational levels in São Gregório.

This preliminary study concluded that there was a need for action and so planning began for a community development project, which was launched in April 1988. The project was divided into three stages: (1) diagnosis of problems, (2) execution of programs and assessment of results, and (3) transition stage towards full independence of the gypsy population. We are now in the third stage of the project.

Project design

Since it cannot subsidize projects directly, the Regional Social Security Office began by establishing a link with the Portuguese Red Cross, whose status as a nongovernmental organization (NGO) made it eligible for funding. In this way, it was possible to make available the resources necessary to carry out the project that was taking shape.

To launch the project a staff of four full-time field workers was appointed by the Social Security Office, consisting of two social workers and two educators. Support and coordination was provided by a team made up of representative staff members from the various agencies involved and including the author of this report.

Several basic questions had to be answered before the project could be designed.

Since the target community consists of an economically depressed group belonging to an ethnic minority, it was essential to find out what differences existed between this and other marginal groups whose outward signs, behaviour and attitudes otherwise appear to be identical.

How do we perceive the gypsies? Is there any truth to the more or less common impression of a group of sordid individuals, cunning swindlers, cheats, liars, and dangerous, violent thieves?[1] Or are these false preconceptions based on external appearances developed in self-defence, while their real personalities are only revealed within the group? And what do the gypsies think of us? How do they see us? For that matter, how do they see themselves and their role as a group within a dominant foreign culture?

Thus, we should start by questioning the accuracy of our preconceptions about them and discovering how they perceive us. By examining the socio-cultural fabric of the community, delimiting areas of conflict and opposition, and clearly defining the openings that will permit assured access to the gypsy people, we hope to remove obstacles that prevent interrelationships, gain their confidence and convince them to take part in the project.

Next we asked ourselves what approach to take. Should we begin with their culture, and work towards that of the dominant community? Or should we develop the project entirely within the context of the latter? This option may lead to complications in the make-up of the project since the gypsies do not carry on their daily life in a vacuum. As a merchant people they must have contacts and negotiations with non-gypsies. They are Portuguese citizens and must relate to our institutions. And they are immersed in a society which is full of challenges and rapid change, particularly now that the pace of modernization is accelerating in Portugal as the European Economic Community approaches complete integration.

We concluded that they could not be self-sufficient if they remained locked in their own little world, that they could not develop in cultural isolation. For it is by having contact with, and confronting, other social values that a group can grow. In theory it is possible to confront these other values without undermining what is essential in one's own culture. The aim then is to integrate the new into the traditional way of life, recognizing that traditions are not absolutely immutable, that they do evolve over time reflecting the progress of the society that cherishes them.

There was one other risk to consider. In the process of undergoing change, the gypsies must be prevented from falling into hybrid behaviour patterns that might strip them of their group identity and leave them in a cultural no-man's-land. Experience teaches that gypsies, like other disadvantaged minorities who found themselves in these circumstances, might then retreat into themselves, closing off all access and preventing the hoped-for changes. Or, driven by their insecurity, they might lash out with even less desirable behaviour.

To ensure against this, it was decided that the project should include constant monitoring of the target group (hence the need for four full-time field workers), as well as promoting cultural activities that would facilitate the restructuring process or the eventual emergence of an internal framework enabling individuals and the group as a whole to understand the phenomena taking place within their community.

Another question that needed answering was how to approach the community. Should we go in as big brother claiming to know what is best for them, or should we take the opposite tack and try to identify with the community and its problems, letting them decide what it is they want and what can be done?

There is a very real risk with the first approach that once the project is over and the last field worker has left, the community will go right back to the way it was before. To avoid this, we chose the second approach. The project was thus designed as a participatory development effort enabling the community to acquire the necessary skills that would lead it gradually in the direction of real autonomy.

The first step was to sit down with them and reflect on the root causes of their poor health conditions, poverty and marginalization - in short, to analyze with them their problems, needs and aspirations; to help them examine their objectives and realize that these are not cast in stone. It was important to make them see that the persons intending to work with them in the community had no wish to take them where they did not want to go. Rather, they should sit down together and decide what path to take and which solutions are best. They must be made to see that before they can gain access to the benefits of the larger society in which they are immersed, they will have to take certain steps to prepare themselves for the enjoyment of these benefits - steps which require effort and involvement on their part.

With this as background, the general philosophy of the project can be summarized in the following beliefs:

- Everyone has a right to both cultural diversity and individual variations from the norm.

- There is no such thing as a superior or an inferior culture, only dominant and immersed cultures.

- People have an innate potential for learning and thought, which well-designed activities can release.

- To be free (not subservient), people must have the right to participate in the changes taking place in their own lives and the life of the community.

- There is need for an ongoing study of communities to obtain deeper and more extensive knowledge of the dynamic inter- actions taking place within the community.

From these beliefs are derived the guiding principles on which the social action plan of the project are based:

- Respect for persons and their diversity.

- Objective analysis of cultures permitting critical examination of diverse cultural values and facilitating dialogue and comparison with the new values of today's interdependent world.

- The starting point will be a continuing study of the community, seeking suitable ways of meeting its needs and solving its problems, based on the objectives set for the project.

- The people themselves must take part in all phases of the project through their legitimate representatives, and particularly in any final decisions that are reached. All aspects of the project must be designed by and for the people it is aimed at.

- The emphasis is on developing people skills (rather than on the intellectual level or cognitive learning); encouraging the relational, behaviourial and organizational skills that will permit change and relativization of social roles; and acquiring the essential tools required to take control of one's own life and that of the community.

The literacy campaign

As theirs is a culture based on oral traditions, the gypsies cannot be faulted for not writing their own language. It is with respect to the dominant language, Portuguese, that they are illiterate.

This illiteracy, in the midst of a society in which writing is omnipresent, denies them access to information essential to their daily lives - information needed to improve their living conditions and ensure their welfare.

Although they have no need for these skills in their own language, their inability to read and write the language of the dominant culture complicates their daily lives, makes it hard for them to relate to Portuguese society and hinders access to public services. Above all it cuts them off from the advantages and privileges reserved for citizens, including training opportunities.

This being the case, it was immediately obvious that an adult literacy campaign should be one of the first tasks undertaken in São Gregório.

Accordingly, a program was launched even before the diagnosis stage of the project had been completed, with the added benefit that it helped field workers obtain information and gain familiarity with the gypsy community.

Harking back to Paulo Freire, there is solid philosophical evidence for expecting this approach to work. For in following this path, we are recognizing man's universal capacity to learn wherever he has the means to do so, as well as the absence of these means within certain structural segments of society; and attempting to develop self-awareness among the gypsy people, thereby encouraging a critical reappraisal of their circumstances as well as new respect for their practical experience, cultural identity and traditional values. At the same time, we hope to promote respect for the written word, not for its own sake but as a means of enabling the community to decode and encode the world around them and society. For as a creative process, as an act of self-understanding, literacy aims ultimately at reducing the risk that a society's cultural identity can be manipulated, or that it will disappear altogether.

Based on these principles, the literacy campaign - which from the beginning has been under the direction of one of the social educators and a co-author of this report - has been and continues to be the most effective common thread linking and supporting the other aspects of the project. All of the other questions and issues, from health problems to difficulty finding employment, and all of the individual aspirations go to make up the universe of discourse brought forth in the literacy campaign. There everything is discussed and debated, mulled over and raised to the level of consciousness. Virtually all of the other activities of the project converge in the literacy classes, and from them flow many of its practical results. In the end, literacy training has played a crucial role in preparing the gypsies for the changes that are taking place within their community.

2. Studying the Community

The aims of research

In attempting to deal with an ethnic minority, and one which is a disadvantaged group to boot, we are entering a variable and complex area fraught with interconnecting social problems and cultural contrasts. One, moreover, in which it is essential to carry out applied and participatory research designed to serve at the same time as an innovative strategy in the qualitative transformation of the social practices of those who are serving as both researchers and subjects of research.

The following guidelines were formulated to ensure that such research is balanced:

- The need for quantitative, statistical studies;

- The opening of a dialogue intended to reveal how the gypsies see themselves and what it is that determines their actions, i.e. phenomenological analysis;

- Understanding of centres of social activity: in public services, shops, markets, fairs, etc.;

- Identification of community leaders and legitimate representatives that can serve as participants in the project;

- Obtaining of information from as many people as possible among those who deal directly or indirectly with the gypsies;

- The earliest possible involvement of the gypsies themselves in the project (so that they can be the protagonists of their own development), and delimitation of specific areas of interaction and commitment between members of the community and the field workers;

- During research, efforts would be made to create the right conditions (by disseminating ideas and proposing self-reliance) which would enable the community to develop the attitudes necessary to improve the lot of the gypsies.

As demonstrated in the above, our line of reasoning was to make the project participatory from the outset, and to ensure that the research phase is one of reflection/action. For making contact with the people in the community - even if only for information purposes - inevitably raises questions and leads to the establishment of informal ties, compromises and commitments: *He who questions is involved; he who responds is committed.*

Rationale and objectives of the study

By studying the community we hoped to obtain information and knowledge that would enable us to:

- Find rapid and effective solutions to a host of problems inherent in achieving balanced socio-economic development without upsetting the cultural framework of the gypsy community;

- Find comprehensive means for meeting the needs - actual or perceived - of the gypsy community, which is subject to enforced idleness while at the same time undergoing a process of change resulting from their insertion into the broader and dominant society that surrounds them;

- Identify and set overall objectives for the project;

- Identify priority sectors or areas of intervention taking into account the problems, needs and aspirations of the community and the resources available;

- Determine the objectives and field of activity of the various participants in the project;

- Identify the cultural and educational implications of community development work within an ethnic minority;

- Adjust the project strategy to the specific conditions among the gypsies and to their socio-cultural dynamics.

To accomplish these tasks, the following objectives were set for the community study stage of the project:

- To identify the main problems facing the community, in particular those relating to basic infrastructure;

- To identify needs that can be met through education;

- To learn what are the main aspirations expressed by the community;

- To understand the socio-economic and cultural organization of the community;

- To assess the psychological, ideological and cultural determinants of, and existing impediments to, the success of the project;

- To discover the collective interests of the community;

- To find out how the various groups in the community occupy their time in order to choose the best time of day, days and season in which to carry out the activities of the project;

- To determine the institutional framework within which the project would be carried out;

- To survey human support services and other resources;

- To choose a site for the project;

- To assess the importance which the gypsies attach to their lack of ability to read and write the language of the dominant society;

- To determine to what extent this lack of literacy causes difficulty in daily life;

- To evaluate their predisposition for learning/literacy, given the high level of illiteracy among them;

- To determine the failure or drop-out rate among the young and identify its causes.

Methodology used in the study

A plan was developed encompassing three phases:

1. Consult documents and records of the various services which have contact with the gypsy community;

2. Interview the people in charge of these services, as well as neighbours and the gypsies themselves;

3. First-hand observations.

1st phase
We began by ordering and analyzing all existing documents and records of the services that usually deal with the gypsy community (social security, municipal council, health services and primary schools). This entailed a great deal of red tape but with a little persistence we managed to compile a list of the community's needs.

2nd phase
While collecting the above-mentioned data, we were also interviewing those in charge of these institutions and any other employees who normally have direct contact with the gypsies.

We also interviewed the owners of the local grocery, butcher's shop and pharmacy, and everyone who lives in the surrounding area. In this way we learned the degree to which the gypsies are accepted in the community, how they are seen to behave and their relations with their neighbours, as well as identifying the natural leaders among them. This information facilitated direct contact and our introduction to the gypsy families.

Early on in our contact with the gypsies we discovered that it was not possible, in most cases, to conduct an "interview". Rather, we had to proceed in a normal conversational style with open questions, and allow the subject to take the response in any direction he/she chose. Often our questions elicited "life histories" which were rich in tradition and extremely useful.

We began by choosing for these informal interviews heads of family, all of them men and mostly elders of great prestige in the community. Meetings had to be arranged in advance as they were generally gone all day attending to sales at the fairs.

At first contact the gypsies are very reserved and distrustful. Little by little they will begin to accept a stranger, and once their confidence is gained they become open and loyal friends. At that point they are warmly receptive and attentive, and will even invite one into their homes. However, it took a year of assiduous courting to gain their complete confidence.

From the start we maintained a systematic scepticism whenever it appeared that the informant was capable of deceit.

Group discussions were more problematic, particularly at first. They became inhibited in the presence of other gypsies, avoiding our questions or diverting them into other areas. It appeared to us that a group psychology was operating, and that all of them were afraid to answer our questions. Once their confidence had been gained, however, the misgivings gradually disappeared and they became more open and consistently spontaneous.

3rd phase

It was first-hand observation which was most effective in giving us a real sense of their culture, their traditions and their psychology. We saw them at various times during their day-to-day activities, observing their family and group relations, and little by little we came to understand their *modus vivendi* and to change the negative preconceptions we had about this people. They invited us for coffee and for meals, and took us along to their weddings. We even observed their religious ceremonies.

In short, we came to know the people and accomplished our first objectives, and the project team was thus able to proceed with greater consistency and confidence in carrying out its tasks and interacting with the community. The knowledge gained enabled us to identify with greater precision what it was that had to be done, and to select the right strategy to be adopted.

We came to the conclusion that an approach of this type is not suited to large-scale projects or those that cover extensive areas; that it is entirely suited to a project centred on social problems; that it is most effect when dealing with qualitative rather than quantitative data; and that it is only possible where the necessary means are available, namely full-time staff.

3. The Gypsies

Socio-historical context

Little is known of the history of the gypsies of São Gregório (Braga). Their oral traditions and the lack of written documents prevent us from full investigation. Not even the oldest members of the community can tell us where they came from. Any memory they have of their forebears goes back no more than four generations, offering little hope of finding out their origin. They only know that their forefathers came very early on to settle first in Andalusia, Spain. However, the families that live in São Gregório originated more recently in various parts of Portugal, and no longer know of any Spanish relatives. According to them, they came to our country because they can live better and there are more social benefits here.

The São Gregório gypsy community initially consisted of 17 family groups totalling 94 inhabitants, with an average of 4/5 children per family. The situation is somewhat different now, with 23 family groups and 115 inhabitants.

They live in one-room huts with earthen or cement floors. The huts have electricity, but the only access to water is through communal taps. There is no sewer system and the only road into the community, which is situated at the top of Mount São Gregório, is a steep and difficult one.

Public transportation is available but the nearest stop is 750m from the community. There is a grocery store and butcher's shop approximately one kilometre away. They buy things on informal credit, to be paid when they receive their social security benefits.

The gypsies are essentially small businessmen, selling their wares in open-air stalls or as street vendors, and acting as horse traders. Some take temporary work as basket makers, but only when business is bad. The women assist their husbands and are housewives.

Despite their living conditions, some gypsy families are well off, having money, colour television sets, VCRs, washing machines, telephone, automobile, refrigerator, furniture. Most own cars as part of the cost of doing business, and not as symbols of wealth or prosperity.

At the same time, begging is an activity they can fall back on in times of crisis to obtain enough to survive. The women and infants engage in this activity. They often resort to social security for subsistence, exaggerating their poverty and wearing more tattered clothes than usual.

Their health is always precarious and frequently at great risk. Their low income levels, poor living conditions and sanitation, lack of education and, especially, their life style lead to serious errors in the prevention or cure of illnesses. They have little protection from the elements (rain, cold, heat). They often sleep in the same clothes they wear during the day. Children go to bed and get up at the same time as the adult members of the family. They have no fixed meal times; they eat when they are hungry and have no idea of what constitutes a balanced diet. They drink a lot of coffee and eat a great deal of fatty pork. Children are raised primarily on potatoes.

The main diseases recorded among them are bronchitis, asthma, flu, colds, intestinal illnesses and psychiatric problems.

Children up to the age of five are most affected by disease. We learned this from the local clinic and hospital where we found that most of the prescriptions handed out had children's names on them. These children had not been vaccinated and did not have a regular pediatrician.

School attendance is poor among children and adults. Of the 27 school-age (6-14 years old) children in the community, only 14 go to school. The failure rate is close to 80% and attendance is very low.

There are many causes for the absenteeism and the poor pass rate including rejection on the part of most teachers, either as the result of culture shock or because of their appearance of neglect and (often) body odour. Allowed to run free at home, gypsy children have difficulty adjusting to schedules, rules and discipline in general. Their parents cannot help with their school work, which they find hard and time-consuming. Abstract knowledge holds little interest and has no practical application to the life they lead. When children turn 12 their parents are reluctant to allow them to go to school. The girls, in particular are tightly controlled once they reach the age of puberty.

In their intercultural relations with local and national institutions, the gypsies face two large difficulties. One is their status as a despised ethnic minority, and the other is their low level of education in the Portuguese language. About 80% of them are illiterate and another 10% read and write only with great difficulty. The gypsies felt little desire to learn these skills at first, but began to come round as a result of our efforts to make them aware of the advantages of reading and writing. As a result, 23 adults signed up for our first literacy class, although in the event only 16 of them showed up.

Most of their free time is spent watching television, and by far their favourite programs are the Brazilian soap operas. They are also very fond of Indian films, virtually the only ones they watch. Their principal recreational activity is singing and dancing "in the Spanish style". They frequent festivals in their own and other communities, and are often seen at wedding celebrations, baptisms, dances and Christmas parties.

The gypsies of São Gregório speak *caló*, which is a dialect of Romany. The basic roots of this language are of Indian origin with some Greek additions and borrowings as well from Gallego, Portuguese, Catalan and French, in that order. Its grammar is heavily influenced by Spanish, which most of the older generation speak. All of the inhabitants speak Portuguese.

Their own language constitutes a sort of taboo, however, and is only used when others are not present. With us they always spoke Portuguese.

The gypsies' language is unwritten. For this reason, communication between them is either by telephone or by personal contact. To communicate with distant relatives they use intermediaries or public telephones. They put little trust in the written word, even in those rare cases where they are forced to rely on writing.

Their cultural heritage is transmitted orally and handed down from father to son within the family. A saying of theirs is that "one learns not by speaking but by listening". All of their traditions are passed along through stories and instructional narratives. The youngest among them learn and remember.

Forced to live submerged in foreign and more advanced cultures, unable to read and write their own language and surrounded by suspicion and rejection, the gypsies have internalized their marginalization/victimization, as a result of adverse social contacts and non-acceptance stemming from their being different and their status as a cultural minority. The constant pressure to which they are subjected has instilled in the gypsies a tenacious will to survive and has led them to develop different defence mechanisms to protect the original family nucleus.

These mechanisms usually manifest themselves in aggressive behaviour, distrust and intolerance - which serve only to widen the breach that separates the two societies they must deal with, and to increase their segregation.[2]

The psychology of the gypsy

The focal concern of the gypsies is their own subsistence. To them, thinking about what is past serves only to disturb the spirit. The future is uncertain - the only thing that counts is the present moment. Hence the gypsy lives day to day. When he feels a need, it must be satisfied immediately. If he must wait for it, the object of his desire loses its appeal.

The gypsies have no desire to get ahead, nor any sense of saving for the future. They possess little, have no wish to accumulate goods and do not envy others. They only work when they feel the need for money to survive. They have an aversion to working on a fixed schedule or in an enclosed space, and generally seek to avoid manual labour: "A gypsy does not dirty his hands".

Young men drafted into military service usually desert as they are unable to adjust to rules and discipline.

They are endowed with practical intelligence and have an intuitive grasp of things. At the same time, they believe in magic and accept the supernatural without critical thought.

They have difficulty concentrating and are fond of emotional display - the spectacular flourish that appeals to the emotions.

They value their freedom greatly, yet identify strongly with their group. They are never lacking in trust for each other, and generously share their food with their fellows.

They are famous for their gratitude for any favour, whether by a fellow gypsy or a *gadjé* (white).

They fear solitude (taking refuge in the family and the clan) and disease - making use of magic and resorting to witches and wizards who live nearby to fool the demons that cause their misfortunes.

Gypsies are fatalists: "sky above, earth below - and in the middle, the gypsies". This characteristic means that they accommodate easily to social problems and thus do not feel many of the needs inherent in our society.

The gypsy lives a happy and passionate life. He grasps life with both hands, yet is not afraid of death. Rather, he accepts it as his destiny with the phrase: "It is written".

The gypsies do not have a religion of their own and accept only with reluctance those of the countries in which they live. The gypsies of São Gregório have adopted the evangelical religion and are led by a pastor in religious services held in a local hut at 6 p.m. every day.

They are in fact very superstitious and it is our opinion that most do not know the difference between superstition and religion. They accept that religion which does them the most immediate good. The evangelical religion forbids certain attitudes and behaviour such as alcoholism, violence, bearing arms and the use of drugs. These were all problems in their community, especially among the young. Through religion they are trying to overcome delinquency, and they are succeeding. But their level of fanaticism, as well as their attendance at church, varies in direct proportion as the above problems wax and wane.

The gypsies have a primitive notion of theft. To rob a *gadjé* is perfectly acceptable. In fact, stealing is simply a means of subsistence made necessary by their way of life, their reluctance to accept regular work and the unreliable nature of their businesses. But among themselves stealing is prohibited.

Gypsy law is seen as prevailing over the established laws, and their own rules (always keeping one's word to another gypsy, extreme love for children, marital fidelity, respect for elders, fraternity and solidarity with the group, guarding a girl's virginity before marriage) are strictly obeyed.

They have a deep-felt love for their children, allowing them every possible freedom, saving the best food for them, giving loving care and protecting them from any harm.

They also have a fierce sense of fraternity and solidarity, despite the many arguments and fights between them - which, however, are invariably resolved without recourse to outside law. They defend each other fiercely and complain bitterly when one of their members is arrested, hospitalized or sought by the police.

When one goes to jail, the rest immediately band together and come to his defense, offering to pay fines, go bail or testify in his behalf. When a member is in hospital, they stay by his side, bring him food and make camp nearby. The same rallying takes place when there is a funeral, which they see as an occasion to turn inward. All will pay their share for a member's funeral if the family cannot afford one.

Gypsy law is very demanding of its womenfolk, especially in matters of love, honour and privacy. Young girls are virtually betrothed from birth, and are zealously guarded by parents and brothers once they reach puberty. A gypsy woman is expected to marry once only and in church, to be faithful to her husband and to remain a perpetual widow should he die. She must also be hard-working, bear children (it is considered a curse to be childless) and avoid showing legs or knees.

The family

The family is one of the pillars of gypsy society. Not just the nuclear family (parents and children) but an extended group, which includes several nuclear families related by blood. This extended family ends at the level of the clan, which is a single organism in its social actions. The clan, in turn, relates to other groups with which it is related to make up a tribe or community.

Authority within the clan increases with age, so that it is generally the elders who organize tasks, give orders and take important decisions.

But the "chief" of the clan is not necessarily the oldest individual. For in addition to age, there are other factors to be considered in the choice of leader: prestige, money, experience in general, number of sons and relatives, connections with the outside world. The tasks of a "chief" can range from financial matters and relations with the dominant society, to settling minor disputes between members of the clan that the *batós* [father/head of family] cannot resolve.

Within the nuclear family, the father is the authority figure but he is primarily preoccupied with business outside the home. As he reaches an advanced age, he leaves these responsibilities to his sons.

Marriage itself is not the beginning of the family; it is simply a rite of passage from young man to adult. After his marriage, a son continues to be dependent upon his father and works to repay him for the wedding expenses. A young married woman (*bori*) passes into the family of her husband and is subordinate to her mother-in-law.

Only with the birth of their first child does the husband become a man and the wife achieve full stature as a woman. At that moment a new nuclear family is created.

A gypsy woman's lot is one of subjugation. When single, she is dependent on her father and brothers; once married, she must obey her husband. Her mate has the exclusive right to inflict any punishment on his wife who is considered weak and inferior. The role of the woman in gypsy society is summed up in their stark social hierarchy: "the aged, children, men, women, animals".

On the day of their marriage, young women must undergo "virginity testing" which is carried out by an older woman who specializes in this art, in the presence of the mothers of the future bride and bridegroom, plus godmothers and other respected female elders.

The wedding ceremony itself is usually in late afternoon during the warmer months so that it can be held in the open air. It is a time when extended families reunite - usually the families of the couple invite all of their relatives, friends and neighbours.

It is on these occasions that the elders get together and make long-term plans for future marriages.

Today, however, the gypsies want to be free to choose their own mate, so that it is not uncommon for a pair of young gypsies to elope when their parents disapprove.

Elopement is in fact traditional among the gypsies. The young couple does not go far, however, returning in a matter of days - sometimes hours - to beg the forgiveness of both sets of parents. This is almost always given, and the young couple are allowed to live together until their marriage can be formalized with a wedding ceremony.

If, externally, the gypsies have altered their ways and adopted many of the cultural habits of their surroundings, the same cannot be said of their traditional family structure or their basic psychology and ideology, which they have managed to perpetuate in their culture despite constant pressure from the cultures of those societies that surround them.

4. **Implementation of the Project**

The overall objective

Having attained this minimum level of knowledge of the community and characterization of its inhabitants; having identified their problems, needs and desires - from their standpoint as well as from our own; having assessed their socio-economic and cultural level, we turned to defining the type of intervention to be carried out, taking as our guiding principle the idea that individuals have the potential to change and to participate in transforming the means of their socialization.

Rejecting the use of charity, we chose instead to lead the gypsies to discover the causes of the problems that afflict them, so that in the light of these problems, they themselves - both as gypsies and as Portuguese citizens - could seek the best solutions. "If a man asks for a fish, give him instead a fishing pole and teach him how to fish." This in a nutshell is what we have sought in our project.

The gypsies are aware of their poverty, their low standard of living. They know that living is more than merely surviving. They know of no other way to improve their lives than to beg, but this "solution" only increases their dependence at every level.

This was what we wanted to change. Not to deprive them of their legitimate civil rights, but to train them in other means of improving their lot, or at least help them find other ways to earn their living which both respect their nature and retain their dignity as human beings.

The team of field workers did not root out some of the gypsies' convictions which had not been expressed at the start, but these came out eventually after some consciousness-raising efforts and much questioning.

The overall objective of the Social Development Project as worked out in cooperation with participating members of social agencies can be broken down as follows:

- To ensure that all family units have access to adequate housing, and that they know how to take care of it;

- To help the gypsy community be less dependent upon social service benefits;

- To improve their employment situation and wages;

- To provide the camp with basic sanitation;

- To ensure minimum standards of hygiene, both for individuals and for the community as a whole;

- To create a standard of living acceptable to the surrounding (non-gypsy) community, so as to avoid social marginalization of the gypsies;

- To promote the integration of the gypsies into the mainstream of Portuguese society along their own cultural lines;

- To make the surrounding community aware of the cultural idiosyncrasies of the gypsies;

- To change the negative and strongly-embedded stereotype of the gypsies within the new Portuguese society;

- To create links between the gypsy community and the society which surrounds them - links which respect their differences.

Plus the following which relate to their schooling:

- To reduce basic and functional illiteracy among the community's adult population;

- To bring down absentee and failure rates among school-age children;

- To promote family participation in the education of their children;

- To encourage a flexible and varied approach in the school system at social and institutional levels alike.

Methodology of the study-action project

To attain the objectives proposed, a number of different entities were called upon to coordinate their efforts. In order to respond to the variety of problems perceived in the community, it was necessary to develop a unified approach in which their several efforts would converge in achieving the total success of the project.

To this end we contacted and eventually obtained the participation of the following institutions: the Municipal Council of Braga, the Health Centre, the Employment and Vocational Training Institute, the School Extension Program (Adult Education Division), the Sports Directorate, the Manufacturers Association of Minho, the Social Security Office and the Portuguese Red Cross.

The broad outlines of the project's context contained many elements indicating what methodology should be adopted in a study-action project of this sort. It would be mainly concerned with pointing out differences, since in carrying out the project only explanations - not generalizable knowledge - of what was studied would be produced (this was compatible with the nature of the project). Its field of interaction was compact and limited: its activities would concentrate on social problems, attempting to change practices and thereby alter the social context of the gypsy community and its intercultural contacts. Participants were available from social agencies serving the community to act as animators in promoting cultural activities. We were confident that the actual contents of the project could be worked out and formulated as problems arose and made themselves known. A team of full-time field workers had been appointed to work on the project, and financial and material resources were at hand.

But, on the other hand, we knew that the study-action method is both complicated and demanding, and is not fully compatible with the difficulties and limitations foreseen. It is a method which can only be applied by a multidisciplinary team which includes diverse specialists not available to us (sociologists, psychologists, educational experts, etc.). The contracts with local cooperators who would help carry out the project had to be in writing (the method does not allow verbal contracts), and yet our counterparts in the community were not in a position to sign these. The method assumes that everything has been negotiated in advance, that whenever strategies have to be changed, new contracts can be made redefining the commitment and recording the changes. This we could not do. It would require that the theory behind it be developed at the same time as the project is being carried out, and we knew that we did not have the capability to do this. It would presuppose a degree of control that we feared could not be provided at all times. At the same time, there are many intangible aspects of the community that are complex and unknown, and that create a chasm between the team of field workers and social service cooperators, on the one hand, and the members of the community, on the other hand, so that we could not predict exactly the degree of participation we would receive from our counterparts within the gypsy community.

Changing social practices implies disturbing the thought processes of the community, and in view of earlier references to this sort of phenomenon we could not be sure that we might not unleash adverse effects. Aware of our limitations, we were afraid that we might not be able to control these.

In view of the above, yet recognizing the advantages of this method - tighter control of results and greater scientific rigour, stronger commitment and higher level of participation and involvement by local cooperators - we opted for compromise. We would attempt to apply the method's stages and procedures, but in a more flexible and less bureaucratic manner.

Consequently, the methodological orientation adopted included the following objectives:

- Using the direct experience and daily life of the gypsy community, to stimulate the thought processes and engagement of the participants toward changes rooted in both personal and collective experience and requiring systematic study of the medium/community;

- To set the operation within the study/action methodology, combining its stages and phases with social dynamic principles, attitudes and procedures;

- To promote participation or involvement in the form of initiative and commitment as a means of articulating knowledge, skills and attitudes;

- To formulate plans for bringing about economic and technical improvements, including consideration of the means (human and institutional resources) and repercussions of the decisions taken;

- To devise means for integrating the action of public and private institutions and services on behalf of the community in carrying out the project activities;

- To design the project so as to include a wide range of activities (training, creativity and recreation) and technical measures (diverse resources: written, oral, audiovisual and other materials);

- To aim at systematic (and systemic) intervention not restricted to practical applications only. To do this it was necessary to balance the following levels of the project:

  • regular and continuous contact with the community
  • classification and study (assessment) of previous projects and experiments
  • study and basic research for the training of agents, systematic organization of the materials and tools used in the project

- To get the community involved in its socio-economic organization, bearing in mind its cultural roots and tradition as a source of regeneration;

- To encourage expression and participation (recreation, festivals, research, artistic creation, cultural interaction, preservation of heritage and the environment, local radio, sports, etc.);

- To promote solidarity and social support programs (aimed at children, the elderly, disease prevention, the handicapped, illiterates, etc.);

- To foster action groups (parent-teacher associations, neighbourhood programs, renters, consumers, etc.);

- To secure the help of local and regional governments as an essential condition for success;

- To decentralize control and encourage initiative and autonomy, avoiding the formality and uniformity inherent in central controls.

Strategies to be carried out

Following the negotiations with institutional participants, a plan was worked out (it would be unrealistic to say it was "agreed" since nothing was in writing and everything depended on verbal agreements). The various services agreed to cooperate by making their personnel and support materials available so long as they were used in accordance with the rules governing their operations and duties.

The project was divided into three stages so as to make its introduction gradual, always subject to readjustments or changes in its basic strategies.

The Adult Education Division played an important role because of its experience in programs for the disadvantaged, its capacity for stimulating self-awareness, and the assumption that illiteracy was a major stumbling block to success in school. Another key element in the equation was the fact that one of the young social educators appointed to the team had been trained in adult education, primarily in literacy programs. She was thus fully informed and prepared to direct a course of this nature within the context of a community action program. In the first stage of the project, then, she was kept busy working as social educator and at the same time developing the literacy course.

In developing this course, she was able to explore issues and expand into areas which the respective social services are not prepared or equipped to tackle within specific community action programs: the environment, consumer awareness, women's issues, the law (two young gypsy men had recently been arrested in São Gregório for drug trafficking).

As part of the effort to ensure that the efforts of the various services did not take place in isolation and would not simply disappear the moment the project ended, the literacy program took on an integrative role by organizing its teaching materials around these issues and frequently expanding its scope to include activities outside the usual school curriculum.

The Health Centre took the lead in the area of personal and collective hygiene, as well as diet, children's vaccination programs and family planning. It was also instrumental in involving family physicians and making the gypsy community aware of the need to consult them.

The literacy program took on all of these topics and, using an interdisciplinary approach, worked to inculcate these ideas and make them a part of the new awareness which the gypsies were developing of their community.

The Municipal Council took on the task of ensuring that the gypsies had decent living quarters, primarily by building several houses and upgrading their shacks, installing sanitation and carrying out negotiations aimed at regularizing ownership of the area where they live. Their shacks are located on private - albeit not very valuable - land. It was proposed that the project buy the land for them, and the Council has offered to seek favourable conditions for its acquisition.

The literacy program brought up for discussion many topics that were then extended throughout the community and roused many people to action. By means of this course, solutions were worked out, means of carrying out these solutions were devised and subsequently adopted by the head of the community, and the necessary documents and requirements were prepared with the help of the animator.

An agreement was reached under which the Employment Institute (Ministry of Labour) tried to help those gypsies who successfully completed the literacy program to find their first jobs.

The business of operating street markets is becoming increasingly difficult and some members of the community have begun to express the desire to find regular employment as electricians, mechanics, drivers or night watchmen. However, there is virtually no chance that this will happen since they lack the employers' confidence and any tradition of working at "normal" jobs; do not exactly subscribe to the work ethic (they are said to look for employment without work); and have a very low level of education. The only other possibility would be for them to find positions in the construction industry. They tried this but quickly quit because the work is hard, and because the gypsies look down on manual labour in general. Accordingly, the Employment Institute has so far been unable to place them and never having worked they are ineligible for unemployment benefits.

Still on the topic of employment, the literacy course also showed that there is a need to provide pre-employment preparation within a socio-educational setting. To this end the Adult Educational Service of Braga, with the support of the European Social Fund, introduced two training programs of the sort needed: a sewing and dressmaking class for women and an electrician's course for men. Those who attended these classes obtained a sort of semi-qualification which helped them gain access to jobs; this shows that they were beginning to feel the need to overcome the idleness that was part of their life style. At the same time, the women who participated learned a few techniques that enabled them to improve their quality of life by mending their own and their children's clothes, and making a few new articles using available resources. In this way too, they were able to contribute to family income.

Another innovation within the community was a multidisciplinary work group called the Leisure Time Activities Group (ATL) which included both children and adults, and which acted as another focal point for various actions and levels of community participation.

It was decided that priority would be given to activities directed at children in this program, since they represent the best segment of society in which to begin - from the standpoint both of influencing their behaviour and of possible multiplier effects. On the other hand, their parents are in some circumstances more susceptible to change.

In planning these activities, we began by researching studies carried out under the Educational Support for Gypsy Children Program of the Ministry of Education in various locations around the country.

In addition to the pedagogical difficulties themselves, the poor adjustment of gypsy children to school, on the one hand, and the failure of teachers to understand their cultural differences or to accept their habits and manner of thinking, on the other, were the biggest obstacles.

It was decided that the program should concentrate on preparing the children for beginning and staying in school, encouraging parents to take an active role in their children's schooling, and making teachers more sensitive to, and understanding of, their cultural differences.

The first step was to define the areas in which activities were to be carried out. For this it was necessary to understand what motivates gypsy children and which skill development to take as a model for stimulating their interest in school.

The teachers who carried out the above-mentioned studies had thought about this and made recommendations on how to integrate gypsy children into the school system:

- Make parents aware of the importance of their cooperation with the schools;

- Create pre-school or kindergarten groups to make later adaptation to school easier;

- Develop support and remedial activities, particularly in the initial stages of school programs;

- Develop both oral and linguistic skills so as to enrich their vocabulary;

- Set up and support sports activities;

- Organize courses for teaching staff on the culture and ways of the gypsies;

- Promote literacy among their parents;

- Develop self-sufficiency in the children who have lived over-protected lives with their families.

Plans were included for activities to overcome the problems they encounter with the work and the difficulties they have integrating into the school system, while at the same appealing to their known interests: keen enjoyment of music, dance and theatre; strong attraction in the plastic arts, for which they show real ability, skill and balance; and enthusiasm for sports and games.

The activities developed and presented in the program were intended essentially to create the necessary conditions for successful adaptation of the gypsy children to the school system (the results are increasingly positive), to get parents involved and make them aware of their children's education (benefiting their own training as well), and assisting the teachers to become more aware and receptive of these children in their schools.

School support activities were organized. In addition to extra-curricular help with their other school work, activities were carried out involving manual training: wood, clay and straw. These activities involving motor skills and creativity fascinated them, and contributed much to motivating them and keeping them involved in the schools.

Verbal skills in language were developed through various topics which were taken up in school wherever possible, presented in films, slides and other teaching methods, especially games, songs and dramatic presentations.

Various lessons on personal hygiene were taught, including bathing and washing. These activities helped to form good habits and encouraged within the gypsy children the desire to keep themselves clean, above all in school, and helped ensure their acceptance by teaching staff and other non-gypsy children.

Sports activities were carried out every week with the help of the Sports Directorate: track and field, handball and soccer. At present the children are getting to know the parish by taking part in a brush-clearing project. Most activities take place on a borrowed sports field and are directed by the project's cultural animator. This summer the children are going to compete in their own small championships and tournaments.

They have also been taken on excursions to visit museums, exhibits, shows, the circus, etc. for recreational and educational purposes. They have been to the nation's capital, Lisbon, where they stayed for five days and saw the zoo, monuments and museums. They have also visited the university town of Coimbra where they went to see the show *Portugal dos Pequeninos*, always a delight for children. They have toured Gerês National Park, a brick factory in Barcelos, a print shop and a newspaper. They went to this with a view to starting their own neighbourhood newspaper. They also had a full tour of a vocational school so that they could begin to think about possible future job training. The purpose of these activities, of which only a few have been mentioned, is to broaden their horizons, let them learn about the country and its natural and cultural patrimony, and to let them have fun.

Week-long holiday outings to the beach were organized and represented the first time most gypsy children had ever been away from their parents. At first they were disconcerted at the daily routines to which they were not accustomed: set hours for getting up and going to bed, regular meal times, use of bedclothes. After two or three days they settled down to the routine. This was their first step towards independence from their parents - and it was also the first proof of the community's confidence in the project personnel who accompanied the group of children.

Special events were planned for World Children's Day, Environment and Consumer Awareness Week, International Literacy Day, etc. During these times, the special topics were taken up with the children in the ATL Group, and with adults attending the literacy course. Various activities were carried out producing various items (posters, pamphlets, photographs, etc.) for display at the end of the special day or week.

Christmas, Carnival and St. John's Day festivals were held in which the gypsies took an active part, accepting assignments and helping with dances, sing-alongs, and even short skits. Despite the fact that these were alien celebrations to them, the gypsies took part with enthusiasm and real enjoyment. They have absorbed much of Spanish and Portuguese culture as can be seen in their costumes and rituals. Helping out in these festivals provided good motivation for them. Together they planned events, organized and arranged for appropriate locations, prepared food and, under the supervision of the project staff, put on small plays or skits - often nothing more than the dramatization of an anecdote or funny episode that had happened, and more than once with a *gadjé* or non-gypsy as the butt of the joke.

Exchanges were organized with ATL Groups in other (non-gypsy) communities, together with adult exchanges with other literacy courses in order to take part in each other's activities and festivals. The purpose of these exchanges was to promote intercultural relations and mutual acceptance, as well as to demystify the gypsies. Events were planned which would promote the cultures of those involved, and included plays, popular music, regional dance and folklore festivals. The gypsies were generally reluctant to mix with non-gypsies - nor were they the only ones to show such reluctance! But they listened attentively, laughed and enjoyed themselves. By the end of the social events (generally they ended with the serving of refreshments), the gypsies were more relaxed and were easily coaxed into singing and dancing to flamenco music.

Practical courses in cooking for women and basketmaking for men are planned, although they have not yet begun. In line with the other training they are receiving, the cooking classes are designed essentially to teach the women how to prepare low-cost meals. The basketmaking course is intended to give the men one possible avenue of self-employment as an alternative to the street market trade which has fallen on hard times. The gypsies have few other employment opportunities. Lacking both education and trade qualifications, and with their poor reputation as workmen (partly because of the racial stigma), they are unlikely to find an employer willing to hire them. Until they can improve their image, self-employment appears to be the best way to counteract the threat to their street market operations.

One method adopted to help salvage their historical identity and their culture was to help both the children and adult members of the community create family albums. These would contain photographs from as far back as possible, life histories, stories and instructional narratives that have come down to them and are part of their cultural patrimony and oral tradition to be appreciated and preserved. They became very interested and worked hard on this activity, gaining new respect for their social and cultural inheritance. Seeing this effort to reconstruct their family histories, even though sometimes without success, made them aware of the importance of recording traditions so as to ensure that these are preserved for handing down to future generations. Compiling these albums is a difficult task and many may never in fact be completed since the gypsies have no writing and many details may have been lost forever along the byways travelled by this people.

A workshop on gypsy culture was held in one of the area's primary schools, and all teachers who deal with children from the community were invited. Once again we noted the general intolerance and lack of comprehension on the part of the teaching staff, and how this leads to racist behaviour which contributes to the failure of children to adapt.

This initiative represented an effort to give the teachers insight into the world of the gypsies, to get them to understand the key elements of the other culture and, hopefully, reexamine their actions in the classroom. The ultimate objective was to make the teachers aware and give them practice in redefining and adapting teaching materials which take into account the cultural differences. It was suggested that coordination be set up between the school and the São Gregório Project, and that the teachers could organize intercultural activities as part of a school project involving teachers and both gypsy and non-gypsy students and parents.

As part of the workshop, a gypsy couple was invited to speak about their culture, their experience with their own children's schooling, and their feelings about the school's failure to understand their socio-economic and cultural situation.

It is worth noting here that we who are in daily contact with the gypsy children in the ATL have an altogether different impression of them than most of the teachers. They are above all sincere in everything and, not understanding the way things are organized, they react strongly when provoked - behaviour which is generally interpreted as rebelliousness or impertinence. They have a strong and determined character; they are clever and intelligent, although their abilities have not been developed. They learn quickly provided the right teaching methods are used. They are obedient when they understand the reason for the things they are told to do. They are affectionate and loving (despite the close relationship with their parents, they are not used to open displays of affection). To gain their trust, one has to establish the kind of relationship that will exist from the very first day.

Methodological aspects

It is not easy to distinguish between project activities aimed at adults and those for children. For in the event they became completely intertwined, with the adults taking part in the activities intended for children and the latter often attending the adult literacy classes (to the benefit of their school work). This was not the way the project was designed; rather, it sprang from the dynamics of the community itself.

On the one hand, the gypsies' natural affinity for their children means that they want to keep them close, or at least to know what they are doing. And on the other hand, many mothers took their children with them to their own adult classes.

Not that this method - which was forced on us - did not have its positive side. As it turned out, often the best way to get to the parents was through their children.

In the beginning we approached issues gingerly, afraid of offending their sensitivities and losing the confidence of the gypsies. Later, when an air of confidence had been established, those who worked with the gypsies began to change their roles and the way they approached tasks. They realized that it was often necessary to be tough and openly critical, virtually scolding them, to get results.

One thing was crystal clear: with the gypsies it is necessary to set definite rules from the start, and both to follow them oneself and insist that they do likewise. Another obvious conclusion was that, in our first contacts, the natural defensiveness of the gypsies led them to attempt to make fun of the "outsiders", acting distant, suspicious and even hostile at times. However, as soon as they felt secure and confident, this attitude was replaced by natural friendliness and hospitality. Once they decided you were a friend, they were loyal friends indeed, even asking for and accepting advice readily, and acting on it without qualms.

It was never the intention that the people taking part in the project should remain neutral. The nature and the reality of the situation we hoped to change were virtually unknown; and we were aware that the better we came to know the community, the problems they faced and their reactions, the more likely it would be that we would have to change and adopt new strategies. It was also difficult to predict how involved the members of the community would become in the project.

Therefore, it was clear from the start that flexibility and adaptability would be the order of the day, as staff responded to circumstances and adjusted to the reactions of the gypsies.

Many different strategies were used in carrying out the activities, some of them mentioned above. Wherever possible (although with moderation), audiovisual materials were used. Great care was taken in selecting these to ensure the right type of message, form of presentation and selection of images, so as to ensure that they could be easily understood and decoded. Posters were prepared to raise the gypsies' awareness, provide information and publicize the materials. Talks and debates in the form of open discussions were organized with guest specialists in the various areas of interest. Work is going on now to produce a community newsletter to come out every three months. The purpose of this publication is to promote the gypsy culture and provide information on the project for exchange with other gypsy and non-gypsy communities and other similar projects.

The newsletter is to be divided into three sections: one for articles and stories relating to project personnel; one for gypsy reaction to project activities including their experiences, needs and aspirations, and their own stories and legends; and one for news items of interest to members of the community and to those running activities for children.

One way or another everyone in the community is involved, especially a group of young people who will have the main responsibility for putting out each issue.

Everything was done at each stage to involve as many members of the community as possible in the activities, either through their representatives or through direct contacts with those in charge of activities. The details of activities were worked out by the participants themselves. In the literacy courses, the organization, contents and methods used - even class schedules - were decided by common accord. Husbands invariably accompanied their wives to family planning sessions. Parents went along with their children to doctor appointments and for vaccinations. And women participated in anti-smoking and anti-alcoholism activities.

5. Difficulties and Conditions Encountered

It was expected from the outset that the project would have difficulties to overcome. At the very beginning, the problem was lack of knowledge about the gypsies and their circumstances. Little was known about their social dynamic or the functioning of their traditions. We were not even sure how they would react to the activities carried out under the project.

We began with notions gathered from reading, plus the common preconceptions about gypsies. We found that many of these were false impressions very far removed from reality.

At the start, before they realized how the project was to work in the community, the attitude of the gypsies was akin to begging. They wanted - indeed demanded - that they be given what they needed, claiming they were entitled to this and showing no interest whatever in the project being proposed and in fact scoffing at it. It was difficult to make them see that only they could secure, by their own initiative, what was required not only for their subsistence but to better their living standards.

This tendency to beg was most obvious when the Minister of Education visited the literacy class. On his arrival, all of the gypsies in the community crowded into the hut where the classes were held and began to recount a long litany of complaints about the way they live, all the services they don't receive, etc. and made endless requests for assistance in areas outside the Minister's competence. However, they did obtain promises of a proper building in which to hold the literacy classes, plus several other items of interest to the community.

On the other hand, several of the barriers to change were difficult to overcome. Among those remaining, the most problematic cultural obstacles are:

- Tradition in general continues to resist change, so that only certain utilitarian accommodations were possible. A few external changes resulted from the contact between cultures (clothing, housing, food), which they recognize as being to their advantage.

- Lack of education and illiteracy continue to be cruelly oppressive, and it was noted that it is the new generation with at least some schooling that is trying to break down the barriers of tradition.

- Cultural ethnocentrism - the belief in the superiority of one's own culture - plus fear of losing face among their fellows, prevents the gypsies from replacing traditional behaviour with what are deemed foreign customs.

- The solidarity of the clan means that each one feels he/she is an integral part of the group and is prevented by peer pressure from accepting changes that may be interpreted as being a traitor to the community.

- The family structure is such that their cultural values are zealously protected and any attempt to change these is viewed with resentment and almost always rejected.

- Their provincialism and lack of initiative means that the gypsies will do little to improve their living standard and socio-economic status.

- Communication (in both directions) was an obstacle to establishing relationships with the gypsies at the beginning. They are not fluent in Portuguese, so they had trouble understanding us and were none too clear when trying to use our language. At times they intentionally used *caló* among themselves to criticize the program or talk about us without being understood, or sometimes to deceive us.

This latter problem has been partly solved, as those working directly with the gypsies, although still far from fluent, have learned a few words and phrases in their language.

There were other problems having nothing to do with the gypsies, such as lack of agreement between public services, which did nothing to make our job any easier.

In Portugal, public service institutions traditionally have a strictly vertical relationship with their clients. In general they are not prepared to give specific responses, especially to minorities. They have rules and procedures to follow which are fairly rigid and unbending.

Because of the diversity of its field of action and the general philosophy of the institution, the Social Security Office was, from the beginning, willing to break with this tradition and take part in a cooperative effort to provide training and upgrade their socio-economic status. It developed specific projects, cut through red tape, applied rules flexibly, and formed special work teams to help the gypsies. Coordination with the School Extension Program was excellent as well, and the attitude of this organization was, from the start, in sharp contrast to the remaining institutions with which the project had to deal. The diversity of backgrounds of its students and their different needs already required flexibility and adaptability, so that its officials were very helpful. However, it lacks the material, human and financial resources necessary to respond to all the requests made of it.

The policies of certain institutions regarding their duties and regulations gave rise to confrontations with the members of the project. Their lack of vocation in this area, particularly when dealing with minority groups, and the little experience they possessed in training programs, led to the adoption of strategies not always in accord with the objectives of the project. There was also the problem of lack of continuity in their activities, which sometimes resulted in ad hoc solutions. In the end we were able to fill these gaps using other strategies as mentioned earlier.

There was also a noticeable divergence in the educational principles espoused by the Extension Program staff who devised the literacy courses and the officials from the Social Security Office. Despite the specific training in the social aspects of adult education which the extension people receive, they tend to restrict their view of the learning situation to student/teacher/classroom; whereas the Social Service workers take a wider view of the social context and concentrate on interpersonal relationships, which are influenced by the subject's place in his environment. These misunderstandings were taken in our stride and worked out by the staff in joint meetings and planning sessions for organizing the activities.

Institutional rules and bureaucracy also hindered progress under the project, as well as a general lack of human resources and a reduction in financial support.

Lack of a suitable site with at least minimum facilities was another difficulty we faced. The literacy course was held in a run-down shack with poor lighting and a leaky roof, making it generally uncomfortable for everyone. Teaching materials and students' work could not be put on the walls. The shack was so cramped that students had to huddle together at two small desks. Children had to take turns sitting on worn-out benches as their mothers came to the classes in shifts. The path to the shack was difficult, winding and muddy.

The teachers complained about the poor conditions and the effect they had on the course. Indeed, only enormous goodwill, immense sacrifice and much courage made it possible to carry on under such adverse conditions.

The first signs of change

We begin by noting the construction of a bathhouse consisting of four toilets and four shower units, now ready for use. Also nearing completion is the pavilion building which will house a number of activities. The following sections list other results obtained under the project.

Health

The children have been vaccinated. At present, mothers are taking their children for their booster shots. Moreover, they are making the appointments themselves.

All the gypsies have been registered with family medicine clinics and the number of visits are increasing. Several referrals to ophthalmology, dentistry, neuro-pediatrics and psychology have been made. Teams of pediatric physicians visit the school on a regular basis to carry out child health programs.

Changes in eating habits are slowly making themselves felt: the children drink more milk than before and are bringing lunches to school more often. In general, they seem to be trying to arrange a more balanced diet.

Use of tobacco has not changed. It seems there are powerful cultural values attached to this habit. The men affirm their manhood by smoking, so children begin to smoke while still in school. At least we can be sure that the gypsies are now aware of the dangers of smoking and drinking.

Most of the women now practice family planning with the consent of their husbands and only after having at least one child. They have put aside their preconceptions and are now open to trying different methods of contraception, even the most radical types. As a result the birth rate is just beginning to register a slight drop.

Housing

Not much has changed in this area. Some huts now have cement floors, and a few people have reinforced their roofs with plastic.

The gypsies are giving more attention to the arrangement of their living space. Many have split their one room into several areas using curtains or wooden partitions in a attempt to obtain more privacy.

Employment

Here too the results are not very significant. Several have applied for their first jobs and are awaiting an answer.

A request to have the Employment and Vocational Training Institute create a class for automotive mechanics was rejected. The regulations of the institution do not permit training courses for persons with a very low level of education.

Personal and group hygiene

The gypsies are now taking more care with their personal hygiene and clothes, and are cleaner in appearance. The common area of the community is cleaner and garbage is not simply tossed out, but is stored in bags and kept tidy.

Maintenance of the bathhouse is the responsibility of the community and the chief collects the fee from everyone to pay for water, electricity and gas. Up to now such an arrangement would have been unthinkable - their attitude would have been that the institution building the unit should be responsible for its upkeep, not the community.

Children's education

The gypsies are becoming increasingly concerned with their children's education. As a result, the relationship between the school and the gypsy community has improved. Parents are more concerned and now go to the school on occasion to make sure their children are attending and to find out if there are any problems. The project staff started this practice, but the gypsies are now continuing it on their own. Parents, and especially mothers, now participate in school activities.

Changes are being noted in the instruction the gypsies give to their children, e.g. with regard to stealing from the *gadjé*.

School situation

During the 1989/90 school year, the failure rate among gypsy children dropped by 25% (at the start of the project it had stood at 80%).

That year the school was fortunate to obtain the services of a young teacher who understood the problems faced by gypsy children and tried a new teaching method aimed at producing an intercultural school. She established links between the school and the parents' group, and opened a dialogue attempting to understand their way of thinking, their concept of learning and even their aspirations for their children. She managed to create a more welcoming atmosphere, made the teaching/learning process more attractive for them and gave them the needed motivation. In short, she brought a new dynamism to the school, setting an example for her colleagues and creating an open atmosphere of acceptance for the children.

However, for administrative reasons she was replaced near the end of the school year and her departure had an immediate effect on the behaviour and performance of the gypsy children. This year (1990/1991) the failure rate is expected to jump by around 50%. The new teachers do not know how to maintain the dynamism that was beginning to be created in the school. The children and the community alike have a low opinion of them and have not accepted them.

The awareness created among teachers, the activities carried out in the school, the encouragement of the gypsy children and the changes in their behaviour, as well as the responsible attitude being taken by parents - all are in danger of being lost by the end of the school year.

Literacy courses

With regard to the adult program, the question is of an altogether different order and a linear analysis is not possible.

It seems likely that faced with their growing concern with their children's education, the adult gypsies have begun wondering about their own lack of schooling and asking themselves to what point this has affected the schooling of their children. It is also possible that this thought has awakened their interest and their awareness of the need to be able to read and write the language of their country - an area in which their own children are beginning to outstrip them.

Clearly there are other factors at work in their decision: the consciousness-raising effort to which they were exposed, concern for employment, and the need to obtain a driver's licence and apply to various social institutions.

One thing, however, has certainly been established: they have the desire to learn. This is clearly seen in the fact that they come back year after year to the literacy courses.

In 1988/89, there were 16 people in the course; in 1989/90 this went up to 23 adults; and in 1990/91 there were only 8 gypsies in attendance despite the fact that 18 had signed up. The teacher opted to work with smaller groups in order to give more individualized instruction. The gypsies require a great deal of attention since they generally have a very low level of education and need much extra help. Larger groups do not allow enough individual attention, nor are the teaching methods appropriate to larger groups very successful with the gypsies.

Often they are not able to attend because of their work (for example, when they attend fairs far from the community) and may drop out as a result. At times they simply stop coming, and then show up some time later saying that they were simply tired of studying!

This had a direct effect on the results obtained. Progress was very slow and this led to much disappointment.

It is difficult to give a quantitative assessment which will provide a realistic view of the progress made and the successes achieved in the course. To date twelve gypsies have obtained their first level certificates (equivalent to successful completion of the first four years of primary school). Meanwhile, many other gypsies have learned how to read with some facility, and others can no longer be said to be illiterate in the Portuguese language.

The real evaluation of the literacy program remains to be carried out in the broader context where the results of their achievements can be judged in other than academic measurements.

6. Continuation of the Project

It is now three years since the project began and the first two stages have been completed. The first stage (research and study of the community) is in fact ongoing in the sense that it is always open to adjustment. The second stage (planning, execution and assessment) was characterized by disorder resulting from two phenomena: the conflict created by the confrontation between the ethnic characteristics of the gypsies and the challenges and stimulation to which they were exposed; and the changes required in altering habits, dress and behaviour.

The third stage of the project (transition) will be characterized by assimilation and internalization of the knowledge, skills and attitudes released in the earlier stages.

It is hoped that the gypsies will develop and reorganize parts of their experience, retaining those elements of our culture that are of immediate use to them, and that help in their adaptation to the socio-economic environment in which they find themselves. The aim is not to replace the aspects typical of their culture with elements from our own. Rather, we hope for gradual change that will allow for improvement of their standard of living, without losing sight of the need to preserve their cultural characteristics and to safeguard their originality.

Our participatory research and close direct contact with this community for almost three years has helped us to reach the conclusions outlined below.

Effective assimilation of the gypsy in our society will be inversely proportional to the amount of force applied. This assimilation will take place slowly over a long period as a result of the impact made by the advantages and demands of the dominant society, which the gypsies will be obliged to accept simply in order to survive. Previous experience has shown that attempts more or less to impose automatic integration on a minority such as this will have the effect of creating small pockets of culturally static individuals resistent to all efforts at change.

The motivation for change will grow stronger in direct proportion to the number of items that are borrowed and successfully adapted to their cultural values and aspirations. For the gypsies, the strongest motivation or stimulus for change comes from, among other things, the desire for status, the wish to obtain the material conditions that will ensure their survival, and to better their economic situation; but above all, the hope that they can provide a safer and happier future for their children.

Literacy and schooling (especially among the youngest segments of gypsy society), the gradual acknowledgement of the work ethic, and the need to accept regular employment, will be essential ingredients in their development and are therefore vital to bettering their standard of living.

Following their own cultural dictates, and avoiding acculturation while promoting socio-cultural exchange, appears to be the answer as it is the gypsies themselves who must decide their destiny. For this they must have at their disposal all of the necessary means that we can provide: knowledge, skills and abilities.

The cultural changes and social arrangements must be desired, accepted and, ultimately, structured by them. Overcoming their idleness must be something they want to do.

Our overall opinion is that the gypsies, once they become aware of their problems and realize that some of their habits and customs determine their own welfare and ability to participate in the surrounding society, generally manifest a desire to adopt and adapt those aspects which they recognize as useful for improving their standard of living. However, they refuse acculturation and will oppose an alien civilization, vehemently defending their traditions and their concept of freedom. Like any other minority group, they fear most the possibility of being swallowed up by a society they reject.

It was never our intention to transform them into Portuguese of the gypsy race, but rather to enable them to retain their gypsy culture while teaching them how to "mix" with Portuguese society. Thus we tried throughout to respect their experience, their traditions and the essential values of their culture, especially their language. We encouraged them to demonstrate gypsy culture, only participating ourselves when asked to do so. We did not view the project as an effort to break down their resistance to change. Rather, we strove to nurture cultural change of the sort that would bring the two cultures closer together, without accentuating the differences between them. We had in mind an integration of the gypsies into the larger society that would come about naturally in the course of the gradual evolution of their culture. However, it was not always possible to organize activities in such a way that this aim would be clear to them.

All change represents a threat to them, causing the members of the community to seek refuge within the group. Here there is no conflict with their own ethos and they have a social shield and effective network that together defend them from external dangers which could threaten their solidarity, traditions and cultural identity.

In such circumstances, change is slow and marked by frequent retreats and advances. While on the one hand they may be encouraged and feel the desire for change, on the other they are held back by the force of a culture which demands that they resist change and retreat into their traditional universe.

Therefore in their conservative instincts, the gypsies come up against a conflict: to progress by shedding their "gypsiness" or to eschew progress in order to continue to be gypsies.

It is worth pointing a critical finger here at a certain imbalance noted between the value attributed to culture and the importance attached to integrating the gypsy community. There seemed to be a bit too much insistence on integration, sometimes at the expense of cultural values. Not all programs have succeeded in distancing themselves enough from non-gypsy cultures, thus losing sight of the fundamental principle summed up in the motto: "To progress while remaining a gypsy". When they can get this message across clearly, and when the gypsies can be made to understand it, then the community's fears will disappear and they will accept the proposed changes unconditionally.

This said, there are many signs of change as discussed here: what might be described as hybrid, fluctuating or ambiguous behaviour.

Help must be given to facilitate this process, and we can begin by removing the stigma attached to the gypsy in our collective subconscious, by rehabilitating the gypsies in the eyes of our society, particularly among those groups with which they must interact. We must help them to be understood, or at least better known, to such groups. This help must not be in the charity or social assistance mold, or provided with an air of paternalism. Instead, such help should take the form of projects to promote socio-cultural understanding, with full recognition of their dignity as human beings.

A systematic theoretical-ideological framework for these thoughts might look like this:

-   social crisis as (dis)order and challenge, from which emerge signs of gradual change;

-   culture as the essential factor of change;

-   the principle that it is within man himself that the capital energy for development is to be sought - in his need for subsistence (bettering his standard of living) and his need for expression and participation (improving his quality of life);

-   individual values, the sense of difference, personal realization, freedom, creativity, justice and equality that permit alternatives for personal and collective development;

-   the right to freedom of action directed toward reforming social practices within the common pattern so as to achieve socio-economic advancement for these people.

As a result of this assessment of the project, its main objectives and guidelines, certain conceptual principles and action strategies were revised:

-   Strengthening intercultural relations to facilitate understanding and the overcoming of contradictions, conflicts and the growing disorder inherent in a complex and divergent minority in a society undergoing rapid change;

- Making constructive use of the challenging nature of the gypsies;

- Continuing the project with a view to resolving problems, meeting subsistence needs and improving standard of living;

- Creating conditions for development of abilities (knowledge/awareness, relations/behaviour and organization /change) as the objective and result of the project, so as to minimize the feeling of helplessness noted in the expression of their desires and in the satisfaction of their natural needs;

- Developing, especially in the youngest gypsies, the ability to learn by providing them with the tools needed for self-learning, and encouragement of their growing independence;

- Promoting direct application of the rights of man in relations between the two societies;

- Lessening the weight given to the need for integration and increasing the emphasis on cultural aspects;

- Endorsing regional and local development, and democratizing and decentralizing it as much as possible.

7. Conclusions

My work with the literacy program under this project gave me the opportunity to examine and reflect on theory based on practical experience and discussions, teaching me a great deal and enriching my personal and professional experience. Certain aspects of this learning process stand out in particular. New ideas and new convictions were acquired. Work of this sort ought not to be approached with rigidly held belief, preconceived ideas, unalterable opinions, inflexible plans or immutable objectives. The study-action approach is the method best suited to projects of this nature, which deal with a complex community with characteristics so markedly different from our own.

The focus should be on schooling and literacy, placing the highest priority on the children since it is the young that represent the best means of reaching the parents and the community at large, and that are best placed to influence the future. Literacy programs and the school system are of fundamental importance for the development of the individual, the socio-cultural integration of the community and long-term understanding of the society of which one is part. At the same time, these activities are best able to adapt the individual to the challenges he will face, enabling him to respond to stimuli coming from societies that are themselves undergoing rapid change.

We are witnessing today the slow but sure dilution of the gypsy tradition owing to the pressures to which it is subjected. If relations between the two cultures cannot be changed, the gypsies will surely suffer a form of cultural genocide. Yet despite this, all the gypsies are intimately in touch with their cultural particularity.

Those wishing to approach the gypsies must do so with a certain minimum acknowledgment of that cultural particularity in order to establish through dialogue a dialectical relationship. The gypsy has a different view of the universe from ours; therefore, one must define a strategy that attempts to enhance contacts between the two cultures based on mutual enrichment (as shown in our project). In carrying out social discourse it is essential that information should be conveyed in both directions, as this is an important factor in avoiding undue conflict.

If we fail to remove, or at least ameliorate, our own ethno-centrism, which is just as strong as theirs, if we cannot rid ourselves of racism, rejection of the stranger and our preconceptions about the gypsies, then we will not be able to assist their social integration or help overcome their marginalization, which is encouraged by the strength, force and dynamism of their culture. In view of this attitude on the part of the gypsies, it is legitimate and advisable for us to promote mechanisms of change that meet the needs and expectations of a group which is an integral part of the multicultural mosaic of our country.

We feel that the underlying problems in this process are ethnic and that therefore the development of gypsy communities should be considered from the standpoint of their own culture. This approach might avoid some of the inter-ethnic conflicts and facilitate development of the personality of the individual while respecting his differences.

In the case of minorities, development projects must act as mediators between the different communities and cultures, promoting mutual acceptance and recognition of all peoples.

The encounter between such diverse cultures - the gypsies' and our own - entails a constant process of investigation, and continuous redefinition and rethinking of strategies and methods of intervention. For this reason it is not possible to make long-term predictions or plans. Rather, planning must continue all the while the project is being carried out, with constant reassessment and adjustment throughout.

Finally, we close with a lesson which we learned from the gypsies: a culture is valid only when it can bring together within man the various components of his existence, and when his values and beliefs have a specific and primordial role in it.

Notes

1. As defined in the *Diccionário Enciclopédico Koogan Larousse Selecções*.

2. Some of the data referred to here have been taken from: Olimpo Nunes, *O povo cigano*, Livraria Apostolado da Imprensa, Oporto, 1981.

LITERACY AND COMMUNITY DEVELOPMENT IN A LOWER CLASS NEIGHBOURHOOD

Madalena Dias
Matosinhos, Portugal

The community development program described in this report reveals the strategies of social intervention generated in the course of literacy campaigns and socio-cultural movements. The fundamental principle on which these strategies are based is that of positive social policy supported by educational practices integrated within consciousness-raising models of socio-cultural identity processes.

The conception and execution of socio-educational and cultural programs are viewed not as the task of a particular institution, but rather as a coherent program involving several layers of society - a program, moreover, which calls upon the resources and is the responsibility of the community at large.

Thus, a literacy campaign is understood as a complex social process which acts in support of planned development by halting the spread of illiteracy, one of the social inhibitors preventing full enjoyment of the rights of citizenship.

The action taken, as well as the effects achieved, would not have been possible without the synergy generated through the coordinated, interconnected and converging efforts of many people and agencies which cooperated to create an opening for social solidarity.

1. The Social Context

The program has been underway since October 1988 in an area of housing developments called Biquinha on the outskirts of the city of Matosinhos. Matosinhos is the regional centre for the northern district of Portugal and falls within the metropolitan area of Oporto, which has a total population of 1.2 million.

Beginning in the 1950s the district experienced rapid growth as a result of large-scale migration from inland areas to the Portuguese coast. This created great pressure on the housing market and required the construction of numerous subsidized housing units.

In Portugal, when low per capita income groups have to relocate it generally means moving into one of these subsidized developments, according to such criteria as the type of housing unit, family size and income, but without regard to relations between families, overall neighbourhood composition or community life. The result tends to be social segregation.

Material factors

The Biquinha subdivision is divided into two separate housing developments belonging to different agencies and built at different times: the "old" development constructed in 1973 and the "new" development which went up in 1979. The area also contains a large number of shacks inhabited by ethnic families of gypsy origin, plus a stretch of single-family dwellings whose residents are referred to locally as *Queques Rafeiros*[1].

These developments consist of 3- and 5-storey buildings, the two together containing 544 units (including basement apartments) with close to 2800 inhabitants, plus another 2400 people living in the above-mentioned shacks. Construction of a third housing development is currently nearing completion, with a fourth one scheduled for completion late in 1992. These developments are somewhat smaller, containing 118 and 45 units, respectively. All four developments combined are expected to provide subsidized housing for at total of 3500 people.

The area is deemed one of the most depressed in northern Portugal, with the zone around the "new" development containing the worst slums and socio-economically depressed living conditions in the district.

Most inhabitants are not from the district originally and have come to the development from poorer areas (islands, shanty towns, etc.). Families are often numerous and overcrowding is common. Many are single-parent households.

There is a predominance of young adults with very little schooling[2]; high failure and drop-out rates obtain among those still in school. Low wages, lack of qualifications and general unemployment in the area make finding a job very difficult. The average income level is very low[3] and in some segments of the population less than half of those of working age have jobs, the rest being made up of housewives, the unemployed and young people in search of their first job. Most of those who have jobs are employed in the construction and metalworking industries (men) or in the textile industry and canning plants (women).

One individual related the following:

> I was sick of being in the second grade and knew I wasn't passing; I sat in the back with the other dunces and had no use at all for books and learning. So I went to look for a job. When I said that I lived in Biquinha, the boss laughed and sent me packing. Eventually I went back to apply again, and this time I lied and said that I lived with my grandmother. A few days later they found out and fired me.

The general underdevelopment in this area includes a great deal of physical degradation of the housing and facilities in the area. Public lighting is inadequate, the area is not properly maintained, buildings show numerous signs of decay, yards are nonexistent, there is garbage everywhere. In short, the picture is bleak indeed and there is plenty of room for change.

Social relationships and values

Daily life among the inhabitants of the developments is characterized by squabbling among neighbours, the coming and going of transients, and virtually no respect for social interrelationships or common civility. Public property in the area serves only as a pretext for discord: the children's playground has been completely destroyed by vandals, entrances to apartment blocks have been defaced and the area contains no collective hygiene facilities. Even children get into fights and often end up in the emergency room of the hospital.

The gypsy residents are an exception in that they do not get involved in fights between neighbours, have close-knit family units and are generally respected by the other inhabitants of the development. So much so that people in the community often employ them to guard their property.

Alcohol abuse, drug addiction and prostitution are rampant among all age groups. The family structure is under enormous pressure with frequent arguments and physical violence by one or more family members against another.

Young women in particular are treated as virtual slaves by their parents. For example, it is common when a child is born in the development for the oldest daughter of the family to have to quit her job or drop out of school in order to take care of the new arrival. The same thing happens if her mother decides to go to work. Children barely 12 or 14 years of age are sent out to do hard work, and are not even allowed to keep their meagre wages. The exploitation of children in general is widespread and takes many forms, including begging and prostitution.

The spiritual life of the community reflects the general instability among the inhabitants. There are a number of different religions and sects established in the area, and it is their members who give some stability to the development. They are generally the most respected members of the community and the ones with the least divisive family structures.

For some it is religion, and for others it is possessing a VCR and television set that provides social status. Most are very fond of soap operas, action films (especially westerns and war movies) and pornography.

The young people and adults of the community alike are very active in several sports and are said to be especially good in athletics and soccer.

Infrastructure and facilities

The development includes the following infrastructure:

- A primary school with an enrolment of approximately 300 and, since January 1988, a cafeteria at which meals are served for the children;

- A nursery which opened in 1988 and is intended for children three months to three years old (capable of handling about 50% of the day care needs of the community);

- Two local associations, one of which is now inactive. The other is the Biquinha Workers Association (CPTBB) which is mainly involved in carrying out sporting events at the local gym. In December they were put in charge of running this. They also have their own headquarters, which includes some space used as a coffee shop;

- A multipurpose pavilion which can be used for any social, educational or cultural activity. It was opened in December 1989 and is also run by the CPTBB;

- The development has no stores or commercial establishments of any kind.

Finally, the area has a new Council which took office at a time of economic growth and which, in cultivating a progressive social and democratic image, could no longer tolerate the adverse conditions resulting from the area's rapid growth. While responding favourably and attempting to solve the disorganized proliferation of housing, they could not ignore the serious social problems arising within these low-cost housing developments.

2. **The Community Action Project**

Origin of the project

The local community complained with increasing vehemence about living conditions that caused such disruption in their day-to-day relations, pointing out that the new housing system was the cause of so much aggression. They frequently took their ill feelings out on the social institutions of the area, complaining that "You stuck us here and now you just want to forget about us". Because of the difficulty they had integrating in the community, some people kept a hut nearby with a garden, where they could go to spend the day.

The residents of the development besieged various social institutions in an attempt to get help for their situation and improve their future prospects. They were looking for answers to their questions, help with their expenses and low wages, some way out of their many and complex problems.

The teachers at the local primary school warned the local government authorities that children were coming to school hungry, that they frequently fainted in the course of normal school activities and had to be taken to the hospital in Matosinhos suffering from malnutrition. This urgently required a solution and gave rise to an unusual agreement between the Matosinhos Municipal Chamber, the Regional Social Security Centre and the Parish of Aldoar, which resulted in the opening of a school cafeteria. These children were the victims of a total lack of any kind of basic public health care and had no knowledge of personal hygiene. Many of them suffered from specific learning disabilities as well.

A process was thus begun that had to be self-sustaining from the start because of the lack of response on the one side, and the welfare or functional approach taken to the problems, on the other. The experts involved began to learn from practical experience that this sort of intervention was gaining them little, only making the people even more dependent. The concern was to change the common linear model to a complex dialectic model coordinated through a communications network (Fig. 1) in which all would participate in a process aimed at changing attitudes.

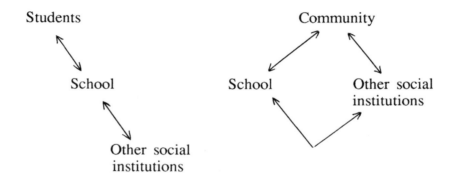

Fig. 1

In March 1988, the Matosinhos Municipal Chamber sponsored a meeting with representatives of the people living in the development and the various institutions that up until then had been acting independently of each other in the community. The idea was to have them join forces in setting up an interdisciplinary team for the purpose of creating conditions that would promote active participation by the community in a process of social rejuvenation. In a meeting that went on for some time, the community, politicians and experts came together and worked out a voluntary declaration of solidarity, under which all agreed to set to work immediately to form an interactive network to facilitate and ensure cohesiveness of purpose in their endeavours. And so was born the Biquinha Integrated Development Project.

A study was carried out of the population living in the development, and a new meeting was held in May 1988. It was agreed that public opinion should be persuaded to change the general rejection of the community's inhabitants. All of the people seated around the table at the meeting, questioning each other and reflecting on their own attitudes, were in accord concerning the need for opening up and agreeing on the strategies to be followed in the project. From these discussions, two overall objectives were decided:

- To prevent any further deterioration in the standard of living of those living in the development;

- To stimulate/create conditions for participation and organization of the community with due respect for individual and common rights.

The number of institutional cooperants increased and the total number of institutions taking part was about 15, representing areas such as health, social security, government employment and social re-integration services, and education. For those already active in the area it was a matter of reformulating their community action plans; the others faced the challenge of coming up with strategies for intervention in the development. Those of us who work in the Educational Extension Service were in the latter category. Thus we set about creating an operational structure for the project linking the various institutional cooperants in the course of their participation in the lengthy meetings, and setting up a two-fold system of institutional cooperation: in the vertical direction, establishing a chain of command within the institution itself, preparing and mobilizing resources; and in the horizontal direction, promoting the formation of a dynamic, multidisciplinary team, and implementing local strategies. Participation in the project was at all times voluntary.

The overall plans worked out in these long meetings and in the course of normal activities in the area, included the appointment of a group of four - two social service workers (one from the Matosinhos Municipal Chamber and the other from the Regional Social Security Centre) and two teachers (the principal of the primary school and the head of the Educational Extension Service) - who would act as the executives in charge of implementing an overall strategy for promoting socio-economic and cultural activities in the various groups, within a varied program.

First activities, first results

The end of the school year was almost at hand in June 1988 and the primary school was trying to adjust its teaching program to the current situation. But attempts at holding meetings with parents were getting nowhere so far as the level of participation and the achievement of interdisciplinary goals were concerned. Instead, they served only to articulate discord, with each side complaining about the other.

In attempting to project and disseminate a participatory methodology as our basic approach, we planned an initial joint intervention counting on the catalyzing effect of the local community association movement and the willingness of the school to go beyond the ordinary scope of its educational activities.

The theme chosen for study was garbage disposal within the development, and the children were to produce various types of work. These were then placed on display in the multipurpose room and a discussion was scheduled on this topic one afternoon. This was open to the community, and the council member in charge of the department responsible for garbage collection, plus other officials involved, were invited.

An information network was formed to publicize this event, consisting of the CPTBB and the children attending the school. Men, women and children came that afternoon to experience new ways of approaching their problems.

To animate discussion we produced and mounted a slide presentation entitled "The Garbage". The audiovisual material was intentionally polemic, bringing into question the actions of the municipal government in this area.

The people in attendance reacted in kind, offering examples of similar problems. They began to tell stories of neighbours who "use their bathtub to salt down sardines, so that they always smell like rotten fish", or who "bring their donkeys indoors so that you see them staring out the window". The triumph was one comment, "The problem is they should only put one pig per block, in which case he will keep clean by example. As it is there are four per block, two of them clean."

They put the blame squarely on the government because of the procedures in its operations for cleaning up the neighbourhood, and the aggressive manner in which it communicated.

Both parties accepted responsibility for the problems and proposed a change in attitude. The government made a commitment to send a work crew to the development to clean it up, and to increase the number of containers available. The people from the development agreed to cooperate in the clean-up campaign and to dispose of their garbage in the areas set aside for this purpose. They spent much time in studying the works produced by their children, as if something new were beginning to happen to them.

This first activity enabled us to observe the power of an intervention of this sort and the reaction of the people to a challenge that touched on a specific problem affecting the neighbourhood they lived in every day. The effect was concrete, immediate, palpable and plain. They were thus able to observe and participate in the clean-up activities, and they could easily understand the relevance and changes that were clearly perceptible.

For us, the next step would be to promote participatory strategies leading to the creation of a project related to educational needs.

The people living in the development began to sense an opening-up to participation. They had many complaints and began to feel that the school was their space, adapting easily to discussing "their" problems - that is to say, the problems of their neighbours.

3. Literacy and Development

Our model of integrated development...

Our participation in this development project was attended by a certain expectation, resulting in particular from the fact that we proposed to intervene in the educational sphere with a neighbourhood literacy program to be coordinated with socio-cultural and socio-educational factors. The focus of development would be the community, and the plan was to challenge it gradually to learn how to apply its own management.

In the first stage of setting up the working group with the various institutional cooperants and representatives of the people living in the development, in the extended meetings and within the executive group, we attempted informally to promote the concept of literacy (which for most purposes is simply a matter of teaching basic reading, writing and numeracy) as "cultural dialogue". The educational activity, means and practices were agreed with the inhabitants of the development, assuming an operation aimed at clarification of their manner of living, with social instruction as a common task involving the roles of teacher and learner alike, as equal to equal, creating individual and group instruments of defence for the cognitive and affective rights of each individual.[4]

The intention was to raise the consciousness of the community through action/reflection on the concept. The action would, first of all, have to stimulate social co-responsibility and facilitate the creation of networks for internal (i.e. within the community) and external cooperation in a spirit of solidarity, permitting the community to take advantage of its existing resources and, using these, to respond to the wide range of needs created by the local educational dynamic.

The inhabitants of the community were launched on a process of social intervention which demanded little of them in the way of participation and interaction in the development process, with the result that they had no say in the choice of its long-term goals. It was a matter of providing subsidies so they could pay their debts, of reviewing incomes and of watching their children go hungry.... The effectiveness of these ad hoc remedies belonged to the past, and a new cycle of dependence was setting in.

Their relationships with the outside world did nothing to stimulate development of a conscious sense of controlling their lives. On the contrary, their capacity for personal intervention had stagnated, in part because of their low income level and depressed economic situation.

Now they were beginning to experience new ways of tackling their problems, of undertaking new attempts.

The Educational Extension Service came into this project more as the result of an evaluation of the educational status following the failure of young people and adults to fulfil the compulsory education requirements, than in response to any public demand arising from the consciousness-raising effort or based on complaints about their inadequate level of schooling. The target groups chosen were young unemployed people with low levels of education, and housewives.

Our project presupposed the capacity for group identification of the need for education. We were constructing an experiment in which the inefficiency of ad hoc literacy programs would stand in sharp contrast to the results obtained in multidisciplinary initiatives pursuing socio-economic and cultural goals.

The social foundations were laid over a long period of time through local development initiatives, with the participation of individuals, groups and organizations belonging to the target segment of the population.

The manner of approaching and promoting adult education was based on opening up and drawing out local sources of knowledge and know-how, and on the role of government agencies and local associations as participants. The main obstacles were the rapid turnover in educators taking part in the project (owing to the lack of full-time professional staff) and the resultant loss of confidence, and a lack of financial resources. Today we have the opportunity to plan and implement operational programs of basic education which combine elements of general and technical-vocational training, with the integrated development of the individual's capacity to change both his social and work environment. The two together constitute an innovation in the use of education in the field of local development.

We were aware that we would be breaking new ground in relying on a strategy of commitment and the possibility for change, in making room for inter-active communication, and in optimizing the resources in each of the subjects as an active protagonist in building his own cultural identity.

Our operational skills, as defined in the theoretical and practical aspects of our frame of reference, would have to be adjusted in the course of the project as circumstances either confirmed or contradicted them.

...and its application

Of the means at our disposal, some were promising while others were problematic:

Training in civics

The government, as the promoter of the project initiated a program of training in civics for residents of the development, so as to open the way for an attack on the housing problem by encouraging the effective participation of those to be the beneficiaries and social agents in the project. This involved obtaining commitments from the other local organizations and institutions, and providing funding and incentives that would mobilize other sources of financing.

The multidisciplinary team

The executive group, whose formation is referred to above, was able to obtain assistance from various sectors, instilling in them a spirit of educational cooperation in a training development program as part of a series of community work operations.

We met every week with the CPTBB at their headquarters where we drew up plans, scheduled and evaluated the progress of events, struggled with the difficulties, optimized the accomplishments and considered the available alternatives. All of these questions and others which arose during day-to-day activities were taken up and dealt with more specifically and in technical detail at yet another weekly meeting, with the Municipal Chamber. At these encounters we tried to balance and perceive the social consequences of the problems identified, with a view to lessening their impact. Officials from the various other social organizations were also invited to these meetings, whenever the activities required their help. Often, where it was deemed more effective, we would pay a visit to these other institutions instead.

Physical site

We had decided that the project would take place within the development, in the broad sense, but there still remained the choice of a specific site to house the educational activities. The alternatives were few and far between. The CPTBB headquarters were too cramped, consisting of an area of only about six square metres with virtually no equipment, and they were not necessarily available on a regular basis anyway. The only other location was the primary school. In one way this would be a good location, in that our preliminary study of dropout and failure rates pointed to a need for early-age literacy training as one of the problems to focus on. On the other hand, the very institution we were considering had been responsible for the marginalization of these children in the first place. Their own experiences had imprinted in their minds an indelible negative impression that could be a major obstacle from the outset. However, it also represented an educational structure waiting to be conquered, and it was the duty of the project to find the key that would open it up to these children.

Planning of activities

In October 1988 we had reached the planning stage for our project. Until then our contacts with the development had been sporadic. We had established a good relationship and common purpose with the CPTBB, and had participated (albeit virtually anonymously) in a first joint effort at breathing life into the community. Our path was laid out in the aftermath of that first effort and we had the feeling that an important first step had been taken. But where the project would lead us was not known. The only certainty was our faith in the effectiveness of community effort as educationally empowering.

The first task that we set ourselves was to consider the stages required for a development that would have as its goal the formation of a community group for educational purposes. We pondered our roles as teachers and the general objectives that the project should have in order to ensure a multidisciplinary approach. Reflecting on our direct experience, we came up with the following:

- An initial stage devoted to motivation, primarily through regular and systematic contacts in the housing development;

- An intermediate stage of involvement in group identification of needs and problems;

- The development of independence through the formation of groups of individuals who were simultaneously members of the target population and agents for promoting the initiatives.

These stages of the project were to be carried out in what we referred to as the pre-literacy period since it is during this time that a target group for the literacy course is identified.

The projection of a varied agenda for the project called for action to be undertaken on three levels at once:

178

- An educational component, the aim of which was to promote the development of intellectual skills and basic relationships;

- A socio-educational component, the goal of which was the integration of the individual in the world of employment;

- A socio-cultural component, which could cover, bring together and promote the first two components, coordinating them within the local cultural and behavioural patterns so as to encourage participation in and effective management of, social regeneration.

4. Plurality of Approach

The overall development of the literacy program is analyzed within the context of the movements that gave rise to the pre-literacy phase and those which, during the program, also produced a post-literacy phase. The path chosen for the first phase of the project was later adjusted according to new developments in the target population. The activities, as well as the subjects themselves, arranged for the pre- and post-literacy phases, undergo a continuous interaction to which I will return shortly. But the activities can also elicit different reactions in the subjects, which may result in their educational advance. This exists at an overall level, where strategies, execution and results make up an ongoing exercise.

Pre-literacy phase

The community, source of powerful resources buried in its complexity, is the premiss that underlies the entire course of action. Thus, the life of the community has an endless capacity to act upon and mobilize itself in stimulating individual and collective consciousness-raising, and these help the creation and spread of a network of communications which can change living conditions. Therefore, it seems appropriate to us that community projects such as this should rely on the local authorities as cooperants/promoters within a multidisciplinary approach.

As part of the social approach, I began making informal visits to the development, together with a social service worker from the Matosinhos Municipal Chamber who had regular contact through home visits with families living there. Most of these visits had to do with overdue rent payments, requests for a reduction in rent or other matters that threatened the residents. On arrival we were generally met by the mother of the family (who was usually a housewife). Sometimes there were men present who were on sick leave.[5] After introducing me as a "teacher of adults" (adults are essentially anyone over 14 years old), the worker would proceed with the purpose of the visit. Meanwhile I would take advantage of the opportunity to open a conversation (which was challenging because of the problems of communication) and we would almost always end up discussing the education of their children.

We noted frequently that the school situation in the family tended to be regressive in the sense of the children having a lower level of education than their parents. They were not indifferent to this fact, insisting that "They're not cut out for studying and never took to it. They went to school until they were 12 or 13, and then began to play hooky. After that they went to work as a bricklayer or in the canning factory. They don't have work papers so they earn very little, but enough to eat. They do whatever is available because they don't know a trade and didn't even finish fourth grade..."

In the course of these conversations, as we discussed their everyday happenings, little by little we would try to challenge them to change the situation they were relating, explaining that all that was needed was the desire to do so. Thus we planted a concern, leaving open the possibility of talking about this further if they wanted to come and visit us at the CPTBB headquarters where we kept regular hours. Many of them went there in any case in the evening to have coffee, use the telephone, watch TV and chat. There were always a few members at the Centre in any case, so we had daily opportunities to exchange ideas concerning the neighbourhood and their way of life.

Family experiences were here repeated as collective problems, and some related to associated activity. Here were the children playing in the middle of the street and in the entrances of the apartment blocks causing damage, which in turn led to conflicts between the mothers. And meanwhile the local gym was kept locked up so that it would not be vandalized.

The challenge of changing this, of opening up new possibilities, spurred this process and raised the need for creating new impulses. It was the joint search for innovative programs for young people that generated action, and resulted in the creation of three projects co-financed by the Youth Institute. The young people who took part as both animators and participants experienced new forms of organization.

The movement was underway and the people came increasingly to participate in the construction of a matrix of educational interest/needs. We began to sense a certain headway in our effort to relate when the guard of the local gym, a member of the CPTBB and former resident whom we had assiduously cultivated and who usually accompanied us round the development, brought us a list of thirty names and signatures of people living there who would attend a literacy course, or wanted to learn to sew or knit, or to study electricity. We attempted better to understand this movement which had developed slowly over a long period and had now come to fruition, beginning to work with the group in a process conducive to better relationships.

Simultaneously, action was being planned with the association: the setting of specific objectives, the calculation of financial costs and the recruitment of teachers (wherever possible from among the residents of the community themselves). The space limitation was carefully studied and we all came to the conclusion that the primary school was the only possible site. Although the school was immediately made available for the literacy course, a number of bureaucratic obstacles had to be overcome to obtain permission to hold the socio-educational programs (sewing, knitting, electrics) there.

By the end of November 1988 we had four target groups ready to try new experiences: one association to promote new forms of sport, to come together outside the development and to participate in sports/cultural projects and associated initiatives. This group exceeded our expectations with regard to its level of participation and organization.

At the outset it was thought that housewives were under-represented among the groups, which were predominantly young people. We could not ignore their importance as a key group in the families of the community, especially in the case of those who were able and mature. The following development of the action should inspire new indicators of participation.

The literacy program

Education is a double emancipation of the target group and the community: it integrates the agents (representatives of the community and institutional cooperants) and creates models for participation by the population. The programming of the different activities is participatory, leading to progressive achievement of the objectives. As an activity it is dynamic, catalyzing, flexible, and generates new learning opportunities. It unfolds on the cognitive, emotive and relational planes, promoting self-esteem, stimulating and fostering the acquisition of social skills, empowering and freeing individual capabilities within a context of social intervention, unleashing collective solidarity.

The activities carried out within the CPTBB headquarters were beginning to be overshadowed by the regular meetings of the literacy course in the school, a location to which little by little the community was beginning to gravitate. Some 40 people were attending the literacy course, with 26 in the knitting group, 20 in dressmaking and 37 in electricity. This resulted in overlapping of the groups which made for better inter-relating.

The relationship of belonging to groups thus alternated between the literacy course and the vocational programs, with most opting for training in areas with which they were most familiar. Their reasons for attending were varied. For some it was the possibility of obtaining a Level One Certificate and pre-vocational training linked to their employment needs. For others it was simply the need for social interaction - the chance to experiment with new forms of relating. The activities were carried out in a common area (what we refer to as complementary training) alternating with components that had the following characteristics:

- The reading, writing and numeracy components - contents conceived as an exercise in critical comprehension - reinforce and stimulate the different areas, functioning as "stimulus for" and "consolidation of", in a relationship of dependence, according to the objectives for which they are intended.

- The link between knowing as intellectual knowledge and "know-how" (the publicity poster for the soccer match, the skirt produced in sewing class...), projected a new idea of knowing oneself.

What we called complementary training was a time to practise free activities and creativity based on current events and association activities. It was based on the co-planning of peripheral aspects only, and according to the dictates of the particular project could involve other local participants, both individuals and institutions. First came the preparations for the Christmas party with the association, leading to the formation of a choral group. Later there were sports events which gave rise to a debate on the nutritional needs of the athlete. And in March 1989 we held the first exhibition of works produced in the courses, together with the showing of animated movies.

The main promoters were the participants from the literacy course, who took charge of coordinating most of the operations. The populace rallied together in massive numbers. They came to the school, observed what was going on, and then turned a critical eye on their surroundings. The next step was the production of a newspaper, which carried information into homes in a effort to spur greater participation in local initiatives.

This dynamism, which had been picked up by a considerable number of people and which now led to even more of them joining the movement, was also the product of the work of the multidisciplinary team. It soon spread to other sectors of the project, giving birth to the idea of holding a month (June 1988) of cultural activities culminating in what became known as EXPOVIDA I, involving the entire community. The theme of the event was "A Clean Neighbourhood", motivated by the beginnings of the effort to restore the apartment complex. There was a competition for the best block, a parade of decorated floats through the neighbourhood to the accompaniment of music, the exhibition itself, a theatre production in the school, sports events, and a folklore and music festival in the gym which was packed with people. All in all, EXPOVIDA I breathed new life into the community.

"These are good times to last a lifetime. We did things we'd never dreamed of. We've been to events in Lisbon and, honestly, this was like the things you see on TV. It was a full day. It gave a whole new life to the neighbourhood. The association is doing more for us all the time - at the gym and in the school, they're always ready to work. A little while ago we had a great festival with all the schools: the kindergarten, children and adults - suddenly everyone in the neighbourhood is involved in the school." These comments are from a poster signed Sandra.

Socio-cultural movements of this sort, carried out at local level, enrich and consolidate internal and external communication, and promote and stimulate effective delivery of "education". On the one hand, the current participants were indicating a desire to continue during the summer, carrying out vocational programs with the support of the FSE and using general training components in health, industrial safety, social integration and entry to the job market. And at the same time, new groups were being organized and beginning to negotiate their needs.

The lack of social equipment led to the aim of building a multi-purpose pavilion as a cultural centre open to the community and as a support for the development of social skills.

Only by flexible planning, taking due account of the need for raising both human and financial resources adequate to the needs, were we able to respond favourably to the initiatives emerging from the educational context.

Post-literacy period

The educational community was in rapid evolution regarding its organization and active participation in the pursuit of the objectives. It had assimilated, and was now inspiring others to adopt a new active, progressive yet thoughtful model of day-to-day living in which each individual and the group as a whole were finding new ways to promote and realize aspirations. The literacy program will have to be continued, for only in this way can opportunities for real change be made available. The impact of the development inspires the participation of a committed community.

A new set of negotiations followed, balancing the life experiences and adjusting the strategies to newly emerging groups:

-   The literacy program was expanded to continue to the Level Two primary school program to complete the compulsory education of those born after 1967. The Level One program had 42 students, the majority being women and young people of gypsy origin, divided into two groups based on different levels of knowledge. Level Two with 60 enrolments was split into three groups.

- The socio-educational courses organized in vocational fields were offered on an alternating basis (sewing, knitting and electricity/metal working) for different age groups. A total of 90 inhabitants of the development signed up and were divided into three groups with some overlapping. For the first time this group included ten housewives.

- The vocational training program coordinated production of local programs, and counseled those requiring access to more advanced training and seeking qualification for employment.

- The complementary training program chose to promote health education in coordination with the local health centre.

- The socio-cultural promotions program based on participation between institutional cooperants and local agents (i.e. people living in the development) generated a training and information network and worked to create multipurpose cultural and support centres for developing social skills.

The overall plan for developing the teaching methods in the literacy program has been brought together here, and has expanded steadily in a constant search for new resources, and reference materials that will bridge the gap between socio-educational and cultural development.

5. Individual Experiences

The following descriptions of day-to-day interactions and exchange of experiences between teachers and learners are given to show that the purposes of literacy training have been fulfilled in its role as proponent of the basic education which promotes community forces and adjusts them to the dynamics of regional and local development.

An animator

As a scholarship student, I became a monitor with the Biquinha literacy program in December 1988. My teaching experience until then had been in formal education (distance education), where I was used to a more or less normal school routine, although in a media environment. I had some involvement in community development work, but only on a sporadic and ad hoc basis. Working with adolescents has always been something I wanted to do and struck me as challenging.

When I began going to the working meetings to set up the group, I was discouraged to see the difficulties of interpersonal relationships and communication. The key words were: facilitate, promote and empower. The contents of the various materials used were based on real participation by the people using materials taken from everyday life, and these were discussed before reading the words and texts. The organized spaces in open areas created an atmosphere of continuous learning and encouraged the development of independence in the participants, which was supported in the research and thinking on the subject.

The participants had the sense of being an active part of the local community force which was cooperating in the various initiatives.

In short, we created a program within which we all could grow, develop and (re)educate ourselves. It became my favourite school.

To enrich my description further I should like to include here the widely divergent experiences of two among many of our participants:

We'll start with Maria and Monteiro, a gypsy couple. Maria began in the literacy course. She was entirely illiterate at the start and frequently attended the class, bringing her husband with her. Monteiro is a fairly well integrated gypsy, dresses differently from his wife and looks like any other European. Initially he had little interest in the class and seemed unmotivated. When he did become enthusiastic, however, he had no trouble doing the suggested assignments. He helped his fellow students and whenever there was a break he would read a newspaper that he brought with him to every class. Maria learned scarcely more than her name and little more when she became pregnant and had to stop coming to class, promising to return after the baby was born. Later she began attending the crafts class, taking it as a point of honour that she would be able to use all the excellent material made there to decorate their house. From the colloquium she attended Maria learned to make use of the health centre. She takes her baby there regularly and is a model mother. Her husband completed Level One and enrolled in Level Two of the literacy program, but dropped out after a month. He joined the local sports team when his talents were noticed during events held as part of the literacy program. The couple began to see the importance of sharing household duties. They come to see us often and say they aren't going to stop coming for visits. Many of their relatives have also attended the night school program and some are still in the literacy course.

Susana represents the prototype "fishwife". She is known as "smelly" because of her lack of personal hygiene. Her family is among the most squalid of the area and are all referred to as "canoes" because their house is such a pigsty that people say you need a canoe to get through it. Hence the nickname. Her vocabulary was shocking, full of curse words and slang. She went around shouting and swearing at everyone and everything because of her poor family background. Her father is retired and her mother earns a small amount as a domestic during the day. She still has small children who are allowed to roam the streets on their own when she is working. She and her older brother, who was also a student of ours, ran off to Lisbon to escape their unstable home life, returning only when they could not find work. Susana attended the literacy course, although she missed class often, and was progressing at an average rate in reading and writing. She skipped the maths portion altogether. With much prompting and patience she managed to complete Level One. At the same time, she attended the knitting class but showed little interest in it. Eventually she finished one poorly-done item, which was not good enough for the exhibition. She participated from time to time in the debates, meetings and in the parade during the exhibition. She also took one course in decorative art given by the European Social Fund/PRODEP, with barely acceptable marks because of her tendency to disrupt the class with arguments. She attended the Level Two literacy program but did not finish it. She is continuing in this class and has one brother in the Level One class and another in the course on electricity.

Maria da Dores, born to parents who abandoned her, was raised by a woman in the neighbourhood whom she still regards as her mother. Her family are poor and considered social outcasts. She is referred to by the cruel nickname *nhónhó* [contraction and mispronunciation of *senhor*] in reference to her harelip which makes it difficult to speak intellihibly. Mostly she would keep to herself in one corner of the house, lost in her own severely restricted world. The fact that she worked in the canning plant, which left her smelling of fish, meant that her companions mercilessly made fun of her. She must have been one of the typical cases of malnutrition, as she confessed later after her teacher had gained her confidence, and she felt at ease. She was an increasingly avid student in the Level One program and managed to complete the course although not among the best students. At the same time, she was also taking the knitting course; where she was a very enthusiastic student. Next she took a handicrafts class where she turned out to be the one student with real talent. At this point we were witnessing a real turn-around in both her personality and social skills. Then as she entered adolescence, she underwent a change in which she began to smoke and flirt (in order not to be different from her friends) and drifted away from the school. She attended the first session of the Level Two class and then she disappeared from the neighbourhood, causing great concern among her teachers. Their investigation revealed that she was staying home, and that she was in such need that she often had nothing to eat. She had begun working as a domestic but earned scarcely enough to survive. She tried to start classes again, but since they were at night and she could not afford even the transport costs, she had to drop out again, promising that she would get organized and begin again the following year. She told her friends that she misses school, and she sent two sisters and one brother to take courses.

People in the community

My name is Albina Rosa and I am the only married student in the literacy course. I'm 25 years old and have a beautiful 4-year old daughter who is in the nursery school in Matosinhos. Before, she was in the nursery here, but at the age of three she had to change. I have to take her and pick her up every day. We live in an apartment block in Biquinha, off the ring road. I used to live in a hut, but I went to take care of my godfather, who has since died, and now we live in his house. I like the house and the area where we live, as we have all the conveniences that were lacking before. I took the gardening class at the CPTBB centre and am now the official gardener for the neighbourhood. I like my job. I am very fond of plants and like to see them well cared for and used to beautify the landscape and the interior of houses. They are good for the environment, and for people. I'm going to set up a gardening class for others in the neighbourhood. We'll see what happens. To do this I am taking Level One of the literacy course. I'm trying hard not to miss any classes because I know they are doing me a lot of good. I'm learning many things that I didn't know, and if possible I plan to take Level Two, as well. My husband was also in the literacy course for two years, but because of his work schedule he was not able to meet the objectives set at the beginning of the course. The same thing happened last year when he started going to classes with me, and then had to stop. Studying is good for you. You feel that you are growing up like a child. Anyone who has the opportunity to study should not waste it.

My name is Jose Maria. I am the oldest student. I am 32 years old, have five children and I love my family very much. I live in an apartment in Biquinha near the gym and CPTBB centre. It was a great joy to obtain this house with a bathroom, three bedrooms and a kitchen. My wife and children and I do everything to clean the house. Our life is hard because we have to go from place to place to sell our wares. We get up at 4 or 5 o'clock in the morning and my wife and I go to work to earn a living. We work hard, but it is worth it since we live without difficulty. Many in the neighbourhood live poorly because they don't want to work. I go to the literacy centre, and since my house is near the school, I go there every day, but only for a quick bite. What I really want is to finish the literacy course and learn something. I tried going to a course in Matosinhos, but since it was so far away, I quit. Here in Biquinha I have been studying for three years, and this year I learned to read and write. I have a son named Mario who goes to school during the day, and I am very happy to be able to help him when necessary. The oldest ones did not go to school, so when they reach the right age they will go to adult classes. My friends want to obtain the certificate so they can get a driver's licence. I have mine and I drive a big car. Since I work hard, at night I like to go to the centre and play cards with my friends and neighbours. I like living in Biquinha. We are all happy to see that our neighbourhood is the envy of the others around us. It is up to us to make sure that everything is made even better. Before, the centre was only for sports. Now it does many other things and cooperates with the night school for many new programs. School is very important for adults, too.

My name is André Monteiro and I am 19 years old and married. I was born and live in a hut in Matosinhos. Although it is small, the hut is always neat and tidy, and is better than some of the houses in Biquinha. We have a TV set, a VCR and other appliances. I would not like to have to live in that neighbourhood because of all the people and traffic. I like the place where we are and I would be very sorry if we had to move. I found out from my gypsy cousin, who is a school guard, that in Biquinha they have school during the day and at night too. I started coming here and am happy with the school. Every day there is something new to do. My cousin Felizardo is the best student because he has never missed a class. Sometimes we don't even have time to have a bath. We have to go directly from work (we work loading and unloading cars and trucks for the TIR) to school, so that we can be here when the classes start. When we get hungry, we have to go and find something to eat. In the night school (literacy course) we keep a journal in which we write short texts and sign our names. We take photographs and learn to read the signs, then we make posters of them and about things in our lives. With Mario we make wicker baskets that we can sell during the festival. But we do this for pleasure really as we don't make much money. When I want to, I go to the electricity class. So far I've learned how to make connections and use the tools. Back home then, we can connect up with the lines on the street, so we have lights. I buy the paper to read in the café now. I can only read some of the words, and others I learn at school. I want to see if this year I can complete the course and then buy a car so I can sell things at the fairs. That way I can make more money. On my job I can only make three thousand escudos in a day, and sometimes I go for two or three days without making anything. And the family has to eat every day. When I can go and sell things at the fairs, my wife will come and learn to read.

A resident and the Director of CPTBB

I am Manuel da Cruz Dias, married with eight children and 45 years old. I was born in Esmoriz and have lived in Biquinha for 11 years. In the beginning it was hard to adapt, as I had never lived in a neighbourhood like this. In time I got used to it and made new friends. Now my whole life is wrapped up in Biquinha. The only entertainment here then was the CPTBB.

I am one of 11 directors of the centre. We meet once a week, at
night, with the social worker of the Municipal Chamber and the
adult school teacher, to deal with matters concerning the neighbourhood project. Sometimes other people connected with the project
come to the meetings as well. Last week we had a French journalist
as a visitor. Our names appeared in a French newspaper, which told
about the work we are doing, and that everything we do is for
charity. Our gym organizes soccer tournaments; dances for children,
young people and seniors; other sports events like handball and
American football. Fishing, table tennis and track and field are our
latest activities. All these programs are led by our own young people
in their free time, as part of the program of the Youth Institute. We
also organize visits to important places like Inatel and the Antas.
Along with the teachers and monitors, we organize all of the
activities of the Adult School. We have a joint budget and it
requires a lot of work. The association support project pays a young
man from March to December, and he does many tasks for us.

Now our Centre has more than just sports. We have a big
Christmas party and celebrate the anniversary of the Centre's
founding. We sponsor floats and parades for Carnival, and we have
held events for World Youth Day, EXPOVIDA and St. John's Day.
All of this is done by our own young people and in the night school
and nursery. Now visitors are coming from all over to see us.

At one point I had an operation on my back and was off work.
The president of the Centre asked me to go and help the teachers
and students with their courses every night from 6:30 to 11:00
o'clock. I began doing this on January 3, 1990. There were a lot
of students and it was no easy task controlling young people and
adults, 14 to 40 years old. This was serious and responsible work.
With a lot of tolerance, the young ones got used to the discipline
and got down to the work of education. Despite what you might
think, with one thing and another I managed to pull it off without
a hitch.

This year has been much easier because they are already used to
the rules. We all live in the same neighbourhood, so it is well that
I get along with the students, teachers and monitors, and have
developed friendships with all of them. What we are doing here is
important and responsible work, and we have to respect each other.
Some of the teachers have moved away, but we still remain friends.
We are almost at the end of the school year and I can hardly wait

for next September, so I can continue with this task that gives me so much pleasure.

A young teacher/animator in the literacy program

These past three years are worth ten to me. At the end of 1988, several initiatives were started in Biquinha, among which the most important were the literacy program and the socio-educational classes. The objectives were simple, but we never anticipated the results achieved in just three short years. The first problem at the start was to find out whether the people would back such a large project. Very quickly the problem became one of whether we could keep up with the enthusiasm of the people involved!

I was one of the first to take the literacy courses and the class on electricity. Since I didn't know much about them, I didn't hesitate to join up. I knew it would be to my advantage, at least for the comradeship of my fellow students and the monitors. The same thing happened with my mother and two sisters who also joined the course, so we set out with trepidation but also with a great deal of hope.

We began to succeed from the first year, and the proof of this is that we never dropped out. We went to all the classes and had great plans. Our greatest moment was EXPOVIDA I, at which we were able to display the many works produced by everyone in the program. We all had a wonderful time and were very enthusiastic throughout this period. It ended with an enormous festival and dance that everyone attended in the gym building. And since then we have had EXPOVIDA II and III, each one better than the last. It was a fantastic event and I am very proud to have been a part of it.

But in the end, what did this course mean to us, what was its value and importance? Well, it gave us a start and showed us the way to socio-cultural development, and even to finding a job in a community with many problems, and which had never before been able to develop - my community. Many of my friends now have jobs or are self-employed as electricians, mechanics or seamstresses. Others who did not know how to read and could not even write their own names now know how to do these things and are aware of what is going on around them. All of this has been a great success. My mother, who is 47 years old, went out and got a job, and so did my sister. The old saying that "one success leads to another" is still true. This was the case with me too. After these projects, other successes followed and now in my free time I work as an animator. I try to help all of the children in Biquinha, so that they will do something - anything at all -with their free time instead of just wandering around aimlessly.

I am still studying at night. Among the good things we have learned is how to relate to other persons and things. I have taken a course as a computer operator and now Zé Silva of the CPTBB and I are trying to get other young people to learn computers too. I hope everything keeps going like this since we have many wonderful plans and are always opening up new paths.

A monitor in the sewing class

My name is Laura and I have lived in Biquinha for 18 years - in the old development, as we call it. I am married with two children and work as a seamstress. I live with my parents and brother in a house with only two rooms. Three years ago we began to change our way of living and thinking about our problems.

Everything started at the Centre, with the adult education teacher and the social worker from the Municipal Chamber. They were very enthusiastic, and soon had many young people involved in the project. They asked me if I could be a monitor for a class on sewing, and although the idea had never occurred to me before I was very excited about it. First I went to the literacy course that they started to give when the school stayed open at night. The neighbourhood started to come alive and to act differently as people began to understand that here was a way to change their lives and solve their problems. Things changed very quickly once the residents of the development began get moving. These courses were a lifesaver for many and got the neighbourhood going as never before. Something was going on at the gym and in the multipurpose pavilion almost every night, and people began to get interested in finding out what was happening there. Soon they were taking part in activities such as colloquiums, reading classes and movies.

The first class in dressmaking started in January 1989. Now this is the third year that I have been working with one group of young people and another of housewives. The interests of these two groups are different, as well as the types of things they do. Often we work together with the students in the literacy class. Now many of our younger students have gotten jobs in the textile industry. Some have even gone on to a more advanced course, and still others have switched from the canning industry - which they hate - and have now taken up sewing. It often happens that someone in this class feels the need to attend the literacy class more often and work on getting certificates. When they finish this class, almost all of them are able to make up clothes and other useful items for the home, which they see in the fashion magazines. This makes them feel more attractive and saves them a lot of money.

Right now we are looking at some of the problems that will come up during construction of the new blocks. We are going to have a new Centre, offices to work in, a bakery, a small market, a hairdresser's shop and space for children's leisure activities. But our biggest problem has to do with housing. Many apartments have only two rooms and up to 21 people. Every week we discus these problems and we think that a few people are going to be able to solve their housing difficulties. It's a shame that not everyone can do so.

We have much more respect for ourselves now that we are working hard and dedicated to making Biquinha a better place to live.

6. The Results and the Problems

Changes

The success of the community project team has been directly proportional to its ability to develop dynamic action stimulating the people - the social agents - to participate in research aimed at education, increasing their motivation, and putting them in touch with their problems. The relationship established is a complex one, in which everything was taken into account from speech to posture. The educational strategy and the underlying methods were based on diverse and on-going actions in the context of continuing education, which has been planned and is being participated in by all members of the community. The emphasis is on the efficiency and effectiveness of the local community association movement in mounting intervention in literacy, socio-cultural animation and socio-educational courses, through which the challenges were slowly but surely organized into structured and formalized plans.

Literacy training assumed a central role in the local structures. It has come to be understood not as a goal or aim of the educational system divorced from real life, but rather as an active principle from which emanates a series of interconnected activities. These generate cohesion, identification, values, in which each individual finds his place and carries out his role within the community. The people are beginning to understand the movement that is providing the dynamism for changing present conditions and thus building their future. The numbers joining have exceeded the expectations of the organizers. It has now become clear that the movement is unstoppable, as more and more programs are being requested and other ways of organizing the project are taking shape. It is beginning to form a model of participation. Young people and adult participants in the literacy courses are finding their place within the local structures. They are becoming the engineers of their own transformation and animators par excellence. In short, they are adopting a new way of life.

Physically, the neighbourhood is changing as most of the houses are being renovated. Exterior areas are being cleaned up and gardens are springing up. At the local gym, in the pavilion and the school, all over the neighbourhood sports and socio-cultural events are being organized on a regular basis and with everyone involved in the process. These strengthen and raise the awareness of the value of cultural identity. Day-to-day life is more thoughtful. It has been reformulated and recreated, with a pool of ideas produced by the life experiences of each and every one of the inhabitants.

The Biquinha development project is continuing and has just been nominated for inclusion in a national program that would provide funding to ensure its consolidation until 31 December 1995. A low-cost housing development which, until recently, was considered one of the worst slums in the district is now being improved at several different levels; it is promoting exchanges of experience and well on its way to becoming a "model" of development.

Obstacles

The main obstacles were not knowing the difficulties and having insufficient faith in the research approach that was guiding us as participants in a project of integrated development. The project was intended to substantiate the way of life in the community, and designed to take advantage of the rights and resources of the target groups themselves. The inter-active strategy between educational, socio-cultural and economic aspects was based in essence on a relationship of dialectic communication among the protagonists, and between these, the obstacles encountered and the resources. The problem of these relationships entails conceptual, operational and ultimate values, which are the forces producing real changes in living conditions.

In the initial stages of the community project, our status was that of relative outsiders. But in dealing with the other institutions involved, this enabled us at times to defuse the antagonisms that sometimes arose when, in the course of developing cooperation, certain bureaucratic and traditional rigidities were encountered among these institutions.

Only by strict adherence to the principle of building cohesion into the way of life of the community were we able to persevere and produce results conducive to an attitude of institutional openness. This was especially true regarding the use of spaces not permitting a "neutrality" (such as the primary school). This resulted in a constant challenge, which at times assumed the most inelegant forms of aggression. It also revealed another side of the school system.

Those who joined our activities were strongly influenced by outside factors (seasonal employment, weather conditions, etc.), which are indicative of their weak relationship to the outside world. The undertaking of issues related to basic necessities of life (food, housing, etc.), and directly entailing the carrying out of day-to-day educational activities, were those that required the greatest delicacy of treatment.

At the same time, the publicizing of the work done by some institutions on an ad hoc basis in organs of communication, using aggressive forms of communication (e.g. "Parish of Aldoar halts hunger in Biquinha"), at times provoked the inhabitants of the development, and caused subsequent periods to be marked by backsliding and behaviourial problems.

The conflicts were overcome through the consistent encouragement of new collective and individual attitudes.

7. Conclusion

Growth and development are complementary key-concepts relative to social well-being, the market for which - when analyzed from the standpoint of the local community - is based on the law of supply and demand in the socio-cultural and economic forces. Many and varied are the internal and external factors which cause ruptures in social systems and face the people with serious problems related to their way of life.

The regional and national structures call for developments to promote social processes which are participatory and capable of removing the obstacles to overall development of the populace.

The Biquinha integrated community development project is the result of an open policy of empowering people on the basis of internally produced social realities. As such, it promotes the optimization of human resources and the participation and creativity of the social agents, who gradually acquire greater capacity to intervene in their own affairs and control their own actions.

Literacy and basic education are at the top of the agenda for adult education where the latter is to be used as a method of improving the socio-economic position of disadvantaged groups.

It is not enough to patch up the school systems, or to beef them up with extracurricular programs. It is necessary to transform them in conjunction with social practices and strategies. The matrix of educational practices that make up a post-literacy frame of reference are not simply another level in the educational system. Rather, they represent a feedback mechanism and a means of promoting follow-up action. Such activities cannot be dissociated from the political scene in which they operate as the real determinants of participatory democracy. Progress and the distribution of knowledge are dependent upon the structure and division of power, both inside and outside the school.

The initiation of a strategy for change demands reference to social levels and practices which are being adjusted to locally emerging initiatives. This is a slow, informal process whose conceptualization and subsequent implementation affect the motivation of the agents involved, their capacity for active participation, and their commitment to the search for innovative solutions.

When conditions favour the exercise of the right to education and training, and the true meaning and usefulness of learning are made clear, the people are very receptive to them.

Notes

1. *Queques* (cakes) is the slang term for the inhabitants of upper class neighbourhoods; *rafeiros* (sheepdogs) adds a further pejorative note.

2. In 1988 only 12 of the area's inhabitants had completed the compulsory six years of elementary school.

3. Some 65% of families in the area have per-capita earnings between US$ 5,000 and US$ 15,000.

4. Paulo Freire. *Pedagogy of the Oppressed.*

5. The term *baixa* refers to being off work through illness.

Bibliography

Comissão da Reforma do Sistema Educativo (Coordinator: Lícinio Lima). 1988. *Documentos Preparatórios III*. Lisbon: Ministry of Education.

Estudo de Caracterização da População do Bairro da Biquinha [Study of the population of Biquinha]. 1988. Matosinhos: Câmara Municipal de Matosinhos.

Santos Silva, Augusto. 1990. *Educação de Adultos Educação para o Desenvolvimento* [Adult Education, Education for Development]. Oporto: Edições ASA.

BUILDING A REGIONAL PARTNERSHIP
IN THE FIGHT AGAINST ILLITERACY IN BELGIUM

André Chapotte
Françoise David
"Lire et écrire", Namur, Belgium

Our Approach

"1990, International Literacy Year, a Time for Action"

The Province of Namur was the first Belgian province to embrace the UNESCO slogan and join the fight against illiteracy.

In December 1990, 20 of the province's 38 communes, following the lead of the provincial government, adopted the following provincial charter or manifesto.

Namur Manifesto for a Literacy Campaign

THE AUTHORITIES OF THE COMMUNE OF ...., AWARE OF THE CHALLENGE OF INTERNATIONAL LITERACY YEAR

HAVE DECIDED, WITHIN THEIR BOUNDARIES, TO

- conduct a public awareness program,

- give top priority to organizing joint action by the Commune's Centre public d'aide sociale and representatives of all associations,

- organize, individually or jointly with authorities in neighbouring communes, courses designed to meet local needs,

- make available to continuing education movements the infrastructure essential to decentralization, and

- inform national, community and regional authorities of the need for their permanent support if literacy activities are to be expanded in a consistent fashion.

In today's climate of austerity, which has hit social expenditure particularly hard, one may well ask why and how regional and local authorities and administrations have taken such a definitive stand on support for the continuing education literacy movement.

As the Charter states, participating communes agree, not merely to give symbolic support, but to make concrete contributions (e.g. premises, material support, financial support) toward the common objective, which entails, over the next ten years, *offering any individual the opportunity to take classes close to home or to travel to such classes, free of charge, by public transportation.* It was essential to reach these authorities and make them fully aware of the real implications of illiteracy.

How did this partnership develop? What groups were involved (including those behind the scenes); which associations and movements were fighting illiteracy in the province? And who were the illiterate? How long have they been a subject of interest; what methods have been applied? Finally, how many years of preparation were required to focus scattered efforts on a common objective? Our subject matter here is the process of interaction and local complementarity, and integrated co-operation among social, educational, administrative and political participants.

Geographical Context

Before describing the process used to focus effort on the literacy campaign, a few words on geographical context are appropriate.

The Province of Namur, one of nine Belgian provinces, is a French-speaking area in the south of the country, at the heart of Wallonia. There are three main language groups in Belgium. These are, in decreasing order of size:

-   the Dutch-language community, in the north (Flanders) and in Brussels;

-   the French-language community, in the south (Wallonia) and in Brussels; and

-   the German-language community in the extreme east.

For administrative purposes, each province is a territorial subdivision of Belgium (Fig. 1). It is responsible for managing all matters of provincial interest (e.g. social policy, public health, culture, education, public works, economic development and tourism). It is both subject to the federal government and responsible for the communes it contains.

The Province of Namur is located in central Wallonia, at the intersection of the main Paris-Liège-Cologne and Brussels-Luxembourg-Strasbourg-Basel lines of communication. It has a population of 415,000 and occupies 12 per cent of the country's land area. The population density, 110 inhabitants per km², is relatively low compared to the country as a whole (three times greater). It contains 38 communes, the most densely populated being: Namur - largest city in and capital of Wallonia, approximately 100,000 inhabitants; Sambreville - 28,000 inhabitants; Andenne, 21,000 inhabitants.

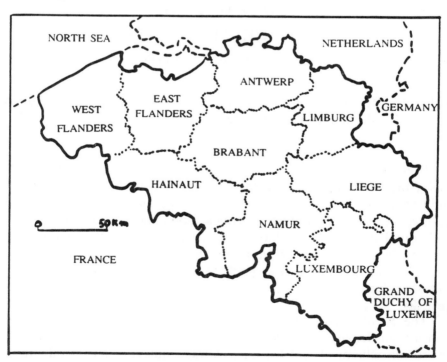

Fig. 1. The 9 Belgian provinces

The three communes are located along the east-west axis of the Sambre and Meuse industrial valley.

Most of the province's other communes have relatively low population figures, an indication of their rural nature: 13 communes have population figures between 5,000 and 10,000; 13 communes have fewer than 5,000 inhabitants (Table 1).

BELGIUM

3 COMMUNITIES	9 PROVINCES	3 REGIONS
- FRENCH		- WALLONIA
- DUTCH		- FLANDERS
- GERMAN		- BRUSSELS

589 COMMUNES

± 9,800,000 INHABITANTS

6,000,000 ELIGIBLE VOTERS

Table 1:   Relative situation of provinces and communes within the administrative structure of Belgium

Both economically and demographically, the Province of Namur has a bipolar structure. On the one hand, it contains the east-west industrial and services industry axis along the Sambre and Meuse valley; and also the industrial zones along the provincial autoroute and round the province's largest city, Namur, all high density areas. On the other hand, the countryside to the north and south of this axis is dotted with a few pockets of service industry and new industrial centres; in these areas, population density is much lower (Fig 2).

The Sambre and Meuse valley has a long tradition of industry and a high density of working population. Its former prosperity was based on chemical works, glassworks, quarries and coal mines. Through the 1960s and 1970s, the coal mines shut down one after the other, producing high unemployment among the population. This included a large number of Italian, Greek, Turkish and Moroccan immigrants who had come to replace Belgians turning their backs on such dangerous and unhealthy work.

The unemployment picture was made even worse by the recession and the subsequent restructuring and consolidation of other traditional enterprises. The number of unemployed workers became too large to be absorbed by the demand for labour in the new automated firms in the industrial estates and the growing service industry centres around Namur. Job distribution by economic sector in the Province of Namur by the end of the 1980s had become:

5.5% Primary sector (agriculture, mining)
32.9% Secondary sector
61.6% Tertiary sector

The rural areas extending north and south from the east-west axis are largely populated by workers in tertiary (i.e. service) industries who have jobs in Namur, Brussels and smaller towns. Although agriculture dominates the landscape in these areas, only 5 per cent of the province's population is currently engaged in agriculture.

However, through family ties, tradition, public opinion and lifestyle, most of the area's population has kept its attachment to rural values. To some extent this mental attitude is widespread in Namur which, although it is the province's largest city is surrounded by countryside.

Illiteracy in the French Community of Belgium

Total illiterates are unable to read, write or recognize letters. This group represents a minority compared with all those who cannot read or write well enough to understand the meaning of what they read or fill out simple forms.

Generally speaking, members of the latter group attended school for a number of years but, for a variety of reasons to be discussed later, gradually forgot or rejected the knowledge acquired. These people are generally known as functional illiterates. In today's urban society, such people, in varying degrees, have difficulty dealing with everyday situations such as reading a bus or train timetable; finding a number in a telephone book; reading directions on a food package;

204

Fig. 2.   The 38 communes in the Province of Namur.

understanding highway signs; reading a highway map or city plan and finding a route; helping a child with homework; reading a contract, an invoice, prescription directions; writing a cheque.

Functional illiteracy is thus generally defined with reference to the demands of a particular society. It is a relative concept based on predefined criteria. Because skills that may appear sufficient in one context are clearly insufficient in another, it is difficult to evaluate the functional illiteracy threshold for any particular population or to assess the extreme variability of statistics emerging from studies, surveys and censuses.

In Belgium the army has produced the only statistics on illiteracy: the partial illiteracy rate among army personnel is estimated at 1.5 per cent. These figures disregard huge segments of the population (e.g. women, the elderly, men exempt from military service, foreigners) and seem disproportionately low compared to quantitative data from neighbouring countries.

The UK reports that 13 per cent of young adults have problems writing and doing simple arithmetic. The data are the result of a 1981 study of a 23-year old population cohort. In France a 1988 survey conducted on behalf of the Groupe permanent de lutte contre l'illettrisme reported that 21.8 per cent of the adult population has difficulty reading and writing. In June 1989 INSEE reported that 9 per cent of adults have serious problems with reading, writing and oral expression.

To arrive at a more accurate estimate of the functional illiteracy rate in Belgium's French-speaking community, the Lire et écrire association, which coordinates the literacy campaign, weighted the army data (tests given to militiamen), Office national de l'emploi data (according to the level of education reached by the unemployed surveyed) and studies done in the various countries of origin of the immigrant communities living in Belgium. The results indicate that between 300,000 and 500,000 adults have a mastery of the written word insufficient to deal with the requirements of everyday life. This represents a bracket of between 7 per cent and 13 per cent of the population, which is consistent with the estimates for neighbouring countries[1].

On a smaller scale, the Province of Namur has approximately 40,000 functional illiterates out of a total population of 415,000. In 1990, 185 individuals took literacy courses. Behind the bare figures there are real people and real stories about the botched lives of so many of the illiterate. Why are people illiterate? Education has been free and obligatory for nearly a century.

It is helpful to remember that the high rates of illiteracy in Europe were revealed during the recession of the 1970s. When the recession hit, people who, in spite of inadequate reading and writing skills, easily found jobs in times of full employment, were among the first fired; once unemployed, they had most difficulty finding another job.

Not only were far fewer of these people hired, but companies operating according to job supply and demand raised qualification requirements. Employment structures have changed radically in the past 20 years: drastic cutbacks in the service industry sector and state-of-the-art technology developed by industry have led to a massive loss of unskilled jobs.

Nearly 50 per cent of the long-term unemployed (unemployed for at least two years) surveyed by the Service subrégional de l'emploi en Province de Namur do not have an elementary school certificate. These people are automatically excluded from the traditional vocational training channels (social development course - tertiary or secondary program given by l'Office de l'emploi - general high school program) for which the entrance requirements exceed their education level. For many of them, the most extreme cases, literacy training is truly the only training available, prior to a personal development course designed to upgrade basic skills.

Now that we have described the economic context in which the social scourge of illiteracy emerged in our country, we still have to explain the odd paradox that individuals, most of whom attended school for a number of years (more than eight), reach adulthood unable to read. In a country where schooling is obligatory, the handicap of illiteracy is far more serious and a far greater embarrassment than in a society where illiteracy is the norm.

A 1985 survey conducted by Lire et écrire and sponsored by the EEC reveals a large number of illiterates who openly accused the school, its methods and its teachers of being the source of their ignorance of the written word, even of their exclusion.[2]

The drastic cuts in education budgets by governments worried about the public debt have led to overcrowded classes, outdated teaching materials, demotivation of education professionals, pupils and teachers, and an undeniable overall dysfunction of the school in relation to its objective of democratizing education.

The school has not found (or not taken) the means to take into account and promote in the learning process the children's own forms of expression, which differ according to milieu. By imposing a single cultural model in an effort to compensate for the shortcomings of the family, it has had, and continues to have, a colonial attitude which turns many children unconsciously against learning and ultimately creates failures.

As things stand, since the school is unable to compensate effectively for the shortcomings of the family, one consequence (at least in Francophone Belgium) is that the family environment (at least in some families) now makes up for the deficiencies of the school.

This doubles the discrimination against the child whose family background does not match the dominant cultural model. If neither school nor parents compensate for the cumulative deficiencies compared to the other pupils, these children inevitably fall further and further behind, and the gap separating the two groups of children continues to widen.

In Belgium 25 per cent of vocational students (one quarter of secondary school students) leave school with no qualifications whatever, deficient in writing, mathematical and reading skills. Because most of them have no solid mastery of these skills, they swell the ranks of the functionally illiterate.

The chasm separating the cultural model transmitted by the school and the experience of children from the most disadvantaged background reinforces inequality and eventually produces a bitterness and aversion to knowledge in these children, which excludes them from all education channels. The figures relating school failure to socio-cultural milieu speak for themselves (Figs 3, 4).

Exclusion from the education framework, which deprives individuals of the training required to find a job and condemns them to all types of assistance, has an impact on living conditions. Most illiterates, excluded from the labour system, live a precarious existence, on a minimum income provided by social assistance or unemployment benefits. The smallest accident or setback drops them into the severe poverty which, according to a survey conducted by the Centrum voor Sociaal Beleid of the University of Antwerp, is the lot of 7.3 per cent of Belgian households.

Severe poverty, defined as a permanent situation of shortage and privation, goes with inadequate housing and poor health. In

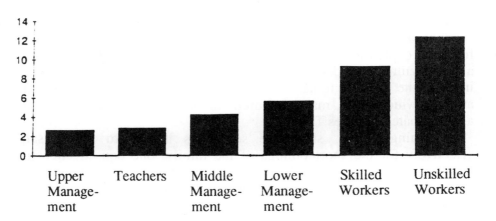

Fig. 4. Percentage of children below standard at end of Grade 6 elementary 1984 (by father's profession)

Source: *Le Ligueur*, 1990 (periodical published by la Ligue des familles de Belgique)

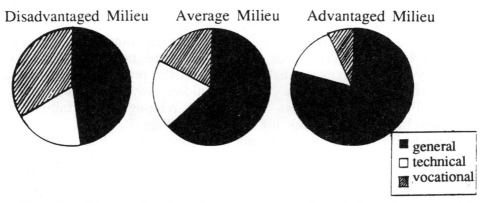

Fig. 5. Type of education program selected based on social hierarchy (1984)

Source: *Le Ligueur*, 1990 (periodical published by la Ligue des familles de Belgique)

Wallonia 107,000 households live in substandard buildings. Conditions in the Province of Namur, where 45 per cent of dwellings are substandard, are among the worst recorded. Rural communes, with a 56 per cent rate of substandard housing, are at the bottom of the scale, as the result of rising rents in Namur, demolition, expropriation and spiralling business and housing real estate prices for commercial and luxury dwellings in the town centre. Some people end up homeless: with no fixed address, they squat in abandoned buildings or sleep at the station.

Considering the appalling living conditions of many illiterates (lack of heating, malnutrition, substandard housing, constant material worries), health is an especially serious problem. The cumulative effect of poor living conditions has a serious impact on overall health. Illness, in addition to producing additional expense for persons already living on the edge, requires them to make sense of insurance forms and medical prescriptions, a considerable task for the illiterate, and one that adds to their feelings of embarrassment and dependency.

Illiteracy and the resulting social exclusion appear as the result of an accumulation of events which feed on one another. A variety of factors (school/unemployment/income/housing) begin the cumulative marginalization process. This is why it is so important, when addressing this group, to coordinate all efforts, especially those of social workers and persons responsible for basic education (teachers, literacy workers).

In the long term, literacy implies fighting for the right to decent housing and providing vocational training for below-average students and, as a corollary, fundamental changes within the school. What is required is joint effort toward social education in the broadest sense, to give the illiterate a real opportunity for education and to reintegrate them into the labour force and society.

Literacy: Institutional Framework within the French Community and in the Province of Namur

Associations and premises for the promotion of literacy have existed in Belgium for twenty years. Until the early 1980s, the goal of these institutions was literacy for foreigners (immigrant workers and their families, political refugees). In 1982, in the recession and unemployment context described above, two Brussels associations began to examine the problem of illiteracy in the Belgian population. The two groups are ATD (Aide à toute détresse) Quart-Monde and the Collectif d'alphabétisation.

In their wake, in the four corners of the French Community, a number of adult education groups affiliated with the Christian and socialist wings of the labour movement (which provided training to workers, groups with low education levels and school dropouts), began to show an interest in illiteracy and decided to co-operate in setting up a literacy structure. The various groups merged to form regional federations. These include Canal-Emploi in Liège, Défis in Brussels, Radio-Télévision-Animation in Namur and FUNOC (Formation pour l'université ouverte à Charleroi). Together they provided coordination throughout the French Community of Belgium and set up an initial awareness operation focusing on 8 September 1983, International Literacy Day.

This joint operation was given the name of "Lire et écrire". The primary objective of the operation was to enable everyone in the French Community of Belgium who wanted to learn to read and write to do so.[3]

As a result of the initial campaign, literacy groups grew out of the various continuing education movements in association with regional federations, largely in the Sambre et Meuse industrial valley. In the Province of Namur, groups were formed in Namur, Sambreville and Andenne.

The next requirement was literacy worker training. At the outset this was provided by previously existing groups (e.g. Collectif d'alphabétisation de Bruxelles); it was then carried to the regions by literacy workers who, within their own groups, acquired considerable experience in a very short time.

In the Province of Namur, literacy groups of various stripes joined forces under an umbrella group known as "Lire et écrire". This was created in 1984 and coordinated the efforts of individual groups, partner associations and community "Lire et écrire" groups. It represented the literacy movement vis-à-vis government and, in the field, coordinated literacy worker training, directed new learners to literacy centres, promoted innovative methods in the groups and acted as a secretariat.

In no time the Namur umbrella group joined with other adult education organizations (e.g. social development schools, Office national de l'emploi vocational training centres, the Centre d'enseignement namurois des arts et métiers, linked to the general high school program, Radio-télévision-animation and various continuing education movements) in an official structure, the Comité subrégional de l'emploi. This committee included, in addition to the education bodies, representatives of heads of companies, workers' organizations and the provincial government.

In the meantime, as a result of annual campaigns and based on observed requirements, new literacy groups sprang up all over the province (at Gembloux, Ciney, Dinant, Rochefort and Marche).

The Development of Synergy Between Associations and Government in the Province of Namur

The Namur umbrella group "Lire et écrire", faced with an increasing demand for training over a larger area and the requirement for funding beyond its means, invited the Province, in the person of the permanent delegate for policy management, to assume responsibility for training literacy workers.

It should be pointed out that each Belgian province has its own education network and a variety of provincial schools within its borders (The Francophone area of Belgium has four education networks: French Community education, communal education, provincial education and confessional education.) In Namur the "Cours pour éducateurs en fonction" [courses for working teachers], a provincial school for social development which trains teachers and literacy workers for the community association movement, already had contacts and worked jointly with the association wing of the continuing education movement, to which the Namur umbrella group, through the literacy groups, was indirectly linked.

When a training program for 1987 was proposed by the Namur umbrella group, the provincial permanent delegate agreed to a 150-hour pilot training module. Some ten literacy workers from all over the province were trained under this program. Actual training was given by experienced members of the continuing education movements and literacy workers from groups which already had four years experience; the project was funded by the provincial government.

The following year, with the co-operation of the Namur umbrella group, the province's courses for working teachers set up a new short-term training module recognized by the national department of education. Those who gave training were required to have national education qualifications and, at the end of the program, a certificate was awarded to those who had followed the courses. These two conditions mark official recognition of such training as part of the social development education network.

As in the preceding year, the team providing the actual training was made up of literacy group workers with several years' experience in the field, but with the required qualifications (social assistant - certified for secondary teaching). Introduction of this program marked the first official co-operation between, on the one hand the umbrella group and community literacy groups and, on the other hand, an administrative body (the provincial government) and a provincial social development school. The synergy between the community associations and publicly funded training for literacy workers has grown with each passing year. This year's group is made up of 18 individuals.

In 1989 the Namur umbrella group became a non-profit organization with the title "Lire et écrire Namur". In spite of its change in legal status, its responsibilities remain the same.

International Literacy Year in the Province of Namur
or, How to Pave the Way for a Concerted Partnership Between Government and Community Associations

Lire et écrire Namur wanted to take all the opportunities provided by the celebration of an international year to promote literacy activities throughout the Province of Namur. Until 1989, literacy flourished only in towns with a population of over 15,000, leaving most of the province's small communes far behind.

Throughout this year, in which media and governments displayed growing interest in literacy action, Lire et écrire Namur prepared an awareness program aimed at three well-defined groups:

1. The provincial and communal authorities empowered to make decisions, assign funds and encourage interested parties to take

the action essential for the various needs of the literacy campaign;

2. The authorities of, and participants in, continuing education movements (associations) and the CPAS (commune level) throughout the province, as priority teams in the fight against illiteracy (CPAS: Centre public d'aide sociale [social assistance centre], a body responsible for keeping records on needy persons and granting financial assistance);

3. The population, to heighten awareness of the problem and ensure public cooperation in maintaining and supporting the illiterate and removing the stigma associated with their condition.

Our proposal entailed a description of the approach to government by Lire et écrire Namur, the means used to heighten awareness and the results thereof.

As we have seen, since 1987 there has been close co-operation on literacy worker training between the province, through social development instruction (Courses for working teachers) and the Namur umbrella group. Within the context of International Literacy Year, the province's permanent delegation was again the first to be contacted.

With a view to extending the awareness movement to the entire province, the permanent delegate responsible for instruction and education invited representatives of all the province's communes to a preliminary information meeting with Lire et écrire Namur. About 50 per cent of them, mainly commune councillors responsible for social affairs and education, and a few burgomasters, replied to the invitation in March 1990.

The awareness program for communal authorities is based on the extent of illiteracy in the province (supported by figures and estimates), the principal types of illiteracy encountered, and the experiences of the illiterate themselves. Emphasis was placed on the concept of citizenship. How can a person enjoy full citizenship without the means for self-expression, faced with the impossibility of exercising economic, social and cultural rights? Depriving an individual or group of access to reading and writing means depriving them of the means of political expression and the basic tools required to participate in decisions which have implications for their present and future.

Literacy has emerged as the condition essential for the effective exercise of most of the rights proclaimed in the Universal Declaration of Human Rights.

Lire et écrire proposed to the authorities the text of a Namur Charter or Manifesto for a literacy campaign (see beginning of chapter). To summarize: through the Charter, the communes undertake to provide material support for literacy programs on their territory and to provide maximum cooperation with the various groups involved (CPAS social assistants, community associations, literacy groups).

It was decided that the Charter would be taken back to each commune, there to be presented to and discussed with the commune council. At the end of the deliberations, each commune would vote to decide on approval or rejection of the Charter.

Two months later, 22 of the 38 communes in the province returned the signed charter. The measures taken in the various communes were evaluated with a view to rendering the process more dynamic and encouraging the less motivated. Preliminary conclusions were drawn.

A second meeting of commune authorities was called jointly by the permanent delegate and Lire et écrire Namur. The communes which had taken action to implement the Charter reported on their progress. Some had organized information sessions jointly with Lire et écrire for target populations likely to be affected by illiteracy.

Meetings had been held, with the teachers and principals of communal schools, with physicians, with association boards, with advisors and CPAS social assistants, all aimed at concerted action toward a common goal. Other communes raised popular awareness through articles in local papers.

In a number of communes, the urgent need for education on the underlying causes of illiteracy and concrete possibilities for reintegration emerged. Lire et écrire Namur and the permanent delegate undertook to respond to the demand.

In October 1990 two one-day seminars on social integration, vocational training and illiteracy were organized for the communes who had signed the Charter. Participants included social workers, psychologists, teachers, educators, instructors and commune employees. The seminars were organized and presented by Belgian and foreign experts. Program organization displayed the same positive synergy between community associations and government: three of its main participants were the Service d'études et de documentation sociale de la Province de Namur, Lire et écrire Namur, and the Cours pour éducateurs de la Province de Namur. Following the seminars, the Governor of the province and all the communal authorities involved came together for a symbolic signing of a memorable charter.

Beginning in September 1990, on the occasion of World Literacy Day, Lire et écrire Namur appealed to every individual involved in the province's associations to think in terms of the overall fight against illiteracy, make every effort to avoid competitive duplication, and give careful consideration to the multiple factors responsible for social exclusion.

Sixty-six associations responded to the appeal and, in a number of meetings, jointly drew up a white paper on social exclusion. The White Paper and the recommendations it contains were submitted to the permanent delegation. Following the meeting, it was decided that the White Paper would be studied at one of the delegation's official meetings and subsequently recommended to the communes.

Parallel to the awareness program, and no doubt as a result thereof, the number of learners jumped from 127 in January 1990 to 185 in January 1991, an increase of more than 45 per cent. Lire et écrire Namur is currently coordinating the activities of 24 literacy groups throughout the province.

To finance literacy programs throughout the province, stabilize even a few jobs (realizing that all the work rests on the shoulders of four ACS* workers and some twenty volunteers), it was essential in the long run to consolidate all the energy available, to focus all the region's forces, toward the common objective: the fight against illiteracy. As explained above, the associations and the provincial and communal governments and related services consolidated their efforts under the Charter. What remained was to motivate other potential partners (businesses, banks, universities) and recruit them to the cause.

---

* Agent contractuel subventionné [subsidized contract worker]: worker status created by Belgian legislation to counteract unemployment.

The Fondation Émile Lacroix, named after a former governor, was established for the purpose. Its objectives are to:

- develop the fight against illiteracy within the framework of an overall course of action to fight social exclusion;

- support the literacy activities of Lire et écrire by providing human and financial resources;

- jointly with Lire et écrire, coordinate action at the commune level aimed at implementing the content of the Charter;

- promote joint literacy projects (e.g. CPAS, Lire et écrire, other movements);

- sponsor literacy program funding drives;

- organize an annual month-long intensive campaign on the problem of illiteracy;

- promote and subsidize production of papers, books and research on the subject of literacy; and

- organize public gatherings (e.g. concerts, sports events, galas) to promote literacy.

A number of prominent companies in the Province of Namur have shown interest in responding to this appeal. It is our hope that universities and banks will follow in their footsteps. The local development which results from expanding the scope of literacy programs is far greater than the sum of its social, educational, cultural, political and economic parts. It is an aggregate incorporating all the links, interactions and complementarity among partners, which focuses and intensifies the joint efforts toward social reintegration and the well-being of a human community.

Conclusion

The construction of a partnership between Lire et écrire Namur, various continuing education movements, provincial and communal governments and authorities and workers in the field (group leaders, educators, social assistants, teachers, physicians, family workers) seems to have been a long process.

In 1985 Namur already had an official structure, the Comité subrégional de l'emploi, made up of persons responsible for adult education organizations (e.g. continuing education movements, Office national de l'emploi, schools for social development), representatives of business, workers and regional authorities working toward the common goal of developing local employment.

By 1986 Lire et écrire Namur (formerly "la coordination namuroise") became a key player in the existing structure when it drew up a five-point strategy for local members of the partnership:

1. making its own action and that of the various literacy groups official;

2. consolidating that action with regional employment and training programs;

3. filling in existing gaps in the region which have a negative impact on the under-educated;

4. spending time with workers in the field, taking part in their discussions, getting to know them, with a view to gaining an overall picture of existing resources and potential; and

5. establishing co-operative links, setting up joint programs conducted by specific partners (provincial school of social development/provincial government).

The fact that Lire et écrire was able to penetrate the excessively official structure of the Comité subrégional de l'emploi can undoubtedly be attributed to its introduction by all the region's continuing education movements, which supported literacy groups or conducted literacy projects and were already firmly established within the structure.

The excellent relationship with the provincial school of social development, and thus with the province, is also based on prior co-operation by "Lire et écrire" with the school (which trains social educators and socio-cultural group leaders) and with the entire fabric of regional associations. "Lire et écrire Namur" has based all its activities on the already solid foundation of co-operative action. To this it was able to add an understanding of the field, and the experience and local presence of its leaders, who included a number of group leaders from the continuing education movement well established in Namur. Lire et écrire, through its constituent literacy groups and associations, already had a reputation for stressing the fundamental requirements of pluralism and complementarity, transcending competition and ideological differences.

Since 1985 the strategy has entailed contact and co-operation among a variety of partners, focused on a concrete objective. This common thread runs through training programs for literacy workers, the Charter campaign associated with International Literacy Year, the wording of the White Paper on social exclusion, one-day seminars on social integration and, finally, establishment of the Lacroix Fondation.

Each individual involved became personally committed to the cause, quite apart from the interests of the association, government or other body represented. In this community process, each one had something to contribute: at one end of the scale, a voluntary literacy worker or continuing education movement representative who works on the White Paper on social exclusion and thus gains new awareness of the necessity for joint action and setting aside the old local quarrels which can still set one association against another; at the other, a social affairs councillor or teacher returning to his or her commune imbued with the message of the Charter and making personal contacts to mobilize an entire local network of professionals and interested citizens engaged in solving the problem (e.g. social assistance centre advisors, commune employees, teachers, physicians, social workers).

Successful completion of a number of steps is no excuse to rest on our laurels. On the contrary, the challenge now is to bring the literacy campaign into the farthest regions of the countryside. Although there is no denying the importance of the geographic expansion of literacy and anti-illiteracy programs, a more in-depth approach to the persons responsible for education, culture and social affairs is even more important.

The job will not be done unless industry and commerce become involved in this enormous plan of action for the right to education. Companies are invited to contribute to the collective effort aimed at implementing the declaration, "The Right to Learn", adopted in 1985 by the Fourth International UNESCO Conference on Adult Education:

Recognition of the right to learn is now more than ever a major challenge for humanity.

The right to learn is:
the right to read and write;
the right to question and analyse;
the right to imagine and create;
the right to read one's own world and to write history;
the right to have access to educational resources;
the right to develop individual and collective skills

and, we may add, to read the truth and master one's environment.

Training is indispensable to the smooth operation of public and private companies, which are investing ever-increasing amounts of time and money in a broad range of training programs, none of which can be effective unless the workers are sufficiently well grounded in the basics. Making companies aware of the illiteracy problem and of the need to invest in a solution is an important aspect of the work to be done over the next decade. This assumes that literacy must be the first step in the long training process aimed at resocializing and qualifying the individual for a job, thus making him or her a better citizen.

A number of courses of action for the future are open. The following paragraphs give an overview of the White Paper on social exclusion[4]:

- sponsoring a permanent statistical record of factors and figures related to social exclusion in the province; this record would enable ongoing adjustment of policies aimed at combating social exclusion on the basis of local needs;

- transmitting to interested government bodies the pressing demand, throughout the Province of Namur, for an increase in the means (jobs and funding) for literacy purposes;

- in programs of study for future teachers (teacher training colleges), including awareness and information modules about the problem of exclusion, a corollary of dropping out which begins in the school, and about the illiteracy phenomenon in general;

- supporting rural schools and schools which play an integrated role in neighbourhood life;

- bringing parents into the school education process, especially in immigrant and disadvantaged neighbourhoods, and setting up pilot projects for schools that are an integral part of neighbourhood or village life;

- setting up literacy and personal development courses close to the homes of marginal populations (e.g. CPAS, shelters, homes for unwed mothers, food banks);

- with regard to job integration, reinforcing the participation of workers' organizations in educating the most disadvantaged job seekers; and

- creating a broader network of information and guidance centres for existing programs, patterned on the COISP (Centre d'orientation et d'insertion socio-professionnelle) model .

This is only a small sample of the proposals to be implemented in the years to come. The success of these projects will demand a great deal of concerted effort and co-operation between the authorities and associations.

In the last analysis, government is responsible for education and literacy. The response to the requirements of the population and the various problems of social exclusion depend on political decisions. It is the duty of government to ensure, by seeking appropriate solutions, that the education provided satisfactorily meets the needs of today and tomorrow.

Each individual is invited to take an interest in literacy, either illiteracy prevention or implementing after-school programs set up to combat the devastation caused by this social scourge. Governments must feel bound to take up the challenge; the future of society and of democracy is at stake. Although the task is enormous, the outlook is promising: the experiences reported on these pages augur well for the future.

As the Director General of UNESCO has said, "Each new reader is a soul that can be mobilized to combat the syndrome of privation, inequality, sickness, and other problems to which illiteracy contributes" (unofficial translation).

Creating a world, a region, a province where illiteracy is unknown may be a long shot; it is not, however, an impossible dream. We know what must be done. We must step up the rhythm and work together even harder.

Notes

1. Goffinet, S.A. and Van Damme, D. 1990. *Functional Illiteracy in Belgium*. Brussels: King Baudouin Foundation; Hamburg: Unesco Institute for Education.

2. Goffinet, S.A., Loontjens, A., Loebenstein, A. and Kestelyn, C. 1986. *Les itinéraires d'analphabétisme*. Luxembourg: Publications Office of the European Communities.

3. Kestelyn, Catherine. 1988. La campagne d'alphabétisation dans la communauté française de Belgique. In Jean-Paul Hautecoeur, ed. *Alpha 1988*. Montreal: Quebec Ministry of Education.

4. Verbeck, Anne ed. Social Exclusion. Paper drawn up by a group of individual members of various associations in the Province of Namur.

URGENTLY REQUIRED: IMAGINATION A WRITING COMPETITION

Francesco Azzimonti
CLAP, Rhône-Alpes, Lyon, France

IF I HAD IN WRITING

If I had in writing the history of my people,

If I had in writing the story of my birth,
from my mother, storm, war, bicycle, fatigue,
work, anxiety, spasm, rain, seven months,
incubator.

If I had in writing gossip from my
neighbourhood, stories about this house, its
children, its women and their lovers. And
the dead too.

If I had in writing the songs of girls shouted
across the fields, and the response of the
boys from the other side.

If I had in writing the story of bread earned,
and of the darkened hands of my father, of
the wine he coveted, of the firewood and
coal, feet warming by the oven, hard boiled
eggs and bitter salad.

If I had in writing the history of a family,
ordinary people, and their passion to improve,
WHAT WOULD I BE READING TODAY?

F.A.

THE BLUE ORANGE*

Once upon a time, a little blond prince lived in a country full of flowers and fruits of all colours and all flavours. He didn't have to travel far: in his garden, there could be found virtually every kind of flower and fruit from the other countries of the world. And all day long in his garden, many boys and girls of all colours from every country strolled and played.

But he, the little prince who was to succeed his father at a later date, was not allowed to stroll in the garden; he could only look at it out of his window. At night, when everything was quiet, he would secretly get up to look through the window at the sleeping flowers and the fruits, with their interplay of fragrances. The little prince was always locked up in his rooms, because he tirelessly had to study and learn, and take one course after another in preparation for being first in the kingdom in due course. He learned grammar and spelling, about the stars and about electronics, he practised foreign languages and learned all the codes of etiquette. He was surrounded by dictionaries and papers, pencils and erasers, pocket calculators and computers, and had wise people all around him to instruct him well and to make sure that he did his homework and learned his lessons. Everything around him was grey.

From time to time, this little prince saw (or dreamed?) between the pages of the books and the keys of the computers, a kind of bubble, like an orange, but of a funny shade, close to dark blue, sometimes with all kinds of colour gradations mixed together.

Little by little, this blue orange-like bubble would appear when he looked through the window into his garden. He was told that he was perhaps colour-blind. He didn't bother to search in his books to see what this meant exactly; he found it so pleasant to see the world in colour that he came to the conclusion that if this was what being colour-blind meant, he would become so willingly. Thus every day he tried a little harder to place his blue orange bubble everywhere to see the world, and discovered soon enough that he could see the changing colours of the flowers and fruits in his garden, the striking variety of faces on the boys and girls who were playing in the garden. He could combine green,

* A story by the author in *Clap Info-bulletin Rhône-Alpes* No. 23/24, February-March 1990

red, orange, sky blue, and purple, and even invent subtle shades that had never been seen before. He discovered that it was really worth the trouble to look at reality with rules and colours that deviated somewhat from the grey monotony of his books, his machines and his teachers.

He took his pens and his pencils, his pocket calculators and his computers, his dictionaries and his grammars, went through the window and descended into the garden. When he arrived, all his pencils had become paintbrushes and coloured felt-tip pens, all his books and machines had become painter's palettes containing all the colours of the rainbow. That is when he began to write and to paint, along with his friends, stories that were full of colour, in which were intermingled travels and tales, proverbs and magic formulae, adventures of men and animals, numbers and letters, drawings and poems.

Colour was everywhere, and everywhere in the garden people could write as they pleased. The little prince showed everyone how to see the world in colour, green-red-orange-gold-blue-purple, and how it was possible to find happiness by writing using colours, and signs of rage and gentleness, passion and fatigue, tears and smiles, memories and anticipation, analysis and love.

Franco

The Comité de liaison pour l'alphabétisation et la Promotion (CLAP) [Literacy and development liaison committee]

The story of CLAP in France

For many years now, the Comité de liaison pour l'alphabétisation et la promotion (CLAP) has had an innovative approach to working with the illiterate and the uneducated: it does not confine the illiterate within a framework of technical and purely linguistic problems, but sets all learning in a context that encourages personal and collective development.

In France, CLAP has grown significantly over a 20-year period, along with the changes that have taken place in French society with respect to the phenomenon of migration and the dynamics of social and employment integration. At the beginning, in 1968, a handful of associations wanted to have a common tool, a liaison committee, to support their efforts to provide literacy education to adult immigrants who were uneducated or who had very little education in their own language; the needs of these people were first dealt with by teaching them to read and write in French, in order to make them comfortable in their new living environment.

Over the years, the network grew. On the national, regional and local levels, including federations of voluntary community associations, the associations that belonged to CLAP worked in information, training, the social, professional and cultural development of immigrants and French men and women, in the battle against discrimination, and in encouraging genuine socialization.

CLAP's goals became broader as it adopted the issues dealt with by member associations: developing literacy education, fostering the social and professional development of foreigners and people who are culturally excluded from society, fighting racism and working towards building an intercultural society. The Committee's primary objective was to support immigration requirements with respect to:

-   training and developing immigrants, in particular the battle against illiteracy, which is a key area in the fight against social exclusion,

-   cultural expression, the rights of different cultures, and education in languages of origin,

-   genuine recognition of the civil rights of immigrants and their organizations.

The steps taken by the Committee to meet these objectives included:

-   combining and coordinating the efforts of member associations throughout France,

-   facilitating exchanges of information and experience among all groups of individuals pursuing common goals, and establishing centres for literacy education and development everywhere the need was felt;

- performing a role as a research and information centre on appropriate pedagogical and instructional methods and, where applicable, conducting experiments;

- enhancing awareness about the socio-cultural problems experienced by disadvantaged groups, and making the public aware of their problems;

- approaching public authorities, communities and other agencies in any way that might contribute to meeting its goals;

- encouraging the creation of regional committees to strengthen its effectiveness and develop closer ties with various associations;

- publishing a periodical journal, developing pedagogical tools, and implementing all necessary information activities.

Now that it has resolutely joined the ranks of those associations, movements and agencies devoted to fighting social exclusion in France, CLAP can now, on the strength of its early experience, become involved in local urban and rural development. Penetrating this field, which is a prime target for dynamic initiatives, highlights the need to support local associations, neighbourhood groups, and even to train development officers. The introduction of the Revenu minimum d'insertion (RMI - Basic Integration Income) along with the job integration contract for participants, underscore still further the priority assigned to this type of action. This new living and working space in neighbourhoods and communes has become, along with schools, one of the best places from which to demarginalize people, to bring outsiders in. The manner in which CLAP has developed its objectives and its practices stems from the changing context and the needs expressed by the associations and publics concerned. It must continue its efforts through new forms of intervention that have yet to be devised and implemented.

Significant phases

1978. The General Assembly debated a report on proposals for a public training network for adults in France. The General Assembly agreed to the gradual implementation of a public training network that would exist at all levels (local, regional, national):

- agencies to carry out training activities

- grass-roots organizations and movements (social partners, particularly union organizations)

- migrants' organizations, which assumes that all impediments to the free exercise of expression and association to which immigrants are victims have been eliminated

- governments and public authorities.

This public network should be decentralized to the greatest possible extent, should receive a public mission from governments, and be capable in the longer term of playing a role in more general forms of continuing education relevant to all adult nationals or foreigners, without necessarily doing away with the special requirements of immigrant training.

1981. "Towards an intercultural society: living together is possible". The General Assembly's motion was hopeful about progress on the immigration front, and signalled that it would be monitoring the situation. The notion of "people in transit" no longer made sense; the migrant phenomenon was treated as "structural". This, however, was something that a large percentage of French society refused to accept. The community association movement had to take into account the facts of a rapidly expanding economic environment, a difficult social context, contradictions that surface within the immigrant communities themselves, and political change. The General Assembly recommended a genuine integration of immigrants into a network of social relations, a fundamental policy whose first goal was to be demarginalization. Mindful of this, suggestions were made about what kinds of action to take to remove the major obstacles to progress towards a multicultural society.

1985. The General Assembly, under the discussion topic of "CLAP and youth", placed an emphasis on the need to give due consideration to the association movement as perceived by young people, who were questioning society, and affirmed its resolve to develop practices that would meet the needs and aspirations of the movement. More concretely, matters like training, culture, the free association of young people, partnership relations, the great need for debate in society and the many issues involved, were discussed.

While CLAP had been in favour of a UNESCO symposium in January 1983 on the topic "Towards an intercultural society", a one-day European conference was held in October 1985 at UNESCO entitled "Monitoring change with a view to action and training".

1988. Towards CLAP in the 90s. The General Assembly policy motion defined a two-pronged Mediterranean and European approach in the context of the implications of the Single European Act.

The Rhône-Alpes CLAP and the Writing Competition

For the whole of the Rhône-Alpes region, CLAP is a place where over fifty associations can meet to discuss and deliberate. It functions essentially with association organizers and members, as well as with educators and social workers, who in our opinion have the potential to effect social change that would make it possible to acquire recognition for, and to improve the lot of, disadvantaged groups, who have a role to play in society now and in the future. Promoting and fostering diversity, doing things "through" and "with" mediators to create a process of change and development for groups and individuals, is the overall purpose of the Rhône-Alpes team.

The idea of a writing competition for people who do not know how to write well was certainly consistent with the logic of celebrating International Literacy Year by, for once, giving those who cannot write, whether French or immigrants, an opportunity to speak and to write, for they are too readily labelled uneducated or illiterate. By urging them "to enter into the world of writing by writing", CLAP Rhône-Alpes wanted to give the battle against illiteracy a living and real face. There is an urgent need for innovation in efforts to deal with illiteracy and literacy education. The contest was far removed from any efforts to provide assistance, because the "illiterates" were asked not only to write, but also, more specifically, to take themselves in hand, and actually express their own desires and thoughts. It was therefore open to all adults who "have things to say, who would like to write, but who have never dared". It also accepted any form of writing (stories, correspondence, poems, proverbs, tales). It was broad enough to allow everyone enough room to meet the challenge in a manner commensurate with their ability.

The project had three primary objectives:

- to make illiterates and uneducated people the producers and the target audience of written matter. To allow people to use their heads and their hands to mobilize the communication resources that they have kept bottled up. They certainly have, given their history and their imaginations, some meaning to express. There are also certainly some ways that they will be able to find, commit themselves to, and develop, in making the transition to a written form;

- through this, to create a climate conducive to creativity at the regional level, to encourage those who did not know how to write to express themselves and to communicate. To suggest networks where those involved would themselves be able to use speech and the pen, and thus go beyond mediation through an official standardized culture and through the delegation of knowledge to educators and social workers;

- to use the occasion to spur a renewal of pedagogical methods in the region, by making it possible for educators and learners to confront the dynamics of producing written work, in which both learning and creativity intermingle.

The regional initiative very quickly became national in scope. At the end of six months, we received a large number of texts: approximately 1,000 persons were mobilized to write throughout France, and about 500 submissions were received. Some were written by individuals, some by groups, some in pairs, and some by families. We attempted to reply personally or as a group to each submission, and asked them to join a writing exchange network. To each, we also suggested that they begin to work with us on reading further submissions: each person was sent the "competition journal", along with the additional submissions as we received them.

Among the submissions, 60 were selected for prizes in various categories: the gifts they received were books, to allow them to continue on their writing adventures. Among the 60, 25 won a trip to and a stay in Paris. An honorary writing jury, composed of Azouz Begag, Laabi Abdellatif and Michèle Reverbel, awaited them to celebrate the pleasure of having written something, and to encourage them to continue to write. A "writing" certificate was given to each, and sent to other winners, signed by the President of CLAP, by a representative of UNESCO, and by the writer Azouz Begag. Emotions in the room were high, for various reasons: the speeches made by the VIPs in attendance, the announcement of the nominees and the awarding of prizes, the reading of a number of the submissions, and the speeches made by the "winners". Writing is an act of love that it was also necessary to celebrate in public: even dreams sometimes need their own theatre.

The lessons learned from the Writing Competition

After introducing this initiative and shepherding it through to its conclusion, I found it necessary to think about and to attempt to understand my "writing aid" efforts (through following up with literacy courses, training educators, direct contacts with persons experiencing problems) and to draw the first lessons to be learned from this "contest". It was also useful to identify a number of theoretical landmarks that guided us along the way.[1]

A wager

Learning to read and write is not a preliminary to training, employment or action. On the contrary, it accompanies all procedures used for social, cultural or economic integration that alone give meaning to the written word.

The uneducated are not without resources: it is necessary to abandon a defensive view of "a battle" against a handicap, and to act instead on the basis of a social transformation and personal development.

It is necessary to renew pedagogical practices, to make it possible for educators and learners to abandon exercises that simulate the school experience, and to confront the requirements of producing written work that can be communicated in a social context.

Our answer was a writing competition for people who do not know how to write, and a proposal to adults who think and say that they are unable to write:

- you have an interesting background and you have things to say,

- you can find new ways to prepare something in writing about this experience that is unique to you. We leave it to you to deal with the problems involved in making the transition to putting it in written form.

In return, a commitment: to publish the submissions (competition journal) and to give them a prize (that is to say value), real prizes, though admittedly modest.

The competition proposed by CLAP was fairly open-ended - its configuration was in part anticipated at the outset, and then modified in terms of the dynamic established by the participants:

- a vertical dimension related to the very essence of the competition: to write, to send and await the results of a reading committee, to undergo a selection process, to receive prizes for reading-writing - a trip and a stay in Paris, or books, a commitment to continue to read.[2]

- a horizontal dimension: to enter into the reading-writing relational dynamic, i.e. to send in written work, to receive mail, to be published in the "writing newsletter", to read the submissions of other writers, to communicate with them in writing, etc.[3]

Learning

From April to June 1990, the proposal was put forward and implemented: approximately 500 submissions were sent in from just about everywhere in France. Some were written by individuals, and some came from groups or from people involved in a training program.

If there are lessons to be drawn, they include both writing and the status of the participants. In spite of the problems involved in writing, people did write: this gives us something to think about with respect to the barriers, background, conditions, and staged learning requirements often given for not writing. In spite of social and professional problems, these people did write: this also gives us something to think about, because through the competition, or through a thousand other similar efforts, people felt authorized to speak and to write, felt recognized, appreciated and listened to (see the many letters of thanks received). The people who wrote spoke about themselves or about issues they hold dear.[4]

It is possible. They did write.

It is possible to write, even if one does not know how to write well. And the work involved was arduous: first draft, corrections, sending it in by mail, reply, reading the mail, discussions, dialogue; the competition journal arrives, and then there are published submissions, more submissions to read, more writing to be done, etc. A thousand persons (whom we call illiterate or uneducated) dared to write: they did not wait until they knew how to write well, they did not wait until they had completed their courses.

Who are these people?

- the vast majority were women (does this reflect a status? does this reflect attendance at literacy courses?);
- age: the majority were between 20 and 40 years of age (but there was also a very high percentage in the 50-60 age group and over 60 - up to age 86! - and there were some under 20 years of age);
- ethnic origin (in order of priority): the vast majority were people from the Maghreb, followed by Portugal, South-east Asia, France, black Africa and Turkey, Latin America, and, lastly, from various European countries.

Special characteristics

The majority of those who wrote prepared their work either in social integration courses in their neighbourhoods, or personally.

Then came those involved in job training courses or enrolled in Ateliers pédagogiques personnalisés (APP - personal pedagogical workshops) or in specific programs like the Crédit formation individualisé (CFI - individualized training credits).

Next came those who attended various social institutions (youth centres, reception centres, community centres, etc.).

Then came persons from specific environments: the mentally handicapped, the physically handicapped, those undergoing psychiatric treatment, gypsies, those receiving the Basic Integration Income (RMI - Revenu minimum d'insertion), and prisoners.

The final category included former literacy course trainees.

How did they go about writing?

The answer is that to write, even if one does not know how to write well, is possible in a thousand different ways. It is not a matter of linear progression or specific methods, but simply of daring to begin to write.

The first step is to overcome fear, and to dare to begin to place things on a blank sheet of paper, and to give shape to one's ideas; and then to negotiate the rules and standards of spelling, grammar and readability; and then to communicate, to send it to others, to receive a reply, to establish a circuit and networks; and then to continue, to improve, etc.

It is true that many of the submissions were prepared while people were taking courses or undergoing training, and showed evidence of group work: this reflected the many people involved in such undertakings, and mirrored the manner in which the educators worked. It was a necessary starting point, like any other.

Many of the submissions were very descriptive, whether about the current unemployed status of the writer, the course being taken by the trainee, or departure from the home country. Once again, description can be an important trigger to leading people to write, and to begin the effort required - one among others.

From all the submissions received, the six categories we were able to identify gave us an inkling of the various approaches that could be taken to writing when a person does not know how to write well; a variety of approaches, to suit a variety of personal agendas:

* beginning writing:
lines, signatures, exclamations, colours, sometimes drawings, something personal marked on a page, short faltering sentences, a hesitant pen;

* writing with others:
a group effort, with various small sections written by different people, finished efforts with photographs, on a computer, large format work, posters, small brochures produced in house, collages and drawings, each time bearing the distinctive mark of their authors;

* writing by others:
obtaining help from the family, children, grandchildren, husbands, neighbours. Work written by several hands: on a typewriter, on a computer, someone correcting an error, someone who completely retranscribes work which is later submitted for correction. And sometimes, help from the educator too;

* developing writing:
small texts are prepared, a few lines or a whole page are developed, there is some sequence of ideas and I speak about myself, my departure from my country, I describe my current situation, I introduce myself, I describe what I see around me;

* writing that takes wing:
progress is made, and confidence acquired; sentiments, impressions and thoughts are expressed, there is poetry in the air, the pen seems to write by itself, and something heartfelt is put onto paper;

* writing that liberates:
there are many things to say, personal pain and joy, events that are provocative - and the pen does not always have the capacity to express it; sometimes there is awkwardness, a large number of mistakes, it is not really like that but the desire to say something and to put it in writing is there. A certain freedom is acquired by writing, even though perfection is not attained.

And some people, after working on their first text, move from one category to another: the important thing is to know that there is more than one possible path, and that there are several registers in which to enter into and advance in the world of writing.

What are they about?

If a person does not know how to write well, but has something to say, then he or she should go ahead. Writing techniques should not be an impediment to anyone who wants to say something about himself or herself, or for someone who wants to send a message to others (whether within the context of a writing competition or not).

No topics were given as guidelines. A cursory glance (which will have to be replaced by a more careful study of the submissions) reveals the following topics, in order of priority:

- a desire to learn, to learn to read and to write (a number of thematic opposites reappear significantly: shadow/light, night/day, walking/not walking),

- narratives about life, about emigration, about current living conditions,

- solitude, sadness, neglect, distress,

- messages of love, affection (and a tiny bit of eroticism, on occasion),

- poetic dreams about one's country, one's home, the environment, but also about inner feelings and passions,

- thoughts about current events (world situation, racism, peace),

- a personal cry, mark, or signature ("I am happy to be able to write because I can shout out my story". "I would like to take a book in my hands". "Hurray, I am happy. Fatima"...).

Comments

At first glance, making the transition to writing appears to be the major obstacle. This is very often said by educators (they do not know how to write, it's too difficult, they'll never manage - writing is not for them - it's too early, they are just beginning). It is also very often felt and expressed by the writers themselves (I do not know how to write, one has to know how to write well, and if I make mistakes, and if it's not nice, writing is not for me).

What are the impediments to making the transition to writing?[5] Most often, these attitudes stem from:

* A concept of language and language learning as a form of "putting into words" (whether oral or written) of something that is already there in thought, of events. Writers write about events that they have previously seen (like a painter painting a model).

The problems encountered by adults in writing lead us rather to an opposed view: that language is not an instrument that someone begins to learn in order to communicate with the environment afterwards. An individual organizes himself or herself by learning, people organize themselves through language and within a language.

* The concept of "apprentices": according to this view, there are people "who do not know", and who one fine day, through the use of the correct method, a proper sequencing of learning and proper technical training, suddenly "know".

Wrong. People learn by doing, by speaking, by writing. It is not experience that organizes expression, but expression that organizes experience.[6] I only remember and memorize that which I plan to use again.[7]

* A concept of "writing": reading and writing, according to some people, are interconnected, through an analytical or syllabic method, and involve a comprehensive approach according to others. We are all aware of the battles raging around these pedagogical methods, and are familiar with the titles of the books that are very often used in courses.

We commend the Association française pour la lecture (AFL - French reading association) in particular, and other French and Canadian authors, for having described the essential processes involved in reading as it relates to a search for meaning, to the formulation of hypotheses, to anticipation, and to communication. There is no need for me to describe these again; I wish simply to underscore the importance of socialization and communication in making the transition to writing, which makes it possible to prepare people to be both capable of writing and of reading written material.

People learn to write because they have something to say to someone. People learn to read when they are interested in what others may have written, etc. It is a matter of learning to read by writing, in real life situations, and learning to read by reading, also in real life situations.

When an adult experiences problems in expressing himself or herself, either orally or in writing, what we are seeing is evidence, sometimes scars, of early education both in the family and at school. Problems with the language system are often no more than surface manifestations of difficulties in asserting oneself, of speaking in the first person.[8]

* The gamble we took with the competition showed us clearly that people, large numbers of people, dared to use the first person and to take pen and pencil in hand. Now that they have taken the first step towards addressing the "I" on their own behalf, comes the need to approach a deeper social "I" through exchanges of writing, which is one of the significant side benefits of the competition.

- A reading and writing network is now being established: people continue to write to CLAP, people are beginning to write to one another about various items published in the competition journal, and people seek out others who have written in the same city, or within the same association.

- Local initiatives have begun to take shape: a neighbourhood newspaper, a course newsletter, an association journal, and it is possible to exchange these between cities, between neighbour-hoods and between associations.

- Regional and local follow-up centres have been set up: Toulouse celebrated the writing competition by handing out a special Midi-Pyrénées prize; Marseille and Nice are preparing to publish the submissions; Grenoble, Lyon, and Saint-Étienne are considering setting up writing meetings between those who have written, who have travelled, and others who are just now embarking on the adventure. Other associations celebrated the success of their candidates in the competition in their own way, and are consider-ing pursuing research into writing. The Rhône-Alpes region is going to launch a regional writing competition. For 1991, the competition will be held nationally and in several regions of France.

- The competition journal will continue to be the permanent link between all those who dare to write, and it will regularly publish competition submissions and be used as a basis for dialogue, both within families and among trainees. It has even become a learning aid for those taking courses. Perhaps we will manage to publish an attractive brochure to showcase the writing efforts of the many contributors who had previously been unable to write.

* Learning to write is essentially centred on conformity to a social and, it must be admitted, very often a school-oriented standard. Hence endless questions were asked about the competition: But what about spelling? And mistakes, do they have to be corrected? Can I rewrite the effort submitted? I'll prepare the fair copy myself. It's not nice, what shall I do? etc.

And "when the written work does not meet all the too precise external criteria (administrative writing, progress reports, exercises based on techniques or even styles that are too precise such as short stories and novels, etc.) the writers establish their own guidelines, their own constraints, their own standards." "Writing truly becomes working on one's own self, and on one's way of thinking and living in the world."[9] The search for personal standards is certainly related to the multiplicity of genres selected: some favour poetry, others biography, yet others songs, letters, a short history, a current affairs essay, a philosophical discourse, a message of sadness or joy, a story, a reformulation of proverbs, etc. It is as if each individual worked on his submission as a function of his or her own representations of the thing written, and as a function of the words that came from the very heart or being (not to mention the stereotypes that everyone may have about such literary genres and the influence of the educator and perhaps his working group). But the personal touch is obvious in all the submissions received. Spelling and mistakes were not important criteria in determining the worth of the written submissions. Each individual worked out the rules for his or her own efforts.

* This is where the important role of a helper, or third party comes in. We are often asked, "Is this all right? Is this correct? Do you understand? Is this readable?" Confidence in the educator, potent and sometimes limitless, can make those he is teaching happy, but can also make them afraid: "What must an author do to learn that speaking and writing always involve negotiating the impossible concordance of self to self, and self to others..., writing is always

giving birth to one's inner being in suffering... but also in pleasure."[10]   One woman who took part in the competition, Mrs. Djellouli, used the concept of giving birth to express the idea: "I have found, since beginning to write, that it affects me like childbirth - painful and marvellous. It is difficult to write about myself and also to know that I will be read. Thank you for your encouragement."

Uncertainties and Proposals

Linking the learning of writing to a writing competition is no easy matter: there is a risk of creating the star syndrome, giving people the idea that they are on the brink of writing careers and that publication, distribution, appearances on literary television shows and celebrity are imminent.

It is true that people need to be motivated to write, and that an increase in self-esteem is also to be expected, but what is essential in all of this is that a network for dialogue and written communications should be maintained, and that impossible dreams, which several of the participants harbour, should not be encouraged.

Most likely, it is in the concrete side-effects in the various communities and training groups that the adventure will be able to continue and consolidate itself.

An initial risk that appeared was that of working essentially in groups and submitting group efforts. Although the process of writing with others is one possible introduction to the world of writing, it is not sufficient and not something that ought to be continued forever. Writing is a thoroughly personal act, and it is something that must lead us to find our own path, our own distinctiveness, and our own way of speaking, which becomes part of a process of reciprocal change and writing networks within a training group that is open to the outside world.

A second risk is relying too heavily on stereotypes people may have about writing and reinforcing them: I like to write poems, I write nothing but poems. I present myself and tell about my life. I describe what goes on during the course. I speak about my country." Discovering different ways of writing and different contents is also a way to advance and to learn - to compare, to confront, and to try another way, to take a risk.

There are two major stumbling blocks: the first cry, the first effort is not necessarily a precious object that warrants veneration at all costs. While writing is a path, the path is pitted with comments, corrections, and revisions recommended by the reader of the first draft, which is sometimes beautiful and finished, but more often needs improvement and refinement. And at the same time, the fear of making mistakes can paralyse us, and the observance of the canonical rules of writing can slow us or even render us powerless. Spelling and syntactical concerns have their role to play in ultimately producing a readable text that can be communicated.

The third risk resides in the attitude of the teacher or trainer. We were often asked, "Can somebody help me write?" And the educators responded, "But it's impossible, they don't know how to write, they are still learning... they still make too many mistakes... this is not for them... what shall I do?". The negative effects that educators can have is not negligible. They are often the ones who have the power to open or close the door, to erect mountains of problems or to move mountains to launch an adventure.

In all probability, each educator falls back on his own methods, and his instructional theories. To being with, is he ready for work that can be somewhat upsetting? Can he identify what are his own relationships with writing... Can he see himself as a mediator-guide to helping others write? The positive reports we have received lead us to suggest that it is essential for people to be themselves, and above all to like writing. It follows that everyone will need others.

Interesting pedagogical processes came to light in the written reports submitted by educators when they gambled on trying to teach writing without being afraid of committing themselves to a way that was somewhat off the beaten path. A positive role can be played by educators in mediation when they themselves take the risk of writing, and when they locate themselves precisely in the process as readers of material produced by others and as guides to others in producing written material.

What is to be done? The question is open, but the spadework has been done

* Places for writing: if writing becomes part of a creative process for non-writers, for those who do not write a lot, and for those who write poorly, to express themselves, then the sorts of places need to

be found where people can produce writing, polish their efforts, make corrections, review what has been written, compare themselves to others, attempt to meet standards, make progress in expressing their ideas, feelings and aspirations. These are just about everywhere - in associations, in training centres, in libraries, and in various permanent facilities (employment, children, adults) - workshops for writing and expression are needed, and appropriate pedagogical methods have to be found.

* Writing helpers or "facilitators": the educator's profile will increasingly become that of someone who helps others to express themselves, who eases the production of written work, who reads and responds to prepared texts, who places people in contact with other writers, who opens up the treasures of writing to them, who accompanies them to places for writing and reading, who puts personal texts in a social context, who raises self-esteem, who suffers along with the writers to make their work intelligible and capable of being communicated.

* Writing networks: communication is never a one-way street. We know today the extent to which exchanges of knowledge and experience play an important role in learning. Likewise, we learn by imparting what we know to others, and we read when we ourselves become writers after a fashion. We are recognized because we are read, and recognized because others correct us; others take an interest in us, we can communicate with others, sometimes our peers, sometimes people who are different from us. All of this occurs when people begin to do relational writing.

Conclusion

To succeed in writing

The deciding factor is that people see themselves as authors-writers.
    It is essential to place an emphasis on production rather than on accepting or copying models or rules.
    The production of written work frequently takes place within a communications network (for friends, within the family, as a member

of a literacy group or a training group, but also for a broader public, such as a neighbourhood, town, etc.).

The texts produced are all related to a unique life experience (remembrances, thoughts, feelings, dreams about the past, present or the future).

There can be pleasure and joy, even when the problems are many, and not everything is solved at one go.

To continue to write

Written work is satisfying and attractive. Each piece of writing has value and deserves a "prize".

A piece of writing needs to be reworked, and improved, because others may read it, respond to it, and because other people write differently, etc.

It must be possible for written work to have a social point, to become a continuing communication activity (community newspapers, collections, correspondence with other writers, and a spilling-over into other language situations or ways in which people act in their milieu).

If we believe that certain people are not capable of writing, and if this assumption is one of the methods used to keep these people in their place, then the ideal would be to prevent them from writing anything at all. If you open the door just a crack, and if you believe they are capable, then you must take the risk that they will enter the "palace".

It is in fact dangerous to say that all of what the trainees write is wonderful, as it was put onto paper the first time. Workshop finishing (to refine, to polish, etc.) is needed. A start is made, but it is necessary to rewrite, to check, to improve.

Writing is an interesting adventure, but one with limitations: you can't make every one believe that he or she will become an author. If writing has to do with oneself and with the world around us, then the adventure can also continue in non-written forms (assuming responsibilities, creating associations, being involved in the community, establishing new family relations).

Changing the role of the educator is the deciding factor in establishing and running active centres for writing and interesting communication networks.

244

Three suggestions

1. People who are uneducated, people who are illiterate, have written. I have given an overview of our project and identified a number of signposts.

   I know that writing can be a process that raises questions and that requires an analysis of situations relating to the experience specific to disadvantaged adults.

   How can the fact that these people wrote, and how can the manner in which they wrote, yield findings useful to research? What role can those who have learned how to write play in analyzing and defining the way in which they learned? What, for them, is writing? How do they go about it once the door has been opened for them and they have been allowed to speak?

   The inner view: what do those who have been unable to write say once they themselves have succeeded in writing? And how do they go about it?

   To be continued - for researchers who take up the challenge.

2. For CLAP, in particular, and for other agencies sensitive to this initiative: is it possible to consider creating a place for publishing and distributing the material written by these people? Making written expression satisfying can also lead us to ask how to go about publishing the texts and disseminating them at a national or regional level. We are on the fringe, it is true, but we have to determine how to make use of normal publishing and distribution channels, on the fringes, obviously, because they are perhaps not always sensitive to this type of activity.

3. For writers (educators and learners): would it be possible one day to have in writing pages of history as told by those who lived it? We know the official history of immigration and racism, and we are familiar with a variety of analyses and interpretations. How can we make it possible for those who have

lived through history, and who continue to live it today, to write about the past and about history in the making?

Allowing those who are Excluded into the Royal Palace of Writing

THE ELOQUENCE OF THE BEDOUIN

At the Court of Baghdad, where, throughout the great Abbasid period, there reigned the highest expression of the majesty and power of cultural refinement and elegance in seigneurial clothing, one day a true Bedouin appeared, who had succeeded, after a considerable struggle, in convincing the guards that he should be allowed to read the King an enchanted poem.

Moreover, we know that it was not unusual for Moslem sovereigns from time to time to have genuine contact with their subjects.

This son of the desert, skin tanned, gaze fiery, exulting in a sacred fervour and bursting forth in a flood of disorganized and grandiloquent gesticulation, began to declaim a poem in which he successively compared the King to the most courageous of goats, the most ardent of rams, to a serpent which, in its meanderings and slitherings was agile and capable of blinding its adversaries with a single sting from its tail, and even to the sober and swift camel, the very epitome of endurance!

This poor presumptuous buffoon was met with a general outcry.

The courtesans drew their veils over their faces. Outraged by so much insolence and vulgarity, they demanded the supreme penalty for this agitator who had insulted the royal person.
Only the King, silent, listened attentively.

Finally, he handed down his sentence:
"Take this Bedouin, wash him, clothe him in the choicest garments, prepare a room for him in the palace and give him the freedom of the court for six months.

He has never known anything but a world of goats, rams, camels, serpents and asses. His speech therefore cannot draw upon anything else. But I heard his music: his speech is beautiful.

Let us give this son of the desert another world, and in six months we shall judge him."

The royal order was carried out and gave birth to one of the crowning glories of Arab poetry.[11]

Notes

1. The following comments were used as a basis for a presentation at the symposium organized by CLAP in Paris, 26-27 November 1990, entitled "non-writers and new integration dynamics".

2. *Alpha et promotion hebdo - la lettre du CLAP* 78, 6 April 1990, Guide d'action.

3. Supplement to *Alpha et promotion*: Le journal du Concours d'écriture, 12 issues May 1990-May 1991.

4. Cf. the many letters published in *Alpha et promotion*, *CLAP Info Rhône-Alpes* and the *Journal du concours d'écriture* (the competition journal).

5. Cf. Revuz, Christine. 1990. Moi, écrire? *Education permanente* 102, April.

6. Quoted from memory from Bakhtin.

7. Quote from a lecture by Philippe Meirieu.

8. See Note 5.

9. Ibid.

10. Ibid.

11. Maisonneuves, G.P. et Larose. [1979] *Traditions algériennes*. Republished in *Alpha et promotion hebdo - La lettre du CLAP* 19, 21 September 1990.

WORKING WITH ILLITERATE YOUNG PEOPLE IN A COMMUNITY GROUP: THE BOITE A LETTRES EXPERIENCE (1983-1987)

Sylvie Roy
Longueil, Montreal, Canada

My experience with the Boîte à Lettres in Longueuil extends from the birth of the organization in May 1983 (at that time, there were four of us, all graduates in remedial instruction from the University of Quebec in Montreal) until my departure in June 1987. Four years full of discoveries, accomplishments, fulfillment and doubts. Four of the best years of my life. The Boîte à Lettres still exists, but I will not say much about its current activities, as it is now being run and coordinated by a different team.

This document expounds the following observations:

- Teaching literacy skills to young adults is an extremely difficult task. Young people come to us after six, seven or even ten years of failure at school that has left them with a feeling of helplessness. They are then forced to come to the realization that responsibility for this failure cannot be assigned only to schools. In spite of all our teaching strategies and efforts, literacy training is still a painful and largely unsuccessful experience. Very few young people left the Boîte à Lettres knowing how to read and write adequately. The fact that there is so little improvement is just as discouraging for the young people as it is for us. Being in an extra-curricular setting, establishing small groups and linking reading to needs, are not enough for integrating reading and writing into the lives of illiterate young people. Our ambition of passing on "culture" does not work for everybody. Much patience and experimentation with new approaches and strategies are needed, in order to succeed in teaching young people, who have already been to school, to read and to write.

- Young people are not easy to recruit, and readily abandon the process of literacy training. For every young person who learns to read and to write, there are maybe seven or more who do not. It is not only a matter of shyness or of shame, but also of the *desire* to acquire this knowledge. There are many illiterates who function in society without feeling the need to learn to read. Radio, television and the oral transmission of knowledge help, in spite of everything, to integrate illiterates into society. However, society is organized according to written language, and thus, tends to exclude those who have not mastered its use.

- Illiterate young people often have other more urgent needs aside from learning to read. If we were able to achieve results, it was through satisfying emotional or social needs: the young people who passed through our organization became more at ease and more independent, took on responsibilities, became more confident, found employment, etc. Literacy training does not bring about such concrete or immediate results, and seems secondary in comparison to the other needs. The two most important needs for these young people remain work and their social and loving relationships (as for all of us, for that matter). It is by meeting these needs that young people will find a place in society, acknowledgement and a sense of self-worth.

Defeatist observations? I do not think so. However, it must be admitted that we are offering a skill that many do not deem essential to their lives, a skill that is pushed aside because of more pressing needs, and a skill that is passed on slowly and with great difficulty owing to certain cultural barriers. Without appropriate strategies where young people are concerned, learning to read and to write is a dead-end, a "school" assignment doomed to failure in all respects. Intervention strategies consist of ensuring that the young people come to the organization, stay, come back, acquire knowledge and the sense of group life, and carry out individual and group projects.

This document, first of all, consists of a brief portrait of the Boîte à Lettres and several profiles of illiterate young people, followed by comments. I then present some advice on the ways of working with young people in a community literacy group.

The Boîte à Lettres is a community group that was founded in 1983. Its mandate is to teach literacy skills to illiterate young people. The target population, initially young people between the ages of 16 and 22, was extended to people under 30 years of age.

The staff consisted of three or four group leaders who saw between 20 and 30 young people every year. The Boîte à Lettres is a member of the "Regroupement des groupes populaires en alphabétisation du Québec" (RGPAQ).

The concept of community literacy training goes well beyond the pedagogical context and underlies our entire work. Louise Miller, a RGPAQ official, defined it as follows at the international conference in Toronto, in September 1987:

> The concept of community literacy that we have adopted assumes that participants should be an integral part of their training, as well as their place of learning. There are three main aspects to community literacy training. The first is pedagogical and broadens the scope of literacy training, in the sense that it should not only amount to the acquisition of reading, writing and math skills. It also aims at developing general, practical, political, social and personal knowledge. It aims at providing individuals with the appropriate skills to be better able to control their working and living conditions. For us, this aspect can be fully achieved only through a group effort, in which the participant plays an active, and not a passive role.
> The second aspect is a political one. We mainly aim to reach out to people or social groups who do not have control of the means to improve their working and living conditions. Community literacy training aims at developing social and political awareness in participants, by developing the capacity for critical analysis, for choice of action and evaluation.
> The third aspect concerns social commitment. Our objective must always be to make the population aware of the problem of illiteracy and to fight for the rights of illiterates.

Here are three examples that illustrate how this definition is lived out on a day-to-day basis at the Boîte à Lettres.

- We organized *group projects* that go beyond the scope of the classes. The project represents something that is shared by the whole group, where everyone contributes according to their potential, and takes on responsibilities for carrying out the project. In 1985, we produced a video, in 1987, a newsletter and in 1989, a calendar. All the projects continue over time: over one year for the production of the video, distribution of the newsletter, calender sales. And soon the projects require the participation of the young people, which gives them a feeling of self-worth and the opportunity to express what is inside them. These projects have allowed reading and writing to become useful elements of communication in the lives of young people.

- We tried to *broaden general knowledge*. Without interest and intellectual curiosity, motivation quickly disappears. When young people are not aware of their environment and get by with secondhand information, it is extremely difficult to teach them to read. We must get young people used to relying on more than oral transmission in what they learn, by giving them the desire to verify the facts and to learn for themselves in books. Through information sessions, video presentations, and discussions, we have tried to give some "substance" to learning to read. In 1984 and 1985, the Boîte à Lettres organized theme sessions that brought together all interested participants. Failure at school, vacations, recreation activities in town, drinking, sexuality and computers were among the subjects that were discussed. These greatly appreciated evenings were an opportunity to get to know the various services in the area.

- We always adapted the teaching material to the reality of young people, in order to develop texts and show them that what they have said can also be written. We also placed great importance on the *composition of individual texts*. Whether it is by way of a book project, a book of poetry or a personal diary, we encouraged the young people to write, and then we used this material for reading purposes. This material informed us of the way the young people expressed their thoughts in writing, the vocabulary used and the mistakes that are generally made. This invaluable information enabled corrections and teaching to be tailored to the actual level of writing.

- We placed great importance on *raising awareness in the neighbourhood*. We wrote about our work, published reports and analyses of our experiences. We rarely refused interviews with the media in order to make known the problem of illiterate young people.

- The Boîte à Lettres always sought ways of *getting the young people involved* in the operation of the organization. There were between two and four general meetings with the young people per year, and a committee of the young people was formed from October 1984 to May 1987. The young people were integrated into the board of directors in September 1987, and staff selection was performed with their participation.

1. The Young People

1.1 *Individual portraits*

Pierre

Pierre comes from a family of nine children; his parents have received little education. His father is a self-employed trucker and Pierre is working with him while waiting to buy his own truck. He is muscular, imposing, proud of his body and of his numerous tattoos - and of the wad of bills he keeps hidden in his socks! He began attending special education classes in grade 5. Up until this point, he was only "annoying" - behind compared to others, he was left alone to sleep in his corner. He says that he was overwhelmed by the many changes in learning methods, by the noise in open-space classes and by individual work on paper. He dropped out of school after the short training program, because he did not want to be used as cheap labour in unpaid work projects. Since that time, he has been a truck driver and a furniture remover, at times living on unemployment insurance, sometimes on welfare - and also "moonlighting".

Pierre participated in the workshops on a fairly regular basis for a period of one year, and then dropped out for good, when the organization left his neighbourhood. Even though he finally felt treated as an equal by the teachers, his impulsive behaviour brought him back to the "silliness" of his childhood.

For a while, Pierre had an illiterate girlfriend, but perhaps they were too similar for the relationship to last. Later on, at a Christmas party, he introduced us to his new girlfriend. She is older than him and has a six-year old child. She also knows how to read and to write, and has no problem expressing herself. Pierre has his physical strength and his job to offer; his girlfriend, her skills in reading and writing, and sometimes her ability to act as interpreter, when Pierre is trying to find the right words. It is a wonderful sharing of strengths. Yet Pierre is no longer motivated to learn to read and to write, if he had ever been.

Luc

Luc was 22 years old when he came to the Boîte à Lettres, all six foot two and two hundred pounds of him, clutching a small piece of paper given to him by the vocational guidance centre: "This the school?" He did not seem too convinced from looking at the room! His wife had just given birth and he wanted to learn to read so as to help his child later on. He was a resourceful and hard-working young man, very aware of his responsibilities as a father.

Luc had been in special education classes since grade 4 and was left alone until grade 9. "I drank, I went out, I smoked; they let me get on with it". He knew the alphabet and recognized a few syllables, but was able to copy sentences perfectly that he did not understand. We were quite amazed at the schoolboy diligence he displayed when writing out the mural alphabet for us! Generally speaking, he behaved like the "brat" of his childhood days in the workshops. He did not do it maliciously, for it was the only way he knew. He stayed for three weeks.

We bumped into him a few years later - when taking a taxi. He had obtained his licence, the car was new and he was very proud of it. His wife was expecting her second child. He had no problem driving us to our destination, even though he did not know how to read. He was making a good living for himself, seemed happy, and the problem of illiteracy did not seem too heavy a burden. In fact, we did not dare to ask him.

Jean

Jean is one of the pillars of the Boîte à Lettres. He has been there since 1984 and hopes to be there for a long time to come. He comes to all the activities and all the workshops. He is the right-hand man for doing all the necessary odd jobs around the place.

Jean lives with his parents and pays them rent. He is a very friendly young man, is not shy, and wears clothes that are sometimes loud and out-of-date. He speaks quickly, mumbles and sometimes has to be asked to repeat what he has just said to be understood.

He has been looking for a job for quite a while, but his experience is limited to workplace training programs offered by the social assistance office. How enthusiastically he would talk about the job promises that his bosses had made him! We tried to make him more realistic, but to no avail. He came back to us depressed and unemployed after a few weeks. Eventually, he found employment through one of the young people at the Boîte à Lettres, but he left after six months. We wondered whether he would prefer to do odd jobs rather than apply himself to a nine-to-five schedule, at a minimum wage.

As far as we were concerned, Jean made little progress in reading and writing, although he himself claimed to be very satisfied. Yet, he still does not understand everything he reads, and writes with no regard for spelling; he is able to do three-digit multiplication, but gets lost when confronted with practical problems. For a period of one year, he worked on a project that was very dear to him: he wrote a book recounting all the years of his school life. Even though he only had a few pages, for Jean, it was a book: "I've succeeded in organizing my memories and I realized that I am not so stupid, it has made me think". He sells copies of his book, which we illustrated and photocopied, and he even visited a publisher to get it published. We do not know whether he should be brought back to reality or should be left to be pleased about himself, perhaps for the first time in his life.

For Jean, the Boîte à Lettres is a home environment. He remembers the exact date of his arrival, which dress I was wearing that day, and especially the time when Pierre listened to him when he was considering committing suicide. His memory, although surprisingly accurate in remembering emotional events, does not have the same capacity for learning to read.

Alain

Alain came to the Boîte à Lettres for two years, after which he remained periodically in contact with us. He had already taken literacy courses for two years in adult education. He was a complete illiterate, and still is and will probably remain so, even though he is intelligent, resourceful and motivated.

He was placed in a special education class starting in grade 2, the year his parents got divorced. At 16, he finished the short technical program in cabinet-making, and then participated in a few workplace training programs. He has always continued to take courses to overcome his illiteracy, which is unexplainable. He has been to see a doctor, undergone a battery of brain tests, has consulted a psychologist, all to no avail. Words always become mixed up in his head, he confuses sounds and inverts letters and syllables, in reading as well as in writing.

When he first came to the Boîte à Lettres at 23 years of age, Alain was a shy young man with a limited and repetitive vocabulary. He always repeated the last sentence that was said to him, without adding anything else of his own. He had a job, lived alone in an apartment and dressed with care. He did everything to be and to feel "normal". Since then, Alain has overcome his shyness, he laughs, has an easier time speaking and shows his emotions. The other young people have always shown him respect; he was in charge of an important part of the finances for the video project, which helped him to believe in himself.

Yet, his progress in literacy is almost nil, and it is extremely difficult to know why. Is it perhaps an emotional or neurological problem? He always says that the problem is fatigue or his glasses. He always carries a book, and says that he knows how to read. Where reading is concerned, as with other know-how, Alain seems incapable of admitting his disabilities. It is beyond him. He stopped coming to the classes for a while. He now has a girlfriend and too much work. It still does not stop him from appearing a little unhappy and from dragging around what he regards to be the problem of his life like a ball and chain.

Gilles

Gilles was 20 years old when he came to the Boîte à Lettres and remained with us for about a year and a half. He comes from a family of educated and well-off parents. His only brother is in a school adjustment class. Gilles is a good-looking young man who dresses in the latest fashions, drives a sports car, has no problem expressing himself and does so in a structured manner. He was considered dyslexic starting in grade 2 and has gone through a complicated and diversified process of school adjustment, which he talks about with cynicism and mockery.

His illiteracy did not stop him from taking a theatre course in college, because his mother did his papers for him. He works in a hospital as a ward master, and is thus the only unionized "young person" that we know. He left the Boîte à Lettres when he moved to Montreal with his girlfriend, who studies at university. Gilles made little improvement, but he reads faster and understands more. Illiteracy does not seem to get in the way of what he wants to do, for that matter. One can speculate whether the fact that Gilles comes from a well-off environment is enough to give him all he needs to succeed, in spite of being illiterate. And whether self-confidence, intellectual curiosity and richness of vocabulary, characteristics often associated with well-off backgrounds, are more important assets for success than literacy training.

Lucie

Lucie was 18 years old when she came to the Boîte à Lettres, directly after the end of her special education schooling and workplace training. She is a shy and sullen young lady. She is considered slightly mentally handicapped and lives with her family, who are not much help to her. She is always well dressed and her hair nicely arranged, but she is bored all day long. She is not on welfare, because her father says he is capable of supporting her. Her activities consist of wandering around shopping centres, sometimes baby-sitting and regularly attending the Boîte à Lettres. In spite of her regular attendance, she has made little improvement. One has the impression that she is playing "school", that she does not know what to do with her time and that her parents are getting rid of her, somehow, by entrusting her to us. After three years, we directed her towards recreation and job hunting activities, because there was no prospect of her learning anything and because we could not meet her needs of social integration.

Lucie experienced her withdrawal from the organization as a painful rejection; she has never really understood this decision. Our main mistake was not to have contacted her parents, in order to get them involved in a process of making their daughter a responsible person. On the pretext that Lucie was an adult, we let things go.

Lucie comes to see us once in a while and is always at the same stage: at 23 years old, she is still unemployed, still spends her time in shopping centres and is continuing her studies, this time in adult education. She still does not have any money, a job, or an activity to motivate her life as an adult.

Marcel

Marcel is an example of someone completely opposite to Lucie. He is slightly mentally handicapped, he knows it and accepts it. He has worked periodically in a sheltered workshop since completing his schooling. He has a difficult time expressing himself, sometimes talks to himself and lacks concentration. He prints in extremely large letters, but is very proud of being able to get by in arithmetic. He stayed for two years at the Boîte à Lettres. During this time, he learned to drive a scooter, found himself a job and a girlfriend. He has come back a few times to the Boîte à Lettres with his girlfriend, who also is mentally handicapped. They live in an apartment together, prepare their own meals, work and look after their budget. Their parents are available, but generally the couple manage without them.

Marcel may not know how to read and write (perhaps he will never know), but his time at the Boîte à Lettres has greatly helped him, by introducing him to young people who were not mentally handicapped and who have encouraged him to become independent and to communicate. The most important factor for Marcel remains the help and support of his parents. His mother has always maintained contact with us, and she has helped Marcel look for suitable employment, which could allow him to be independent.

The difference in the case of Lucy and of Marcel is perhaps between an indifferent environment and a motivating one, the difference between the future of a mentally handicapped young man and that of a mentally handicapped young woman.

Richard

Richard is a lively and resourceful 18 year-old. He is the youngest in a family of eight children. He went through elementary school in regular classes with some problems, and was placed in special education classes at the start of high school. He dropped out of school in grade 9. Since then, he has been doing odd jobs for members of his family. He now wants to finish high school and learn a trade. His motivation seems good and his achievement is relatively high; he understands what he reads and he writes phonetically. During the first class, he fitted in very well, he talked a lot and helped those who were having the most difficulty. It was stimulating. However, he never came back after the first class. I called his home two weeks later; his mother finally admitted to me that he had had the impression of being with "backwards" as in high school, and that he could not stand it. I was furious to think that Richard had dropped out, while he had a chance to succeed, because the atmosphere of the Boîte à Lettres reminded him too much of special education classes.

Ginette
Ginette is a regular of the Boîte à Lettres; she has been coming and going for three years. She is 23 years old and has two children. She is a plump, lively young woman who has been living with her boyfriend for quite some time. Her mother is illiterate and is taking adult education classes; it is through her that Ginette heard about the Boîte à Lettres. Ginette has a speech impediment, which was the reason why she was placed in special education classes starting in grade 1. Her five-year old child is showing signs of language problems, but that does not seem to be a problem for her and for her family. Moreover, she is very touchy in her role as mother, especially when given advice from single people.

Ginette participated in workplace training programs (with the Jeunes récupérateurs, in Longueuil) and found employment in a Montreal clothing factory. She earns \$150 per week, for 40 hours of work on her feet, barely a few dollars more than her social assistance benefits. She still has great difficulty reading and writing, but she is more self-confident and more socially integrated. Her relationship is holding together, her boyfriend works, and she has a supportive environment. Perhaps she will now be better able to help her child at school, if he is ever placed in "maturity classes". Let us hope that we will continue to be of support to her. If not, it will be still another example of illiteracy repeating itself from generation to generation.

1.2 *General comments*

The influence of environment of yesterday and today
Illiteracy, far from being an individual problem, is a problem of society, of poverty and of under-education. It is a phenomenon which has the tendency of being passed on from generation to generation, and which became apparent following the institution of mandatory schooling. Before 1948, lower-income groups did not have access to education. Illiteracy was a common and normal

occurrence. Now that knowledge is accessible, and even mandatory for all, it is disturbing to see that, in spite of the efforts of educational democratization, undertaken since the end of the sixties, lower-income groups "pass" through schools without acquiring the rudiments required in adult life, in an educated and industrialized society.

Parents of illiterate young people have often not received much education themselves. They cannot help their children, because they are quickly overtaken by new teaching methods and by all the requirements of schools. The value they assign to school is theoretical, because they have managed to get along in life without having to attend. Children cannot learn the joy or appreciation of reading, if there are not any books at home and if their parents never read or write. Young people are aware of this indifference and are more influenced by the behavior of their parents, rather than by the wonderful principles expressed by them.

André is a good example of indifference towards education; he was the youngest of a family of ten children and his parents never wanted to send him to school, so as to protect him from drugs and violence. André was completely illiterate at 21 years old.

Disadvantaged families tend, even today, to have a lot of children; it is not uncommon to see families of seven, eight or nine children. The number of children can influence the quantity and the quality of attention that each child receives. When one considers the importance of the role of parents during the first years of elementary school, it is a determining factor of success. It is therefore not uncommon to see several children of the same family all experiencing difficulties at school. The size of lower-income families can also bring about instability: they move frequently because of rent increases or because the parents change jobs. Some children may be temporarily placed in a foster home, following a work-related accident, a depression or divorce. These changes have negative effects on scholastic achievement and learning difficulties often begin from the time of these disruptions. As an example, let us take Stéphane, who was placed in a foster family for two years after his father's work-related accident. His father was in a coma for a year, and Stéphane naively wonders whether it has affected his achievement in school. Stéphane never stayed more than a year in the same elementary school!

If the social environment is sometimes a factor in failure at school, it is also a factor of illiteracy among young people. The environment of a 20 year-old has not really changed from the one in which he grew up at six years of age. Literacy training has to begin with this realization.

Scholastic progress

Illiterate young people are not drop-outs in the usual sense of the term. Drop-outs are young people who leave school before the end of high school, where they were in regular classes, and who can resume their studies at the point where they were abandoned, in schools that have been recently put at their disposal (what are referred to as "drop-out schools").

Illiterate young people do not come from regular classes. They have spent the majority of their schooling in special education. They may have completed their schooling, but without having necessarily achieved a satisfactory result, whether it is basic knowledge in French or mathematics, or learning a trade. Their scholastic achievements can be summed up as follows: special education classes starting in the first years of elementary school until grade 7, then the choice of doing the short vocational program, which offers the basics of a trade, which is sometimes completely outdated (weaving, for young women), or of doing one or two years of unpaid workplace training. This schooling is final and does not lead to a diploma. The young person who abandons the short vocational program at 13 years of age is no worse off than those who stay until they are 17 or 18 years old.

The only way out for a young person who wants to continue his education is to retake literacy training in elementary school, and to repeat, step by step, everything that he has just finished failing. What a great prospect!

"Learning" disabilities

It is difficult to determine the causes and consequences of the current disabilities of illiterate young people. Is it because special education classes are so unruly that they have such little concentration? Is it because they were distracted and temperamental that they were placed in special education classes? It is not easy to determine. What is clear is that these children come, for the most part, from undereducated, lower-income backgrounds and that the problems they were experiencing, perhaps at six years old, have not only not gone away, but have been maintained or amplified.

Young people experience numerous problems. Illiterate young people have a terrible fear of failure, which they have known throughout all their schooling. They consider themselves incompetent and stupid. The principal's office, other children and teachers, have all given them a negative image of themselves. Some have openly identified with it, others have contested it and have hidden themselves in a cloak of toughness or delinquency.

In general, only the minimum has been required of illiterate young people, and they have therefore not acquired work habits and self-discipline. They have constantly been in classes for the "mentally retarded", "poor mixers" and the "socially maladjusted", pupils having "severe or minor learning disabilities", etc. Even though they are not sure who they are, they do, however, consider themselves to be very "abnormal". Their education has been linear and dismal. Nothing really changed in the programs over the years. There was no logical progression towards grade 6 and the completion of elementary school. They also lost the fragile notion of time, and this has restricted their psychological development, as well as the establishment of long-term goals. They did not have the rightful ambitions of children regarding their future, nor goals in terms of improving their scholastic achievement, nor did they experience the sense of accomplishment of finally being the most senior pupils in their school and the most responsible.

They did not acquire the elementary curriculum, whether it be in French, mathematics, social sciences, natural sciences or geography. They did not acquire the idea of measurements; they have a difficulty estimating distances, weights and lengths. For them, everything takes on exaggerated and unreal proportions: they lost 30 pounds in one week, they have been working for two years (when it has been really only six months), they arrive an hour early for a meeting "so as not to be late".

In fact, they have often not achieved the ability of abstraction that is needed in developing concepts. The information they receive from the outside is not very structured: they have difficulty distinguishing the essential from the secondary, linking ideas, deducing and summarizing meaning. They have difficulty concentrating, memorizing and using logic in problem solving. They have difficulty with concepts that are unrelated to their immediate reality; they have difficulty generalizing from a hypothetical example.

Furthermore, they are very passive where learning is concerned. They want to learn to read, but without doing any work, waiting for the work of the teacher to take "its effect". The majority of them never had stimulating projects at school. They only learnt how to do nothing, to fill out pieces of paper and mindlessly to copy without end. In general, they did not learn how to establish objectives, to build a project and discover the ways of carrying it out. Never having been taken seriously, they often did not have any responsibilities to meet and no sense of worth in the assignments they did. For these young people, school was only a bad experience to get through. And for those who were lucky enough to have motivating and dynamic teachers, an atmosphere of happiness and personal development prevailed, to the detriment of a rigorous learning of French and mathematics. Moreover, this also threatens our efforts in literacy training, for it is much easier to observe improvement in social areas than in the area of cognition.

Faced with almost continuous failure, illiterate young people have created ways of camouflaging their problems; they have learnt to imitate and simulate. They have learned to find self-esteem with their peers by being the "worst", the most disruptive and the least good. Those who claimed to be succeeding were pushed aside and scorned. Once they had left school, this attitude of escape continued. They learned to rely on the people around them to offset their disabilities in reading and writing, and this attitude of dependence and of avoidance is so deep-rooted that it becomes a handicap when they now want to learn.

Intolerance and rejection
At a Halloween party, several young people were talking in the kitchen of the Boîte à Lettres, over beers and with music booming in the background. The topic of discussion was the atmosphere of the place. The participants who had been there the longest, who had collaborated on the video, were doing all the talking. Their feeling was that the Boîte à Lettres had changed, that the most interesting people had left because it was a waste of time, that nothing was being learned and that there were too many "morons". Everyone was listening carefully, even those described as being "backward". I was present in the discussion, without knowing how

to intervene. The judgements of young people can be so random! Some young people who are judged to be normal clearly have an intellectual handicap, whereas others are isolated simply because they are different in the way they look or the clothes they wear. The evaluation criteria of young people are very personal and depend very much on their past experiences in school. Those who are the most critical are not necessarily the most motivated to take on literacy training.

Young people scornfully reject the environment in which they went to school, even though they are still participating in the "silliness" they are denouncing. The world of special education classes is their obsessive fear and at the same time their security; they know nothing else. They prefer, without really choosing, to be the best among "problem" people than to risk being the worst among "normal" ones. Anybody who appears to be the least bit abnormal reminds them of their past. They do not have the confidence to break away from it and to define their own personality. They are very intolerant, which is apparent in their jokes, rejections and frequent departures from the organization owing to the presence of "the backward".

As group leaders, we are caught between two fires: encouraging understanding and respect, while at the same time accepting the aggressiveness of young people, who must regain confidence in themselves. They are so afraid of being deficient that it is difficult to ask them to be tolerant towards deficiency. In the same way, it is difficult to make them aware of their "silly" behaviour, as they have never gained self-confidence through learning accomplishments, and have known nothing else.

Communication

Many illiterate young people have difficulty expressing themselves. They repeat themselves, talk by way of onomatopoeia, gestures and without using the correct words. Group conversation is a challenge, with everyone talking without listening to the others. The group leader becomes the hub of eight monologues, which is demanding and unprofitable. Learning to talk and to listen is a long process, which will develop hand in hand with a better awareness of self and others.

The high point of non-communication came about when a group of Belgian illiterates were visiting us. It was a proper Tower of

Babel, and we were all speaking French! The vocabulary and expressions of the young people, both Belgians and Quebecois, were too limited for them to understand one another. The group leaders became interpreters in the discussion of our identical reality, the common feelings and similar failures at school. We realized that, because of literature and knowledge, we had access to an international language that goes beyond the scope of time and regionalism. Conversely, illiterate young people use language in a limited and local way. Their communication is orally based, from popular television and radio programs and no phrases or vocabulary of written language are used. The French spoken by Bernard Derome (a television news announcer) is like Chinese for the young people, as is the French of France or the Belgian French Community.

Luckily, the evening spent with the Belgians was a success. The young people felt the points they had in common more than they verbalized them. We laughed a lot about these linguistic barriers, and it was while doing the washing-up after the meal that we finally came together.

Love relationships

Many couples came together, thanks to the Boîte à Lettres. We saw several attempts as well as the successful creation of a few stable relationships. Many young people feel painfully alone and their main goal is to find a partner. We have found that this can become a good motivator in terms of attendance at the workshops. As it is often their first serious relationship, there are problems of insecurity, jealousy and exclusivity. I had a tricky time with a couple that had come together in my workshop, because the young woman saw me as a threat each time I spoke to the young man in question.

The context of the Boîte à Lettres facilitates interaction and makes it more secure, because the young people do not have to try to meet anyone. We sometimes reluctantly became intermediaries: the young people, incapable of talking directly to the interested person, would come to us to explain their desires and frustrations. We had to pass the message on.

The young people who succeeded in establishing a stable relationship quickly left the organization. One can imagine that they wanted to forget the context of their meeting as soon as possible, because it reminded them of a common past failure. Therefore, they left without having achieved their educational objective. Their main motivation became the material organization of their relationship: a shared apartment, money to be put aside, future plans, the hope of marriage. Learning to read disappeared with their other good intentions, until the pressing need comes back again. We are a long way from offering an essential and vital service, and we realize this each time there is any question of love or a new job.

The situation of young women
As there were generally fewer of them in special education classes in elementary school, there are not very many 20 year-old young women taking literacy training. Owing to their upbringing, young women are often more docile, and conform more readily to the discipline of schools, which gives them a better chance of passing elementary school classes. Young women fall behind in high school instead, especially in science and mathematics. Young women of today still make for traditional jobs, which are less fulfilling and less well-paid than those of young men. This is also true, if not more so, for young women in special education. In grade 8, in the short vocational program, the choices for young women are generally limited to weaving, cooking and sewing. One might as well say that they learn only daily domestic tasks and not the basics of a trade. Although there is not much variety, the choice for young men is somewhat more interesting: cabinet-making, automobile body work and repairs, bookbinding and mechanics.

Regarding workplace training programs, they offer young women a continuation of their position as women and as mothers: looking after children in a daycare centre or working in a cafeteria or in clothing production. Their access to the job market is very limited.

Illiterate young women, being generally responsible for children, are more dependent than young men. They want to have children because it is a sign of social success. They can finally "make something that is beautiful", and do it as well as any young woman who has been to school. While maternity represents a new motivation for learning, it can also bring about greater isolation or impoverishment. If a separation occurs, the young woman finds herself alone with the financial burden of a child. Day-care being expensive, it is difficult for these mothers to contemplate going back to school or work, which requires great amounts of energy and motivation, especially when one is illiterate.

Illiterate young women who have a literate partner often live in a double dependency: financial dependence and that of not knowing how to read. This leaves them unsure of themselves and confines them in a traditional role. They must rely on their partner's money and ability to read. It is difficult for them to conceive of separation, for they have few resources of their own.

In the case of an illiterate young man with a literate young woman as a partner, it is often a much more balanced relationship: mutual dependence establishes equality. The illiterate partner provides his strength of being able to work and financial security, but he needs the abilities of his partner, in order to be able to read and pay bills and to fill out forms. The woman has more respect, because she contributes to the relationship by way of her abilities. The male, who has a job, is nonetheless better viewed socially, work being more valued than the ability to read. We have known several illiterate young men living in this situation of interdependence. In general, it resulted in fairly egalitarian and more stable relationships.

Particular importance has to be given to young women in our recruitment, in order to help them overcome their lack of confidence, to encourage them to go as far as they can with their abilities, to help them, in real terms, to find babysitters for their children, to get out of the house and to find a job.

Expectations regarding literacy training
Young people come to the Boîte à Lettres for very specific reasons: the insistence of a new partner, spare time between jobs, the prompting of a social assistance officer, the birth of a child, etc. They want to read and to write, but they especially want to be independent (in relation to their parents, their family), to have "a job, a boyfriend or a girlfriend". The need to read and to write is associated with being normal; it is vague and imprecise. They want to be dubbed "normal", as if they were wearing a label, but at the same time they have always been capable of managing without knowing how to read and to write. They thus have a difficult time knowing how to integrate this new knowledge into their lives.

Young people want to learn to read above all for practical reasons, such as being able to read the newspaper on the bus in the morning, to read letters they have received and to fill out forms by themselves. Some even want to acquire a school-leaving certificate, but there are not many of these. Reading is a tough necessity that has nothing to do with pleasure, relaxing and the need for knowledge. They do not live in an environment where books and magazines are very common, and their intellectual curiosity is affected by this.

When they come to the Boîte à Lettres, the young people are also looking for a place of social interaction, a place where they will be treated equally and respected as adults. If they are looking for someone to talk to, they particularly want to be taken seriously. For the most part, these expectations have been largely met: the Boîte à Lettres has become a reference point, a stable and friendly place for socializing. The very fact that we existed, that we represented a different type of school and a different image of teachers seemed sometimes enough. The young people derive self-confidence and trust from the Boîte à Lettres, even if they only come once in a while.

We can sum up the expectations formulated by the young people as follows: to learn to read and to write, to have a job, to find a partner and to have friends. Paradoxically, our role is to meet the first need, but it is in relation to the other expectations that we obtain the best results, particularly in respect of improving one's way of life. Reading and writing remain the most ambiguous objective and the most difficult to attain.

2. The Community Group for Literacy

2.1 *Making known the organization*

Raising awareness
Raising awareness consists in making known the problems of illiteracy among the people in the area. This could include the general population, the leaders of community groups and those in charge of public organizations and teachers in elementary or high schools. The facts of illiteracy have to be made known, its symptoms and causes explained and the possible remedies widely circulated, however modest they might be. An action of social importance must be reflected in an articulate way, in order to reach a wide public.

For the Boîte à Lettres, this objective has been a constant worry. We have published two research reports that we have circulated on every possible occasion. We have produced a video that we have shown to various audiences. We have created a newsletter from texts written by the young people. We have rarely refused interviews. All this has enabled us to become legitimate spokespersons. This is also apparent by the various invitations we have received, one of which was to represent Canada at UNESCO, in 1986, at a conference on illiterate young people.

Raising awareness in the area is one of the main responsibilities of community organizations. From my experiences of raising awareness, three thoughts stand out:

* <u>The promotion of awareness must not replace action.</u>

> At a certain point, we had the impression at the Boîte à Lettres that our best work was in raising awareness, and not the work we were doing with young people. In two years of existence, we had not stopped talking about our work. Yet, everything we do is based on our work with young people. It can be dangerous to become experts in a subject: one can gradually lose contact with reality, which is itself constantly evolving. It should be mentioned that the fact that we were the only ones who were specialized in the field of literacy training for young adults pushed us to the forefront of the scene and demanded our constant presence.

* <u>There are certain dangers for the young people who are involved with the task of raising awareness.</u>

> At the Boîte à Lettres, we have always sought the involvement of the young people in this task, because it is a question of their reality. Their quotes were the basis of the first study, their personal accounts were at the heart of the video, and several media interviews were carried out with their collaboration. However, it is disturbing to realize that these young people, who previously were of interest to no one, became the objects of much fascination because they were illiterate! The press is eager for copy of this kind which it can denounce. Journalists look for the worst cases, denouncing the school system, or rouse the public with success stories of people who have overcome their illiteracy.

In spite of ourselves, we were involved with this sudden infatuation, without always considering the consequences. In the face of all this interest, the young people reacted by ending up saying what was expected of them. We were astonished to hear them say that they had never learned anything at school and that, since they had been at the Boîte à Lettres, their lives had radically changed. This was far from being the case! The young people were becoming naive victims of the media. For these young people, who have difficulty estimating time, this sudden review of their lives was not particularly beneficial. I remember very well Alain's indignation while looking at his photograph spread out across a full page of *La Presse* newspaper, under biased quotes from what he had said in confidence.

One must therefore be very careful regarding the role played by the young people in raising awareness, to ensure that the young people themselves get something worthwhile and positive out of it. They are not zoo animals to be put on display to satisfy the curiosity of scandal-mongers.

* The promotion of awareness must especially not be confused with recruitment.

Raising awareness may have a certain effect on recruitment, but this effect is uncertain and indirect. Recruitment is a different task altogether, much more concrete and demanding, which calls on the skills of the group leader and not the explanations and speculations of the intellectual.

Recruitment

Recruitment is an essential task in the operation of a service such as ours. Our challenge is considerable, for illiterates are not easy to reach. On one hand, many of them do not see illiteracy as the problem that society considers it to be. On the other hand, illiterates generally do not call on public or community services. They manage to get by themselves as best as they can, relying especially on the help of those in their immediate surroundings. Those who want to learn to read often live with their illiteracy as a defect that has to be concealed.

Young people live in situations that make recruitment even more difficult. They have just recently left school and feel like doing something else: find a job, get by or "live their life". For the time being, they write off "school" learning and try to succeed in other areas. We offer an essential service, but one that is difficult to "sell", especially to those concerned. Our job consists of informing young people that there are services available to them and that they can use them, when they feel they are ready. The fewer the intermediaries between the young people and ourselves, the better the recruitment.

The most common methods of recruitment include articles in regional newspapers, simple and appealing flyers and visits to community and public organizations to leave posters, flyers and to meet with those in charge. We used these methods for a long time, but they did not bring about as many results as anticipated. After four years, the Boîte à Lettres has become known as a reliable and serious service. However, the number of participants has not greatly increased, maintaining itself between 20 and 25 young people for the Longueuil area and surroundings.

Why has recruitment stagnated? It is easy to feel guilty and to imagine that the young people are not satisfied with what we are offering them. Yet, we are not responsible for the fact that literacy training is not an essential need on the same level as finding food, clothing and shelter. We are not responsible for the fact that literacy training is a long and demanding process that confronts people with their past failures, and whose results are far from being guaranteed. But it seems to me that our recruitment efforts were performed in a timid and limited way.

Through our actions, we can have an influence in the areas where illiteracy is likely to be found. We have to be animators outside of the Boîte à Lettres, before the process of literacy training begins. And this is what is the most demanding. The task is not easy to plan, it must be done as we go, using every favourable opportunity.

Recruitment is a crucial task that involves continuity, objectives, an action plan and the designation of those responsible. This task is similar to that of a "street" worker: it means GETTING OUT of the building, going to hand out leaflets and talking with people in the subway, at entrances to banks on every first of the month, when social assistance payments are sent out, in shopping centres, in youth centres. On these occasions, one often sees the same people, one learns to understand daily problems, and little by little, people get to know who you are. One learns where the young people spend their time and discovers the resource people and leaders in the area. This "street" work can provide us with much information on illiterate young people, drop-outs and the unemployed. It can help us to know what their concerns and reservations are with respect to literacy.

Reception of the young person into the organization consolidates the initial work of recruitment. It is important that this work be done continuously and not only in September and January. The turnover being quite high, the young people concerned must be able to benefit from the service as soon as there is an available space. The effectiveness of the reception and the positive impression of the first interview are elements that will determine whether the young person will continue the process. For each person who agrees to take courses, there are at least five people interviewed who do not.

Waiting lists are, wherever possible, to be avoided. The first interview must happen quickly, even if there are no available places. This meeting enables us to see whether the organization corresponds to the needs of the person, or whether they should be directed elsewhere. The interview is a further introduction for the illiterate person, an opportunity to become acquainted with the place and the people who come to the organization.

At the Boîte à Lettres, the initial interviews lasted one to two and a half hours. We took whatever time was needed, for the interview is very revealing. There was no one in charge of the interviewing, everyone took part in it in turn. This enabled us to be in continuous contact with the young people, instead of being confined to running workshops.

The interviews were conducted only with the young person: the people that accompanied them had coffee with another group leader in the kitchen. The interview was conducted from a series of questions on scholastic achievement, family situation, work experiences, and the young person's own explanation of his or her learning disabilities and objectives. We used a test consisting of three different levels of difficulty in French and mathematics. We also asked questions on general knowledge and geography. During the interview, we avoided taking notes so as not to intimidate the young person. The transcript of the information obtained will be very useful for painting a true picture of the young people who have been to see us and for improving our work with them.

At the latest, we try to give an answer three or four days after the interview. If there is no space available, we try to call the young person often to invite them to a party, an evening information session, in short, to remind them that we care about them and that we want them to continue the initiative.

2.2 *The team*

Two conditions are essential to belonging to a community group for literacy: experience or training in teaching, in elementary school if possible, and experience or ability in leading a group. It is not easy to be a teacher and a group leader at the same time. We have constantly wavered back and forth between these two poles. Sometimes we let the teaching go, to spend time only on suppers, meetings and activities with the young people. We were delighted with the group spirit and the crowd who came to the Boîte à Lettres, but the progress made in French was not substantial. We shut ourselves up in our offices to prepare exceptional material, but we no longer had the time to talk to the young people! In this case, as in others, a balance must be found and constantly revaluated.

"Good" teachers

The Boîte à Lettres was established by four graduates of the Bachelor of Education in school adjustment program. Although the staff has undergone many transformations since the beginning and their experiences have been diversified, I am still convinced that experience in teaching is a major asset when forming a group, because our goal is to teach reading and writing. The training in remedial instruction gave a certain distinctness to the Boîte à Lettres; we had been trained to teach young people six years younger than they were. Through our teaching practice in schools, we had experienced special education classes and saw the qualities that were required to teach them. We knew the reading methods, the school programs and the teaching material at elementary school level.

Our training enabled us to focus on elementary school and high school, to have a certain amount of access and to understand what really goes on there. The lack of ties between teachers who teach in elementary school and high school and those who work in adult education, especially in community groups, is a serious problem.

There is a wall of suspicion and ignorance separating each sector, which divides up the task of teaching and prevents an overall vision of teaching. It has very often happened that we met elementary school teachers who did not show any interest in literacy training, whereas the learning disabilities begin right in elementary and get worse from there!

We met with special education teachers at the elementary school level with the goal of getting to know their teaching methods and their material. Our training in remedial instruction made us more demanding in terms of teaching. We did not want to re-create, as is the case in some special education classes, a free atmosphere of activity and of warm contact in which learning to read comes last. We wanted to offer a program that was as structured as possible, to allow the young people gradually to evaluate themselves and to demand the best of themselves. This was the basis of our faith in their abilities.

Teaching networks
Working in literacy training is restricting and demanding. We continually need to rethink our approach, evaluate our actions, define our objectives and find appropriate material. It is not as if the wheel has to be reinvented: educational research has already been done, and the material intended for children from disadvantaged areas, the methods of training and evaluation, and the literacy learning methods, deserve to be studied carefully. It is a question of taking out what is useful and adapting it.

In 1984, teaching was only one of the many subjects discussed in our meetings, where we also discussed finances, internal management, etc. These meetings were held too frequently (one a week) and had too many items on the agenda to be effective. In 1987, we organized monthly staff meetings devoted solely to teaching. These were prepared and presented by the person in charge of the item, and gave us time to discuss a theme and to expand on it according to our practical experience. We also turned to resource people from the teaching field. We met with other literacy teams to discuss our similar practical experiences: evaluation of teaching methods, strategies to be adopted concerning mathematics, questioning of failures and development of teaching projects.

The most important thing for the staff, whatever the method being used, is to remain open-minded, freely to admit the problems and weaknesses, to define the teaching needs and to go and find resources where they can be found.

Good group leaders

To work in a literacy group, it is not enough to just be a "good" teacher. One must consider oneself a group leader and want to take action beyond that which is pedagogical, in the very lives of the young people. Often, it is through the consistency and the quality of our action that we are able to establish a link with young people, and provide support that enables them to keep going in this very slow and difficult learning process. If this support is not provided, the young people will readily abandon the class and not come back to inform us of their problems or achievements.

The young people come to us for overall support. They do not break down their needs. If they recently went through the break-up of a relationship or left a job, they cannot be receptive to learning. Their world is susceptible to all kinds of disruptions. Young people will not remain long in courses that are difficult and that fail to contribute to their self-esteem. We must therefore take all these factors of motivation and demotivation into account. For the young people who have just spent six to ten hours on our premises, the organization is a reference point.

Being a group leader can involve many different things from the most insignificant to the most fundamental. Going to have supper at Michel's place to help him and his partner with their decision regarding the continuation of a pregnancy. Having a coffee with André, because he feels like committing suicide. Staying after class, sometimes for an hour, because the young people simply feel like talking. Helping Line who wants to leave her boyfriend and at the same time sort out her drug problem. Finding activities for Robert, who is bored. Having supper every second night with the young people who arrive an hour before the class starts. There is no end!

It is obvious that one must not take oneself for God Almighty (or Mother Theresa, depending on the case) and try to solve all the problems. We are, first and foremost, a group devoted to literacy, and the young people should clearly be aware of this. But one must be attentive, agree to listen to them and to talk, and then direct them to the appropriate services. The young people must especially not be left isolated to face their problems.

Service networks

The primary source of services is the staff itself, which represents a place of exchange and mutual help. Group leaders must not carry the weight of their actions alone; the whole team must be behind them. The consistency of the staff will in this way be felt by the young people, and will be a positive factor in maintaining a stable atmosphere. One has to know how to get organized; the team can establish a rotating schedule for availability to the young people.

Following this, other services can come from different sources; the important thing is that they must allow young people to be seen in their total situation, and not just as illiterates. The Youth Advisory Bureau (YAB) is a good service: it offers a series of workshops and conferences on the subject of young people and work, drugs, school and sexuality. The Local Community Service Centres (LCSC), which have the mandate of providing preventive health measures and of organizing community service, can also provide interesting workshops on the health of young people and sexuality. The people who work in the area of preventing school drop-outs can also shed some useful light, as can community groups that deal with housing, prostitution, etc.

I remember a meeting that was held of a few dozen community organizations that work with young people across the province of Quebec. Religious groups had called the meeting to discuss the priorities of young people. This meeting of exchange was very worthwhile and enabled us to include literacy in the overall needs of young people.

2.3 *The life environment*

First of all, the atmosphere of a supper: "happy hour" before classes begin (a memory of autumn 1986):

> Johanne quickly finishes her photocopying; she wants to have the time to go outside before the whirlwind starts. The telephone rings; it's Julie who takes ten minutes to explain that she will be arriving a little bit late. As always, André is the first to arrive at 5 o'clock. He goes to buy himself something to eat in the restaurant downstairs. At the beginning of the month, he has his meal of the day; at the end, he only has some french fries, but then he says that he is not hungry.
>
> Suddenly, a radio is heard; that must be Claude who has just arrived. Dragging his feet, he goes into the kitchen to have a coke

(sometimes he has to be asked whether he paid for it or not!). He then goes and sits down in the living area without taking off his leather jacket, even though it is boiling hot in the room. Ginette comes in and sits down in the kitchen laughing. She is more than likely taking a break from her duties as a mother by arriving early. As for me, I have to go and buy some cheese, I rush out and pass three people coming up the stairs. Soon, there are twelve of us in the tiny kitchen. Six people are sitting down, trying to eat, while the others are standing, jammed between the chairs and the cupboards. The living area is empty. Perhaps Carole has arrived; being a shy person, she must be studying in her classroom. It is becoming very loud in the kitchen; Denis is eating food from the young people's plates. Everyone quite enjoys it really, except me of course!

I have a headache; I am trying to think about my class, but two people are talking to me at the same time. I have to make them understand that I am not a tape recorder! I am also concerned about Jean-Pierre, who has not been heard from for two weeks.

There is discussion going on in the hallway, and this is blocking the way; Denis is talking to Lucien about the articles that are posted on the bulletin board. Johanne takes advantage of the crowd of people in the kitchen and a miraculous lull in the conversation to remind everybody of the agenda of the next general meeting, and invites everybody to attend.

To set an example, we grab two of the young men at random and do the dishes. Denis has already slipped away, because he has to work on the reading text for his workshop, and as it is already six-thirty. Claude has taken over the telephone, talking to his partner for the last half an hour; he most likely feels that it is quieter here than at home! I am going to have to go and talk to the new addition, he looks isolated in his corner. But Alain has gone over there, well done! Michelle is keeping an eye on the door; for two weeks, Pierre has not been calling her and her only chance of seeing him is here. I would swear that right now it is her biggest motivation for coming to the Boîte à Lettres. It is the opposite for Gérard and Manon: since they have been together, we do not see them any more.

The workshops will be starting in three more minutes. I finish my dessert, and I grab another coffee as I pass by. The young people are already settled, except for Pierre who adamantly insists that Denis go and see his "new set of wheels". Quick, it is already seven o'clock!

For the young people, taking courses is extremely demanding. The group atmosphere and the availability of the group leaders are essential motivation factors. We have to create and operate a "life environment"; generally speaking, this begins with the careful choice of location for the classes. The Boîte à Lettres has known three different locations and I will describe them briefly, and then sum up the essential conditions that constitute a life environment.

The initial location was a small, three-room commercial suite, located on the second floor of a pizza restaurant on Chemin Chambly. In the neighbourhood there was a greengrocer's, a garage, a hotdog stand and a shopping centre. The young people lived in this neighbourhood and felt at home there. Inside the premises, the décor was awful, but we left it that way, because of lack of money and time. As one came up the outside staircase, the young people would be sitting on the steps talking and watching people pass by. The place was well liked by the young people. As there was no room for privacy, we spent our time there informally and without fear of getting anything dirty. The atmosphere was very cosy. At this time, our teaching material was very basic and of poor quality, but our availability was unlimited. We were intrigued by the young people, and the literacy training was a learning experience, full of daily surprises. We stayed there for a year and a half.

The second location was very different and so were our expectations; we wanted to have something pleasant, big and clean. We moved onto the third floor of a building in the old part of Longueuil. It had six rooms with hardwood floors. It was wonderful! We decorated it and purchased office furniture. The young people were not too fond of this place, nor of the prevailing atmosphere. Everything was too practical, too defined in terms of its use. Sometimes our office door was closed because one of us wanted to work in peace. The young people felt that they did not belong there outside of class hours, and did not know their way around Longueuil's chic neighbourhood. In addition, the inside stairwell, which led up to the third floor, gave the premises the look of an office. After two years, we moved again.

The third location, which I have not worked in, seems to be a good compromise between the two previous ones. The Boîte à Lettres resettled in the working-class neighbourhood, above a video club. In the area was a cheap restaurant, a garage, some shops and street life. The stairway is on the outside and from the large windows we can see the commercial streets below. The premises are easy to locate and easily accessible. All the rooms open up into a large kitchen.

I can recall these few thoughts on looking for a good "life environment".

*   <u>One should consider the neighbourhood when choosing premises</u>

    Even if the rooms correspond to our needs and the place is easily accessible by public transport, it is pointless to set up shop on a back street, where there is nowhere to have coffee, to shop etc. Setting up in neighbourhoods where the young people never go is to be avoided.

*   <u>The young people prefer to have direct access to the premises from the outside</u>

    The young people like to sit on the steps of the stairway or on the balcony; they can see people arriving. Furthermore, a door that opens direct on the exterior has the advantage of not giving the impression of entering into the waiting room of an office, where no one is supposed to make any noise and must wait their turn. The premises must look more like a house than an office.

*   <u>Find a balance between the likes of the young people and those of the group leaders</u>

    The young people could have a room for chatting without bothering anyone, for watching television or listening to music. In practice, it is difficult to organize this area. The young people do not come there every day as we do, they do not have any shared ideas on decorations, and it is often our company that they are seeking. But it is possible to let the young people have their say in the layout, the decoration and the use of the rooms.

*   <u>Even if the premises are adequate and in a good neighbourhood, they are useless if they are not accessible outside of class hours</u>

    The young people have to feel that they are not bothering anyone when they come to the premises, and that these also belong to them. For this, a permanent and specific schedule is needed, in order to ensure consistency. We were open Monday to Thursday, from two o'clock to ten o'clock. Friday was devoted to meetings or to days off, and the mornings to the individual work of the group leaders.

Yet a life environment is brought about primarily by the availability and the presence of the group leaders. Exchanges should be numerous, spontaneous and not too structured (" Okay, you want to talk to me, how about next Wednesday at two thirty?"). Availability is to drop what you are doing to spend half an hour chatting with a young person. It is to accept the fact that, during the hour before classes begin, there is going to be noise, laughter, the television and the radio, and continual coming and going. Availability happens spontaneously; important meetings are often held on the edge of a table, during washing-up or over coffee. This in no way replaces the need for occasional meetings and for more structured interviews; but spontaneous availability must be the backdrop of communication with the young people.

* A suitable place for learning all forms of reading

Learning to read must go beyond the framework of the courses and slowly become part of the lives of the young people. This is why we built up a library of over a hundred new, appealing and easy-to-read books, with the collaboration of the City of Longueuil Library: comic books, books for the participant's children, fairy tales, short novels and simplified books on science, health, natural phenomena, etc. The books were placed out in the open: by introducing them into the classes and by organizing a personal loan system, an attempt was made to encourage reading. It was still not a service that was used very much, but books were part of the visual surroundings. We also purchased magazines that are likely to be of interest to the young people; we left them lying around in the workshops, in the kitchen and in the washrooms. Furthermore, a lot of signs had to be put up, in order to accustom the young people to look at written messages and to ask themselves what they mean. There was therefore a place in the washrooms for graffiti (that we ourselves conscientiously filled), bulletin boards where photos of the most recent parties were displayed, newspaper clippings, a humorous cartoon, etc. The agendas of general meetings were posted right at the entrance, in order to catch people's eye (we paid particular attention to the visual presentations of our posters). As finishing touches, there were calendars on which the dates of parties and important events were marked, as well as all kinds of posters. The premises "displayed" their raison d'être, and the message has constantly changed, in order to retain people's interest.

Ideally, I would have preferred that the locale should be also a place for working individually and independently between workshops. The young people could have access to material prepared in advance, in the form of graduated and self-correcting work sheets, or diskettes of exercises for working on the computer. In this way, the young people would have the chance to acquire work habits by becoming more responsible, in terms of their learning objectives. We would be available, but the young people could just as well get organized by themselves. It is a project that we have often talked about, but which has yet to become a reality.

3. **The Community Group in its Environment**

3.1 *Knowing the environment*

Community groups are part of a movement that has its own history and characteristics so far as the population, the economy, housing and education are concerned. To be part of a movement, is to take part in discovering all aspects of it. To know a city or a neighbourhood is to discover, through reading, meeting people and strolling around, the history of the city, the crime rate, suicide rate, school drop-out rate, the recreation activities, community struggles and the movements of the population. It is not an easy task, daily work is so engrossing that this examination of the area is often forgotten.

The Boîte à Lettres is situated in Longueuil, a city on the outskirts of Montreal, which obviously does not have all the services and infrastructure of the big city. Longueuil is a "big village" that has experienced a very disorganized urban development. Side by side are gigantic shopping centres, old country cottages, office towers and modestly priced apartments. The city is not divided up into neighbourhoods as is Montreal; the parishes are still very much involved with the activities of young people and the elderly. There are two Local Community Service Centres, three Travail-Québec centres as well as three high schools in a radius of four square kilometres. There are also two libraries, a college and a lone metro station, which is a big meeting place because it is also the last stop of all the bus routes on the South Shore.

According to the 1981 census, there are 125,000 residents, of whom 22 percent are between the ages of 15 and 25. Community groups are also well represented: almost all of the people who work in this district know each other, as either friends or acquaintances. The city provides help to these community groups, and also the possibility of using various premises and its printing services. But its priority remains organizing sports for young people. Communication between community groups, as well as with public organizations, is easier in a city like Longueuil, than in the bureaucratic sluggishness and anonymity of Montreal. Yet, in spite of my four years of work in this city, my knowledge of the area is still poor and mainly amounts to awareness of community groups and public organizations that have ties with young people.

If illiterate young people are considered an entirely separate group having many different needs, literacy training being only one of the many, knowing the area is essential for referral purposes.

Like most young people of their age, illiterate young people are concerned about finding employment; for them, it is the first basic condition of entering into the real world of adults and of attaining a certain financial independence. Young people also want to leave home, find a place to stay and establish a love relationship. As much as having a relationship, the idea of having their own place brings about a feeling of real freedom with respect to their parents. This does not mean that their plans always work out, but they remain a priority in the minds of these young people.

For some, other problems are more urgent: settling a difficult separation, getting out of drugs, finding an apartment or facing psychiatric problems. Even if they were illiterate, many only stayed for an interview and went back to their world, without our being really able to help them. At least we know that they are aware of our organization and could come back.

We must therefore see ourselves as one of the links in a chain of co-operation that unites the organizations working with young people. Mutual awareness of services and fast and direct referrals are essential.

3.2 *Community groups*

Our closest allies in meeting the needs of young people remain the other community groups. Together, we share similar objectives, have a flexible structure and common demands. It would not be incorrect to say that in the beginning, each group considers itself to be the most important. There is a danger of competing against each other for subsidies and for attracting "clients". This attitude in no way helps the work we are doing. On the contrary, open-mindedness and frankness is what should be developed, if one wants to learn from others and better understand our environment.

We can establish our community alliances according to two axes: the horizontal axis, for those who offer community literacy training, and the vertical axis for those who work with young people.

Youth networks

The organizations in Longueuil with whom we are associated are as follows: the Youth Advisory Bureau, the Youth Centre, Entretemps (short-term and middle-term accommodation), the Jeunes récupérateurs (employment program), SEMO (an employment service funded by the Canadian employment service before it disappeared in 1986) and the Young Catholic Workers (YCW). We often work with the same young people, but for different reasons.

The Boîte à Lettres was a member of a youth consultation committee in Longueuil for several years. This coalition wanted to define a series of rights for young people, to provide help to groups and to establish better coordination with respect to municipal, provincial and federal authorities. Participating in this group was a really worthwhile experience for us. We became familiar with our community, its services and its projects. We committed ourselves to defending the other groups, when there was a question of closing down services, the reduction of a subsidy or outside interference. It was together that we were able to establish a common position on the services that were needed in Longueuil, in order to meet the needs of young people, and also on the support we were expecting from the municipality and public organizations.

For our part, we explained the problem of the relatively unknown phenomenon of illiteracy to the leaders of youth groups. We shared our experiences regarding the channels of school adjustment, vocational paths that do not lead anywhere, such as the short vocational program and workplace training programs. Through our work, youth groups are now becoming more concerned with the educational side of their objectives and defend it before the public authorities concerned.

For several years, we have had strong links with the organization, "Les Jeunes récupérateurs", which provides young people with job training and a sense of responsibility. The goal is to provide them with a positive experience of four to six months and to facilitate their introduction into the job market. Several of our young people participated in the Jeunes récupérateurs program. The young people continued to come to their literacy classes in the evenings and the businesses took this into account in their work schedules. We were frequently in contact with the group leaders in order to track progress and to discuss any difficulties. For several young people, this experience enabled them to find steady employment.

Collaboration in referrals between youth groups is not carried out in a bureaucratic way. We know the people who work in the organizations and know that the young people will be quickly and unfussily accepted by them. To preserve a harmonious link between these groups, communication must be continually maintained. One cannot rely on reputations, whether they be good or bad. One has to make the rounds, to learn about other groups and to make oneself known, for the structures change and the staff turnover is quite high. Invitations are sent out about once a year to the various organizations to come and visit the Boîte à Lettres. It is a time for discussion, for showing our working material and the video and for introducing the new staff members. This mutual awareness will help the group leaders when referring young people to an appropriate service.

The "Regroupement des groupes populaires en alphabétisation du Québec"
Since it was founded, the Boîte à Lettres has been a member of the Regroupement des groupes populaires en alphabétisation du Québec (RGPAQ). We have participated in all the meetings and have been involved in working groups as well as the coordinating committee. For us, the Regroupement is essential. It does not simply exist so we can obtain better subsidies. Literacy training is a an increasingly widespread social concern in different segments of the population. Alternate solutions urgently need to be supported in the traditional

school system. There is not only one approach to learning, and non-governmental organizations are the proof of this, through organizing training on a smaller scale, according to the needs of the different segments of society they serve.

Community education is continuously threatened with extinction or take-over. In the province of Quebec, the government spent $25 million in 1989 for literacy training. Community groups only received $2 million of this money, a budget that is frozen from year to year.

We must be a national movement to ensure the survival of community education. Through the Regroupement, we pool our ideas and analyses based on our respective experiences. We expand our vision of literacy through the groups that work with target segments in urban and rural areas. Each contributes to improving the overall picture.

Since it was founded, the RGPAQ has helped to put the question on a political and social level, in such a way as to affect public opinion, as well as that of public authorities. While we are recognized as an essential partner on a national level, as we are internationally (UNESCO and the International Council of Adult Education), the RGPAQ and its member groups receive only a small part of the available funding.

3.3 The "non-organized" partners

The immediate surroundings of illiterate people
Our partners in the work of literacy training are, first of all, the people who are close to the young people in question. The collaboration that we hope for must not be perceived as paternalistic interference, nor as proof that the young people cannot take care of themselves. The immediate surroundings include the parents, partners, friends, and brothers and sisters of the young persons taking literacy training. Their attitudes can have a major effect on the behaviour of young persons with regard to their learning.

Some of those closest to the young people express feelings of indifference and contempt towards those in literacy training. They never ask questions, and do not offer any real assistance in the learning. They have already adopted the opinion of the school system and have classified the young person among the "incompetents". This contempt is overwhelming for the young person and it leaves them completely uninterested, as in "elementary school" times.

In some cases, however, those who are close to the young person are too protective; they write letters for the young person, pay the bills, read the mail and drive the young person to wherever he or she has to go. Although the intentions are commendable, this attitude furthers passivity and brings about a lack of confidence and initiative in confronting and dealing with problems. Continual help from those who are close to the young person is stifling. The illiterate person feels powerless, passive and will progressively become accustomed to this reassuring takeover of control.

Sometimes, however, those close to the young people know how to help: they accept the problem of illiteracy and follow their progress, while providing appropriate help. They constantly encourage them in what they are doing, without doing it for them. First and foremost, these people love the person as he is, and consider him to be *normal*. This is the foundation of all interaction, and we must pursue it with those who play a part in the lives of the young person. If not, the way of life of young people will remain an obstacle to literacy training.

Often, those close to the young person do not know how to start helping. They do not have a clear picture of the steps that need to be taken, and attach great importance to superfluous or inadequate learning. The community group must link the people in the young person's life to the process of literacy training, in order to get them to play a constructive role in the learning process.

This can be accomplished by inviting these people to attend a class or end-of-session evenings, where the results of the work are presented. The young people have the chance to display the projects they have worked on and to explain their learning objectives. Special meetings can be arranged on our literacy approach and on illiteracy in general, in order to assist these people in obtaining a global view of the problem.

These activities make collaboration with family members possible, which regular schools have not always succeeded in doing: getting closer to the home environment and to enabling experiences to be shared on both sides. While the organization has things to pass on, the same is true for the those in the young person's surroundings. This mutual edification will be beneficial in understanding the mental blocks of some young people and the way that they express themselves outside of the limited area of the literacy group.

At the Boîte à Lettres, we have undertaken this activity without giving it a structured form or precise objectives. We have invited those who are close to the young people to Christmas parties and end-of-the-year parties. We have also had "open house" evenings at the beginning and end of sessions. We were scared of appearing paternalistic by involving the parents. Yet, we came to realize that the young people were happy to allow us to get to know those close to them. They were also pleased to be able to show their place of learning, to show the work they are doing, the books or the texts they are reading and the group project underway. The closer and the more constant the ties between the outsiders and insiders, the better the chances of transferring knowledge.

Resource persons in the area
Those who may be our allies are not always organized within group networks. Certain groups or individuals are essential partners because they have been working in their neighbourhood for a long time, because they are known and respected in the area and because they are aware of the needs of people. It could be a person in charge of a used clothing agency located in a church basement, a parish priest, the owner of a corner store or the manager of a credit union. These people work in isolation and often in obscurity. One must make oneself directly known to them. They have valuable experience. They have to be made aware of the work we are doing, be invited to come and visit the premises and be encouraged to refer the young people in need of literacy training that they come into contact with to us. This contact will better help to integrate the organization into a neighbourhood and enable the establishment of numerous referral networks for recruitment.

3.4 *Public organizations*

School institutions
We are in contact with three different sectors of public education: elementary schools, the literacy sector of adult education and "drop-out schools". With elementary schools we have occasional and sporadic relations, which have come about owing to the initiative of teachers who are interested in our experiences. We would like

to be able to meet the staff of elementary schools on a more regular basis, but this has still not been accomplished. However, it is at this stage that scholastic failure or success is determined.

With the literacy sector of the Chambly School Board, we have always maintained ties. In 1984, the budgets of Quebec school boards were more limited and we were able to benefit by contacting the young people who were on the waiting list. This collaboration changed when the literacy budgets in the school systems increased, while our budget remained unchanged. This disparity has always put a delicate kink in our relationship with the School Board. How can a relationship that is respectful of mutual skills be established, when one of the two partners is underfunded and its very future threatened? How can discussions as equals take place between an organization that has a staff of four and provides a service to 25 young people, and a school board that offers courses to over 400 people and administers a staff of around 50 employees?

Recognition of community education takes place on the political level. School boards are not our "enemies", even if they are decidedly privileged at our expense. They are not the ones who can change the situation, only a change in political trends in the long-term development of literacy can accomplish this. As was stated by a school board representative at a regional meeting: "Community groups have certain freedoms and a lot of latitude in determining their approach, but they have no money. It is the opposite with us; we have money, but we are up to our necks in administrative paperwork and have little room to manoeuvre."

The collaboration with the Chambly School Board was slow; mutual distrust had to be overcome. As we were convinced of the importance of our work, which did not intend to replace school but provided a different service, we openly made known our leanings. This brought about a frank and open atmosphere. Nevertheless, all collaboration boils down to a question of personal contact. Our openness and that of the director of the literary section was a determining factor in creating a positive relationship.

The relationship with the "drop-out school" has always been a weak and sporadic one. We have tried to get close to them, for we wanted to know the grade 7 program objectives, in order to refer the young people to the program. But there is strong mistrust; the directors of the "drop-out school" in Longueuil felt as if they were being attacked by our work and public activities. Also the fact that several young people were quite straightforward in talking about their negative experiences in the special education classes of this high school, spoiled our relationship. Even though the idea was not to assign blame for illiteracy in young people, it was interpreted in this way. Sensibilities run very high in high school when there is mention of illiteracy.

Established as an experiment a few years ago, "drop-out schools" have spread across the province of Quebec. Their main objective is to enable those who have dropped out of high school to finish their studies. As such, they are part of the elementary and high school programs, even though they cater mainly to adults. This linking of "drop-out schools" with the elementary and high school program has the effect of distancing them from adult education. These two services often exist side by side without being aware of each other and while providing similar programs. There is duplication of services, and young people are sometimes passed to and fro between the two before finding the appropriate service.

Illiterate young people are rarely good candidates for "drop-out schools". Their learning needs are at the elementary school level, even though they are sometimes in possession of a "diploma" from a short vocational program. In "drop-out schools", the classes are organized in a very similar way to those of colleges. Everyone works independently and at their own pace. Special education classes are not very conducive to initiating the young people to this method of working.

"Drop-out schools" do not provide literacy training; this is not part of the mandate of high school. However, they too are being confronted with failure at school; they are starting to offer prerequisite classes for grade 7. It is not evident that the prerequisite class, like the school adjustment classes beforehand, lead the student to full integration into the regular program. Is this yet another crack in the system? What will be in it for the young person who has spent his schooling in special education classes, to find himself doing the same thing in "drop-out school"? It is better that a young person should become literate and set feasible goals for himself in order to function in society, rather than wasting his time in classes that claim to lead towards high school, without ever really getting there.

The general training that is offered to adults remains a highly compartmentalized network, which is a real maze for the young person who is experiencing difficulties. Some people will move around for several months between drop-out school, failure in a prerequisite class and adult education in literacy. This bumping around is detrimental to the motivation of some, and leads several others to vegetate in inappropriate classes.

Other public organizations
Other services provided by public organizations in the area also have to be investigated: federal and provincial employment centres, the LCSCs, hospitals, protected workshops and the court-house. These organizations come into contact with young people, whether they want to or not. We have to make ourselves known to them, for they know only of adult education or "drop-out schools" for remedying weaknesses in education. For young people, these avenues will often lead to failure, because they are forced into them and because the school structure offered reminds them too much of their past failures.

Public organizations come into contact with a lot of people; their scope is wide-ranging and the services they offer are diversified and not widely known. The LCSCs offer courses on sexuality, provide health clinics for young people, abortion services, drop-in daycare centres and prenatal classes. The organizations involved with employment for the mentally handicapped provide consultation and evaluation services. Employment centres offer rehabilitation programs for women, etc.

Our involvement with these organizations must be planned and vigorous, for it is difficult work. Public organizations want to learn about community groups so long as community groups want to make themselves known to them. The onus is on community groups to take the first step. One must be bold, call back several times, jump through the bureaucratic hoops and have patience. It is difficult to establish contact, there are a lot of staff and one does not always know who is the right person to talk to. Their work schedule always seems to be very busy and civil servants do not necessarily see the use of meeting with us to discuss illiteracy. Once a meeting is finally set up, administrative constraints have to be adhered to.

Conclusion

The work at the Boîte à Lettres cannot simply be evaluated according to the progress made in literacy, given the difficult and demanding nature of this endeavour. Here, therefore, are my own criteria of success in judging the effectiveness of the work, which underlies and is the context of the literacy training process.

-   That young people who drop out of the program without succeeding stay in contact with the organization. If they are able to find employment, feel more self-confident or feel better about themselves, this certainly reflects the quality of our work. A *long-term relationship of trust* has to be developed with the young people, so that they can overcome illiteracy and follow the process at their own pace. The young people who leave here, who talk about the organization with others, who come back to see us because they are concerned about how their child is doing in school, all this represents elements of success.

-   That the organization be socially integrated into its area and that its partners continue to view it as a dependable, honest and permanent service. The organization must be known and recognized, as much by shopkeepers, the municipality and public organizations, as by community organizations. This recognition in the area requires patient and continual work; it is essential for the survival of the organization, especially in the light of budgetary cutbacks and takeover attempts. Our work is only legitimate if it helps to establish *ties of solidarity in the area*. In the same way, we are only effective, if we have a good understanding of the area and its characteristics.

-   That the current staff, as well as the board of directors that supports and supervises it, be constantly evolving. Literacy training is too tricky a task to be carried out in a routine way. The strength of the organization essentially lies in the *enthusiasm and energy of its staff*. This is the cause of the instability of non-profit organizations, whose budgets cannot maintain stable teams. As a group leader, one must have the openness and the courage to question oneself, and to leave if one is worn out. Working in a community group is a very demanding and thankless task; this is not a reason for doing it in a bureaucratic way and with a minimum of effort. Without a staff that is motivated to get involved and to take on the task of providing literacy training, the organization is doomed to fail.

- That literacy remain the basis of our involvement. Literacy training is a relatively new and demanding field. Everything is still to be done, whether it be program-based research, the development of evaluation tools, the development of objectives and learning material, the creation of texts adapted for adults, the introduction of computers, the evaluation of knowledge and so on. *Research and experimentation* must be a part of literacy training, while aiming for the best results possible.

- That our work succeeds in changing the ties that are present in the lives of illiterate young people. That the "partner" or the mother of the young person adopt new attitudes with regards to reading and the young person, so that the young person feels more at ease and can adopt *new "reader" attitudes*. Our work can only bring about results if it enables change to take place, if it completely change the past relationship that was created towards reading.

These five points sum up my vision of the strategies of involvement in literacy in a community group. Nevertheless, I have a dream of another vision of literacy. And, since nothing is impossible, I leave you with this dream that was shared by our initial team, comprising Pierre Stanton, Denis Bourgeois and myself, during endless and energetic discussions.

And if literacy was...
Something else than a new and improved school, in effect the opposite of school, where, behind closed doors, classes, learning, evaluations, etc. still take place.

I dream of a large community building where various community groups could stay. A common objective: to help young people to succeed, in all areas. There would be a work program in automobile body work and repairs, where young people would learn to repair cars, to prepare estimates and bills. There would be a recreation centre where young people would get together to watch videos, organize a dance or plan a sports event. Next to the library, there would be a daycare centre for those who come to the centre; young people would play with the children, supervised by an experienced team.

Of course, there would be a literacy group, integrated with real life and with the other needs of young people, in a simple and tangible way, for immediate concerns such as long-term education. Some young people might only go to the recreation centre for two years, before undertaking the literacy process; they would then approach the group leaders, become aware of the uses of the literacy process while attempting to design a poster to announce a film.

And why not a sewing workshop, a permanent used clothing store for the people in the area? And why not an organization that deals with drug and alcohol problems? It is simply a matter of groups accepting sharing a common place, of consulting each other and of organizing themselves collectively, without losing their independence and without becoming a huge "machine". It is also simply a matter of having enough money to rent or (actually!) buy a building together.

Is it possible that one day literacy training will be integrated with the other needs of young people (that is in the same place, with teams that work collaboratively)? Is it possible that young people can learn basic work skills and responsibility, while providing services in the neighbourhood? Is it possible that this would be a different kind of school, a life school and a school that corresponds to the needs in the area? It is said that dreams are the food of daily life. So do not forget to dream!

Bibliography

Teaching Productions

Jeune sait pas lire, 39 minute colour video, directed by Roch Christophe Payer, produced by the Boîte à Lettres, Longueuil, May 1985. (To order: The Boîte à Lettres, 112 Norbert Street, Longueuil, Quebec, J4J 2Y9. Tel.: (514) 646-9273)

La presse à idées, four-page journal presenting texts written by the young people, inserted into the South Shore regional weekly newspaper in May 1989. (Can be obtained along with a report on the experiences of the Boîte à Lettres.)

Research Reports

Bourgeois, Denis and Roy, Sylvie. 1986. S'alphabétiser après l'échec scolaire. In Hautecoeur, Jean-Paul ed. *Alpha 86*. Montreal: Quebec Department of Education.

Bourgeois, Denis; Roy, Sylvie and Stanton, Pierre. 1984. Sortir de l'école par la porte d'en arrière, être analphabète à 20 ans. Longueil: La Boîte à Lettres, August. Mimeo.

FROM SPECIALIZED TRAINING
TO
GRASS-ROOTS LITERACY EDUCATION

Mario Raymond
Louise Meunier
La Porte ouverte, Saint-Jean sur Richelieu, Canada

Porte ouverte is an autonomous Quebec literacy organization which operates in Saint-Jean-sur-Richelieu and neighbouring towns. When it first began its work in 1984, and up until 1987, Porte ouverte did only pre-literacy work (awareness-recruiting). Since October 1988, the organization has handled all three phases of literacy education: "pre-lit", "lit", "post-lit", and it gives workshops in French and in arithmetic to the people of Haut-Richelieu.

Porte ouverte came into existence through the efforts of a group of educators working for the Honoré-Mercier Regional School Board Department of Adult Education (DAE), who wished to change the pre-literacy education environment; the organization slowly became transformed into an autonomous grass-roots literacy education group. This chapter describes the organization's development.

1. A Comprehensive Literacy Education Plan

Prior to 1978, individual requests for literacy education to the Honoré-Mercier School Board were forwarded to the Chambly School Board. In 1978 the DAE, which had been receiving a growing number of requests, established a basic French course. It was in carrying out these initial experiments that it became clear that it was important to involving the community in literacy education, and particularly in recruitment.

The Honoré-Mercier School Board then submitted to the Department of Education an action plan that had two objectives: to obtain financing for training activities, and, in particular, to prepare organizations in the community to assume responsibility for the pre- and post-literacy education phases. It was at the time felt, quite correctly, that such agencies are in the best position to penetrate disadvantaged neighbourhoods and to enter into contact with illiterates.

In 1982, the plan was implemented. The DAE hired a full-time community organizer to set up volunteer committees responsible for introducing literacy education into each community within the school board's territory. The organizer's role consisted of looking for leaders in each of the local communities. The goal was to make it possible for local literacy committees to assume responsibilities for all non-pedagogical aspects of literacy education.

The DAE defined a model, called a "terminal" model, for the sharing of tasks and responsibilities between the community and the DAE. The model calls for a "local literacy committee" to take charge (responsibility and leadership) of the overall operation in each community: planning, organization, management, financing. The local committee is composed of resource persons in the community. The DAE is the pedagogical resource for teaching, programs, etc., and provides financing for training within the limits of its budget. "The local committee may, on its own initiative, organize and carry out pedagogical activities that complement the work of the instructor, ideally in concert with the instructor (cultural events, outreach, consciousness-raising, functional activities, etc.)."[1]

Implementation of the terminal model

The terminal model specified the fields of action for each of the partners involved. The selected group (ideally a local literacy committee) was to be placed in charge of the overall operation, while the DAE was to assume responsibility for one aspect of the operation only, the pedagogical component. The literacy committees were therefore assigned the responsibility of organizing the community and tracking down illiterates, and then attempting to induce them to take the elementary French course.

Questions of a pedagogical nature (requirements analysis, training, pedagogical follow-up, evaluation of learning, hiring educators) were the sole responsibility of the DAE, which retained the right to monitor literacy committee activities. The only area where the committees had full and total autonomy was financing, which was to be obtained "from a source other than the DAE".

The DAE nevertheless identified a number of risks involved in having community organizations take over such matters:

Like other community agencies, associations or services, the DAE has its own specific role, its own expertise and its own special areas of responsibility... which it must shoulder and not assign to others in the community... N.B.: By encouraging "the community" to develop its specific role, its expertise and its responsibilities in an unrestricted fashion, the curious phenomenon of a parallel structure eventually arises, with paid professionals and employees in certain instances...[2]

Each literacy committee was established around one person responsible for running it - the educator hired by the School Board to give basic French courses. These key persons, supported by the community organizer, created a well-established core group in a number of areas, at least solid enough to supply students for a number of basic French classes for a few years. Literacy groups established under this process carried out a systematic recruiting of illiterates in the area. They had no budget and worked on a voluntary basis to organize pedagogical activities for the students.

The results for the School Board were altogether satisfactory, and the Board expected to withdraw its community organizer after three years. The educator's pay, linked as it was to the number of students enroled, was its only financial contribution. In the medium term, the plan made it possible to teach a good number of complete illiterates to read, and to maintain the number of basic French classes through which under-educated individuals were given the opportunity to learn a trade or pursue their secondary studies through adult education.

In Saint-Jean, the plan was not applied in the same way because the urban environment is more impersonal and the population larger. In the early stages of recruiting, the DAE was able quickly to set up a number of basic French classes. Several educators were therefore hired to teach during the evening at the comprehensive school. Unlike educators working in the regions, the Saint-Jean educators did not establish agencies to assure continuity. That is because at the time, the DAE was afraid that a parallel organization would be established that would encroach upon its educational mission.

The organizers hired to find students for the basic French classes also quickly exhausted potential sources of recruiting. Because they had no control after this initial phase, it was difficult for them to assess how effective their work was. When recruiting ceased to yield results, the organizers were disbanded.

Early efforts

The first literacy education experiment took place in 1982 in Farnham. The DAE recruited a small team of volunteers whose task was to make the community aware of the problem and to recruit illiterates. Seventy-four were recruited and 46 began to take instruction in the fall of 1982. The LE committee was established (Literacy Education, later re-named Adult Education).

Also in 1982, similar work was begun in Marieville. Community leaders established the Marieville local literacy committee, which quickly began its pre-literacy efforts. Sixty-three illiterates were recruited and 28 began their instruction in the 1982 winter session.

Little by little, DAE resource persons withdrew from the committee to let it manage its own affairs. Community awareness work was also done in Saint-Jean, where the DAE recruited 128 persons, 105 of whom began instruction in the fall of 1983. At the end of the year, it was recommended that a local literacy group be established to take the operation in hand.

The birth of Porte Ouverte

The DAE resource persons who helped to set up the Farnham and Marieville groups submitted an application for a job creation program to the federal government to make the public aware of illiteracy and to recruit illiterates in Saint-Jean, Iberville, and in the region (over 56,000 inhabitants). The program, which was sponsored by Relado Inc., an agency that provides assistance to adolescents, was implemented in late 1983. This period was in effect the pioneer phase of literacy education in Saint-Jean-sur-Richelieu.

Three organizers were hired for a six-month period, and assigned the task of making the public aware of illiteracy and of recruiting illiterates to enrol in DAE literacy education activities. These were the people who did the real spadework. Virtually every method of community awareness enhancement was tried (door to door, at-home meetings, leaflets enclosed in pay envelopes, etc.). The results were convincing: 177 of the persons reached began training in the 1984 winter session.

In 1984, the DAE seriously considered establishing a local pre-literacy group in Saint-Jean to perform the role defined in the 1982 terminal model. An interim group was established but, unlike

Farnham and Marieville, the group did not consist of community leaders, but rather members of the DAE (organizers, educators, resource persons). Two names were put forward: "À Livre ouvert" and "La Porte ouverte". The second name was selected.

Porte ouverte was incorporated as an association for the promotion of literacy, with its terms of reference strictly limited to promoting the DAE literacy education program, without any direct involvement in training itself. The agency's articles of incorporation were also very clear: "GENERAL OBJECTIVE: to promote the literacy education program through activities other than training (which is the preserve of adult education)"[3].

At the time, Porte ouverte was more an offshoot of the DAE than a Saint-Jean community group. Porte ouverte could best be described as a DAE appendage assigned the task of independently financing a pre-literacy phase that it would be difficult for the Department of Education to finance. Porte ouverte was given a great deal of freedom, but it proved impossible to give it the means required to make its activities permanent. The problem remains equally serious today.

2. The Financing of Pre-Literacy Activities

The School Board and community agencies were unanimous in considering the pre-literacy groundwork as a necessary and indeed indispensable prerequisite to training. It was therefore of the greatest importance to make sure that such action, which since 1985 had been the full responsibility of Porte ouverte, should be successful. How could an embryonic agency like Porte ouverte shoulder such heavy responsibilities? The mandate assigned to Porte ouverte was enormous: to put down roots among a population spread over 11 municipalities, with a total of approximately 60,000 inhabitants, among whom no less than 15,000 adults were considered illiterate in varying degrees.

To make itself known, Porte ouverte had to find a distinctive personality to set it apart from the School Board. But how was it to do so when its members were mostly School Board employees, and the agency itself was housed in board facilities? Funding bodies did not fully understand why a community agency was asking for their financial assistance for activities that fell within the School

Board's purview. They did not fully understand that Porte ouverte was not funded by the DAE, and that the DAE simply happened to be the prime beneficiary of Porte ouverte's community action.

For all these different reasons, direct fund raising in the community was a failure. Hence the appeal to governments. In Quebec City, the program to provide assistance to adult education agencies, the only possible source of funding, was frozen. The last hope was the federal government. It was thanks to the manpower retraining programs (Canada Works, Article 38, Job Development Program) that Porte ouverte was able to finance most of its activities in the field.

Such programs unfortunately have disadvantages. Their purpose is not to sustain subsidized agencies, but to develop the employment skills of the participants by giving them training and job experience. Agencies that are able to provide the best training, and eventually to hire the participants, are obviously given preferential treatment. Porte ouverte, whose underpinnings remained flimsy, and which could not even hire its own employees, was bringing up the rear.

The agency was nevertheless able to obtain funding for at least one program of this type every year, but in each instance, the projects were temporary. At most, they made it possible for Porte ouverte to continue to work in the field full-time six months of the year, with the other six being the responsibility of voluntary workers, some of whom could at best handle one basic course in French at the DAE.

As was noted in 1987, "for literacy agencies, the piecemeal financing provided by job development programs is obviously not ideal. It does not allow for continuity and makes any kind of follow-up action impossible. Volunteers can fill the gap, but they quickly run out of steam, and the needs of illiterates remain just as pressing as ever.[4]" "The work therefore has to be done all over again, and always for a limited period of time.[5]"

Owing to the nature of federal temporary employment programs, field workers, who inevitably are chronically unemployed, came to Porte ouverte primarily to acquire job experience that would enable them to find work elsewhere once the project was over. This has resulted in a steady turnover in personnel over the years, and a built-in instability in literacy efforts. (From 1983 to 1989, no less than 13 persons held the position of Porte ouverte field organizer.)

This meant that volunteers had an ever heavier burden to bear. They had to do the work between projects, and each year submit new requests to set up additional programs. When the response to their request was positive, they were the people who had to train the newcomers, who were nearly always new to the literacy education field. Such a situation was much too demanding for volunteers who did not have a special interest in literacy education, and perhaps for the educators as well.

The year 1985 was thus one in which many volunteers were demobilized. DAE educators and teaching assistants alike withdrew from Porte ouverte, leaving it in the hands of field organizers hired on contract and the remaining members of the Board of Directors (most of whom were themselves illiterates). This general demobilization was to last three years, during which a handful of determined individuals carried the torch of literacy education. It ended only when Porte ouverte decided to reorient its action.

In spite of it all, the field work carried out over all these years yielded tangible results and gave Porte ouverte recognized expertise in pre-literacy education.

3. Field Organization Methods

Porte ouverte earned recognition in literacy circles as a specialist in the pre-literacy phase. With seven years of field work under its belt, and the experience of no less than 13 field workers, Porte ouverte was able to acquire genuine expertise. We shall now speak of the various communication organization activities implemented from the beginning, and the results obtained, in chronological order.

The responsibilities of the field organizers included consciousness-raising in the community and recruiting illiterates for the DAE basic French course.[6] In 1988, responsibilities were added for taking the action required to make Porte ouverte autonomous from the DAE.

1983-1984: Pioneering phase

The year 1983 marked the beginning of the phase in which agencies took over the pre-literacy area. For the first time in Saint-Jean, organizers from outside the school board worked autonomously in the field. From 1981 to 1982, a small publicity campaign was all it took to recruit enough students for the basic French courses, and the DAE could not accommodate any more than this without running a deficit on its budget.

In 1983, three organizers were hired under the federal NEED Program for 23 weeks of field work. Their first task would require a great deal of preparation and hold a number of surprises for them: "To our great surprise, most people were incredulous when we told them about the statistics we had collected.[6]"

After four weeks of preparation, the organizers left for the field. All agencies were contacted, first by telephone to make them aware of literacy education, followed by a request for a meeting; at the meetings that were held, ad hoc assistance was requested (to distribute publicity material, organize information meetings and, in some instances, to prepare a list of persons who might be illiterate). The purpose of these contacts was to reach as many people as possible in the community, and to penetrate the community.

When all the work was completed, no less than 613 addresses were contacted and 677 persons met. The recruiting results were convincing: 192 persons took part in the exercise and 177 enrolled in basic French courses in the 1984 winter session.

The number of persons recruited was impressive for the amount of time devoted to the operation (23 weeks). Although much remained to be done in the community, literacy was no longer seen as a problem that affected only the third world. Illiteracy at home undoubtedly existed; everyone was now aware of it, and literacy education could become a community affair.

1984-1985: Action focus

After field work had been interrupted for a few months because of a lack of financing, Porte ouverte obtained the services of a new team through another employment program (Article 38). Three organizers were hired for a 20-week period, and assigned approximately the same objectives as those hired under the previous project: to make the general public aware of the problem and to recruit illiterates for the 1985 winter session. In carrying out its terms of reference, the team placed a focus on various types of action:

-      to encourage the development of a literacy education service at Lacolle;

-      to identify unemployed young people, former students and drop-outs;

-      to begin to take action in downtown Saint-Jean.[7]

Porte ouverte's action was defined both by the targets it selected and the manner in which it evaluated its activities. The general comments, recommendations and suggested follow-up action for future programs that were included at the end of the activity report show that continuity was already a concern.

Special attention was paid to young people. Lists were prepared of young people who were unemployed, who had completed the short vocational training course, and of graduates and drop-outs from the abridged vocational course. Approximately 10 youths showed an interest in the courses or enrolled in them. But it could be seen that most of those who had taken the abridged vocational course were working and had little time to devote to any kind of course. Moreover, more than one was scared off by bad memories of school.

An attempt was also made to create a literacy centre at Lacolle, a small rural community.

In the same year, a new program was established. Two of the organizers from the previous program remained, and a third joined the team. Work in the field continued. An experiment to hold kitchen meetings in a rural environment proved to be an excellent way to make people aware of illiteracy.

1985-1986: Between projects

From the fall of 1985 to the winter of 1986, nothing at all was happening. The federal programs were exhausted, and they were the only available source of financing at the time. Porte ouverte submitted a request for interim financing to the DAE while awaiting a new project. The DAE authorities agreed, but on condition that Porte ouverte do the field work over the entire School Board territory (as well as at Saint-Jean and Lacolle, and at Farnham and Marieville).

The two remaining organizers agreed to the DAE proposal, but quickly became aware that "the DAE contribution does not allow for serious action in the short-term in each region.[8]" It was therefore decided to take concerted action to submit a joint project for all the regions, which involved placing an organizer in each locality and a field work coordinator in the region.

During this time, each committee, with the help of the Porte ouverte organizers, did only a small amount of community awareness work. Community groups were contacted in Marieville, Farnham and Lacolle. An effort was made to create an educational workshop for young people on social assistance in Saint-Jean, with the cooperation of the Quebec Work Centre. Unfortunately, the organizers had to abandon these efforts owing to a shortage of time.

One thing quickly became clear to everyone: the rural environment has nothing to do with the urban environment. At the annual field meetings, where each committee was represented, it was noted that there were professional organizers in Saint-Jean and semi-voluntary educators in the region. A leadership crisis quickly developed which clearly confirmed that the DAE method had failed in the city.

1986: Towards complementary services

A major new regional project was begun in 1986. "The federal funding program was requested in order to provide the regions with a full-time employee. But the job was temporary. Employees were to be supervised by the local committees, and they were given the opportunity to think about and to take part in our future in the short term, and not merely be considered recruits for the fall of 1986 session.[8]"

Five persons were hired. Their terms of reference, which went well beyond awareness enhancement and recruiting, included bringing new blood to each of the committees, becoming full members of the committees, and working both within the committee and in the community.

After three years of pre-literacy education work, the results in Saint-Jean were disturbing. The level of recruiting was dropping dramatically. The time had come to disband the Porte ouverte Board of Directors. The educators - all of whom were employed by the DAE - left, leaving the agency in the hands of the organizers.

Porte ouverte suddenly became, like the persons in charge of it, a temporary agency. In fact, "the Porte ouverte agency no longer exists in between course sessions.[9]"

As early as 1985, this realization led to fundamental second thoughts about the agency's role: "Porte ouverte, by offering the service to another agency, is having trouble gaining recognition (remains unknown) and is not included on the list of recognized community agencies. In view of this situation, we believe that follow-up action with respect to the awareness program ought to be to concentrate on establishing concrete activities that directly meet the people's needs.[9]"

It had become essential for Porte ouverte to establish a distinctive literacy service in order to earn special recognition in the literacy environment, and to assume a distinctive role. Porte ouverte existed only for others: the School Board, especially its educators, who benefited from the jobs created for them by recruiting. The agency sought an identity that would break the vicious circle.

Why work for the School Board, which can neither finance it nor recognize a role for it? Simply because the School Board was still the only institution with the right educational credentials in literacy training. To break away from the DAE would have been suicidal. Little by little, it was necessary for Porte ouverte to become involved in activities, which over time would make it essential. The first efforts in the downtown area, the initial attempts to create awareness in businesses, and the workshops, were all attempts by the agency to give it a profile in those communities where the School Board was not present, to acquire its credentials as an agency that complements the Board.

The incumbent organizer and the regional coordinator decided to establish a reception service for illiterates who had been identified. The service consisted of "welcoming individuals (particularly at the group facility) in a manner to create a relaxed climate more conducive to genuine dialogue.[5]" It was presented as an alternative to the depersonalized manner in which the School Board receives people. Both the linguistic and experiential requirements of the individual were analyzed as part of the process. Basic French courses were offered to meet reading and writing needs. Complementary community resources were also recommended when other needs were identified (problems with alcohol, drugs, marital violence, etc.).

Because the reception and evaluation service had previously been exclusively the responsibility of the School Board, it was necessary to obtain approval from DAE authorities to provide such a service. It proved to be no easy matter.

Members of Porte ouverte argued with the DAE that they were more accessible and that they could give all the time needed to everyone because they would be providing the service on a voluntary basis. This accessibility was the most important factor for Porte ouverte which, as we saw, had to distinguish the services it was offering from those provided by the DAE.

The DAE argued that it was dangerous to place a service that was considered indispensable in the hands of a temporary agency. According to the DAE, nothing guaranteed that Porte ouverte would always be there to provide the service, once the project had been completed. Porte ouverte further pointed out with respect to the survival argument that although Porte ouverte might not be there at the end of the project to provide the service, not allowing it to provide the service would almost certainly seal its fate once the project was completed. There was therefore not really any choice, and it was necessary to gamble bravely on its survival.

Negotiations lasted two months, and it was finally agreed that Porte ouverte would be given carte blanche. The results were convincing: the number of registrations increased significantly and, in particular, the withdrawal rate during the session decreased considerably (at least among those who registered through Porte ouverte). Sixteen persons enrolled in the basic French course, including 14 newcomers, 86% of whom were in the introductory levels. Of these, 82% continued their training to the end of the session.

With respect to the indispensable community work, the situation was less sanguine. For the first time, Porte ouverte found itself with only one organizer in the field to serve a population of over 60,000. The challenge was a major one: to make the public more aware, to recruit more illiterates, and to provide a new reception service. All in all, it was necessary to do more with less.

This meant that it was no longer possible to go door-to-door visiting all the community groups, and to survey the whole area searching for places to speak about literacy. Owing to a shortage of human and financial resources, Porte ouverte had to make choices about targets, and had to select targets that were easier to reach.

Hence the organizer and the regional coordinator decided to build a network of contacts and cooperative ventures with those community groups most likely to encounter illiterates. Approximately 20 government and community agencies were contacted. The cooperation agreement took the following form:

> First the group (background) and services (evaluation-motivation-enrollment) are described. Front-line workers are then asked to provide services to the group of persons concerned. If the individual shows interest, he or she is asked whether details can be passed on to the group (name and telephone number).

> If the answer is affirmative, the agency supplies us with the details. We then enter into contact with the individual and volunteer to evaluate his or her reading and writing skills. We then make an appointment to meet the person at home or at the group facilities, depending on the person's preference.

> The group therefore commits itself to two things:

> 1) to provide personalized service to the adult,

> 2) to provide the associated agency with follow-up on the individual's progress.[5]

The results proved to be very positive with respect to community commitment. A process like this assigns responsibility to individuals and to their agency by making them aware of the important role they play in the community. In addition, the regional coordination provided by Porte ouverte generated dialogue among the organizers and each of the localities. The end result was consensus about what forms of action ought to be taken, and a degree of solidarity, and these in turn led at the end of the year to the establishment of a regional representative agency, called the Groupe régional d'intervention Alpha (GRIA) [Regional Literacy Action Group (RLAG)].

1987: Regionalization

In 1987, the recently established Regional Literacy Action Group took responsibility for pre-literacy education work throughout the territory. The RLAG had been created as a result of the desire to combine the efforts of the four local literacy committees and to eliminate the leadership problem, which was making it appear that Porte ouverte was in a strong position in relation to the other three literacy groups and the School Board.

A new program was established. Four persons were hired: three field organizers and one regional coordinator. The main problem was anticipated from the very outset: four points of service, the required coordination, and... only four persons in the field.

Porte ouverte, which till then had provided regional leadership, was assigned responsibility for regional coordination. The issue of leadership was far from being resolved. The three regional local committees demanded the services of a field organizer. It was finally agreed that each sub-region would be assigned a field organizer for the duration of the project. Porte ouverte had to content itself with one full-time regional coordinator, assisted by a part-time organizer.

When an organizer works alone, double duty is required. The field work is kept to a minimum, while the objectives remain the same: public awareness and recruiting, not to mention reception.

In the field, the world of industry, which is closed and which harbours so many individuals in need, becomes a priority. The comments made at the end of the program are eloquent:

> In this era of changing technologies, the basic training requirements for adults are becoming increasingly pressing. This means that efforts to make people aware and to provide them with information become all the more necessary...

> In the short term, industry will have to identify a prime target. Contact with this target group will have to go beyond politely receiving people without any concrete follow-up action. Some industries in the area have too many illiterate workers to be able to pretend that they are unaware of the situation.[4]

From the organizational standpoint, Porte ouverte found itself in a very bad position: a single employee, half paid, half volunteer, surrounded by a micro-team of three volunteers. It was up to the organizer virtually single-handedly to handle the burdensome task of keeping Porte ouverte afloat. In the opinion of the few remaining members, and in view of recent experience, radical change was needed.

At the same time as a decidedly urban strategy was being developed, with efforts made to maintain the best possible contacts with the School Board, it became essential to consider providing training on our own suited to the needs of those identified in recent years. The purpose was to plan an active role in the community, and at the same time search for financing from the only possible source other than the Board, the Adult Education Branch, which had not yet given any grants to an agency exclusively dedicated to recruiting and promotion.

From this standpoint, the year 1988 was to be a turning point.

4. **Summary**

Lack of recognition for the status of field organizers

We saw above that the status of field organizers is precarious in the extreme. While no one working in literacy education really has security, the field organizer is at the bottom of the ladder. From the very outset, the field organizer knows that work will be for a limited time, at most six months, during which efforts will have to be made to learn more about the community, about the work environment, about the services to be provided, and about general literacy issues, if an action plan is ultimately to be formulated. Now six months is a very short time, especially when the post-project phase has to be considered.

In addition, the work of the field organizer, although essential, has little recognition. "The pre-literacy work remains the poor relation in the redistribution of funds, and yet it is the very engine of the literacy education mission.[10]" Because the organizer has become the driving force of Porte ouverte, the agency as a whole has been saddled with the precarious status of the field organizer.

The pre-literacy education phase remains the only responsibility of literacy groups like Porte ouverte. Such groups are therefore required to take responsibility for obtaining financing, for training organizers, and for providing a framework for their work in order to be able to obtain the best possible results (for the DAE, it goes without saying, this means the number of enrolments). At Saint-

Jean, because the DAE's recruiting is primarily among young drop-outs, Porte ouverte's contribution, in spite of all the effort, is perceived as marginal (barely 15 per cent of basic education). It is nevertheless Porte ouverte that recruits most of the total illiterates, but this demanding work is taken for granted.

In fact, the pre-literacy education work, although it is essential, is discreet and not well recognized. This lack of recognition comes not only from the School Board, but also from community agencies, which do not readily understand what role Porte ouverte has to play in literacy education. It is easy enough to understand that people who have little or no education may require basic education, but it is difficult to explain why they cannot go and obtain it where it is available. At best, Porte ouverte is seen as the School Board's publicity department. This lack of recognition extends to those who receive the service; even though they are convinced that Porte ouverte is effective, they have trouble dissociating it from the School Board.

For Porte ouverte, the lack of continuity is an impediment to any form of recognition, and also to any hopes for development. Being restricted to pre-literacy education work results in a lack of knowledge about the overall operation. This means that "selling literacy" becomes all the more difficult. Because literacy education is part of a comprehensive effort to give people autonomy, it is difficult to be effective if one aspect is isolated. We became specialized in one specific area, but remain neophytes in others.

Problems in financing pre-literacy education

The lack of recognition for the pre-literacy education phase naturally leads to problems in obtaining autonomous financing. The Department of Education is reluctant to recognize and finance a so-called autonomous agency whose awareness-recruiting services appear to be supported directly by an institution that is already financed by government.

When financing is obtained for pre-literacy education, it is received only indirectly. Job development programs, which finance employability enhancement for the chronically unemployed, and not the activities of the group, are an excellent illustration of this. Porte ouverte has had more than its share of federal programs (eight in six years). In recent years, it had become obvious that the well would soon run dry. The welcome received from the federal MP gave an ever-clearer indication of what was to come. It was explained that Porte ouverte had already received considerable funding, always for the same type of activity, and that other agencies which were generally more innovative, were still waiting for seed money.

Where we stand

In 1988, after five years of pre-literacy education work, the time had come to take stock. No less than 11 persons had held the position of field organizer. Of these, one was still - temporarily? - in the field. The Board of Directors had run out of steam and been disbanded. Porte ouverte was still awaiting another employment project, and this time, the battle was far from won. A great deal of effort had been expended on the RLAG, and the results had been lean. Our services remained little known and barely acknowledged. Prospects for development were virtually non-existent. The four remaining members of the Board of Directors, who were tired of regularly having to pull from its death-bed an agency in which they had invested a great deal, needed to take stock.

It had been noted, for example, through contacts with those who took the courses, that the DAE services did not meet all requirements. Some more practical needs (such as preparing a shopping list, budgeting, reading work instructions, etc.) were not being met. Moreover, training at the comprehensive school had disheartened many, particularly among young drop-outs.

For Porte ouverte, it therefore appeared to be of the essence to assume the whole literacy education operation, which basically means that people in need ought not to be left without services, and that they should be provided for as effectively as possible throughout the process.

This new direction involved three major objectives:

- follow-up throughout the learning process;

- implementation of an adult education literacy program;

- recognition and financing of our action (and at the same time handling of the pre-literacy education phase).

The end objective of doing so was to develop the autonomy of the group and earn recognition for it. This was already a concern of the field organizers in 1985: "In view of the situation, we feel that, following the public awareness work, it would be important to concentrate on consolidating an autonomous group to provide leadership in a comprehensive literacy education program.[9]"

The new direction certainly created shock waves within the DAE and member groups of the RLAG. Among the former, there would of course be concerns about duplication of services, while among the latter, there was talk of backroom politicking and a change in the agency's role. Today, one year later, people have calmed down and the initial reluctance has given way to a degree to understanding and confidence.

With this important change under way, opportunities for development, and for financing, appear to be much more numerous. The targeted activities remain the same: industry, research, preparation of instructional materials and the establishment of a documentation centre, a project which has now been completed. In short, these are certainly all activities that can be financed by job development programs, but by various departments and agencies whose mandate covers the social and economic sphere.

Formulating new objectives is one thing, but meeting them is another. One needs the means to guide the ship safely into port. In this, the 1988 job development program was to play a determining role.

5. From Piecemeal Action to Comprehensive Action

Two organizers succeeded one another in the field. It was clearly established from the very outset that their committee work was as important as their community work, as was also the case in 1986. Their very broad mandate consisted of making the agency as autonomous as possible in the eyes of the community, and of continuing to pursue awareness-recruiting and reception work.

The first organizer, who had solid experience as an educator, was committed to creating pedagogical tools. She prepared an analytical grid of practical requirements and a bank of teaching materials for practical workshops. Unfortunately, she had to leave her position in the middle of the project. The work begun remains unfinished.

The organizer who took over from her had more experience in public relations, and the agency therefore made an effort to make use of her specific skills. She quickly established an action plan:

1. Make the agency autonomous
    - through a board of directors that is representative of the community
    - through more satisfactory financial arrangements.
2. Provide the agency with recognized expertise in literacy education.
3. Take steps to obtain financing.
4. Make approaches to industry.[11]

Board of Directors

To establish the agency's credibility in the community, the organizer set about recruiting people with a high profile in the community to serve on the Board of Directors. Six new members joined the Board. Included among them were two retired teachers, one educational consultant, one person who was in charge of a group of parents of children experiencing learning problems, and one librarian. The members of the previous Board of Directors, the members of Porte ouverte, and a former student remained to oversee the transition. Somewhat later, it was jointly agreed that in order for the agency truly to set down roots in the community, the field organizers would withdraw from the Board. It quickly became apparent that it was both difficult and demanding for the Board and for the field organizers to function in such a way. Because the role of the Board is corporate administration and policy making, it required constant input from the grassroots. For the field organizers, who were already overburdened with work, such an enterprise quickly proved to be exhausting. Moreover, the Board sometimes got the impression when issues were submitted that the decisions had already been taken.

The situation rapidly created pressures: the Board felt useless and the organizers increasingly questioned its role. Members of the Board soon resigned from their duties, leaving Porte ouverte in the hands of its organizers.

An agency that has been entirely controlled by its organizers for years does not readily accept such radical change in its decision-making process. A Board of Directors that includes members of the community is nevertheless desirable. It makes it possible for the agency better to penetrate the community, and allows the community to gain a better understanding of the overall illiteracy and community literacy education issues. But any such efforts to improve relations require proper preparation and regular follow-up on the various matters in hand. This means that having organizers on the Board is more than desirable, it is inevitable.

New services

The idea for comprehensive action in the literacy field had been around for some time: all that remained was to put it into practice. As International Literacy Year approached (1990), we seized the opportunity afforded by the lifting of the freeze on the program to provide assistance to voluntary community education agencies, and decided, in order to be able better to meet the needs expressed, that the time had come in September 1988 to move wholeheartedly into the field of training.

The organizer decided to publicize the new services, and Porte ouverte held a regional public awareness day to inform community groups about its new directions.

The reception in the community was more than enthusiastic. Everyone quickly recognized the soundness of our approach and the need for a new type of action. Everyone also recognized that they had to bear their share of responsibility in the battle against illiteracy, and said that they were ready to support our efforts. The idea, so dear to organizers, of getting the community involved in the battle against illiteracy was finally beginning to take a concrete form.

On the strength of this support, the organizers enthusiastically set up the first literacy workshops. Educators were recruited, initially within the agency. The authors of this paper, who are already working there, added two voluntary educators chosen for their commitment to literacy rather than their CVs or their academic credentials. Ordinary people to teach ordinary people to read and write: that was the selection criterion.

Two groups of participants were set up. The first, which came from the working world, consisted of female workers from the textile industry. Their needs were very practical: prepare a budget, prepare a curriculum vitae, familiarize themselves with resources in educational and job-related orientation, etc. The workshop, called "social training", had three objectives: to make the participants aware of their strengths, to help them individually and collectively take stock of their situation; to develop their personal autonomy and their determination as a social group. The contents of the course still included teaching them to write. Essays and exercises in writing French were also part of the workshops.

The second group consisted of participants who were taking the DAE basic French course. The workshop, called "functional workshop", was designed to reinforce the subject matter covered in the classroom. For the educators involved in this workshop, the task required presenting the course material given by the DAE educator in a new way. This, as one might well imagine, required a considerable amount of creativity, because some people who were slower learners had to attempt several different approaches before being able to assimilate the subject matter. The workshop had six objectives: to get all participants involved in the process; to make them feel comfortable with the process; to keep motivation up; to play down the difficulty of learning French; to encourage mutual cooperation, to make participants aware of what they had already learned and experienced.

Participation

But above all else, the Porte ouverte workshops made it possible to develop a new attitude among the participants, who quickly progressed from being simple students to being partners in the agency.

To begin with, the workshops encouraged participation. As a result, the participants had a considerable impact on how training activities were carried out: the workshop contents were decided by them on the basis of needs expressed; as for timetables and length of training, they decided these matters in concert with the educators. It was, for example, at their request that the daytime workshop was changed from one to two periods a week during the year.

The participants felt that they had genuine decision-making power about their individual and collective training. No longer were they required to follow training that was defined in advance and to which they had to adapt.

This new participation dynamic was soon to spill over well beyond the workshops into other areas. Some participants wanted to play a more active role in the activities as a whole. One participant is currently a member of the Board of Directors.

Conclusions

We now find it much easier to promote literacy in the community. We know what we are talking about. Porte ouverte is therefore gaining increased recognition as a community resource. There is no longer any hesitation in referring to Porte ouverte people who may have had difficulty fitting into adult education programs. A new solidarity, and a new partnership, have emerged from the community.

Training experience made it possible for the agency to acquire new expertise. Porte ouverte was able to create new pedagogical tools, as well as a distinctive approach. We believe, as the maxim says, that in all fields "practice makes perfect". Restricting oneself to only one facet of the business would be like a blacksmith lighting the fire and using the bellows, while leaving to others the task of shaping the metal.

But above all else, what broadening the field of endeavour will have brought is the recognition that has been so highly sought after by all organizers who have worked with Porte ouverte. Their tireless effort has finally been recognized at its true worth. Organizers are no longer simply passing through, but truly feel a part of a cause that they dearly believe in.

Today, an increasing number of volunteers and voluntary groups who are sensitive to the literacy issue are coming to lend us a hand. The "literacy family" is growing every day. A new Board of Directors, consisting of organizers, illiterates and members of the community who are very well versed in the literacy issue, are doing remarkable work in providing a framework and performing a representative function in the community. The results of their work are tangible. Two social clubs got together to pay rent for the next two years. Religious communities have made a commitment to keep Porte ouverte operating for at least the next three years. Equipment donations have made it possible to furnish and organize efficient facilities. A weekly column in the local newspaper allows us to reach a wider public.

Porte ouverte now runs four workshops per week for 35 persons. Because demand is so heavy, negotiations for the financing of course hours have begun with the School Board. Since the summer of 1989, the agency has had a completely computerized documentation centre with no less than 500 titles.

Today, Porte ouverte is a member of the Regroupement des groupes populaires en alphabétisation du Québec (Quebec Association of Community Literacy Education Groups) and of the Table régionale des organismes volontaires d'éducation populaire de la Montérégie (Regional Federation of Voluntary Community Education Agencies in the Montérégie Area). These new links stimulate dialogue and the resourcing of our organizers, and at the same time strengthen our common cause: the recognition of autonomous grassroots education. Given that illiteracy is a social fact, we believe that it is only together that we can truly deal with it.

6. Future Prospects

Only the future will show whether our decisions have been correct. The change that has been effected was the logical outcome of a process and a review that have been under way for some years now.

Let us recall the highlights. To begin with, the awareness-recruiting work, which led us to question the way in which illiterates ought to be reached, and further led us to want to work more directly with the people. Then, the establishment of the reception service, which made it possible for us to identify more accurately the needs of illiterates, and hence to provide a more accurate evaluation of the usefulness of the services provided. And lastly, the findings concerning these practices, which underscored the need for a form of training that was different from that provided in the adult education mould.

Porte ouverte therefore went from being an appendage of the School Board to a complementary resource and then an alternative resource. Current prospects must be seen as an extension of this process.

With respect to public awareness, industry remains a priority target. The work has begun, but much remains to be done to open up this sector, which has long been off-limits to literacy education.

The development of services also remains a constant concern. It is necessary to consolidate what we have learned in pre-literacy education, and to develop post-literacy education, by getting illiterates involved to the greatest extent possible.

The development of educators is also a priority. Our participation in the training program of the Regroupement des groupes populaires en alphabétisation du Québec allows educators to familiarize themselves with the various practices in use in the literacy field.

The commitment of all sectors of the community to the battle against illiteracy remains our objective. We believe more than ever that illiteracy is a social problem which goes well beyond the mere educational dimension. That is why we plan to continue to work towards having the community deal directly with the problem.

The road travelled by Porte ouverte since it was founded has been mined with problems, some of which led the agency to the brink. It was only because of remarkable individual effort, as well as collective effort, that it is still possible today to speak of a Porte ouverte in Saint-Jean-sur-Richelieu.

Porte ouverte, which began as a volunteer sub-contractor, with a shaky status, working in the shadows, has today become a full partner in the community. Its principal objective, which has always been to involve the community in the battle against illiteracy, remains a constant concern, and Porte ouverte believes that it is better equipped than ever before to meet it.

We hope that this short history of Porte ouverte has given the reader some idea of the role played in our society by grassroots literacy education. We also believe, modestly, that it could perhaps inspire a new generation of literacy education organizers, and that it might enable them to avoid the pitfalls that stood in our way.

Notes

1. CSR Honoré-Mercier, Service de l'éducation des adultes. *Projet d'alphabétisation: rapport d'activités et évaluation, année 1982-1983,* June 1983.

2. CSR Honoré-Mercier, Service de l'éducation des adultes. *Projet d'alphabétisation: rapport d'activités et évaluation, année 1981-1982*, June 1982.

3. La Porte ouverte, inc. *Charte constitutive*, December 1984.

4. Raymond, Mario. 1987. *Rapport d'activités*. Saint-Jean-sur-Richelieu: Groupe régional d'intervention Alpha.

5. Raymond, Marion and Poulin, Claude. 1986. *Rapport régional d'animation en alphabétisation*. Saint-Jean-sur-Richelieu: Porte ouverte.

6. Côte, Nicole and Gousy, Nicole. *Animation Alpha 1983-1984.*

7. Courville, Lise; Tarte, Martin and Poulin, Claude. 1985. *Rapport animation Alpha*. Saint-Jean-sur-Richelieu: Porte ouverte, May.

8. Nolet, Diane and Poulin, Claude. 1985. *Bilan du mandat SCRHM (automne 1985 - hiver 1986)*. Saint-Jean-sur-Richelieu: Porte ouverte, May.

9. Courville, Lise; Nolet, Diane and Poulin, Claude. 1985. *Projet de sensibilisation "Alpha"*. Saint-Jean-sur-Richelieu: Porte ouverte, autumn.

10. Blais, Hélène; Hautecoeur, Jean-Paul and Léoine, Lucie. 1988. *Recherche-action sur le développement de l'alphabétisation au Québec: Evaluations*. Montreal: Quebec Ministry of Education, DGEA.

11. Meunier, Louise. 1988. *Rapport d'activités*. Saint-Jean-sur-Richelieu: Porte ouverte.

WOMEN AND LITERACY: A VITAL MOVEMENT

Elise de Coster
La Jarnigoine, Montréal, Canada

In Touch with Realities

The popular promotion of literacy consists of a set of practices and actions directed at disadvantaged social groups, and essentially aims at producing greater autonomy in individuals. The popular groups working to eliminate illiteracy have the will to anchor themselves in the reality of the environments in which they work so as to act in accordance with the needs, values and interests of illiterate persons. To them, the elimination of illiteracy is not simply teaching people how to read, write and do arithmetic, it is also a process of reflection and of individual and collective expression.

Learning to read and write is only one of the aspects of the battle for autonomy. In order to act effectively, it is necessary to take into account the factors that condition or determine the reality of illiterate persons so as to be able to attack the root of the social problems which foster and produce illiteracy. From this point of view, to act is to make a political gesture with the aim of sparking awareness, of arousing a will to change and of adapting literacy to social realities.

In the course of their work, the women who act as group literacy leaders have learned certain facts[1] which have led them to ponder a little-known reality: illiteracy among women.

Women attend the popular groups, places traditionally reserved for the most deprived persons, in great numbers. Their average age is generally high. Their access to literacy resources appears to be limited by factors related to their role within the family. Highly motivated, they nevertheless receive little encouragement from those close to them, and the reasons for absences or quitting are often connected with family pressures.

In the workshops, they say little and rarely discuss their preoccupations. While illiterate women may be able to manage in situations familiar to them, they are nevertheless lacking in resources, or even completely at a loss when confronted by the unexpected. Humiliated and made to feel inferior, they are little inclined to communicate.

Above all, women want a place that is completely free of any form of behaviour produced by the relations of dominance and subordination which, for the most part, have characterised their lives since their childhood. Sexist attitudes end in submission and reduce them to silence. This type of relationship continues to be very common in mixed groups. The women feel trapped and reduced to a condition which they no longer want to experience. They desire henceforth to concentrate and work in a context which encourages learning.

At present, the idea of conceiving and setting up workshops exclusively for women is very rare in Quebec in the field of literacy work, both in the educational institutions and in the popular groups. Lack of resources and non-recognition of the problems of women are the two principal reasons. Even so, in the groups in which certain activities are addressed to women only, the group leaders have quickly noticed a change: the participants are able to carve out a niche for themselves, to occupy the space progressively and to create a favourable climate for expressing themselves. They talk about themselves and the various aspects of their lives more easily. They soon show the desire to come together in order to define the conditions they consider essential for learning as well as to experiment with educational tools which meet their expectations.

In order thoroughly to understand the need to establish non-mixed groups in popular education centres, it is necessary to look at learning in the broad sense. Cognitive functioning, the acquisition of ideas and the habits essential for mastering reading, writing and arithmetic are only one of the aspects of the process, since illiteracy often appears as a general difficulty in self-expression. The act of learning, that is, of receiving and transmitting information, of modifying one's knowledge and grafting new elements onto it, is intimately associated with the capacity for communicating with others. In the context of adult education, this should be kept in mind and related to the motivations of individuals, their previous experiences and their attitudes with respect to learning. Workshops reserved for women therefore offer new advantages.

Isolation and lack of information limit the access of illiterate women to the resources within the environment that could give them the means to change their reality. On the other hand, group leaders who work in fields other than literacy training have difficulty in approaching the issue; they cannot recognize the various forms of illiteracy, discern the problems it creates and determine which literacy resources should be used to assist the illiterate.

Very little documentation can be found on illiterate women. The statistics, which are rare and often contradictory, frequently relate to the amount of schooling or the general phenomenon of illiteracy. Its particular nature among women is never presented as a point of departure for work. Once again, women seem to be ignored or absent from the story.

In order to remedy this situation, the group leaders have attempted, by means of research work and various projects, to draw a more accurate picture of the illiterate women who attend their centres, in order to assist them more effectively in taking charge of themselves and of the world surrounding them.

Examining the Details - Developing the Theory

Women experience a personal oppression which gives rise to specific conditions of life

Spurred on by the desire and will to involve the women of the Centre as "active and motivating" subjects of their research project[2], the group leaders of the Centre de lecture (CLÉ) chose the form of life histories in order to define better the reality of illiterate women.

From interviews with eight participants, there emerged an exchange of life experiences, a communication rich in emotion. Twelve hours of tape were set down in about 200 pages: a collection of witness statements which were dissected and organized by subject matter in order to protect the anonymity of the participants and to produce a synthesis which transcends the personal. As the details are examined, the theory is developed.

At the same time, the group leaders[3] in Villeray, at La Jarnigoine Literacy Centre, undertook a study conducted jointly with the shelters for women who have been victims of violence, and with the centres in the Island of Montreal. They organized information sessions on illiteracy among women. About 150 women, including group leaders, residents, participants at the day centres, immigrants who have worked on literacy campaigns in their native countries and literacy group leaders, participated in discussions on illiteracy among women.

Even though they followed one another, the two research projects were conducted in a completely independent fashion. Without consultation, the same subjects were tackled, similar observations were made, conclusions were drawn which confirm that the existence of a particular problem must be recognized and the necessity must be emphasized of offering women adequate resources, as is presently done for other groups such as youth, immigrants and ex-convicts.

Certainly, there are factors which women and men have in common: all types of illiteracy result from various forms of oppression caused by social relations which exclude and marginalize. For everyone it is linked to poverty, and it reduces people to silence. Illiterates are exploited, stifled by fear and shame. But there are differences: within social contexts, illiteracy is manifested and experienced differently.

A common vision

The two research projects had the objective of defining the characteristics of the female illiterates who attended community groups while establishing relationships between illiteracy and the traditional education of women, sexist experiences, sexual division of labour, access to employment and, more broadly, the traditional role of women in society.

Isolation and discrimination, which mark the socialization of women, play a determining role in the outward expressions of illiteracy and the way in which it is experienced. Indeed, many of the causes of illiteracy in women are directly related to the discriminatory attitudes and behaviours to which they have been subjected. The history of illiterate women, like that of women, is piecemeal, painful and characterized by discrimination from childhood on. Generally born into large families in which the mother takes care of the children and the home, the girls receive an education focused on their role within the family. They leave school if one parent becomes sick or if the mother is not up to her tasks; they abandon their studies in order to take on family responsibilities. The old mentality persists: boys are encouraged to study, girls are discouraged. At school, long and repeated absences frequently result in severe judgements regarding their capacity to learn. Finally, discouraged or forced by family pressures, they leave school very early.

They have a very firmly determined social position and rapidly identify with the role imposed upon them. Family relationships and, by extension, social relationships gradually influence and delimit their environment. Although they develop many skills, their personal freedom still remains greatly reduced: they work alone and have little means of action. Many of them live or have lived in a state of dependence upon their spouses, which limits their autonomy even more.

The majority of them have desired, at one time or another in their lives, to have a job which is interesting, stable, well-paid and recognized socially. In the fields in which they apply for work, the hiring criteria are often unrelated to the tasks to be accomplished: they are arbitrary, unjust and generally based upon discrimination by race, age, sex and physical appearance.

According to statistics established by women's groups working on employment issues, those who take part in information sessions on the state of the labour market and hiring opportunities are between 30 and 50 and are generally on social assistance, are receiving unemployment insurance benefits, or are employed in temporary and part-time work. Twenty-five to 30% of them are returning to work after a prolonged absence due to family responsibilities. They turn to these services after repeated rebuffs, setbacks suffered in their efforts, or because stress and lack of confidence in themselves prevent them from taking written tests.

These women are little inclined to emphasize their experience, otherwise rarely accorded recognition. Because they are poorly educated, they find themselves in female labour ghettoes, con-centrated in non-unionized jobs characterized by a fast pace, lack of benefits, and instability. Many take two jobs while remaining underpaid; others work strictly illegally. Many obstacles related to illiteracy and the insecurity arising from the non-recognition of their skills prevent them from gaining better paid jobs or from demanding better working conditions.

Discrimination, isolation, a social role lacking in recognition, repetitive tasks, a restricted personal space and economic dependence characterize the conditions of life for women, aggravate their situation as illiterates and help to create a particular profile. Conditioned at a very young age to occupy a peripheral position in various cultural and social fields, they are seldom called upon to use the ordinary channels of communication and, consequently, to perfect their knowledge of the written code.

An itinerary of ideas and projects

Social projects have been launched to arouse awareness and to provoke change. Although conceived independently, they have the same goal: to combat illiteracy by improving the conditions of life for illiterate women. Based upon the will and determination of certain group leaders, they nevertheless remain marginal. Lack of time and of financial resources currently prevent the pooling of experiences which could lead to joint action within the scope of a general action strategy.

At CLÉ, a supplementary activity parallel to the literacy workshops has been created via a Women's Committee.

At the Atout-lire[4] and the La Jarnigoine centres, a functional practical workshop has been initiated for women.

At La Jarnigoine, literacy action tools have been produced, adapted to the needs of the group leaders of shelters and day centres on the Island of Montreal.

At La Gigogne[5], literacy workshops have been added to the usual activities of welcoming and sheltering women and children who have been victims of violence.

"Educating oneself to understand how to change one's situation, one's state of being a woman"[6]

The CLÉ research project had the goal of creating a place for exchange and reflection. The will of the women at the centre, both participants and group leaders, to gather together and to share their ideas was the determining factor. They decided to launch a feminist literacy process by creating a Women's Committee. Trials, periods of stress and periods of uncertainty have characterized the three years in which this collective experience has existed.

The participants are motivated to organize themselves by the desire to instill a sense of confidence and to strengthen the ties uniting them with other women, whether they be housewives, wives, mothers or employed. Together, they define the goals of the committee: to create a place for exchanges and reflection, for expressing one's views, for support and solidarity, for organization and action to change their condition as illiterate women.

Conceived in the form of exploratory encounters, the initial activities of the committee served better to define the goals and to address the questions relating to the lives of the participants. The discussions inevitably led to reflections on illiterate women and by extension, on women in society. The meetings focused on topics chosen by the group: the 8th of March, the division of labour at the centre, menopause, interpersonal relations, fears and worries. Generators of complicity and new ideas, these exchanges of opinions, information and experience, both happy and sad, are always very stimulating. The interest of the women is obvious. The committee is composed of up to 18 participants.

The realities of illiterate women are recognized in the same way as those of women living in better known social situations. The women talk about their strengths, their weaknesses, their desires and their mistakes in a world dominated by men. The sum of these experiences which have been lived through is impressive but difficult to analyse. It is hard to define the realities, to find a common thread among them and to derive new knowledge from them.

Faced with the committee's feeling of impotence, the situation was examined and it was concluded that certain steps needed for developing a feminist process had been skipped. Nine women, group leaders and participants, studied the course of the encounters in order to redefine the operation of the Committee. An attempt was made to organize the more significant meetings by integrating the topics in a planned process. For example, beginning with "sexism, harassment and fear", the focus was placed on defining the reality of sexism and of harassment in daily life. Each participant expressed herself, recounting her own experiences and those which she witnessed. One gradually became aware of facts and their consequences. Emotions and reactions to these events were explored. Together, the members grasp the reality, name it, explain it in their own way, and this then constitutes new knowledge. The analysis develops, gradually the theoretical aspects of the question are underlined from each person's point of view. The matter is then illustrated more concretely by the staging of various situations involving ideas and emotions. On the basis of the facts, the means of taking action are explored; a way is found to make the realities visible and to transform them.

A new step is taken: the members talk about change, they look for ways to provoke it, to organize it, to make it possible. The commitment grows: the individual and the private becomes collective and political. The members organize together according to the goals to be attained and choose to act at the centre itself. A collective writing workshop is organized: the women address themselves to the men close to them. The text is published in the journal and in the agenda; it circulates, provokes reactions and stirs discussion.

In theory and in practice, the activity represents a feminist model of literacy. It enables women to become aware of their situation, to acquire a theoretical knowledge of their experience and to exert a real power in their lives, by making a change affecting both the female condition and literacy. It fits in with a literacy practice which takes into account the lives, socialization and attitudes of female illiterates.

Using the feminist ideology "the personal is political" as a starting point, the Committee of the CLÉ prefers the "consciousness-raising group" approach throughout its program, the cornerstone of the feminist movements. Instead of internalizing problems and developing a sense of guilt, the women learn to share their experiences, to go beyond individual responsibility, and to grasp the collective significance of the problems. For the women involved, this underlines the common character of the experiences and situates them in a society where the oppression of women is general and institutionalized. In establishing the link between the personal and the political, the women of CLÉ are better able to give their reality a name, to become more aware of their situation and to implement a change in improving the quality of their relations with the participants at the centre.

The Way of Women[7]

We have decided to write this text with the aim of sensitizing men to the situations which we regularly experience with them and which make us feel uncomfortable. For example, at the centre, we are often the object of disparaging remarks regarding our persons: "You're getting pretty fat, you're really silly, you always have the same hairstyle" and it goes as far as looks that undress us. There are also the stupid jokes about us women. At the centre, just like at home, we often have to repeat the same things: "Men, pick up your dishes, wash your cups, help us to collect the ones that are left..." It's tiring always to have to repeat the same things and to feel responsible for the cleaning and decoration of the Centre. It is true that we learned young how to do domestic chores. "There were nine of us at home and it was the girls who did the housework." We quickly learned what it means to keep house and we would like it if the guys would learn as well. And it isn't just with regard to housework that they were raised differently. That's why they don't think the same way. We learned to get along, we did not learn to affirm ourselves and to take our place in society. We were taught not to talk back because it was not polite for a little girl. And even today we have trouble reacting when we end up in disagreeable situations, such as getting stuck with someone, being kissed, being called sweetheart when we're not interested.

We think that it is important to react because we don't like being bothered. We tell ourselves that there are ways of dealing with it. We can't make them understand by being stupid. Sometimes humour is the best way to get out of it. Other times, we decide to be deaf to disparaging remarks. Sometimes they don't realize they are hurting us, they should be told or else they will never know. We must have confidence in ourselves, we must respect ourselves. Basically, we're not the only ones to experience this, if we talk more to women, at the centre or elsewhere, we could stick together. What we want is to be equal, not to have to struggle all the time, not to be always on guard. We want to feel comfortable, to take our place without being told to shut up. We want men to listen to women and to stop thinking that they are only good for housework, washing, cleaning up and bed. At the centre, the women have decided to give themselves a place for discussing and reflecting together on the subjects that interest us. There we can express ourselves comfortably regarding things that we do not often have the opportunity to talk about: our rights, our fears, violence, harassment, our health... In these meetings, we find ways of taking our place in the centre more effectively, means of learning about ourselves. We can hear our own voices. In fact a Women's Committee is intended for the solidarity of women.

A Place of Learning that Measures up to the Expectations of Women

Workshops for and by women, and defined in the course of experimentation

The Atout-lire[8] staff wanted to facilitate access to education by opening a supplementary workshop during the day, after having discovered that the fear of having to travel the streets of the neighbourhood at night constituted an obstacle to literacy training for many women. Thanks to this initiative, women registered in the advanced group henceforth have the choice of working in a mixed or non-mixed workshop.

At La Jarnigoine, the functional illiterates group[9] has been composed solely of women for two years, although it was open to all. The women have created an atmosphere of confidence and have been able to gain recognition for themselves. Cooperative and united, thy have gradually learned to define the content of the workshop according to their life experiences, their values and their fields of interest.

In the two centres, what initially appeared to be a simple combination of circumstances has rapidly transformed itself into a common will to exert an assertion of power over reality. The participants want to create a place of learning which is suited to their wishes and meets their expectations. The idea, the very concept of these workshops is defined by experimentation.

Learning means communicating with others

In the workshops, the group leaders have gradually discovered the importance of defining the factors which will interact in the process of achieving literacy. What influences learning? What restricts or increases the chances of success? Can certain difficulties be resolved more easily by creating workshops especially designed for women?

For the latter, the decision to learn how to read often emerges from a situation of change and is directly related to an irreversible will to take control and achieve autonomy. Whatever the reasons - the death of the spouse, the breakup of the couple, the children entering school, the desire to enter the labour market - this decision gives rise to distressing awareness. It reveals, often brutally, that the factors which caused the illiteracy and the extreme precariousness of living conditions - sexist teaching, sexual division of labour, lack of space, repetitive tasks, isolation, economic dependence and non-recognition of skills - are determined by the position which women occupy and by the role they play.

Their principal motivation, when it is a question of becoming literate, is often to break with their past. They must henceforth assert themselves, break certain habits, refuse to be constantly available, allot time to themselves and recreate their emotional freedom. In turn, these changes risk setting in motion reactions on the part of those close to them who, in many cases, do not accept the changes. External pressures intensify the women's doubts as to their ability to learn and often discourage them systematically. Gradually, the group leaders help these women to create a climate of confidence which enables them clearly to articulate their motivations and to use them as a source of stimulation.

If we wish to be able to draw from our experiences the resources to permit the acquisition of new knowledge, we must first of all recognize their worth. It is noticeable that illiterate women in particular have a very marked tendency to deny the value of the intellectual skills they have developed in their activities. At home, the lack of confidence is reinforced by the non-recognition of their participation in cultural and social life. They have internalized a negative image of themselves which strongly conditions their attitudes toward learning.

In the workshop, we try to discover with them the various forms of knowledge they have acquired, among other things, through the specific tasks such as planning and organization within the family, as well as the education of the children. We validate their role in interpersonal relations. Gradually, they gain more confidence and establish contact with an interior world which they wish to share. They go beyond the simple acquisition of a particular skill, the mastery of the written code, and express what they feel, what they think and what they experience.

Tools which meet their expectations in the learning situation

The educational experiences which follow illustrate well how the fact of taking into account the lives and attitudes of women in the practical work of teaching literacy influences the content as well as the orientation of the workshops and determines both the place and the role of the participants in the choice of subjects and methods.

At the Atout-lire Centre, the thematic workshops are organized according to the concerns of the women in the groups as a whole. In these workshops, verbal expression by the participants play a very major role. The work sessions are set up on the basis of subjects chosen by the women. Initially related to reports of experiences with the personal circle, the discussion gradually shifts their focus to the condition of women and finally moves on to their relations within society. It is noticeable that the participation of immigrant women in the workshop leads to greater diversity of exchanges. The thematic workshops, designed in accordance with the needs, fields of interest and preoccupations of women, stimulates them to seek out information in other groups and subsequently to share it with members of the workshop. Reading and writing exercises are grafted onto various organized activities.

At La Jarnigoine, the women's workshop has participated in writing a guide intended to facilitate the work of sensitization and orientation of group leaders in the shelters and day centres. The illiterate women first learned about the project as a whole and then participated actively in it by writing a collective text. In this way, they emphasized their experience as participants in a literacy group and reinvested their learning in a socially-oriented activity. They are particularly proud of their participation.

This experience is based upon the oral expression of each participant and its success is owed in large part to the desire of each woman to express herself and to share her ideas. They talk in turn about role, they compose sentences which translate their thoughts. The interest given to the discussion and to communication with others enables them to establish a distance with regard to writing. They almost forget they are writing. The teaching of grammar and orthography does not intrude until the last stage of work.

Power in One's Own Hands[10]

Once I was an illiterate who did not know how to count, or read, or write; it was very difficult for me; it made me think; I wasn't any stupider than anyone else; it was then that I decided to take courses.

I am very happy to be able to read and write; it gives me a purpose in my life and the courage to go on. It is not easy. It is a source of satisfaction to me. Now, knowing how to read and write better gives me confidence in myself to confront situations that I consider very embarrassing; for example, when my godson asks me to read him a story before he goes to sleep.

It is very important for me to see that I can solve my problems and can talk about a lot of things.

The need to know how to read and write is so that I can have a better job and a better salary.

I am very proud of myself.

Finally I am no longer afraid to write.

Louise Nadon
Évelyne Petit
Sylvie Sévigny

Literacy workshops in a women's shelter at La Gigogne[11]

The recruitment was done mainly at La Gigogne. The group leaders of the shelter were in a position to provide information on the literacy workshops and to bring the persons in charge of these workshops together with interested women. It is often the case that the latter have acquaintances or friends who are also illiterate. There is also collaboration with the CLSC (Local Centre of Community Services) and other community agencies which are in contact with people who could benefit from this service.

For two years, two literacy group leaders have run a workshop composed of functional and complete illiterates. The more advanced come to the assistance of those who are less advanced, the discussions have been enriched, and the life of the groups has become much more interesting. For the group leaders, the important point is to utilize capacities and affinities. Faster progress has been noted, especially among the complete illiterates.

Given that the activities take place over the course of one day, one can go into depth in developing a subject and finish in some degree that which has been started. Overall, learning takes place as part of a process of personal growth.

Once the needs have been defined and discussed with each of the people, the topics corresponding to individual needs and to subjects of interest to the entire group are brought out. It is in fact the common denominator which must be found.

If there is a problem which concerns only one person, there is provision for a mechanism for individual assistance. The activities connected with the theme must encourage learning the grammatical and linguistic code, basic arithmetic, the metric system, oral expression, and reflection, and lead to new comprehension of the topic, a concrete application of learning in daily life and the adoption of new attitudes.

There are various blocs of activities during a day. The morning is devoted mainly to what may resemble group therapy, although all possible opportunities are taken for writing (personal diary), for reading (texts which add information) and expressing oneself.

When one talks about oneself, one's fears, one's questioning, one's wishes, one gets caught up in the activity. In this way, one improves the construction of one's sentences, corrects one's faults, learns new words, talks so as to be understood by the others, learns to have confidence in oneself, to comprehend the reality of others and to respect it. Obviously, not all are at the same level, a fact which enriches everyone.

In the afternoon, one period is devoted to practical work: how to write a cheque, address an envelope, read a pattern; another is devoted to arithmetic and to the metric system. Finally, there is one reserved for grammatical exercises in which each person can work at her own speed on her own difficulties.

Before leaving, each person evaluates her progress and discusses the tasks to be accomplished during the week: not only reading and writing work, but challenges to be met as well.

During the week, each person attempts to do things which she has never dared to do and the experience is shared with the others at the next meeting.

The session generally ends with a trip or an activity which is intended to enlarge the members' vision of the world, to open them up to other realities and to go a bit beyond what they have always known.

An Obvious Need: Cooperation

A woman who is a victim of violence can be blocked in her progress if she is illiterate.
An illiterate woman can have trouble learning if she is a victim of violence.

In the course of recent years, women have set up a network of service and pressure groups in which they fought in accordance with the priorities they have defined. In the autumn of 1986, the staff of La Jarnigoine decided to add a section to their popular education activities by developing a joint project with other women's groups in order to understand how, under the circumstances, to include the struggle against illiteracy in a broader action strategy to change the conditions of life for women.

This activity was intended to make it possible to understand the importance of illiteracy in situations in which it did not necessarily appear to be a grave or first-priority problem. The intent was to define its manifestations and consequences in order to sensitize group leaders of women's groups to the necessity of examining together the set of problems of illiterate women and to formulate with them demands concerning their situation "in a society in which knowledge is supposedly egalitarian and democratized". The intent was to enable women to gather together, to express what they were experiencing and to organize collectively. The intent was to create a network for screening, support and orientation.

For practical reasons, the La Jarnigoine staff initially decided to approach shelters and day centres: the type of activities offered by these bodies appeared to be suitable for the launching of literacy activities adapted to the procedure already undertaken by the group. A mobile group was established to determine what resources a popular literacy group could offer, taking into account both its means and the needs of the group leaders and participants of the shelters and day centres.

About thirty groups located on the Island of Montreal were contacted and the proposal was made to meet them, to present a video on illiteracy and to hold an information session. Designed in the form of thematic sections - illiteracy, a social fact; who are the illiterate? the special character of illiteracy in women; literacy resources - the information session proved to be a flexible and effective tool of communication. In addressing both women who are victims of violence and illiterates, as well as group leaders, a permanent place of exchange was created which enables the former to reveal themselves and the latter to discover techniques of screening and the sources of documentation which they lacked at the time. The social and political realities which affect schooling and the process of becoming literate were examined. Together, the needs of illiterate women were defined in the process of autonomy undertaken at the centres they attend: signing a lease, looking for a job, making banking transactions, taking legal measures, registering for a course, in order to offer them adequate resources.

If the information session is well integrated into the operation of the day centres, and responds to the expectations of the participants, it has proved to be difficult to reconcile with the work done in the shelters which experience crisis situations and indescribable stress every day. The multiple problems of the women and the urgency of their situation consumes all the available energy.

Nevertheless, conscious of the problems caused by illiteracy and the insurmountable obstacles which paralyze the residents in their progress, the group leaders of the shelters have demonstrated a desire to be trained in order to be able to act on the spot and to diminish the shame, fear and impotence felt by these women. By joint agreement, therefore, the meetings have been suspended and tools intended to facilitate work with illiterate women are being developed together.

In the groups, a questionnaire is being tested which concerns primarily the obstacles which the women have to overcome when they take measures: what are the constraints and limits imposed by a lack of mastery of reading, writing and arithmetic? This questionnaire helps the shelter group leaders to address a subject which they often prefer to ignore. By determining clearly what obstacles illiterate women encounter, they are acting concretely and quickly.

We are waiting for a second version of the questionnaire before encouraging a larger number of group leaders to use it. At present it appears to be a valuable tool of sensitization and communication between participants and group leaders. It breaks through the isolation and encourages women to take their own measures.

Furthermore, in order to respond to the need for training expressed by the group leaders, a support document[12] has been produced which has been distributed to groups that may be interested in this issue. The document is intended to sensitize shelter group leaders to the social character of illiteracy, to the difficulties of illiterate women and to the work accomplished by popular groups in order to facilitate screening.

Meetings are organized with the centres that have participated in the project, in order to discuss its repercussions and the possibility of collaboration. There is an exchange of information on practices, an attempt to clarify certain points of the theoretical research and an evaluation of the possibility of adding literacy workshops to the activities of shelters. This last point, moreover, frequently gives rise to controversy. The mobile team of La Jarnigoine has expressed certain reservations, both in practical and educational terms, regarding the usefulness and effectiveness of such a workshop.

It is interesting to compare the observations of La Jarnigoine with the testimony of the staff of La Gigogne, which has taken the initiative of establishing a workshop of this type. For the two staffs, the initial goal was the same: to act while taking into account both the violence and the illiteracy. The contexts are different and, it appears, determining factors in the conclusions which can be drawn.

The launching of workshops within the shelters, designed and run jointly with the group leaders for women who have been victims of violence, remains a feasible but long-term objective for the staff of La Jarnigoine. In the course of the project, the literacy group leaders learned that information and sensitization work must be done before the establishment of workshops outside the popular groups or educational institutions. It is thought to be preferable, for an initial period, to offer resources that require less organization, funding and energy, such as the production of a video on the subject of illiteracy and on violence, which would be distributed to all the women's centres.

The staff of La Jarnigoine is also pondering the educational aspect of its action. It distinguishes two types of action: short-term actions, which help women to take certain urgent steps, and workshops presuming a process of acquiring literacy stretched over several months, if not several years. The first possibility appears more realistic to them, however, and better adapted to the context of the shelters.

The staff of La Jarnigoine considers that learning to read, to write and to do arithmetic is a difficult task, sometimes even arduous, and can only be accomplished under certain conditions. In order to concentrate, it is necessary to distance oneself from certain preoccupations, at least temporarily. Before undertaking such a step, one ought to take into account such factors as availability, safety and stability, which influence learning. For these reasons, it has been concluded that it would probably be preferable, for an initial period, to encourage popular literacy groups to run these workshops themselves rather than the shelters, which are not a suitable place.

We note that this hypothesis could not be verified in practice. It is at the limits of the project that the experience of La Gigogne adds its message in emphasizing the point of view of a shelter which, thanks to its consciousness-raising with regard to illiteracy, utilizes the links between violence and illiteracy and acts comprehensively to solve the problems of its residents.

Literacy Consciousness-Raising at La Gigogne [13]

Initially, La Gigogne wanted to have a house designed, organized and managed by women who were victims of violence, who came from a socially disadvantaged class, who would be supported in their action by several group leaders. It was at the request of women that a first group of functional illiterates was set up for the autumn of 1982.

These women were the heads of single parent families, poorly educated, economically poor and, for the most part, with experience of violence in one form or another. However, this portrait is not static; it has evolved over the years. Many of these women, still in most cases the heads of their families, have been trained, have returned to their studies and now occupy paid positions at La Gigogne or elsewhere. Their quality of life has greatly improved in general. Obviously, we are speaking here of the members of La Gigogne who have remained loyal for several years; for those who have joined the staff along the way it is almost always a matter of beginning again.

The depiction of literacy consciousness-raising also developed in La Gigogne. The first workshops did not make their appearance by chance. They were born of the will to take charge of La Gigogne by its members. In their steps toward autonomy, despite all the efforts made to take them in hand, the fact of not adequately mastering the written and spoken language closed many doors to these women.

How can one lead, teach others, make a radio or television broadcast, organize a press conference, deal with correspondence, gather information, form an opinion on subjects such as violence, abortion, nervous depression, etc.? And do all this when one's self-esteem is at its nadir.

Teaching reading and writing is done on the basis of tasks made necessary by the operation of a shelter which is just starting up. The importance of this project rests in the fact that it has been the source of motivation that has promoted learning, the ideal place for their reinvestment and the place where a more critical consciousness was born.

Two years later, given that the women did not know how to read or write, or only very little, when they came into contact with La Gigogne, a second group leader was added and it was possible to welcome complete illiterates.

Currently, workshops are offered every day to members of La Gigogne, but also to other women in Matane who live in the same situations. The needs change with the years and the groups. Or rather, it is the circumstances which change because the deep needs themselves remain the same.

A practice of consciousness-raising continues to be combined with the acquisition of literacy. What good are the tools of reading and writing if one does not at the same time acquire the means of utilizing them? Self-knowledge, understanding what is going on in one's environment and the capacity to exert an influence, the improvement of one's manner of entering into relations with others and of communicating, the development of one's personal potential, learning how to read, to write and to do arithmetic are the main concerns of La Gigogne.

Beginning from the lives of the women, from the point at which they are, is undoubtedly of paramount importance in the achievement of these goals. Depending on the participants, the topics may be more political or closer to day-to-day life, the lessons may lead to involvement in La Gigogne or in another agency, or simply in one's personal life.

In the light of two initiatives, those of La Gigogne and La Jarnigoine, it has been learned that the awareness and the will to change on the part of illiterate women has an influence not only on the choice of projects but especially on the determination to supply resources. For example, in Matane, the success of the workshops was due in large part to the fact that they were set up at the request of the residents. In the same way, the La Jarnigoine project derives all its value from the fact that, owing to information and sensitization, it is intended to provoke just this awareness and that it is committed to supporting concretely the actions that can follow. Thus, what could be an additional concern and extra work for the group leaders of women's groups becomes a means of action all the more effective in that it makes it possible to work at the same time on various facets of the same problem and encourages collaboration on various issues relating to women.

A Constantly Evolving Work

This text and the experiences related in it can be compared to the formula "work in progress" used in the theatre. The reflections concerning illiterate women and the actions undertaken to date are part of a work in constant evolution. The practice and the theory develop simultaneously and nourish each other: the ideas trigger and justify the actions; the experiences call the theory into question and promote more thought.

If the group leaders working with illiterate women want to draw a more precise and more complete profile of the latter, it is essentially for the purpose of creating adequate resources and using the most effective means to counter the problem of illiteracy as a whole, in order to work more accurately to improve the conditions of life for women. As has already been mentioned, illiteracy is a serious social problem that affects both men and women and concerns the entire population. Men and women have common problems, which are as serious for one as for the other. The issue here is not to compare or to measure them, but fully to understand the differences, often brought about by the discrimination practised by society, in order to enlarge the range of our actions and increase our chances for success.

The picture of the situation of illiterate women may appear grim, but it is nevertheless true and faithful to the realities of the majority of those who currently attend popular groups. Conditioned very young by their education, they are strongly influenced by sexist stereotypes: they feel responsible both for organization within the family and for the quality of interpersonal relations. They are alone in the face of realities that are difficult to grasp. If they know their situation well, the precariousness of their conditions of life block any prospect for change they may have within themselves.

In taking the step toward literacy, they break that isolation; in communicating with others, they gradually become aware of the reasons for their choices, for their desires and for their will to change. In many cases, it is the motives of the participants that determine the setting-up of activities designed for them. In participating actively, they learn to use these resources and gradually to appropriate them for themselves.

At CLÉ and at Atout-lire, it has been learned that women participate more in workshops and various activities designed for them. They can talk about their experiences and their preoccupations; they take their place and gradually open up to the outside.

At La Gigogne, one of the group leaders having set up a program of community organization at the CÉGEP, some of the participants now have a work certificate and others have enrolled in various programs after having completed their secondary 5 in continuing education.

As for the project of La Jarnigoine, it was lived like an adventure: no certainty and hypotheses reformulated many times. The only index: the experience of groups already working to combat oppression among women. The mobile team thus had the possibility of going to check the rightness of its action among the women who share their socio-economic preoccupations.

Taking into account the experiences described, we understand that illiteracy among women cannot be isolated from the set of their problems as a whole, and that studying it presumes the understanding of complex social relations, cogs in a giant mechanism. Whatever the spheres of action, whether one works on an individual or collective basis, actions and research concerning illiterate women must be in keeping with the social realities and connect with the preoccupations of the women's movement.

The experiences described serve as models, as reference points. Some of them could be retested in the development of new strategies, in order to determine clearly where to act, which aspect it is preferable to work on and in what way. They can be divided into two main categories: actions taken in the literacy centres, where activities are created solely for women, and social projects developed jointly with other groups.

In this way, a group could decide to set up a special activity during an election campaign to inform women as to what was particularly at stake for them. One could invite the candidates to discuss certain subjects, participate in public meetings or encounter groups of women involved in the campaign.

One could also facilitate women's access to community resources as a post-literacy activity - legal aid, tenants' associations, groups of people on social assistance, unemployment action, health centres for women, labour market re-entry programs - or promote their involvement in the community (parents' committees, women immigrant collectives, tenants' associations or citizens' committees).

One could also organize pressure groups to influence political decisions concerning the struggle of women against illiteracy and study the literacy campaigns and programs addressed to women which have been tested in other countries, for the purpose of better adapting ourselves to a reality which goes beyond our national frontiers.

Other groups could examine more closely certain laws concerning women in order to understand the consequences for their literacy training, for example the measures concerning day care, continuing education, social assistance or unemployment insurance.

The position given to the realities of illiterate women will be determined in large part by the energy devoted to developing the knowledge of the women's groups, pursuing the reflection begun in the popular education centres, enriching experiences, defining the new directions of research and making known and recognising the problem. This task cannot be accomplished except by the increased presence of women in public manifestations and their involvement in joint projects set up with prospects for collaboration.

Notes

1. These observations were made in CLÉ and La Jarnigoine literacy groups, located respectively in Mont-Royal plateau and the Villeray neighbourhood in Montreal.

2. Boucher, Andrée; Gladu, Nicole and Reid, Josée. L'école, ça me rentrait pas dans la tête. (I couldn't get school into my head). Reading and Writing Centre, 3684 Mentana, Montreal, H2L 3R3, (519) 527-9097. 1984.

3. Élise de Coster et Hélène Quellette, La Jarnigoine, 6815 St-Denis, Montréal, H2S 2S3 (514)273-6683.

4. Atout-lire, 325 Rue Ste-Thérèse, Québec, G1K 1M9, (418)524-9353.

5. La Gigogne at Matane.

6. Cf. Gladu, Nicole. 1988. *Une démarche féministe en alphabétisation* (A feminist approach to literacy work). Montréal: CLÉ.

7. Collective text written by Women's Committee, published in 1987 in the CLÉ journal.

8. The Atout-lire Women's Workshop was set up in 1984 and has been run by Francine Loignon for two years.

9. The group leader was Hélène Quellette.

10. Collective text by participants at la Jarnigoine.

11. Excerpts from a text by Allard, Lise. 1987. L'alphabétisation-conscientisation à La 'Gigogne' (Literacy consciousness-raising at la Gigogne). *Alpha Liaison* vol. 7, March.

12. *Le pouvoir entre les mains* (Power in one's hands) produced by the team of La Jarnigoine, Montréal, 1987.

13. Excerpt from Lise Allard, op.cit.

Acknowledgement

The author wishes to thank all those who wanted to share their experiences, such as Christiane Tremblay and Maryse Perreault, for their attentive reading and their commentary. All documents are available at the Documentation Centre for Adult Education and the Female Condition: CDEACF, 1265, Rue Berri, bureau 340, Montréal, H2L 4X4, (514) 844-3674.

THE ALPHA MONS-BORINAGE EXPERIENCE

Omer Arrijs
Alpha Mons-Borinage, Quaregnon, Belgium

1. The Situation

After 15 years of experience, we are still asking ourselves such simple yet weighty questions as, "What should be done? Why? How?" Very specific questions. We have experimented day after day, discovering how much the interests of communities, groups and individuals termed "illiterate" differ from those of the institutions which apply this label -and thus relegate them to society's fringe - and which draw up literacy training strategies in the name of a universal right to education and knowledge. Communication lies at the heart of our activity. But we have been unable to establish any real communication between society and those who society guarantees will remain "fully illiterate" or "functionally illiterate" simply by applying these terms to them. Contrary to the official line, does not society feed on illiteracy, which it produces to ensure that its unequal structures are perpetuated? Society needs both illiteracy and literacy training in its current, ineffective forms.

This is what a group of poor, illiterate participants in an adult education program in West Bengal wrote in a poem entitled "Why should we learn how to read?"

...But we must know
Why we should learn how to read.

We have taken literacy courses before,
But we wised up after a while.
We felt we were being tricked,
So we quit.

Do you know what we found out?
Those bureaucratic stuffed shirts were turning this work
To their own advantage.

Perhaps elections were coming up,
Or maybe there was a government grant,
Or something else that had to be used up.
What they taught us was useless.

Being able to sign your name means nothing.
Being able to read a few words means nothing.

We agreed to attend the courses,
If you taught us how not to be dependent on others.

...Can literacy help us live a little better?
To die of hunger less often?

...Will this program teach us
How to think and work together?
Will it include practical training?
If it does all this, we will all attend the literacy courses,
And it will be to learn how to live a better life...[1]

Of course, we must not over-simplify matters. We must acknowledge that literacy training has produced results both in industrialized societies and in the South. But we must reveal that these results have been slim and have not touched the root of the problem.

With a few changes, the questions which these common people of Bengal asked their instructors are also valid here in Belgium. Most of the "illiterate" set little store by our resources[2]. We have not communicated with them. We have not got below the surface. We have not really analysed all the issues, because, among other reasons, we have failed to put the "illiterate" themselves at the centre of the process and have not sufficiently analysed the relationship between literacy training and a wider process of liberation that affects the very way in which democracy operates and the way our societies develop. Literacy training has in many respects been only an excuse for continuing to do all the same old things. Literacy training remains a component of the marginal management of marginality.

An evaluation of our activities has prompted us to level these criticisms. Will we find solutions?

2. The Initial Period of Alpha Mons-Borinage

In Belgium's former coal-producing area of Mons-Borinage, the question of social exclusion is a burning one. The official unemployment rate of 26 per cent (36 per cent for women and 18 per cent for men as of June 1990) is the highest in Belgium.

The *Association Alpha* was created in Mons-Borinage in September 1976. At first, it organized courses in spoken and written French at several locations in Borinage for immigrant workers, including Moroccans, Algerians, Turks, Italians and Spaniards. We reached about 80 people a year. But there are approximately 47,000 immigrants in Borinage. And most of them have been here for 10, 20 or 30 years without any real language training having been organized previously. (For the reader's information, Belgian authorities halted immigration in 1974.) It was not surprising then that these courses were not wildly successful. Most immigrants had developed their own version of everyday French which satisfied them.

Recruiting participants involved a great deal of work visiting associations, neighbourhoods and the homes of possible trainees.

The declared objectives fell into three categories:

- utilitarian objectives: to provide people with the tools they need to survive in Belgium, so they can successfully handle procedures related to employment, housing, food, health, education, and so on;

- cultural objectives: to encourage immigrants to express their identities and personal histories in the face of Belgium's dominant culture; and

- political objectives: to develop a critical consciousness and a movement for social change, especially as concerned immigration, which our analyses indicated was a mechanism for perpetuating exploitation. A further goal was to create political projects in which the common people could express their vision of society and create their own history.

Liberation pedagogy

Literacy training claims to be a tool of liberation. It is a political act.

Literacy groups are both vehicles for learning language and venues for discussing, on the basis of everyday life, the key issues that concern immigrants: survival, immigrant identity, work, housing, education, the right to vote, and trade unionism. The issues widen toward an analysis of society itself. The speech of the immigrants is the starting point for everything. Learning a language means learning a specific way of expressing oneself, in the form of thoughts in tune with the realities one has experienced, about the representations of social relationships. Literacy training opens the door both to everyday processes and to sociology, law, economics, political analysis and the search for alternatives. Beyond the courses, literacy training puts people in contact with (or prolongs their contact with) other associations, other groupings, other struggles. It ties into a wider network of immigrant activity.

These options and this methodology are inspired by Paulo Freire, who said, "Knowledge cannot be transferred. It is created in and through actions that affect reality."[3] We believe that people liberate themselves, that developing the speech of all, even the oppressed, is the motor for social change. We refer to UNESCO, which declared in Persepolis in 1975 that:

> Literacy training, like education in general, is a political act. It is not neutral, because both exposing the social reality in order to transform it and hiding it in order to perpetuate it are political acts. Accordingly, there are economic, social, political and administrative structures that are favourable to the implementation of a literacy project, and others that stand in its way.

In our view, speaking, reading, writing and communicating involve expressing one's social situation as defined by exploitation and exclusion. All speech is the speech of a class or social group created by specific interests. The issue for the common people is liberation, not insertion. They achieve this liberation by affirming their identity, their right to a specific popular or immigrant culture. This liberation rejects conforming to the dominant standards. But this does not mean we think marginalization is a good thing. What we are talking about here is critical integration. Language itself is not seen as a system of socially and politically neutral symbols. The popular codes are different from the dominant codes[4]. The main purpose of language is not to convey the messages it claims to convey. Its main purpose is to serve as a marker of social position[5]. Phonetics, grammar, vocabulary and the semantic system are always marked socially. They immediately tell others where we stand on the social ladder and where we are speaking from.

Language, as actually used in the here and now, is like an article of clothing, a sign of belonging that can be used to develop linguistic or non-linguistic strategies for establishing relationships with other groups. From this viewpoint, it is essential to promote the development of popular speech forms that express popular identities and at the same time develop speech forms that make it possible to communicate in the official languages.

Dynamic, liberating pedagogy for the common people is complex. It begins with the participants expressing their views of reality in their own terms (their speech, their writing and their re-reading of a text). We reject all scholastic approaches, textbooks, exercises and grammatical or linguistic formalism. The goal is to bring into being a specific system of symbols, meanings, relations and forms. A given utterance is spoken in relation to a concrete reality: the neighbourhood, immigrant history, school, the power which people seek, work, or the trade union.

This is used as a base for expanding, for enriching the linguistic resources used in the preceding stage. Using precise seriation techniques, we make the linguistic system operate in relation to what has been said and what forms have been produced (whether correct or incorrect). Enriching the forms permits and invites further expansion of the contents and meanings. A dialectic develops between work on the content and work on the form. Our literacy project tries to get below the surface to the bases of social change through language activity.

In the beginning, we worked almost exclusively with volunteer instructors, many of whom gave up when they realized the scope and difficulty of the task. "Literacy training" is more than just a few hours a week spent with immigrants who either do not know French or do not know it very well. It means investing in a complex pedagogical process that challenges the instructors and organizers themselves. Later, we had access to programs for getting the unemployed back to work called Unemployment Reabsorption Plans. These programs are aimed at putting the unemployed to work for a limited time in socially useful projects. There are several formulas: Special Temporary Staff, Third Work Circuit, Unemployed Put to Work, Interdepartmental Budgetary Funds, Subsidized Contract Officers and Regional Labour Market Insertion Programs.

We had access first to the Special Temporary Staff program, then to the Third Work Circuit program and the Interdepartmental Budgetary Funds program. I will speak later about the precariousness of these types of job. At first, they were looked on as a golden opportunity, both for the literacy project - since it acquired a "more stable" work force (some people stayed with us for several years in this sort of arrangement) - and for the worker able to escape unemployment (even it not all the worker's rights are respected). Later on we shall analyze this situation, more radically, as a sham.

We organized instructor training on an on-going basis for the volunteers and for the Unemployment Reabsorption Program workers, who did not enjoy the usual statutory rights. Our purpose was to enable them fully to understand the issues, goals and methodology. This training had sociolinguistic, methodological and political components. We also took part in instructor training programs for associations other than our own.

Our methodology was written down in the form of pedagogical reference materials for instructors. These were neither recipes nor manuals, but simply methodological indicators[6].

The écoles de devoirs (Homework centres)

Shortly after launching the literacy courses for adult immigrants, we created "écoles de devoirs" with similar objectives at various locations in Borinage. In so doing, we tried to answer the call for a linkage between literacy training and *écoles de devoirs*, a call which Véronique Marissal made in *ALPHA 90* when she wrote: "It seems to us that *écoles de devoirs* and literacy centres could work together both in prevention and in promoting literacy among people who have little or no schooling."[7]

Six centres were set up serving approximately 100 children. Is this a lot? Is it a little? We think there should be a centre in every neighbourhood, but that would require an army of instructors.

The objectives of the *écoles de devoirs* must take into account scholastic constraints and the reality of scholastic failure. Children of low-income families (Belgian and especially immigrant) often fail at school because no one there recognizes their language and distinctive culture, and because the teaching methods, even when revised, are foreign to their lifestyle and view of life because they are based on the dominant lifestyle and standards. Schools select, perpetuating an unequal society. Those who are able to overcome the cultural barriers will occupy a respected, even dominant position, while the rest are pushed into vocational training (one "drops down" into vocational training) and can expect either manual jobs or social exclusion pure and simple. School thus reinforces cultural, social and economic discrimination.[8]

Combating scholastic failure is therefore a prime objective of the *écoles de devoirs*. Beginning with the school work and going back to the prerequisites, the goal is to help students understand the mechanisms of language or mathematics. As we struggle against scholastic failure, we try to develop means of expression that are specific to the children of low-income families and encourage an openness toward an analysis of society. But scholastic constraints are so strong that it is difficult and often impossible to detach oneself and step back far enough to introduce the analytical components that we would like.

3. Initial Evaluation

An initial appraisal of literacy training for adult immigrants and the *écoles de devoirs* prompted us to ask some basic questions about the effectiveness of our actions beyond the sincerely declared objectives. We could see some results.

Adult immigrants made progress in their acquisition of French, improved their ability to express themselves and even took part in defending their rights. In Hensies, for example, a group of Turks acted to defend their accommodation after they were threatened with expropriation.

Children did better in school, or failed less dramatically. But they were still being streamed into vocational training. And we found several of them a few years later in a training program we organized for young unemployed people.

A certain collective consciousness developed or strengthened around immigration in the neighbourhoods, families and networks of associations.

But, at the same time, we reached very few of the people who could potentially have benefited. We offered no real solution to the overall problems. Basically, nothing changed. In fact, it was clear that most of the people we wanted to reach had no interest whatsoever in what we were doing. Their lack of interest matched our lack of resources. What was the point of working with such a (relatively) small fraction of the population that was supposed to benefit? To put it bluntly, the "illiterate" did not want to be made literate. Literacy was our project, not theirs. And those we reached the least were precisely those who, in our view, should have been reached first: the most completely excluded of the illiterate. We were chasing a will-o'-the-wisp.

There is very little mobilization of resources around a project aimed at liberating others. The ideology of individual consumption is strong in society as a whole, and the common people are no exception. The mass media reach them much better than we can. How can we get our message across? Literacy training itself is more a product to be consumed than a mobilizing project. And raising the level of consciousness without the means to act and bring about change only produces a new and deeper apathy.

How can we communicate literacy training that is by definition based on a negative view of the people described as "illiterate", and therefore deficient culturally, socially, economically and politically? They are viewed in terms of their shortcomings, their lack of language ability, their lack of everything, whereas they do in fact have a culture, experience, thoughts and dreams, even if these are stunted, attacked and trampled on by a cultural and symbolic combination of forces that is not in their favour.

Yet dignity is possible. It must be able to emerge, but it lacks the means to do so. Literacy training is not what is needed. The starting point lies elsewhere and has not yet been formulated. Literacy training defines and underscores the very isolation it is intended to eliminate.

4. **The Second Period**

To cope better with these contradictions which our analyses highlighted, we adopted a new, more global approach. Literacy training became part of a more complex educational process based above all on the motive forces that make people tick and determine their behaviour and languages strategies, on the forces that can bring them out of their isolation, form them into groups and make them act. Once this is the goal, it does not matter where we begin, whether we start with literacy training, photography, the theatre, vocational training, dancing or cooking, so long as the teaching methods constantly expand upon possibilities that either already exist or are at least in the germination stage: possibilities of expression, analysis, understanding and action. The starting activity is a device for catching their attention, a conjuring act designed to make them see the issues. Diversity is desirable in that it creates a larger number of access points and thus responds to a range of expectations. So in addition to the literacy training and *écoles de devoirs* which we were administering, various other activities were also developed.

Multiple activities

Cultural expression activities

- *Théatre Alpha*, an action theatre, was initially set up by a literacy group and later expanded to include other participants. Two plays were discussed, mulled over, revised and performed by the group. The first, entitled "Dream of a Suitcase", tells a story many immigrants have experienced dealing with their never-realized dreams of returning to their home countries. The performances are an occasion for celebration and discussion. The entire production process is analysed, and the performances are a way of spreading discussion. The second play, entitled "The Beans of Hunger", analyses the loss of purchasing power and its consequences for low-income families. Its production and performance methodology parallels that of the first play.

- The multicultural *folk dance* group did not operate for very long. It was designed to juxtapose the various identities and encourage openness toward the various histories of immigrant groups.

- *Photo workshop* introduces participants to a method of expression centred on images, but in the framework of a critical approach to the relativity of our society's dominant image language.

- The multicultural *cuisine exchange* pursues an objective similar to that of the folk dance group.

Training activities (other than literacy training and the *écoles de devoirs*)

- A *sewing workshop* brings people together and has them exchange ideas. The workshop is aimed above all at Turkish women, who do not appear interested in any other activity. This is the means we have developed for establishing contact.

- Literacy *instructor training* ties into more general pedagogical training, centred on the key question of how to use these various activities to foster discussion capable of raising new issues and spawning new activities and projects that will help transform relationships within society.

     Theoretically attractive as this approach may be, it is very difficult to implement. Instructors very often experience a great deal of difficulty getting beyond the well-organized initial activity in order to identify paths of action that will allow their students to progress. People reach their limit very quickly. Yet instructor training remains a central component.

- The program for *helping people get a driver's licence* met a major need. Many people with low-income backgrounds have a great deal of difficulty passing the test, and the main difficulty involves language. Repeated failures have serious financial consequences. We helped almost everyone who turned to us get a licence.

     But an irony quickly appeared, in that people vanished as soon as they got their licence. They had got what they were looking for when they turned to us for help. Invitations to continue learning with us were quite unsuccessful. So our goal of providing continuing education was perverted into offering no more than a one-off repair service. This led us to abandon the program.

- *Arabic, Turkish and Spanish courses* for both native speakers and Belgians are an occasion for multicultural contact. The courses are intended to remodel the speech of immigrants with reference to their mother tongues. Exchange and multiculturalism are possible only if we at the same time strengthen identities and restore positive status to cultures which, through immigration, have become backward and suspect. This is no exercise in nostalgia nor an attempt to restore cultures to the way immigrants knew them when they left their native lands. It is an attempt to encourage a specific discussion of current relationships between immigrants and native Belgians in the here and now. By studying their mother tongues, immigrants can develop a positive self-image. When Belgians learn and respect the language of another group and themselves experience culture shock during this intercultural linguistic exchange, foundations are laid for new social relationships that reflect this difference.

- *Vocational training* is aimed above all at young unemployed people who have failed at school or have dropped out altogether. It includes workshops on and courses in mechanics, electricity, video, photography, sewing, crafts, knitting, masonry, typing, bookkeeping and computer science. These technical courses and workshops are complemented by remedial French and mathematics and by courses in English, current events and law. The accent is on incorporating participants into society, but also on training them to analyse society and work for basic rights.

  This training responds to a clearly-defined expectation. It undeniably remotivates participants, brings their education up to standard and offers a second chance to unemployed people with a history of scholastic failure. But it offers practically no real prospect of a decent job. Although 33 per cent of the participants either find a job or go on to more in-depth training after their training with us, it has to be said that all the rest go back to being unemployed. And the jobs that participants do manage to find are generally unrewarding ones, such as temporary, part-time or odd jobs. Enthusiasm thus gives way to discouragement and scepticism.

- *Socio-political training* sessions deal, among other things, with North-South relations. This type of activity has produced a twinning of our association with a pilot school in Nicaragua. In October 1987, we organized a North-South Week in conjunction with other organizations.

Activities of a social nature

- A *clothing exchange* recycles second-hand clothing, offering affordable clothing to low-income families. The exchange is always open and serves as a place for the poorest people to meet. The difficulty lies in getting people beyond the stage of simply selling things or helping one another socially to one of taking part in continuing education or training.

- Social and legal *consultation rooms* have been set up for immigrants; they also attract low-income Belgian families. They have given rise to a collective project involving "Fourth World" families called *popular economic workshops*. The purpose of these workshops is to bring together low-income families that have been excluded from society, so that they can together take charge of their future, rather than depending exclusively on the social services and public social assistance centres (CPAS)[9]. The popular workshops consist of various activities of an economic nature that the families themselves organize. These include gardening, wood recycling, preserves, meals, a furniture sales room, a second-hand goods bazaar, carpets, painting and clothing recycling. They are a place where participants learn about group living, project management, bookkeeping and written French. Weekly evaluations form a framework for on-the-job sociological training.

    But conflicts arise quickly. It is hard to develop solidarity among those who are most completely excluded from society. Many seek immediate, personal benefit before anything else. It is hard to keep activities going beyond the short term, and the group easily breaks up.

In addition, there are often conflicts between the paid staff and volunteers from Fourth World families because of differences in status and in the degree to which they are involved in the project. There are always questions as to who is in charge of the project.

Activities of an economic nature

- *The Alternative Bookshop* was a co-operative bookshop, but it did not last.

- A group of trainees and instructors from the unemployed youth training program set up an association called *R for Recovery* for recycling household wastes. It is currently independent of the Alpha program.

Participation in action networks

Our association takes part in various activities, such as an immigrant rights defence committee, Co-operation for Peace, efforts to protect socio-cultural workers (by campaigning against legislation that makes employment in our sector so precarious), networks aimed at combating poverty and activities that show solidarity with the Third World.

Insecure jobs

The second period was marked by a major increase in activity. Not all the activities were organized at the same time. Some had a shorter life span than others because of a lack of interest on the part of participants, or because we were unable to ensure continuity or attain our educational objectives. This increase in activity was possible because we successfully petitioned the Department of Employment for workers on a temporary basis. Because of this, our staff at the beginning of 1990 consisted of 22 people on Third Work Circuit contracts, four permanent employees, and one person hired under the Interdepartmental Budgetary Funds program[10].

This kind of employment status deserves a great deal of criticism. Several factors ensure its precariousness:

- The revolving door principle, by which the program puts an unemployed person to work for a while and then makes him unemployed again by giving the job to some other jobless person. The first unemployed person should theoretically have already found a job, but the job market is all but closed to people who have few qualifications and have been out of work for a long time.

- These programs are designed to reduce unemployment, and not to further the activities of associations. Because of this, the worker's qualifications (if he or she has any) are rarely those needed for the association's literacy program and other activities. And any training the associations provide ends as soon as the worker leaves the job, so it counts for little when the worker applies for other jobs.

- The rights of workers are restricted. For example, their seniority on the wage scale does not extend back beyond January 1, 1987. Any work they did previously is not counted[11].

- The unstable nature of the jobs means employees are often treated like second-class workers. And they seldom work in management-union partnerships.

In the beginning, both the association and the workers felt that, despite the precariousness of the jobs, they were better than nothing, better than being unemployed and better than being unable to carry out socially useful activities that met real needs. Everyone agrees the situation is not ideal, but everyone - the associations, workers, public authorities, unions and businesses - find some benefit in it.

This produces waste and reinforces an arrangement that exploits the associations, which need more permanent, trained staff; the workers, who go from unemployment to sub-standard jobs that only marginalize them even more and make it harder for them to hold on to jobs; employment policy, which becomes nothing more than an unemployment reduction policy; and social and cultural policy, which becomes subordinate to the foregoing.

5. Second Evaluation

Accomplishments

- The quantitative expansion and diversification of our activities enabled us to reach a larger number of people, up to 300 a year. Even if they were often irregular participants, many took part in our activities, which were linked to those of other associations. Our expansion was also geographical in that we acquired a stake in several new locations in the region.

    Of course, not everyone we reached became involved to the same degree. Imagine a set of concentric circles, beginning with consumers of the social and educational services and passing through various intermediate levels of participation to those individuals or groups who sustained the project and were concerned with its objectives. We tried to show everyone that literacy training is a collective project for social change using continuing education and based on the diversity of their realities. The responses, of course, were varied and complex.

- A popular methodology was designed and is now functioning. At first, it was based on literacy training, but was later expanded and adjusted to include other starting-points and activities. It aims not only at insertion into a specific experience, but also expression and analysis. It involves "applying speech" and "applying action" to the social reality that concerns us. The pedagogical approach is socio-linguistic and has been put down in writing (in part at least) in the form of pedagogical reference materials. It is applied in the association's instructor training program and in other associations as well.

- Obvious individual and collective progress has been made, both by "trainees" who stayed with us a few months and by "participants" who remained involved for longer periods and made up the nucleus of the project's "militants". Other progress, although more difficult to quantify, could be observed in improved linguistic, technical and professional abilities; a bringing up to standard of basic knowledge; better understanding of legal, sociological and socio-political matters; acquisition of reading and writing skills and French by immigrants and political refugees;

increased capacity for both verbal and non-verbal expression; greater self-confidence, a better self-image, greater independence and a greater sense of responsibility; development of an ability to analyse, discuss and act; improved project design and management; development of a critical consciousness of social mechanisms; collective action in the immediate environment and the region; and integration into other training programs and activities.

- About one in three recipients of "continuing vocational training" finds work or receives training at a level higher than what we offer. But most of the jobs lack security. Alpha's vocational training is intended above all for young people who have quit school and experienced failure. We can put them (back) on the road to socio-vocational integration, but major barriers still face those who are most excluded scholastically, since they are most often unable to find decent jobs once their training is over. We expect miracles from training programs, but the labour market is glutted!

- Fourth-World individuals and families have experienced solidarity, especially in the popular economic workshops. They have acquired management and organizational skills and have themselves organized a collective survival project that made them less dependent on social services. They have used this project to train themselves and analyse. But we have not got beyond the survival stage. The perspectives refused to widen beyond a given point.

- A great deal of work has been done training literacy instructors, social workers and educators in our region and in other parts of Belgium's French Community. This training of trainers is based on an analysis of language as a medium for expressing the relationships of power that confront one another in society. Training does not mean just teaching a neutral, formal system. Language is based on a system of speech, with which it has a dialectic relationship. The form is constantly being used in the light of political, social, economic, cultural and symbolic interests. If the popular linguistic codes are specific, then popular language teaching methods will also be specific.

- Alpha has promoted in public opinion a "brand image" that is contradictory and often challenged, but which raises basic questions about social exclusion, the universal right to knowledge, immigration, racism, multiculturalism, solidarity and our model of society. We constantly emphasize that literacy promotion, training, education and social action are political acts that influence the orientation of society as a whole.

Innumerable difficulties

The Alpha project has survived, but only in the face of great difficulties. The difficulties are so numerous that it often seems as if one has to be crazy to go on working in these conditions.

- The public authorities have often been very late in paying the subsidies. But it is quite impossible to finance ourselves. Our staff is large, but most are in substandard jobs of a temporary, insecure nature. What we really need is an activity that goes deep and extends beyond the short term. The jobs lack prestige, and this saps motivation. We have to hire staff who are for the most part poorly qualified, and this is incompatible with literacy training, which requires competence. We therefore experience a great many problems related to the quality of the training we provide.

    In June 1990, the Walloon Region replaced the the TCT, the Third Work Circuit system with a new one called the Regional Labour Market Insertion Programs (PRIME). This requires sponsoring organizations to shoulder a major share of the staff's wages. We cannot afford this cost. Because the new program perpetuates job insecurity, the association's workers refused to be transferred from the TCT program to the PRIME program.

    The result was that the number of posts dropped from 28 to 2. To continue operating, we have had to turn back to volunteers. We have had to restructure our activities and make more use of shoestring solutions than ever before.

- Our declared continuing education objectives run counter to the "mass culture" that defines instructors, organizers and the public. Our attempt to mobilize people for social change runs up against the ideology and values of consumption. Has not the very idea of freedom become a product for consumption? In the face of an arrogant market and reinforced inequalities, exclusion affects great masses of people. We deal with this exclusion every day. The excluded are offered no real hope. For the moment, we operate like resistance fighters, calling on others to join the resistance. Many people are deeply discouraged.

- The current crisis and this worsening exclusion have placed greater demands on assistance organizations. Working in partnership with the people, providing continuing education, organizing training in social criticism, and getting at the causes of the problems we encounter tend to be put off in the rush to respond to more urgent matters. Continuing education, once seen as an education in critical analysis and in action for social change, has become nothing more than training aimed at integrating or simply inserting individuals into society.

    At Alpha Mons-Borinage, we realize that this need to provide emergency assistance prevents any real strategic reflection. We respond to those in greatest need. Must things continue this way?

- One considerable difficulty arises from the fact that it is hard to maintain an attitude of continual learning and redefining. After a period of research and progress, most people (and this applies to instructors as much to participants) quickly slip into an attitude of complacency because of the modest powers they have acquired.

To continue advancing, we must widen the perspectives and provide more motivation. But the necessary links are lacking.

- Our activities have greatly suffered from a lack of truly dynamic links with other sectors of society. We are sometimes criticized for working in a ghetto, for trying to do too much by ourselves, to the point where our project becomes partially unmanageable.

    It is difficult to find linkages that are truly open to the special characteristics of the excluded, to their history and their identity. Changes are needed in the practices and methods of many institutions, which, by operating in a highly bureaucratized way, really do more to reinforce the mechanisms of exclusion than to correct them.

- Our activities reach hardly any of the six per cent of people in Belgium's French Community who live in poverty. Nor do we reach the "illiterate" people most marginalized in terms of the written language. The people we reach are those who already enjoy a certain amount of social mobility. We share these difficulties with many other associations. Without a specific communication strategy based on the specific interests and speech of the excluded, we will never make any progress. The approach cannot be merely technical. It must be cultural above all. Will we invest in this sort of cultural activity?

Is our appraisal of the second period completely black then? No. I have emphasized our accomplishments, which are undeniable. But we must also admit that in many areas we run up against a brick wall. But the story is not over.

6. What Now?

We are two appointed workers: one permanent and the other hired under the Interdepartmental Budgetary Funds program (FBI)[10]. Another ten or so people work as volunteers. We are in the process of restructuring our activities to reflect this manpower shortage and respond to the results of our more all-encompassing evaluation. How can we overcome the obstacles? What activities should have development priority? How can we, on the basis of these activities, act on a general level as well, on a level that addresses all the issues of literacy training and continuing education?

Two sectors remain at the moment: literacy training and the campaign against poverty.

Literacy training

Literacy training comprises three levels of activity:

i. Literacy courses

We continue to offer *literacy courses* to both immigrants and native Belgians. We are beginning to organize ourselves in order to expand within our region the network of courses, in co-operation with other associations and institutions, including schools, libraries, public social assistance centres[9], consultation centres for foster children, and the Youth Protection Committee.

In addition to courses organized in our own facilities, we want to see courses offered in other venues where communication has already been established with excluded individuals and groups, and could be expanded by introducing a literacy training approach based on teaching writing[12] and reading skills. We hope this will enable us to add new dimensions to our socio-linguistic teaching methods for encouraging the emergence of spoken and written speech and language that are most closely linked with an actual history, with effective social relationships. The immediate, strategic goal is to establish and construct communication, not to promote literacy. We must therefore establish communication in which the speech of the excluded is recognized as valid, to the point of becoming the core of the whole approach. Introducing into our teaching methods a simple style of questioning which nevertheless solicits complex responses, would open up new perspectives and no doubt unblock a number of apparently dead-end situations: Who says what? Where? When? To whom? How? Why? This new style of questioning does not negate the value of the specific action of literacy training, but may give it a new breadth[13]. It also presupposes that various actors in the struggle against exclusion will be able to agree on common strategies. That is the goal of action-training activity.

ii. Action-training

Action-training implies that the training process is aimed at setting up new strategies. It is organized at two levels: training instructors, organizers and liaison personnel for the struggle against cultural exclusion; and training literacy instructors.

Training instructors, organizers and liaison personnel for the struggle against cultural exclusion involves various social agents, including organizers, educators, librarians, trade unionists, infant-care nurses and parents. The goal is to establish a training process that is tied in with the activities of various kinds of agents involved in communication or non-communication with excluded populations, in such a way that their practices further the struggle against complete or functional illiteracy[14] as a factor in re-establishing communication. The literacy centre would thus cease to be the only place where people identified as completely or functionally illiterate would be sent (most of these people do not report to the centre anyway). Instead, the centre would interact with other agencies willing to revise their strategy for acting as agents of communication.

We are just at the beginning of this process. Other associations are trying to work in the same direction. The contacts we have made so far will enable us to offer an action-training program of this type beginning in September 1991.

The Organizer Training Service of the French Community Department[15] is also preparing a training project for the various categories of socio-cultural organizers that includes literacy training. We are associated with the preparatory work for this project. It will involve approximately fifty hours of training and is intended for actors in a position to spread such approaches throughout the territory of Belgium's French Community.

The literacy instructor training is designed to develop methodological abilities in a socio-linguistic perspective. The training tries to promote constant interaction between practice and theory through a chain of activities: initial description of practices $\rightarrow$ theoretical approaches $\rightarrow$ strategic and pedagogical pathways $\rightarrow$ experimentation $\rightarrow$ evaluation and analysis of practices $\rightarrow$ theoretical reinforcement $\rightarrow$ reinforcement of the strategies and teaching methods, and so on.

Our literacy instructor training includes: the initial and on-going training for our association's instructors, training we offer to other associations, training which other associations request from us, and participation as designers and/or instructors in training sessions co-ordinated by or with other agencies. Examples include:

- Training 16 literacy instructors in Namur province[16]. The training consisted of 150 hours of class time plus 60 hours of on-the-job training. Participants received certificates showing that they had passed or attended the courses. This training was important in that it gave participants a chance to develop real competence and gain recognition as literacy training professionals.

- Literacy instructor training in Hainaut province. A training program consisting of 220 hours (including 60 hours of on-the-job training) is being prepared and should start in October 1991.

- A 50-hour training course for literacy program personnel is being organized by the French Community Department's Organizer Training Service and should start in November 1991.

- An approximately 100-hour instructor training program (EAP) in a vocational training business[17]. The purpose of the program is to provide in-depth training in literacy promotion techniques and socio-linguistic methodology.

iii. Creation of the Mons-Borinage Committee for the Struggle against Illiteracy and Cultural Exclusion

This *committee* too has brought together various kinds of social agents to create pathways between the various levels of activity, although the main goal is to develop concerted strategies. The group, which has just begun to operate, is intended to play an active role in setting up local networks in the Mons-Borinage region.

We have begun a study involving teachers, librarians, parents and students that looks at ways of developing the pleasure of reading. We will use this study as a basic tool for discussing common strategies, especially with certain schools and libraries.

Without abandoning literacy courses (on the contrary, while expanding them), we have nevertheless chosen an orientation less centred on our association as the one and only agency combating illiteracy. We do not have the solution; society does. It is therefore essential that we create networks within society, while at the same time clarifying the significance of the actions to be undertaken. To do this, we need a concept of language and socio-linguistic teaching methods, plus active research into ways of integrating it into all educational and organizational activities and the struggle against cultural and social exclusion.

The campaign against poverty

Activities include:

-   popular economic workshops to promote survival through solidarity (see above),

-   providing social and legal support to families in difficulty,

-   basic training in writing, group living, typing, bookkeeping, and so on,

-   a writing workshop,

-   a street library for children (with a female worker reading with children in the streets),

-   a sewing workshop,

-   thematic sessions on social issues that concern low-income families and individuals,

-   a network for co-operating with other organizations and associations, and

-   studies conducted in local neighbourhoods.

We hope to co-ordinate the two kinds of activities: one of a more social nature aimed at combating poverty and expanding the field for literacy training, and one of a more cultural nature that offers precise tools for understanding, analysing, expressing and acting - tools that are necessary for acquiring independence, developing a sense of responsibility, communicating, and therefore for solving the social problems that face us. We constantly evaluate our activities in their various dimensions.

But this socio-cultural articulation is insufficient. It does not solve the problems of poverty. The duo of social action and continuing education, however dynamic it may appear at first, very often only highlights the problems. Closed-circuit management of poverty is a definite factor in perpetuating exclusion. Poor people run into too many walls involving under-employment, health, accommodation, education, the police, income, administration, the myths of the consumer society, and so on.

At our level, we believe that co-ordination in networks is necessary not only for achieving global, in-depth action, but also for evaluating the appropriateness of the methods used. Is offering services to the poorest people likely to encourage them to become more independent? In extreme situations, it is often the only way of showing tangible solidarity, but it exacerbates dependence and does little to encourage people to undergo training. The relationship created by offering services and that created by offering education are different and necessarily contradictory. And when we offer services and education at the same time, the offering of more immediate interest generally wins out.

We want to go beyond simply managing poverty and imper-manence, but such a step is beyond the capabilities of a single association.

7. Conclusion: Networks are Necessary but have yet to be Sufficiently Developed

The history of Alpha Mons-Borinage can be summed up as a series of efforts that have yielded results, but results that are limited and have sometimes led to dead ends. We have fought alongside many others for social change, not only in the realm of ideas, but also in reality, in people's everyday lives. But it seems as if many of them and of us live worse now than before and that our prospects are even more limited.

Overall, poverty has increased in our societies. There are 44 million poor people in Europe, approximately 20 per cent of socio-vocational positions are insecure, and many young people live as if part of a sacrificed generation. The aggravation of social problems is manifest in everyday life. Our actions in most cases do no more than help people better integrate themselves in a marginalized fringe that includes larger segments of society.

Many of us in the literacy, continuing education and social action associations wonder what meaning our actions have. Are we a kind of socio-cultural police force designed to impose order on the excluded? Are our services supposed to fill in the gaps of the social system? Are we factors for integrating people into society? Are we agents for social change? Many of us think fundamental social change is necessary if we are effectively to improve the everyday lives of the excluded, and especially if we are to bring them out of their exclusion. Teaching methods based on the liberation of speech systems that are today considered marginal and on developing a new dignity, cannot succeed unless we change the more general relationships in society.

Reorganizing associations into multidisciplinary networks that precisely co-ordinate, through the implementation of concerted strategies, the actions of teachers, literacy instructors, social workers, cultural workers, and so on, is definitely necessary if we are to discover a way out of the dead ends in which we currently find ourselves. But this alone is not enough. We cannot avoid a more complete socio-political re-evaluation. Otherwise we are only shifting the blame.

Public authorities have a well-defined responsibility for setting policies that effectively implement socio-educational priorities. Community associations can act in this regard as a social movement, exerting pressure, initiating debate and pushing for discussion of what priorities to adopt in the management of society as a whole. Should the market and gross national product have priority, with whatever is left over going to culture, education, social services and employment? Associations are starting to group together to address these political issues[18], to redefine themselves as a pole of activity within society, to think out political strategies and to build alliances.

But better resources and networks and new political priorities will produce no fundamental change if they are all designed and implemented *for* the excluded and not *by* them. The best-tailored and most indispensable resources will never do more than simply create the conditions in which the excluded themselves can gain access to expression. The excluded must be the principal actors in the drama of their liberation. Democracy is not just the right to vote, not just a body of lofty ideas, not just a component of the program for promoting the rights of the excluded. Democracy is communication through action. The point is not to integrate the excluded into

society but to recognize that they are social agents no less capable
of speaking and orienting society than any other agents. Our main
goal must be to introduce this final truth into our pedagogical and
political strategies.

The excluded are not illiterate in the same way as, for example,
a one-armed man is handicapped. They are rich in knowledge,
experience and history. This should be the motor driving alternative
teaching methods. But educators often set themselves up as con-
trollers of accepted knowledge and ability. There are other, more
creative approaches, but on the fringe. The role of the networks must
be to expand these approaches and give them general application.

Teaching methods will come face to face with politics. Literacy
training is currently only one of many factors that perpetuate
inequalities, but it could transform its logical basis and become a
voice of freedom for society, a factor that trains and educates not
only the excluded, but all those who learn to communicate with the
excluded. But by that time it will no doubt have ceased to be
literacy training.

Notes

1. Cf. Lalita Ramdas. 1987. Alphabétisation et capacité d'agir: pour une
   définition de l'alphabétisation (Literacy and the ability to act: for a
   definition of literacy training). In *Point de mire sur la pratique* (Focus
   on practical training), an unpublished, international conference on
   literacy training in industrialized countries held in Toronto from October
   13 to 15, 1987.

2. The literacy associations together reach only 3,000 or so of the 300,000
   to 500,000 illiterate people who are thought to live in Belgium's French
   Community. And the people who are reached are rarely those most
   excluded from knowledge, such as the so-called "total" illiterates.

3. Freire, Paulo. 1987. *Pédagogie des opprimés* (Pedagogy of the
   oppressed). Paris: Maspéro; and Freire, Paulo. 1975. *L'éducation,
   pratique de la liberté* (Education: the practice of freedom). Paris: Cerf.
   See also Hautecoeur, Jean-Paul. 1987. Paulo Freire: politiques
   d'alphabétisation ou alphabétisation politique? (Paulo Freire: literacy
   training policies or political literacy training?). In *Introduction aux
   pratiques et politiques d'alphabétisation* (Introduction to the practices

and policies of literacy training). Montreal: University of Quebec in Montreal, pp. 295-325.

4. Bernstein, Basil. 1975. *Langage et classes sociales* (Language and social classes). Paris: Minuit.
   Labov, William. 1976. *Sociolinguistique* (Sociolinguistics). Paris: Minuit.

5. Bourdieu, Pierre. 1979. *La distinction. Critique sociale du jugement* (Distinction: a social criticism of judgment). Paris: Minuit; Bourdieu, Pierre. 1980. *Le sens pratique* (The practical sense). Paris: Minuit; and, especially, Bourdieu, Pierre. 1982. *Ce que parler veut dire: L'économie des échanges linguistiques* (What speaking means: the economy of linguistic exchanges). Paris: Fayard.

6. Publications of Alpha Mons-Borinage:

   Situation sociale et enseignement linguistique (Social situation and linguistic training)
   Fiches pour l'apprentissage du français (Resources for teaching French)
   Évaluation (Evaluation)
   L'apprentissage du français de base (aux travailleurs immigrés ne connaissant pas le français) (Teaching basic French to immigrant workers who do not know French)
   École de devoirs. Pour une poignée d'idées en plus. (Écoles de devoirs. A few more ideas)
   Calcul, mathématique. Initiation, mise à niveau. (Arithmetic and mathematics. Initiation and bringing up to standard)
   Apprentissage oral - Apprentissage écrit (Oral learning - written learning)

7. Marissal, Véronique. 1990. The Role of Homework Schools in the Prevention of Illiteracy. In Hautecoeur, Jean-Paul. *Alpha 90 - Research in Literacy* (339-358). Montreal: Quebec Ministry of Education/Hamburg: Unesco Institute for Education.

8. Bastin, G. and Roosen, A. 1990. *L'Ecole malade de l'échec scolaire: Pédagogies en développement. Pratiques méthodologiques* (The sick school of scholastic failure: pedagogy in development and methodological practice). Brussels.
   Bourdieu, Pierre et al. 1964. *Les héritiers* (The inheritors). Paris: Minuit.
   Bourdieu, Pierre and Passeron, Jean-Claude. 1970. *La reproduction* (Reproduction). Paris: Minuit.

Snyders, G. 1976. *Ecole, classe et lutte de classe* (School, class and class struggle). Paris: PUF.

9. Public social assistance centres are funded by the communes and the Department of Social Affairs. They provide a regular monthly allowance or emergency social assistance to people without resources.

10. The main unemployment reabsorption programs available to associations are:

a) The Unemployed Put to Work program, under which the unemployed remain unemployed but are put at the disposal of an association (or public body) for one year with a possibility of renewal. It was cancelled as a separate program in 1989 and incorporated into the Subsidized Contractual Officers program (see below).

b) The Special Temporary Staff program, under which an unemployed person is given a work contract for a set period (often one year) and is paid the same basic wage as public servants at an equivalent level.

c) The Third Work Circuit program, under which an unemployed person is given a contract for an undetermined period and is paid the same basic wage as public servants at an equivalent level. Seniority is recognized, but only as of January 1, 1987.

d) Programs (b) and (c) have been cancelled in Wallonia and replaced by a new system called the Regional Labour Market Insertion Program. This program requires the hiring organizations to contribute a major share of the wages. Consequently, many associations have had to give up many of their positions. In addition, the minister responsible in Wallonia has cut a large number of Third Work Circuit positions: 4,000 out of 10,000.

e) The Interdepartmental Budgetary Funds program, under which the unemployed person becomes a full-status employee. The Minister of Employment may agree with another minister, whose budget is insufficient to pay for the positions to which associations are entitled under the legislation governing their activities, to assume responsibility for funding these positions. However, these interdepartmental agreements are concluded for limited periods subject to renewal, and there is a ceiling on wage contributions. (The current ceiling is 590,000 Belgian francs, whereas the wage which the hiring organization must pay is at least 800,000 Belgian francs.)

11. Another discriminatory measure requires beneficiaries to work for two years in a substandard job before they can obtain a revision of their "unemployment code", the basis on which their unemployment benefits are calculated. Benefits during the first year of unemployment equal 55% of the beneficiary's previous wages and 35% from the second year, except for heads of households. Many participants in the Third Work Circuit program were paid 35% of their previous wages from the moment they were hired. "Normal" workers have to work six months before they can have their code revised and receive 55%.

12. More than simple technical ability, the goal is to provide access to "the act of writing", the act of signifying through the written word strategies for social positioning and for the creation of meanings. This is fundamental to our search for a pedagogy that promotes democracy through action.

13. The sociolinguistic approach we are suggesting is based on a theoretical framework that analyses the functions of language. Language represents the whole of human experience, of life in society. Action that affects human relationships is itself language. So our practices would benefit greatly from a better understanding of language's functions in relation to all the complex and contradictory interactions that characterize communication, non-communication (since we also speak in order not to communicate, to protect ourselves), desires, thoughts, the creation of meanings or the relativization of meaning, social positioning or marginalization, the imposition or challenging of authority, and the promotion or subtle destruction of independence.
There has been a great deal of research done on these subjects, including:
Jakobson, R. 1963. *Essais de linguistique générale* (Essays on general linguistics). Paris: Minuit, esp. Chapter 11: *Linguistique et poétique* (Linguistics and poetics).
Kristeva, J. 1981. *Le langage, cet inconnu* (Language: the great unknown). Paris: Seuil.
Schaff, A. 1969. *Langage et connaissance* (Language and knowledge). Paris: Anthropos.
Barthes, R. 1978. *Leçon* (Lesson). Paris: Seuil.
Sapir, E. 1967. *Anthropologie* (Anthropology). Paris: Minuit.
Bourdieu, P. (see Note 5)
B. Bernstein and W. Labov (see Note 4).

14. The distinction between complete illiteracy and functional illiteracy was explained by Jean Foucambert. Approximately 70% of the French-speaking population are functionally illiterate in that they cannot effectively read a text of intermediate difficulty. Complete illiteracy affects only the most excluded of the functionally illiterate.

15. Belgium has become a federal state comprised of three regions (Wallonia, Flanders and Brussels) and three communities (French, Flemish and German-speaking). Belgium's French Community is administered by an Executive composed of four ministers, one of whom has responsibility for continuing education and organizer training.

16. Training organized by the Higher Provincial Socio-Educational Training Institute (formerly the course for actively employed educators).

17. In keeping with the spirit that guided their creation, the vocational training businesses are both vocational training centres and small businesses. They are intended for people (preferably young people) who have no employment income and are therefore the responsibility of the public social assistance centres (see Note 9).

18. See, for example, the special edition of the magazine *Alternatives wallonnes: "Monde associatif: la cinquième roue? De la question sociale à la société en question"* (Walloon alternatives: The world of associations: the fifth wheel? From the social question to questioning society), March 15, 1991, No. 73-74.

ADULT EDUCATION:
LITERACY FOR THE MASSES

José Luis Corzo
Julio Lancho
Madrid

Salamanca's Santiago Uno Boarding School

When children come to seek admission to Salamanca's Santiago Uno Boarding School, they do not usually hide their problems, since they all know that those with the most difficulties will have a better chance. It is easier for those who fail than for those who pass, easier for difficult students than for those who are easy to teach, for those without families than for those with families, for those unable to pay than for those who have the money to do so. Some of their initial profiles are truly alarming, especially their academic records. All are fourteen or older. Some have thus far completed only five or six years of schooling, or have repeated the sixth grade twice. They are very bad readers and hate school. They feel that they are failures. Some of their classmates have gone on to finish high school, whereas vocational training is their last chance. They have been hooked by the idea that, instead of studying, what they should do is learn a trade. "He likes working outdoors, you know," say their mothers or the adults who bring them, "but he has no interest in books. You see, he doesn't like to study. Not everyone has the same bent. Now take his eight-year-old sister. Every day she has her nose buried in her schoolbooks and notes. But the boy is happy when he's driving a tractor or tending the cows with his father, whatever you want him to do along those lines."

The teacher who welcomes the new student knows in his bones what a challenge he is taking on. Without his realizing it, the boy must be made to become accustomed to a school routine *on a full-time basis* (Saturdays and Sundays included, except for one day a month). Every day during school hours, he will go to Lorenzo Milani Agricultural School, where he may enter a special remedial course until he catches up with the rest; at the boarding school, in his free time, he will be tutored daily by another student who has volunteered for this purpose, and he will take part in many weekly group activities. Above all, he will read the newspaper. Reading the newspaper is the miraculous tool by which a boy whose teachers have given up on him will be turned into an active student.

Every night after dinner, at 10:15 p.m., the whole boarding school gathers to read the newspaper. The headmaster leafs through it, sitting in a circle with all of the junior and senior students, teachers and kitchen staff, as well as Consuelo, the housekeeper. They are all ears, eager to find out what is happening in the world. They are not naturally interested and attentive when they get here; you have to keep working on them day after day. (How could teachers who maintain that the interests of youngsters must always be used as a starting point manage with students like this?) To whet their appetites, we recommend starting with what is most difficult for the boys and least familiar to them (not soccer). We must also ask ourselves who would benefit from keeping these youngsters ignorant, and why they would want to distract them and keep them out of the mainstream.

The headmaster reads a headline and begins asking questions to ensure that the students have understood. What does this word mean? Where is this country? ("Point to it on the map, Johnny.") Is it rich or poor? Who is its leader? What led up to this event? What is happening? What are its consequences? Does it affect us? Can we shrug it off? The main thing is to promote solidarity. Instead of dividing the world into Spaniards and foreigners, those near or far away, we divide it into those who take action and those who are left out; we feel close to the victims of every event in each place. We delve into each news item until students see that it affects us or others like us, even if they are far away, and we connect it as much as possible with what students already know. We never ask anyone what he does not know; rather, we ask each student what we know he can answer, no matter how simple some of his answers may be. Giving an answer makes a student more self-confident and raises his esteem in the eyes of the rest, even if he only names the king or his son. Answering questions about the newspaper has given many boys at Santiago Uno their first taste of academic success, their first and only intellectual satisfaction. They may have learned what they know outside school, probably on television. What better opportunity to make connections with real life on the streets?

Once this exercise has begun, its possibilities multiply a thousandfold. One has only to see this in the older boys. "Ask the history teacher." If the question is about economics, "Ask the maths teacher." "Ask your grandfather and see if he remembers." It is useful for students to make a note of the new words they learn each day and a few of the most interesting events; they will use this later as a diary and a reference.

This daily practice, which lasts twenty to thirty minutes, lays the foundation for many things. It arouses an undying interest in whatever happens to the world's poor. Broader and more serious subjects can be discussed with the older boys. Above all, this daily exercise arouses their suspicion and shows them that not everything printed in the newspapers is true, making them very aware of the news industry (owners, agencies, advertising, pressures and so on). This is essential in today's world to safeguard the freedom which you lose if you are misinformed.

Long-range developments can then be followed over a whole quarter. News items can be carefully analyzed to see their inner workings as well as their snares, and we can write them ourselves, using the rules that journalists follow, so that we never forget what experience has taught us. We can even put together a school newspaper in eight hours, such as Santiago Uno's independent newspaper, *La Bronca* [The Uproar], which comes out from time to time. Above all, students become informed and critical citizens who participate and seek the truth.

Roots in the School of Barbiana (Lorenzo Milani, 1923-1967)

This Spanish experiment in adult education and literacy, in the broadest sense of the word, stems from, and is modelled on, the work of Lorenzo Milani, an Italian whose students lived in the hills of Florence's tiny parish of Barbiana. In 1967, they wrote *Letter to a Schoolmistress*, which was translated into Spanish in 1970 and had a significant impact on the experiments that we are describing.

Letter to a Schoolmistress summarized and was the culmination of Milani's contribution. He died a few weeks later at the age of 44, a victim of his illness. But the *Letter* was not his only achievement, and we must explain his work as a whole to gain a better understanding of our own educational experiment in Spain.

Milani was twice a convert. First, when he was already twenty years old, at the height of the Second World War, he converted to Catholicism from his family's agnosticism (his mother was a non-practising Jew). Second, and at almost the same time, he was converted to solidarity with the poor and underprivileged social classes, whereas his family had been well-to-do and culturally sophisticated.

The first conversion landed him in the parish of Calenzano, on the industrial outskirts of Florence, immediately after the Second World War, when the people were emerging from hunger, the backward rural conditions of many areas, and the defeat of fascism, and turning toward industry, progress and freedom. The young assistant parish priest, who had recently embraced the gospel of Christ, found his fellow parishioners to be a brick wall of prejudice and conditioning created by propaganda and custom, without any ability to reason and therefore incapable of resisting. Milani felt that it was impossible for the life-giving Word of his faith to have the slightest effect on minds hampered by a poor mastery of language, since words were the only vehicle for the Word made flesh. He then decided to devote his priestly work to education, mainly for young people who are the fodder for all propaganda, including ecclesiastical propaganda of the worst kind. Apart from his theological intuition that saw faith in the Word of God as impossible unless it can be heard in the only medium in which it can be spoken, which is the world around us, Milani understood that each person must freely name reality from within himself. That is what being an adult means: not learning what others have said, but calling things by their true names. In this inner echo, which uses the words of everyday speech to call each reality by its rightful name, and not the name dictated by others, people hear the call of reality that is meant for them alone. This call and response, this mutual encounter in which reality is illuminated by its true name and every individual's inner being is summoned to the cause of reality, is humanity's most noble experience. (For believers, it is also an encounter with God.)

Although Milani and Paulo Freire did not know one another, an admirable kinship exists between them. Milani's second conversion to the poor inspired the second part (also akin to Freire) of his intuition as an educator that the poor are closer to reality. To colonize them, to teach them our words for things, is to do them violence and thus destroy any likelihood of a truly liberated and liberating culture. Milani exhaustively analyzed the colonization of the poor by the dominant bourgeois culture. Amid the euphoria of world peace, he intuitively perceived all of the dangers that have now become a reality: the mass media's invasion of the fabric of society, creating popular culture and information usually biased in favour of capitalist interests, the destruction of class consciousness that this entails, and the shunting aside of the exploited into regions of the Third World that are less visible from here.

Milani devoted a book - the only one he ever wrote under his own name[1] - to a study of the Church and whether or not it had been an accomplice in the domination of the poor through education or the lack of it. Despite the long foreword by an archbishop and the *nihil obstat* of the Cardinal of Florence, the book was withdrawn from bookstores as untimely.

There were to be two other major clashes with the civil institutions of this free and democratic world: with the courts and, even more, with the legislative authorities to which justices inevitably defer; and with compulsory education. The first clash occurred because Milani defended conscientious objection to military service, and thus also trampled on the army and the concept of the nation as the protector of individual interests. In line with this thinking, however, Milani made it very clear that conscientious objection is the habitual state of modern citizens, and not only where the military is concerned.

In his most famous document, *Letter to a Schoolmistress*, this time signed by his young students in the hills of Florence, Milani opposed compulsory education as a truly selective and taming institution. Yet Milani saw this institution as the last hope of awakening awareness and clear thinking.

In Spain, this experiment - whose protagonist (he was so fond of each individual being his own protagonist!) said that *loyalty to the dead is the greatest disloyalty* - produced the Milanian Educators' Movement (MEM), part of the trend toward educational reform in recent years, which sees education as taking a stand against domination and thus reacting to rather than conforming to the modern world.

This movement's educational techniques boil down to becoming aware of reality in terms of the interests of the poorest of the poor. At the same time, this movement involves mastering language, a feat no less historic than the storming of the Bastille, although it is a quieter, more tenacious battle that is much harder to win. The final step is action, the individual and collective attitude that stems from taking a conscious stand.

Everything we have said above explains, if only to a slight degree, why people are tremendously unaware of, or fear the stigma of, Milani's message. This is because Milani left those who have continued his efforts on the slippery and unfavourable slope of a paradox. This yes-and-no situation - which means developing educational theory solely on the basis of practices to which one is committed; radically opposing all types of institutions, from the Church to the courts or legislative authorities, from schools to the mass media, showing absolute respect for the orthodoxy of each of these institutions; opposing the dominant culture while claiming its achievements for the oppressed - is shocking and uncomfortable in our world of those who either aspire to become part of the Establishment or who, having done so, rebel against it.

Of all possible paradoxes, however, the one that professional educators find most unsettling is, once again, Milani's ambivalence toward his own methods. He developed magnificent teaching methods, which would in themselves have made a significant contribution to our educational heritage, except that he saw them as being of secondary importance:

> Friends often ask me how I manage to keep the school open and full. They insist that I write down a method, that I spell out curricula, subjects and educational techniques. They are asking the wrong question. They should not be concerned about *how to teach*, but about *how to be teachers*.[2]

This pronouncement, as well as the other statement quoted above about disloyalty to the dead, render virtually impossible the servile imitation that has been the curse of famous educators, both living and dead, with Freire and Freinet heading the list. In many cases, their methods have been adopted but not their underlying intentions, thus watering down their message. This is relevant because each of the experiments being carried out at the Santiago Uno Boarding School and at Lorenzo Milani Agricultural School, both in Salamanca and at other schools and centres for adults in Spain's suburban and rural areas, is unique, irreproducible and intentionally heterogeneous. The same can be said of the methods applied there: reading the newspaper, collective writing, visits and field trips.

The common thread in all of these experiments is not so much *how to do things* as *how to be*. That is why we do not distinguish between doing and being in the description of educational strategies which follows.

Literacy and Education through Reading the Newspaper

First, let us agree on the meaning of "education". For the students of Barbiana, *true education, which no one has ever possessed, consists of two things: being of the people and mastering language.*[3] According to this definition, everyone should be regarded as uneducated, and the vast majority of people as illiterate. The reader should be careful to note that we are not talking about education in the conventional sense. Taking this argument to its extreme conclusion, we might infer that this vast majority of *illiterates* would be found at opposite ends of the spectrum: the masses and the educated people (?), farthest removed from the concerns of the majority.

However, not all *illiterates* and not all *uneducated people* are alike. Some are unaware of the forces that motivate most of their fellow human beings; they have the good fortune of possessing the dominant culture. Others belong to a world traditionally more inclined to co-operation; they are unfamiliar with the keys and mechanisms of the dominant culture.

For some, the logical process of *enculturation* and *literacy* occurs by acknowledging and practising such unfashionable values as solidarity; for others, it occurs by learning the passwords of official culture - mastering language - without abandoning one's own cultural milieu. In school, however, the latter is the problem.

The process of literacy (in the broad sense in which we are using the word) thus cannot be a one-way street - with culture being bestowed and received - but implies give and take: both teachers and students exchange their respective cultural models to produce a new reality. The fact is that this process of literacy never occurs on a level playing field, which means that there are serious difficulties in applying theory to practice. What thus occurs in many cases is a patchwork literacy, a cultural invasion that Freire described as banking education.

This is often true despite the good will of educators, who are more often concerned about methodologies than the meaning of their task. Let us examine one of the methodologies that we have examined in detail: the educational use of newspapers. This is one of the strategies most susceptible to the bankers' approach. As soon as a group of adults get their hands on a newspaper, they take for granted its wonderful benefits, its supposed ability to result in the liberating education that books describe so well.

This superficial view of the matter is fundamentally based on two very widespread myths regarding the use of newspapers that must be debunked. The first is that newspapers bring real life into the classroom. This well-intentioned and very widespread statement is potentially fraught with danger, since it gives rise to attitudes of complacency. It would thus be sufficient to introduce the use of newspapers in schools to establish a very close connection between the classroom and real life; we could then talk about adult education serving those for whom it was intended, and modern educators distancing themselves from outmoded styles of teaching. However, things are not that simple. This approach is simply a cliché for public consumption. Newspapers are not real life. Moreover, newspapers bring biased views of life into the classroom, which is cause for alarm. This should not lead us to conclude that their use is thus inadvisable, since books also present biased and unquestioned views of life, and text books - even mathematical texts - are no exception, for the existing educational system and all foreseeable systems present a biased view of the world.

The advantage of newspapers in this regard lies in the fact that their biases are more obvious to informed readers. Newspapers also focus on specific situations and do not claim to have all the answers. This makes it possible to demystify the printed word and thus the guarantee of infallibility that written culture ("what books say") enjoys in the eyes of the man in the street. Seen in this light, newspapers can be used, not so much to bring real life into the classroom, as to ensure that students think above all.

The second myth is that using newspapers is liberating. This statement, like the one above, confuses the end with the means. Simply using newspapers in adult classrooms without carefully thinking about the role that newspapers play is merely stultifying.

It would be rather like transmitting the same old values, those of traditional schools, only more effectively. That would be like running to stay in the same place. It is not the means that liberates. It is not sufficient to change educational techniques. Using newspapers would be liberating only if its ends were liberating and clear to those taking part in the educational process.

But now that we have debunked these myths and know the enormous potential of newspapers for influencing opinion, what approach do we take when faced with a group of boys from a rural area or a group of adults from a suburban community?

The paradoxical approach, of course. Newspapers must be used precisely because they are biased and slanted like everything else. They must be carefully analyzed precisely because they express the world view of those in power. They must be translated precisely because they use a secret jargon accessible only to those who have mastered the code. Their true nature must be exposed precisely because, when used in a naive manner, they may entail a cultural invasion and a travesty of *literacy*.

All of these things must be done precisely with people who belong to the vast majority of the dispossessed, those for whom newspapers are not written, those mentioned only sporadically and in a negative light as "the masses". This must be done precisely with the intention of making people *literate*, that is, enabling them to gain a better understanding of the world. We must also bear in mind that newspapers are a distant reality for these people, and we must ask ourselves why.

The answer to this question is of fundamental importance in addressing this task. It seems clear that a vast majority of Spaniards lack the specific tools required to read newspapers. They lack not only the mastery of their secret jargon but also the linguistic tools and the level of culture necessary for an adequate understanding of the mechanisms that govern the complex world we live in. Furthermore, undoubtedly as a result of the woeful legacy of the previous régime, we Spaniards lack a sense of community, that is to say, of political life. Spanish society continues to be without a backbone; very few people join organizations of any kind. Thus, the life described in newspapers, which revolves around the community, does not interest the majority of people in the slightest, since they do not understand what they are being told. As a result of their historical legacy and the current passion for privacy, the people seem to have been pushed into choosing the path of fierce individualism.

Are newspapers an appropriate vehicle for literacy, then? Without a shadow of a doubt. They might even be called an ideal and essential vehicle, where institutional and human failings cross paths and come face to face. However, this is not obvious at first glance. That is why we must use newspapers, analyze them carefully, translate them and expose their true nature, thus blending into a single process both learning and an understanding of what reality means to each individual.

In practical terms, this means avoiding the easy and immediate tendency to make the content of newspapers *educational*, that is, to turn them into useful aids for language or mathematical games, as we used to do with compositions about what we did on our summer holidays. This practice, which characterizes the banking approach as we have indicated above, is misleading and isolating.

Opposing the Culture of the Owners of Information

If we wish to avoid misleading and isolating students and turning them into mere clippers of newspaper articles, they must first know who is who in Spain's media industry. This knowledge is not always easy to obtain, but it is essential if students are to begin reading their output with a minimum of safeguards. We must find out who controls information, the economic, financial, ideological and political groups that pull the strings of the national news. Basically, we must review:

- the major national and/or regional newspapers;
- press associations;
- news agencies;
- advertising agencies and advertisers.

We must pay attention to changes in ownership, capital investments and the invasion of Spain's communications market by large multinational groups. All of these changes are currently taking place at an accelerated pace and are significantly altering the information scene in our country. The information given in the mastheads of our newspapers rapidly becomes outdated and may be misleading.

This difficult job is absolutely necessary, however, since it is a complicated matter to decode messages without knowing where they are coming from. Performing this task also teaches us to see the apparent pluralism of information in its true light; every day, this pluralism is increasingly jeopardized by the inexorable trend toward concentrating many media in few hands.

Next, it is necessary to analyze how newspapers are organized: their corporate structure, their technological development and, most importantly, their sources of financing. This special emphasis on financing sheds new light on another type of influence on the output of information that the reader ultimately receives. Figuring out how much revenue a publishing company derives from newsstands and advertising is a necessary and enlightening exercise.

After studying how publishing companies are organized, we must formally analyze *newspapers as objects in themselves*. Here we begin the task of decoding, since not all newspaper readers are aware that the way in which information is presented is already a manipulation of that information. It thus seems important to spend some time analyzing how space, sections and supplements are laid out, as well as the priority among them and the criteria for establishing this priority.

In descending order, we then come to a study of how news items are structured. Knowing how news items are put together subsequently makes it much easier to work with them and also provides an opportunity to begin learning about the different types of journalism.

Only then can we begin decoding the content of news items and the linguistic codes in which they are written, and *translating* newspaper talk - another *cultured* idiom - into popular terms that ensure that the reader will fully understand the messages that news items convey. This is done in a variety of ways depending on the context and the group that undertakes this task. We may read the news in a group as described above, trying to grasp day-to-day reality. We may make an in-depth analysis of the news that is of greatest interest to the group each day, taking it apart and putting it back together from the perspective of those who will never write for a newspaper. We may monitor a specific current event over a period of time, usually three months, to gain a full grasp of the issue studied and the circumstances that surround and shape it.

Other approaches may be equally valid, as long as newspapers are used, analyzed, translated and seen for what they are.

In connection with this task, groups of students may develop newspapers such as *La Bronca* at Salamanca's Santiago Uno or *El Loro* [The Parrot] at the Alcorcón Centre for Adults in Madrid. They must be newspapers, however, and not literary magazines as is common practice at the vast majority of educational centres. They must be fast-paced, put together in a period equivalent to that of daily newspapers. They must be informative, containing news of interest to the communities in which they are based. They must be self-sufficient, financed by the means usually available to newspapers, such as advertising and sales. All of this must be done with two purposes in mind: to discover *from an insider's perspective* the determining forces, the conflict of interests, the pressures and the limitations of the news profession, which is so frequently idealized by the illiterate; and to serve as a means of expression, however modest, for those who never have a say.

In any use of newspapers in the classroom, it is essential to rewrite the news. Passive acceptance of the press is the reader's greatest pitfall; to overcome this, it is not enough, as some maintain, to allow readers the occasional, limited opportunity to have their own say. It is not enough to produce school newspapers, no matter how well. Doing so teaches students the tricks of the trade, its limitations and dependencies, and this knowledge is very valuable when they pick up a real newspaper. However, it may produce habits of general scepticism and indifference so great as to be impervious to any news, and that is not good, either.

Bertrand Russell said that *schools should teach children the art of reading newspapers with disbelief.* That is something entirely different. Unlike scepticism, disbelief is active and involves becoming an active interpreter rather than passively and bitterly cutting oneself off.

Interpreting does not always mean being right, much less grasping, the truth by and for ourselves alone. Nor does it involve becoming know-alls, but rather restless searchers for relative truth. Relative does not mean absolute, of course, but that is not what matters. We mean *relative to the masses*, from whose vantage point we have already said that we read: the truth of a matter that affects us.

Let us look at an example. After following the same news story for several weeks (what we call monitoring), or after carefully analyzing a single news item, the group must develop its own written version, giving the background of the event to provide a proper framework for more recent developments and then asking the questions of traditional journalism, the five W's (who, what, when, where and why), as well as how. To this we add how events are interrelated, the background in question and the consequences. When the news is read from the viewpoint of the poorest of the poor, those who pay the price of history, everything is turned topsy-turvy. The protagonist of the news story (who) may not turn out to be the mandarin but rather the victim. When ceases to be an immediate date and becomes the exact number of years spent waiting for greater justice or for a demand to be met.

This is an amusing and exciting exercise that allows room for future consequences. It is also a bitter pill for teachers who believe that schools should be neutral, or that they should keep their own opinions to themselves. Many adults believe it is their duty to avoid controversial issues that would disrupt the school's tranquillity. On the contrary, such controversies represent a golden opportunity to practise true democracy, for teachers to become the absolute guarantors of the freedom to express all of the opinions - including their own - of those who are present and those who are absent and hence unable to speak for themselves. Dissidents deserve to be paid attention, especially if they are in the minority. This is a good opportunity to write the viewpoints of the respective sides on the blackboard along with the reasons they give, and to force students to think about and even expound the arguments of others. (It is also not a bad idea to do a few exercises in classical rhetoric every now and then.) A diligent search is made for the truth that is missing; the longing for neutrality is replaced by a nobler respect for one's opponents. This is how it should be, both in the classroom and in life itself.

The group's rewriting of the news does not have to be un-animous. It may be appropriate for the text to note differences in interpreting facts, accept the account of events as it appeared in the official press, or anticipate consequences of one sort or another.

Renaming the World together: Collective Writing

The best technique for this new and active writing based on the dictates of newspapers is once again Milani's discovery of *collective writing*. The genuine high point of this pedagogy, collective writing seeks to give voice to those who live the day-to-day existence of the silent majority of the earth. Until now, books have not been written by the poor, by farmers, fishermen, labourers and shepherds. To tell the truth, the poor have not read many books, either; almost none of them buy books or have a place to put them in their homes. When they do read, it is what others have written. We have all heard the works of the great authors explained in school; they are a few isolated geniuses whom we must admire and imitate if we wish to write. As a result, we have held several mistaken beliefs: that the art of writing is a privilege, almost a gift of the gods; that it is something individual and not collective; that it is of the few and consequently for the few; and that, in order to write, it is necessary to read the authors that have gone before, the way all authors read each other's works.

The practice of collective writing follows a procedure that is the reverse of developing ideas outlined in advance. Instead, it involves an inductive process based on each person's disconnected, inarticulate ideas and intuitions. Written on little slips of paper, these individual starting points are classified, separated or grouped into themes through simple analytical and comparative exercises that result in the various chapters or aspects of the topic. Nothing is eliminated except what is strictly repetitive. Once the little slips of paper are put in order within each chapter, complete with their contradictions, they are written one after the other on large sheets that everyone can see. This is the time for collective revision, for contrasting opinions, for finding the best sequence and the best word to express exactly what was meant. At first, the participants did not know what they meant; none of them would have been able to write it all down on their own. They now learn to do so as a group; an idea is born, the word itself, while collective writing forges a collective we.

This is also the time to create a thing of beauty, to eliminate the superfluous, to prefer what is clearest to readers who belong to the masses (and not the élite). It is a time for creativity as well as discovery: reality is out there in the harsh shadows of that which we do not control, but when we name it, it is transfigured and appears in all its brilliance. Teaching people how to talk means teaching them how to obey, giving them the world as it is named by those who order and master it. That is why it is important for these adults to become protagonists, naming everything around them for themselves. This fundamental human task has more safeguards if it is performed as a team by the masses who live in and bear the brunt of the world around them. We have already pointed out that there is room for differences, for making contrasts and for paying attention to the reasoning of others. If agreement is not reached, the final text will be enriched by the pros and cons of certain arguments.

At the school of Barbiana, collective writing became craftsmanship in the service of art. *Letter to a Schoolmistress* defines art in a surprising and profound manner that is already well known to and highly esteemed by aesthetes and sociologists alike. It should be equally valued by Christians:

> ... only insults and four-letter words came to my lips. By setting them down in this document, we have been able to contain these words with a little effort and to transform them into arguments. In so doing, we have come to understand what art is. It means loving the evil in someone or something, thinking about it at leisure, seeking the help of friends and working patiently as a team. Little by little, the truth underlying the hatred rises to the surface. A work of art is born: a hand outstretched to the enemy so that he may change his ways.[4]

This entire educational experience continually depends on the motivation to learn. It is far removed from interest in becoming part of the established order, and is rather concerned with avoiding marginalization and the world that causes it. Transforming even hatred into an outstretched hand is a truly inspired, delicate educational task. Other educators would have avoided or soothed this hatred. Milani provokes it. In the pedagogy of non-violence, with which he expressly aligns himself, Milani does not show contempt for aggressiveness but rather channels it. From his initial phase as a teacher, when he discovered that he was one, comes this surprising and extremely lucid statement:

> I do not radiate sanctity, nor am I even a likeable priest. Instead, I have all of the characteristics needed to alienate people. Even in the

classroom, I am merciless, intolerant and provoking. I do not get along with young people by virtue of some special gift for drawing them to me. I was merely astute. I knew how to push the button that released their innermost qualities. I did not have any wealth of the soul to offer them. They were the ones who were full of riches, and no one knew it. I appealed to their pride, their natural generosity, the social angst that is the atmosphere of our time, and in so doing I touched, deep inside them, man's instinct for rebellion, for affirming his dignity as a servant of God, and nothing more.[5]

Letter to a Schoolmistress is itself the product of this technique of collective writing and, more importantly, of this pedagogy. In our own country, the same is true of *Escritos colectivos de muchachos del pueblo*[6] [Collective writings of working-class boys], developed by the students of Santiago Uno. It is also true of many other unpublished works of different lengths and purposes that have been written by various groups of people: adults who have just learned to read or belong to groups studying basic courses, young people from underprivileged backgrounds, and school-age children.

All of these works have a common thread, something too often forgotten by schools that usually devote much of their time to routine repetition of dull and meaningless things. This common thread is the first rule of writing: *one must have something important to say* that is useful to all or to many. This means not talking for the sake of talking, not engaging in empty and rhetorical verbal diarrhoea that is an end in itself and sterilizes any attempt to link writing to the real world.

This something important must be said - and written - to be read, that is, to explain one's own position where appropriate, to express views different from the opinions of those who do all of the talking in various forums, to try to influence people by speaking out together as a group, and even to give vent to internal differences.

The form varies from fully-fledged books to reflections on and evaluations of work done as a group, including letters written to newspapers in protest or support, articles providing information about activities or expressing opinions on matters of concern, or any other form. Whatever the form, all reflect a profound and passionate discussion, understanding and clarification of one's own views and those of others. There is no room for frivolity here. This is not a matter of writing compositions for school or playing at democracy.

It is something quite different from what the students of Barbiana described with reference to certain educational practices:

> I have been told that in some American schools, every time the teacher says something, half of the students raise their hands and say, "I agree." The other half say, "I disagree." The next time around, they change sides and continue chewing gum in all seriousness.[7]

Learning in Real Life: Conscientious Objection

One last educational practice deserves our attention: *visits*. Field trips from the boarding school are a required assignment in which students both learn and measure what they have learned, a good educational technique for study and evaluation. But carefully planned meetings with visitors to the school are the training ground for such field trips. A weekly ninety-minute session would be enough to get students used to asking questions and, as they themselves say in a collective text,

> That is how we learn to master language, to speak in public, to converse with people, and to overcome fear and shyness. We study and write in the classroom, but mainly we talk. The classroom is the parliament of our boarding school. We talk about things in our lives, and outsiders come and let us ask them questions.

In other words, visitors agree to allow themselves to be questioned and are free to answer or not as they wish. They do not come to lecture or to take advantage of any question to expand on their ideas. All students are required to participate, and any student may interrupt an over talkative interviewee by saying, "You are not answering the question."

As with newspapers, students must be active interpreters and not merely passive listeners. Some visitors are VIPs but, in the final analysis, all are important people even if they do not hold high positions. The school is thus also visited by students from other places and by common people, who are interesting simply by virtue of being who they are. When visitors leave, students naturally spend time thinking about the experience, polishing the notes they took during the interview, highlighting key words that generate basic themes, and so on.   Then they pool this information and calmly analyze what happened.

The same thing occurs every time the students return from a field trip.   They go out in twos rather than in groups, even though group visits are also useful.   The other students ask them questions, and the teacher raises issues and aspects initially overlooked. Interest grows from one field trip to another.   Students open their eyes and ears.   As active interpreters of reality as they experience it (and not merely as it is described in the newspapers), students become freer - but not always more effective.

Understanding reality is a step toward transforming it, but it is not enough.   Few things change in this world.   In this method of teaching, it is very necessary to cultivate *conscientious objection* as a habitual attitude toward the law, both formal law - which is the bastion of the strong and not the weak - and the social laws of custom and the masses colonized by the propaganda of those who hold economic power.   Objection is a means of expression, of conveying meaning, of knowing who is who; it is not a guarantee of effectiveness, as if one were always seeking to achieve something. Sometimes it is more than enough to achieve one's own independence and to say no when everything conspires to force you to say yes.   The educator's attitude is fundamental in this regard:

> ... I cannot tell my boys that obedience is the only way to love the law.   I can tell them that they should have such esteem for the laws of men that they should obey them only when they are just (that is, when they strengthen the weak).   When they see, on the other hand, that the laws of men are unjust (that is, when they condone abuses by the powerful), my boys must struggle to change them.

> Voting is the official mechanism for changing the law. The Constitution also adds another means: the right to strike.

> But the real force behind these two instruments of power is the ability to influence other voters and strikers by word and by example.   When the time comes to do so, the greatest school of all is personally to pay the price of conscientious objection, that is, breaking a law that one considers unjust and accepting the penalty that it prescribes.

... Having the courage to tell young people that every man is supreme, that obedience is not a virtue for them but the most cunning of temptations, that they must not think obedience can shield them from man or God, that each of them must feel solely responsible for everything[8]

A liberating education, one that does not seek to co-opt people but to affirm and liberate them, runs the enormous risk of provoking clashes between students and the established order, the risk of failure and bitterness. That is why it is essential to create and encourage *celebrations* of life, as opposed to vacations free of the effort of work, and diversions from the monotony of routine. Celebrations must have a reason, a meaning, and must be warranted by something or some event. In short, we must celebrate our students' lives, even though we cannot rejoice in owning many valuable possessions. Celebrations must affirm our being on the side of good, which is not the same as owning material goods. Distinguishing between the two is the breath of life for those learning to live in a world of power and emptiness.

Notes

1. Milani, L. 1975. *Maestro y cura de Barbiana, Experiencias pastorales* [Pastoral experiences of the parish priest and schoolmaster of Barbiana]. Madrid: Marsiega. Italian edition: *Esperienze pastorali*, 1958, Florence: Libreria Editrice Fiorentina.

2. *Experiencias pastorales* (see Note 1), p. 223.

3. Alumnos de la Escuela de Barbiana. 1982. *Carta a una maestra* [Students of the School of Barbiana, Letter to a Schoolmistress]. Barcelona: Hogar del Libro, p. 107. Italian edition: *Lettera a una professoressa*, 1967, Florence: Libreria Editrice Fiorentina.

4. *Carta a una maestra* (see Note 2), pp. 131-2.

5. *Experiencias pastorales* (see Note 1), pp. 226-7.

6. Casa Escuela Santiago Uno. 1979. *Escritos colectivos de muchachos del pueblo* [Santiago 1 Boarding School, Collective writings of working-class boys]. Madrid: Editorial Popular.

392

7. *Carta a una maestra* (see Note 2), p. 129.

8. Milani, L. 1976. Carta a los jueces [Letter to the judges]. *Sínite* 49: 117-118 and 126.

Additional Bibliography

Corzo Toral, J.L. 1983. *La escritura colectiva, Teoría y práctica de la escuela de Barbiana* [Collective writing: Theory and practice of the school of Barbiana]. Madrid: Anaya.

Corzo Toral, J.L. 1986. *Leer periódicos en clase, Una programación para EGB, Medias, Adultos y Compensatoria* [Reading newspapers in the classroom: a program for basic general, secondary, adult and remedial education]. Madrid: Editorial Popular.

Corzo Toral, J.L. 1981. *Lorenzo Milani. Maestro cristiano, análisis espiritual y significación pedagógica* [Lorenzo Milani, Christian teacher: spiritual analysis and pedagogical significance]. Salamanca: Pontifical University of Salamanca.

Lancho, J. 1972. *El periódico en la escuela* [Newspapers in the schools] (video). Madrid: San Pablo Films.

Marti, M. 1972. *El maestro de Barbiana* [The schoolmaster of Barbiana]. Barcelona: Nova Terra.

Milani, L. 1973. *L'Obbedienza non è più una virtù. Documenti del processo di Don Milani* [Obedience is no longer a virtue. Documents from the trial of Father Milani]. Florence: Libreria Editrice Fiorentina. Spanish edition in *Sínite* 49 (1976): 111-134.

School of Barbiana. 1967. *Lettera a una professoressa* [Letter to a schoolmistress]. Florence: Libreria Editrice Fiorentina.
There is a Spanish edition: *Carta a una maestra*. Barcelona: Hogar del Libro, 1982.

Students of Milani and others. 1978. *Contraescuela, Por una escuela popular* [Counterschool: in favour of a people's school]. Madrid: Zero.

TRAINING -- A TOOL IN THE STRUGGLE AGAINST ALL TYPES OF EXCLUSION? THE HISTORY OF *AFER*

Francis Gosset
Christophe Caron
Didier Andreau
Action-Formation-Etude-Recherche
Lille, France

Introduction

The main weapon against illiteracy in France today is what might be called "pedagogism".

We are among those who believe that what should be studied is the practice of and the reasons for reading; no one can learn techniques in something he or she cannot do. Reading can be taught to persons who are involved in development projects where learning to read is necessary for success. "If I live in a society that does not require me to read, I will not read."

It may seem contradictory for such a belief to be held by a training centre whose mission is educational. We may therefore wonder what can be the place of a document from a training centre combating illiteracy using extra-pedagogical practices.

In France, we are used to dealing with paradoxical situations. While we believe illiteracy is mainly a political problem, which in large part goes beyond the context of educational research and mere technical responses, we have to work in an educational area, namely training, so that we can try to provide solutions.

Apart from great conclusions announced with much fanfare, and a few initiatives taken by interdisciplinary partnerships, we have almost no real co-operative methods for the development of innovative practices in the fight against illiteracy. We have to work within the structure of the educational authorities which provide our funding, which means we must adhere to conditions that do not allow the greatest possible latitude.

Our association, which promotes political and ideological choice by offering training providing an alternative to exclusion, has been trying since the beginning to better manage this contradiction. This is what we shall attempt to demonstrate.

We shall first attempt to describe what we have done by giving a history of our association - how, starting with an ideological choice which guided our choice of actions, these have led in turn to further reflections, which in turn have led to other actions, and so on. The battle against illiteracy has throughout held the principal place.

In part two we shall try, through description of the personalized educational workshop and the section for reintegration of the long-term unemployed, to show how, in training sequences, we try to avoid "pedagogism" by allowing individuals to take charge of their training and to develop projects in which knowing how to read makes sense to them.

1. The History of Action-Formation-Etude-Recherche (AFER)

In 1978, a training school for social workers in the Lille suburbs and the jobs of its instructors were restructured. After long and hard struggles, there were those who were not resigned to the situation. At the end of the 1970s there was a mounting wave of hopes of self-management. The discussions were long and difficult, "alternativism is the coming thing". At all events, alternative politics in France were beginning to grow.

Instructors who were victims of economic lay-offs at the School of Social Service formed the Action-Formation-Etude-Recherche [Action-Training-Study-Research] association (AFER) as a collective, proposing training that was to be "different in content and form, setting up new kinds of collaboration, new relationships within the working collective ...."

The gestation period (1978-1982)

The creation of AFER was the fruit of several years of reflection, experience and interventions among social workers in the Nord/Pas de Calais region.

"AFER's purpose is to promote, encourage and develop all methods suited to health, social and cultural training. This action is to be pursued at all stages: design, studies, contacts, training, research" (extract from the statutes). It offered to staff working in the health and social sectors an approach different from the daily professional reality.

All the actions taken in training were part of an alternative process. The object was to construct methodological and pedagogical tools for training adults. Because we were self-managed, all members of the collective played a part in planning the day-to-day work. Each was master of his or her own actions, from the birth of an idea through design, negotiation and completion to evaluation (extract from the planning text for creation of the *Atelier pédagogique personnalisé* [personalized educational workshop] 1986).

A dual goal was set for the first year: to continue intervention in continuing education with employees in the health and social sector and to make ourselves known.

Training was principally centred on psychiatric personnel. It was supplemented by the creation of a structure for putting forward our ideas to others. This took the form of action through regional, national and international media, discussion evenings, and study days on themes in the anti-psychiatry sphere.

Along with the work in continuing training and the building of our image, we reflected on other actions to be implemented and other areas for intervention. AFER wanted to offer something broader, a mutual sharing of resources. This was the birth of "AFER-dissemination", a three-year experiment to provide musical and theatrical groups with part-time secretarial help to manage the administrative tasks related to cultural activity.

Four main ideas thus regulated the life of our emerging structure:

- continuing training of personnel in the health and social sector;

- making the association permanent by creating a permanent mechanism for discussion and confrontation concerning practices in the battle against exclusion;

- promotion of cultural enterprises through sharing of technical resources;

- experimentation with new kinds of relationships in the enterprise.

Emergence of the problem of illiteracy

The goal of becoming known through creating a place for debate on exclusion began to bear fruit. Intervention with employees in the health and social field gave birth to new examination of, among other things, the suggestion of joint intervention among employees and the public in the sector. Following technical training experiments with handicapped workers in the *Centres d'aide par le travail* [centres for aid through work] (CAT), which were sheltered workshops for adult handicapped persons considered unable to work in an ordinary milieu, AFER was asked to set up training aimed at integrating young handicapped workers into a regular workplace.

The success of this project brought about the first big change in the organization. New measures put in place by the new socialist government, particularly the plan for social and professional integration for young persons 16 to 25 (the Swartz Plan) gave rise to AFER's work in the area of integration.

Measures accompanying the creation of the mechanism for integration of young people would henceforth provide a legal and financial framework for actions taken to train young job-seekers.

At the end of eighteen months of operation, these training courses were not as successful as we had hoped. First conclusions were roughly as follows:

- The goal of integration into the ordinary environment did not seem to work, at least in the short term, with these people, who were too marked out in society, too circumscribed and in a poor psychological state. The time period allowed and the methods used for these courses were too limited to achieve the goal of integration into the working world given to the organizations.

- The tools for intervention were not adapted to this public, especially those concerning the approach to illiteracy. It became increasingly clear that this problem was the main obstacle to access to training and, by extension, to employment.

At the time, the organizations working in the field of illiteracy made the same observation: the enormous difficulty, if not inability, to deal with illiteracy using traditional teaching methods, without training for the instructors and without policies and research. Since up to that time illiteracy had been considered non-existent in France, the lack of research and therefore of teaching tools suited to coping with it was understandable.

Faced with these observations, AFER took two types of measures:

- review of the strategy for intervention. The public was too young, too troubled, to be integrated into a job, even in the medium term. The legal framework, means and time periods were not suited to any in-depth action. AFER reoriented its work towards an older public, within a framework of experimental actions for a two-year period;

- assignment of two permanent staff members to study national and international teaching methods and experiences in the battle against illiteracy. The investigations resulted in a meeting with the *Association française pour la lecture* (AFL). It was love at first sight! All the members of the organization took teacher-training courses at the AFL's school and became committed to a very clear reading policy.

From the meeting with AFL to the regional illiteracy day

Meeting with AFL: a resolve taken
We had met with an association where the practices and concepts echoed what we had perceived in the field. According to AFL's Jean Foucambert, changes in the reading situation in France depended on the implementation of a comprehensive policy.

An action limited to a single area only benefits those who have no need of help in other areas. Improving the technical level of reading without doing anything else only helps those who can already read. New measures were called for:

- A continuing information campaign about reading and its significance, so that the social status of reading and non-reading could be examined;

- Reading means to accept sharing power, taking on responsibilities and agreeing that the greatest number of people possible should take responsibilities;

- Helping to increase the number of readers means questioning one's own experience as a reader;

- Promoting the use of collective equipment that would allow choice of what one is going to read;

- Designing action to promote reading as an aid to exercising a skill, going from assumed rejection, through questioning and change of mind to choice;

- Developing new written material with different values and terms of reference;

- Reading begins processes whose nature and complexity is far different from those that require the rudimentary use of literacy, which is still that possessed by close to 70% of individuals today. That is to say that an important methodological investment had to be made, both in initial learning and in the subsequent phases of improvement.[1]

To teach reading, to empower the greatest number and help them to share this power, is our project and the goal our actions have been aimed at since our association was created. It remained for us to learn AFL's pedagogical methods in order to use our training tools better and then to take up our pilgrim's staff to meet new adventures and new debates.

Regional illiteracy day (17 October 1984)
Following the methods adopted at AFER, the investment in AFL's pedagogical methods could not remain a secret. Preliminary observations of our experiences with adults had to be discussed in public. The reality of action being taken to deal with illiteracy, along with the rising curve of unemployment, concerned not only educationists.

After a series of interventions concerning the illiteracy problem, working committees set out a list of questions and directions for future work:

- Action should be taken to provide information in order to demystify accepted ideas about the matter;

- Is it useful to know how to read today, given technical progress, particulary the development of robotics?

- Is combating illiteracy not a kind of normalization?

- Existing training methods and their limitations should be assessed;

- Is a specific mechanism needed?

- A file on organizations working in literacy in the region should be made up and distributed;

- Preventive actions against illiteracy should be taken in early childhood. Interventions should be made and support provided in schools and school-related activities for those under 16;

- Training adapted to literacy trainers is needed;

- Is it necessary to be in a pleasurable situation to be a reader?

- These days the non-reader is increasingly inundated with written material. Without tools to decode them, he or she becomes more and more marginalized. What are the best ways to develop these tools?

The number of those who participated in this regional day (250) demonstrated the significance of the problem and the powerlessness of many trainers.

The third stage: experimental actions to help long-term unemployed and handicapped long-term unemployed persons when the APPs were set up.

Following the orientation day, the organization put to use what it had learned at AFL and at the conference on continuing education. Sensitization courses were offered to teams of professionals who wanted to take action concerning reading in their establishments. Joint training sessions suggested to users and to professionals that they question their status as readers, and reflect on the act of reading and on what methodological and pedagogical methods could be used.

At the same time, between 1983 and 1985, AFER set up experimental actions for long-term unemployed persons over 21 and long-term unemployed persons with handicaps who were recognized as being able to work or were working in a regular workplace. At the time there was no mechanism for taking charge of these persons. Training was aimed at social and vocational integration of a public with difficulties (illiterates, persons with behaviour problems or difficulties in relating with others, persons with motor or mental handicaps, persons leaving prison or being followed up after psychiatric treatment, and so on).

Our knowledge of this public in the context of various institutions, and the questioning of these in the face of barriers and exclusion, led us to take action for integration into the ordinary milieu, outside of an institutional framework.

Our experience with young people led us to set up long-term actions. It takes more than a few weeks for us to help people become autonomous, find or recover their place in space and time, open themselves to the social, vocational and cultural world, move beyond strategies to avoid or circumvent written material after years spent withdrawing and turning in on themselves. We wanted to lead these persons out of a circumscribed life, caused by long-term unemployment or a mental health problem, by using real situations.

The experience of these two courses led us to the idea of individualized training where self-evaluation and self-training could be acquired in real situations in which the trainee could bring about a positive result.

There were conclusive results from work with these persons: they became more autonomous, more open, they had more self-confidence, which allowed them to cope with constantly recurring situations leading inevitably to failure; they achieved integration into the world of work, and sometimes into training leading to qualifications, which had been previously unimaginable.

It is in precise projects to be carried out that people become aware of the relationship that everyone has with written material (whether it be use or avoidance of this material) and it is starting with this awareness, encouraged by the training context, that learning how to read can begin. Any demand that did not respect these steps would place the individual in the role of student again, setting up between trainer and trainee the ambiguous relationship that exists between one who has the answers and one who needs them.

AFER today. What remains of our original passion?

Today, *AFER* has 24 salaried staff working in the following 8 areas of intervention:

- Personalized teaching workshops (5 paid workers and one conscientious objector).
  Clientele: all members of the public over 16, whatever their level, project, problems and status.
  Partners: State, region, department, communes, *Fonds d'action sociale* (FAS), *Agence pour l'emploi*, social workers, businesses, reception and counselling organizations and so on.

- Long-term unemployed, Lille (5 employees).

- Long-term unemployed, Tourcoing (4 employees).
  Clientele: young people and adults looking for jobs, workers who are handicapped, persons who are leaving prison or psychiatric institutions.
  Partners: State, region, department, commune, *Agence pour l'emploi*, social workers, *Direction du travail*, businesses, reception and counselling organizations and so on.

- Continuing education (3 employees).
  Clientele: personnel in the health and social sector, business employees, etc.
  Partners: mainly businesses.

- Multi-media (2 employees)
  Clientele: no direct clientele. Multi-media teaching tools are produced.
  Partners: State/region, businesses involved in new technology and audio-visual materials, social workers, reception and counselling organizations.

- Secretariat (4 employees)

- *"La petite Maison"*. This operates with the participation of full-time staff from the other areas.
  Clientele: any person accompanied by a child under four who wants to discuss early childhood.
  Partners: as with the other areas, plus all structures dealing with early childhood and partners in the neighbourhood where the project is set up.

- Two employees are now seconded to a regional mission called *Nouvelles qualifications* in Villeneuve d'Ascq.

The idea of different areas is related to the nature of the intervention, the public affected and this public's legal structure. Some employees work in several areas at the same time. In principle, any employee can change his or her area of work,

As well as these sectors of intervention, we have co-operative groups. These research groups are where practices are compared, in an area of work (reading for example), with a specific public or with tools (the multimedia section and the *Petite maison* are tools created after multilateral discussion in these groups). One permanent employee is assigned as resource person for this group.

Since the beginning we have maintained the principle of self-management. Each full-time employee is paid the same salary. There is no director. Each can carry a project through from conception to negotiation, completion and evaluation. Each is careful to play his or her role as an institutional representative. Each is a member of the association and as such participates in the monthly general meeting with voting rights.

The day-to-day and central management of the structure is looked after by a pool of representatives designated by those working in the various areas; each area uses the management method most appropriate to its work.

In terms of organization of working hours, we have: time for institutional negotiation, time for research and preparation, time for co-ordination and time for intervention. The time is divided up in terms of area of work and period of reference.

Our area of intervention is mainly regional. It is concentrated on Lille, Tourcoing and Villeneuve d'Ascq for publics with problems, spread over the whole territory for continuing education.

We have many partners. There is no central place in the institution integrating outside partners. Each area of work, and at times each individual, deals with the network of partners. One area might invite partners to a pilot group to discuss a certain problem (for example in the APP, see the next section); another might meet its partners in an evaluation meeting after action has been taken, or in a working group.

This is also true for the public using our services. Each area deals with things on a case-by-case basis. Trainees might set their own schedule in one project, in another they might have an operating budget and have to manage it themselves.

Overall, we encourage persons to define their training goals and we suggest a course of self-training to them (self-management of training, see the following section). One of our objectives is to have trainees take responsibility for their own progress.

The question of their integration in the central management of the association is a perennial one. That said, we have not yet found a formula to make this possible. It is the same problem as with the partners - those providing funding and other institutions - with the difficulty of limits of training time on the one hand and, on the other, the difficulty these people have following this kind of procedure. Since they have never been asked to share power, when we attempt to have them do so it seems bizarre, almost indecent, to them.

Another problem is the lack, locally and nationally, of efforts to bring together persons with problems who could represent these people in the structures that concern them. Because of the deterioration in the state of the union movement and its traditional lack of interest in the jobless, we do not believe that the unions - given their present structure and orientations - would be the best representatives.

This, briefly, is the institutional context in which the AFER collective exists. We have become considerably more active in the last twelve years. This increased activity and institutionalization is not without a certain number of problems and questions, particularly with regard to choice and forms of intervention with the public. We shall come back to this question in the conclusion.

Now that we have painted the backdrop, we shall describe two kinds of intervention with the public in which reading plays a prominent part.

2. **Two Examples of Intervention**

2.1 ATELIER PÉDAGOGIQUE PERSONNALISÉ [PERSONALIZED EDUCATIONAL WORKSHOP] (APP)

In 1985, the national network of APPs was set up, and AFER formed an APP in October of 1986.

In principle, the APP is an open, individualized educational facility, allowing all persons to develop a training activity, a link between the course of training and vocational integration, due in particular to emphasis on use of self-training methods.

The primary objective of the APP is to provide general training that can be supplemented by an approach to basic technology (such as understanding and using a technical tool in various situations). In no case is this training of a vocational nature. The APP does not provide career counselling or evaluation.

The APP is meant mainly for individuals who have a personal or vocational project that is sufficiently defined and who are voluntarily undertaking training. It is intended for a public at all levels and of all origins (employees, young or adult job seekers, etc.). There is no minimum level required to make use of APPs.

The requirements also stipulate that all publics (except salaried workers) must be referred to the APP by an information and counselling reception centre, a local mission, the *Agence nationale pour l'emploi* or other such organization. If a person comes directly to the APP, he or she must be put in touch with a reception centre so that follow-up can be done. For this purpose, a liaison sheet is filled out at reception to inform the APP of the number of trainees they have referred.

The APP's goal is to supplement other mechanisms for continuing education (regional program, special examination for university entrance, social advancement and so on).

The following steps take place in the training period:

- a phase in which the training is defined before a training contract is signed;

- training evaluation periods, in which the trainer provides the learner with immediate information on his or her progress, shortcomings and ways to remedy them, through discussions;

- self-training using tools provided to the trainee;

- personalized support provided by trainers and resource persons;

- evaluation phase at the end of the training contract;

- return to the reception organization.

In its field of competence, the APP places the trainee and defines a contract with individual goals, which on average does not exceed 150 hours. The contract can be renewed in exceptional cases and in no case can it replace training that could be given by a training organization for the job market. It is signed by the trainee and the trainer. It makes clear:

- the objectives;
- the content of the training;
- the overall duration of the training and minimum weekly attendance by the trainee at the APP;
- the work plan;
- the ways the expected skills will be recognized and/or validated.

The reception organization is informed of this contract when the liaison sheet is returned.

At the end of training, each person receives a certificate, part of a portfolio of competencies, on which is recorded:

- the name and content of the training taken through this contract;
- skills acquired at the end of the contract;
- validations achieved in general training.

How we operate

The APP is not a training course in the traditional sense of the term, that is, training that starts on a certain date and ends on another with X persons taking the same course, selected with regard to pre-established terms of reference, with presupposed educational levels. It is a training structure that is constantly moving, intended for all persons (job seekers, employees, handicapped workers, persons receiving health and social support), no matter what the training project might be. The project in this latter case can be the act of developing the project. The idea that the APP is not a course is explained by the fact that each trainee comes to it at a different level, with different expectations. It is impossible for the training centre to develop a common program or length of training period, given the heterogeneity of its public and of their status, levels and needs. In this sense, the APP is a tangled web of workshops with the individual's training project at its centre. Training is without salary, free, and takes place part-time on a weekly basis. Time spent in training is 300 hours for those over 25 and 150 hours for those who are younger. Trainees spend an average of 15 hours per week at the APP. Training may be stopped at any time if the person has managed to enter certificated training, returns to work or simply finds the services we offer unsuitable. Training does not lead to qualifications (we cannot grant qualifications nor do we wish to be able to do so). Training begins after a weekly information meeting for the purpose of explaining the goal of training. At the end of the information meeting, persons state whether or not they want to become part of the APP. For those who do, a time is set for an individual meeting and discussion. This meeting of about an hour allows us to get to know the person and to sketch out a possible project in the APP, dates, times and content.

A preliminary plan is worked out in terms of what the person has been able to express; this plan can be modified at certain times during training (we shall return to this). A six-week period of self-evaluation and an individual meeting are also scheduled. The first six-week training evaluation allows the trainees to see where they stand in their training and, through exchanges, to develop their expectations from training.

Training is now begun, and we shall continue this presentation later.

Self-training

The situation when training ends is not the only parameter for evaluating the progress in training of a trainee in the APP: self-training provides another.

Our training objectives in the APP can be summed up as direct or indirect vocational integration. However, we feel it is indispensable to take other fundamental aspects into consideration, such as social integration and autonomy.

Our training process aims at considering these two inseparable aspects from the beginning. Because of this, all training has indirect effects on the life and behaviour of the trainee: revitalization, a new rhythm of life, a different social status. But because of the kind of public we serve, we must emphasize this implicit role of training to give it an explicit training character.

Making this clear means leading the trainees to take part, to become active in working towards their future and, as a beginning, in their own training. It means causing them to give up their wait-and-see attitude of being merely spectators.

To achieve this result, we have to create learning situations. The first learning situation, which is most likely to bring about change, is training. To exploit this training situation we must give trainees freedom to take an active role. They are no longer the "trained", they have the potential to have power over themselves during the ensuing period of respite, thanks to the neutrality possible in the training situation. Participation in the APP is not to receive pay, but because of a desire for training and reclassification.

We suggest to the trainee an area of action which is certainly within a structure but is empty, without content, and he or she possesses the key to it. This is our primary objective at the APP: to give the individual tools to become an actor in the training.

However, self-training has limitations:

- denial of any support from others (I trained myself all by myself).

- ideological use of self-training: having persons work their way alone through constraining systems of social relationships, persuading them that they have power that they do not, in fact, possess.[2]

But it is by keeping these limits in mind that we can work in the right direction. At a time when cracks are appearing in the educational system's primary function - social reproduction - some patching up is required. Self-training seems to be a good method.

The practice of self-training as analysed by Gaston Pineau cannot be separated from a project where a person takes personal power over his or her life and training.

Self-evaluation

In the same way that trainees tend to become actors in their own training, they want to plan the course of their own training, seeing what is at stake.

A first training evaluation at six weeks allows trainees to see where they stand with regard to their training and to develop through discussions their expectations from training. We have chosen to formalize this first phase, knowing that each of the trainees negotiates the content of training every two weeks.

Working from requests from trainees, we have planned activities with three objectives:

- to bring about evaluation and self-evaluation;

- to work out personalized training projects and the necessary content of training;

- to lead the trainees to more autonomy in taking charge of their training, in both content and method.

The trainees work following an activity plan that allows them to evaluate themselves and their training project in terms of vocational orientation. These activities must also provide time for individualized work and relate to the existing mechanism for training.

An evaluation is carried out systematically after each workshop. The tool used is the self-evaluation booklet, in which the trainee reports what he or she has learned in a session and what he or she is in the course of learning. An evaluation workshop takes place every two weeks with sub-groups of trainees supervised by an advisory trainer. This evaluation is done in relation to objectives to be attained, thus allowing content to be improved. A monthly individual evaluation meeting allows for verification of the whole project for social and vocational integration.

The self-evaluation booklet is an aide-mémoire for trainees. It is a written record of their progress and also verifies the coherence between the initial project and their requests for modifications as the project goes along.

Although we have revised it several times, we are still not satisfied with the trainee's booklet. It is very awkward to use and some trainees have a great deal of difficulty with it from day to day. They do not understand our insistence on its use and on what they consider repetition (for example, several reminders of the project evaluation every two weeks). Some people have a very academic view of training and prefer results to the process, independent of goals.

However, there are significant benefits:

- fewer discrepancies between the trainees' objectives and the content of the training;

- ease of follow-up, especially for trainers who were not in charge of the trainees in question;

- the trainee has the pleasure of accumulating a written record of his or her progress and the booklet is the best tool for validating the program.

In spite of everything, we think the booklet is indispensable. We are at present thinking about modifying it, and in particular about ways of having the trainees get involved in these deliberations.

Heterogeneous public and individualization

We feel it is desirable to serve a heterogeneous public, starting from the observation that it is not very relevant to address a public which has difficulties while shutting them into training that is all aimed specifically at a public with a low level. We have chosen rather to open the APP to a heterogeneous public, both as to level of projects and of education. Thus we can offer to all trainees a structure centred not on mass integration of knowledge, but rather on reflection on use of this knowledge. This is also so that we can meet the growing demands for training from a public that we have not traditionally served.

A heterogeneous public is necessary to stimulate group dynamics, while not preventing the individualization of training.

Management of schedule of conditions

We are also faced with a paradox: our work involves self-training; but the framework imposed on us, and certain ideas of control that have been introduced, do not always encourage this method. The APP is involved in constant relationships with local partners.

Because of the specificity of the APP's operation, these relations are difficult to manage. They are formalized by:

- individualized meetings;

- follow-up groups for trainees (partners who take over);

- pilot group;

- thematic groups (illiteracy, minimum wage for integration, research).

The partners with whom we collaborate are representative of the APP's identity. This identity is chosen by the organization, which has developed its competencies and strategies by favouring service to a marginalized public having problems with social and vocational integration. We continue, however, to accept a heterogeneous public, because the APP should never be seen as an APP ghetto, reproducing the image of failure among the public it serves.

We must respond to any request for training that can be done at the APP, whatever it may be. The APP wants to have a real representative image of the local demands and needs for training of a public that is experiencing exclusion.

Examples of intervention through workshops

There are three types of workshop, offering different training, even if at times the dividing lines remain intentionally blurred to allow for adaptation to individual situations and to persons looking for a place suitable for them.

"Theme" workshops
These workshops bring together persons who at any given time show similar needs in the same area (reading, arithmetic). They offer to publics with a low degree of autonomy (new arrivals, for example) the possibility of learning basic knowledge in a group. This is also the best place to start reflection or the process of self-training (What does it mean to be a reader? What does it mean to learn? How do we learn?).

This is also where teaching can rely on group dynamics, on collective projects such as production of a newspaper. Work with a public with problems requires going through phases of socialization, which is not easy in other training situations, in individual work, for example.

Without these workshops we would not be able to motivate certain persons whose primary problem is more a need for structure than for training.

These different objectives may or may not exist simultaneously. They are regulated by how the groups are made up at a given time. Similarly, certain themes emerge, others fade away, depending on the persons' interests at any one time. Thus, at a meeting of a group of women, the desire to set up a workshop with early childhood as the theme emerged, a workshop that no longer exists except in the form of attendance at the *Petite maison* (reception centre for mothers and children, managed by AFER).

Newspaper and writing workshop
The aim of this workshop is not to cover all the skills involved in writing the French language, but to touch on all work that can be done on writing: summarizing, planning, construction of a text and so on. The main support of this workshop is the newspaper. Trainees write articles which, once completed, are assembled as a newspaper, which is then distributed internally to instructors, trainees and also to certain persons outside. It is not strictly necessary to know how to write to participate in this workshop. Each person works at his or her own pace, although the date the newspaper is to come out sets a goal for the person to reach: "What must I do so that my article will be in the next newspaper?" This leads to setting up a schedule, organization of work and so forth.

In theory, a trainee goes from using paper and pencil to using a computer for desktop publishing. Not all trainees work on the computer, it would be too difficult to manage. The texts are revised, corrections are made in a group. In this way we touch on the rules of grammar and spelling, which have more effect when work is done in a group on a text which means something to the trainees.

Several possibilities are presented to the trainees:

- they can choose one or more common themes;

- each can choose the theme best suited to him or her and work alone or with several others on the same theme;

- they can choose a subject such as their work, their life or a topic in the news and work on an individual article.

Reading

In this case we ascertain the different kinds of writing in the person's immediate life and, starting from this basis, try to integrate reading behaviours into his or her life. It is of prime importance that the reading trainees be able to reconstruct the experiences and written material they meet with in other workshops (this point will be developed later). It is important to go back to them in the reading workshop.

Arithmetic

The trainees participate in this workshop following a work plan defined in the course of the initial interview. First of all the work program is fixed, then the trainee works out a program with the instructor and makes use of files with exercises suitable to the chosen level.

Other workshops will then "feed" this one, especially the cooking workshop (budget management), book-keeping, and anything that trainees may meet with in daily life which causes them problems. .

Job-search techniques

Apart from the purely practical aspect of job-search techniques, (CVs, letters and so on), time in this workshop is also spent on working out projects since many have difficulties in immediately starting on production of a CV or letters.

Often the method used is for a trainee to come and go throughout the workshop, with use of job-search techniques either validating or invalidating the initial project. This is also the workshop where we can help people looking for training.

Functional workshops

The purpose of these workshops is to facilitate basic learning, in reading and arithmetic, for example, for persons with major difficulties. They allow for use of different support material, stimulating interest in completing projects and relating the work to daily life.

These workshops (photography, oral expression, computer science, cooking) are not meant to train photographers and so on, but to offer technical frameworks where, according to liking for a particular field, the trainees will try to verify the relevance of their projects.

For persons with major difficulties who thus feel excluded from any traditional learning situation with pencil and paper, these workshops offer a place for success, and often start up a process of regaining self-respect, which is necessary for undertaking any training.

The evaluation that we do of our work means that we modify these workshops either in form or content or by using other tools. They also evolve in terms of demand from the public and are thus often constantly changing, especially in the course of the monthly trainees' meeting where trainees can make suggestions. This time for expression is meant for the trainees. We try to have them run this meeting as far as possible, which poses certain problems. Preparation can be done in certain workshops, such as oral expression. A suggestion box is available. Ideas collected allow the schedule to be set and they are dealt with by the group of trainees present at the meeting: questions, suggestions, etc.

Workshops for individual work

Persons work autonomously and have at least one opportunity a week for individual work. The goal for each trainee is to succeed in managing time and pace of work, to use the most suitable tools or those which suit him or her best, not to deviate from the planned project and to become an active participant in his or her training.

The process should be facilitated by the trainee record booklet. The content of these workshops is prepared in the theme and/or functional workshops.

Links between workshops

These three kinds of intervention are closely linked and only make sense in relation to each other. It is the trainee's project that must be the common thread in participation in the workshops.

Thus, the workshops interact among themselves, making requests and responding to them, ensuring a link in the trainee's progress as well. For example, at one point, the group in the reading workshop, who were working on daily writing, sent an order to the photography workshop for pictures to illustrate a recipe. The trainees made their request explicit: they wanted photos of the different steps in the recipe with the various ingredients and utensils pointed out and named.

These persons then participated in the photography workshop, which was transformed into a cooking/photography workshop. Then the texts and photograph captions were worked out in the newspaper workshop and in the individual work periods. The photographs and text were assembled using desktop publishing software on the computer, the recipe and pictures were published in the newspaper and then used again in the reading workshop.

It is essential for the trainee to be aware at the time of the initial interview that his or her training will be constructed around his or her project (even if the training project is the construction of the latter). The project evolves and involves giving value to intermediate projects; it allows the trainee to measure results.

A workshop, whatever it may be, never has defined content. It offers the trainee different tools and situations so that he or she can achieve immediate objectives, never losing sight of the fact that what he or she has achieved is never without value, but is well integrated into his or her own project.

Tools to combat illiteracy

Newspapers

Since the creation of the APP, we have been trying to set up a training period that would help people to produce written material: a workshop time sufficiently open so that people mastering this tool at various levels could work together but also so that there would be readers for what was produced to make it meaningful.

The newspaper quickly came to seem the most suitable format. Newspapers are a mosaic of written material, allowing each person to give free rein to imagination while respecting the production pace of all.

After a long odyssey with trials and errors, after many "zeros" in quality that improved along with our stock of equipment, we have succeeded in structuring a permanent workshop and publish this newspaper relatively regularly.

How is this done?

The writing workshop takes place every Tuesday morning. Each trainee, whether registered or not in the workshop, can think about and write a piece with a theme of his or her choice. These texts will appear as columns in the newspaper.

Following this there is collective discussion to determine a common theme to be used in one issue of the paper. Brainstorming is the method used, which then allows ideas to be structured into a plan where each person can participate according to interest in some aspect or other of the subject. At the same time, discussion is begun on what is to be written and who the readers are.

The next phase is production of texts, either in this workshop or in others such as individual work, reading or others (for example, in the context of documentary research in the library or in other outside resource centres).

When the writing has been completed and corrected by the writer (at the end of the process we correct the remaining errors), the text is entered on computer.

We then move on to an exchange of texts and each sums up someone else's text so as to come up with a headline and work on the technique of summarization. At the same time we look for pictures to illustrate each article.

A collective session works out a preliminary paste-up which will be used again in the workshop for introduction to computers as a tool for learning desktop publishing and computer-assisted design software.

Each cycle ends with a discussion on the content and form of the last issue. This organization is, of course, theoretical and managed according to who is registered in a given period. In principle, the process goes on for a month or six weeks.

We have described the structure, let us go on to the tools available to the trainees. Apart from the time for discussion and co-operation, paper and pencils, we have good supplies of paper board, photo supplies for developing and printing, a video-camera, editing equipment, audio-visual documentary collections, a Minitel with which we can call up data on computer - AFP press dispatches, for example - newspapers and periodicals, books, tape recorders, IBM-compatible PCs with word processing, desktop publishing and design software, a scanner, a laser printer, a photocopier, access to all the other workshops and, of course, outside resources.

The structure and resources used by this workshop make up a mechanism that is open and constantly changing for the production of written material.

Educational software: ELMO (Entraînement à la lecture par micro ordinateur) [Reading instruction on microcomputer] and MAC6 (software for self-teaching in mathematics)
ELMO is used in the reading workshop and is an obligatory part of this workshop. This tool is worthwhile in so far as the exercises it offers for reading training are constructed from texts produced by the trainees. The trainee types in his or her own text, then the work is corrected with the help of a trainer. Also, the results are quantifiable and it is possible to analyse the different aspects with the trainees.

MAC6 is used in the mathematical workshop where the trainee progresses as the sessions go on, according to the project and work area chosen.

Library-Documentation centre
The library and documentation centre is of interest because it has a whole series of files with exercise sheets that can be corrected by trainees according to each one's area of work and level. It also provides a central area for information available to trainees in their different areas of interest.

The concept of the library-documentation centre allows the trainees to find answers, to use the files independently, according to the work program set up. Of course, that is not obvious, especially at the beginning of training, but this is the direction the trainee should aim for.

We are at present working on other training tools: software for management of pedagogical resources is being studied and experiments are going on. The purpose of these studies is to:

- facilitate and thus encourage use of the library-documentation centre by an illiterate public (they can learn to use software based on symbols);

- restructure this area using statistical analysis of frequency of use of various support materials;

- correlate content and pace of learners' training and profiles.

Video

This tool is especially used in the oral expression workshop: work on televised daily news, simulated interviews and so forth. These are filmed and then used again in the workshop, where they require a story board.

Also planned is a self-service audio-visual area. This project will come about through setting up of a video and audio library, whose resources will support all the workshops.

Intervention, other areas

Remaining faithful to our past (artistic expression course) and our original intentions (to promote and develop all means suited to health, social and cultural training ...) we intend to continue to work on research for alternatives to any kind of exclusion, including cultural ghettos.

The collective desire at AFER is to integrate artistic expression with all other training processes. We do not want to set up culture as a pedagogical-therapeutic tool, as is often done in the health and social sector. We are trying to bring about a juxtaposition. We believe that there is a difference between occupational or therapeutic educational techniques and an artistic practice calling first of all on the creative possibilities that each of us has or may have, no matter what our social status. This is why we attempt to have professional artists intervene in some organized meetings:

- courses for social and vocational integration for long-time job seekers, co-animated by AFER and a theatrical director;

- participation in activities and administration of the "Arts and Health" association, whose aim is to promote artistic practice among handicapped, aged and infirm persons;

- transformation of our premises into exhibition rooms and concert halls for our tenth anniversary;

- continuing education for personnel in the social sector, providing training with a cultural dimension.

This idea also exists within the APP, where we have had:

- a professional photographer in a workshop on job-search techniques;

- a sculptor in a reading/writing workshop;

- an actor who works full-time as animator in an oral expression workshop, using theatrical techniques.

We are going to be able to continue to introduce the cultural dimension because the City of Lille and the local youth mission have agreed a scheme for funding leisure activities. The purpose is to encourage our trainees to "digest" shows (theatre, concerts, films) at a minimal price of 10 FF per show and to then make use of these experiences in training (research for information on the shows, making reservations, organization, production of written material, use of desktop publishing software to produce a special issue of the trainees' newspaper).

The APP is thus a structure constantly seeking to be more relevant in its field of action. There are problems in achieving this.

The practice of self-training that is intended faces difficulties that are mainly due to:

- change in the public served: the training sought is expressed more often these days in terms of upgrading skills. Persons contacting the APP have an increasingly distant perspective on integration into a job, which more and more is becoming a remote goal for them. The desire for upgrading gains in urgency what it loses in meaning. It hinders development of various interventions possible in the APP, interventions that are not directly related to training, but which are an unavoidable framework for achieving fixed goals;

- the fact that there is no pay for training, which presents a problem for people who are voluntarily working in the APP but who see themselves hampered by the fact that this training is not paid. However, it is obvious that if there were pay, we would be faced with other problems: persons would certainly come to the APP not because what was available there would met their needs but because their participation was paid for.

2.2   Integration of the Long-term Unemployed

At the end of the 1970s, training schemes that were said to be the means to combat unemployment began to be set up. These were very quickly made so complex that it was difficult to make sense of the proliferation of measures, which were sometimes complementary, but at times duplicated each other. It was only in 1985 that the scheme for training adults over 25 was really structured, with the setting up of modular courses.

A specific program was set up aimed at the long-term job-seeking public, comprised of the hard-core unemployed, unaffected by favourable fluctuations in the job market. This specific scheme was to improve the chances of a job for these categories or, to quote Foudi and Stankiewiz, to "improve their place in the line-up".[3]

This program is managed today by the departmental employment branches under the name AIF (*Action d'insertion et de formation* [Integration and training initiative]). Job seekers affected by this measure have the status of job trainees and are paid. This program serves three functions:

- slowing the process of exclusion and marginalization, aid taking precedence over placement for one segment of the public;

- to increase the "intrinsic employability" of the job seeker through training oriented towards resocialization, motivation and job-search techniques;

- to improve qualifications so as to narrow the gap between the qualifications of the job seeker and those required for the job.

The public

A recent study by the departmental employment branch attempted to draw up a profile of long-term job seekers served by the AIF in the north-east part of Lille:

Type 1
Over 40, loss of steady job, often after an economic lay-off. According to their social competence, the individuals have been able, more or less successfully, to move into temporary employment. The

scarcity of jobs not requiring qualifications in this specific market and the competition from younger persons supported by the mechanism has pushed them all into total unemployment.

Type 2

Mostly under 40, they intended to obtain a stable job, but the redeployment of industrial jobs has deprived them of this opportunity. According to their social competence, closely related to their level of general culture, they have been able to live or survive with temporary jobs. Some have never been employed (or never worked for a long enough period to obtain rights).

Type 3

Often women, often immigrants. They seldom know how to read and write, they have great difficultly with oral expression, and have no working experience. When their partner or relatives become unemployed and their children find it impossible to find jobs, they are forced into the job market.

Type 4

Often under 40, male, with immigrant parents, they realize the impossibility of finding work and their elders' experience is no longer a role model. They are very likely divorced from the dominant value system, which gives an important place to work. They exploit the possibilities (the only ones) that "the system" offers to them, which are "courses" that they tend to substitute for work.

Type 5

These are adult males over 35 who have never had a steady job. From the most proletarian fringe of the working class, they have grown up with uncertainty (families with major problems, social assistance, in child care institutions during their childhood, and so on). They share the value system of the working class: attachment to the patriarchal organization of the family and to the "work ethic", but it is in this class that "moonlighting" is over-valued. They cannot all be classed as illiterate, but the great majority of them have difficulties dealing with the written word.

Some aspects of our intervention

The teaching method that we are developing in our integration work fits in with the work already described for setting up a process of individual and collective self-training aimed at the autonomy of groups and individuals.

In a context of self-training aimed at vocational integration, persons meet with many experimental situations requiring use of written material: the telephone book for setting up meetings, street signs to get to the meetings. administrative papers, job advertisements, and so on. We try to the utmost, in all training sequences, to set up situations that require the trainee's having direct contact with writing and which usually lead to action (learning to read).

The group

The pedagogy for self-training and making individuals responsible that we have developed plays an important role in the training group. One might think that self-training, by reinforcing the idea of personal qualities to the detriment of the idea of being a member of a group, omits the idea of the group. This is not the case at all. Our teaching methods are based on negotiation: trainers must have trainees agree to what they suggest, which obliges them always to take into account each person's project. Trainees cannot obtain the assistance of trainers unless they prove that this assistance will be useful to their project. This process introduces a balance of relationships: the weaker the rights of the group members, the more the group resembles a group of "school kids"; the stronger they are, the closer the group comes to resembling a group of social actors.

By making the trainees responsible for the space and time for training, we in fact give them a grasp of all its dimensions. Management of constraints of time, space and resources and taking the environment into account (social and administrative rules, for example) are no longer only the jurisdiction of trainers. Through sharing responsibility, the constraints become the concern of both trainees and trainers, and make mutual management necessary. Management of constraints of all types means that trainees will have to deal with more writing; they have to argue, prove, and justify their position to be able to intervene directly, with real significance, in the resolution of problems.

The effect of socialization that the group and this pedagogical method has on the individual is fundamental. The person becomes aware of his or her differences and finds external responses indispensable for working out his or her project. Finally the person becomes aware of where he or she fits into society.

Rotation

Training does not take place only in training centres, but also, for periods of varying lengths, in commercial enterprises. This rotating training provides good opportunities for dealing with writing.

First, the trainee has to find a corporation that will accept him or her. This requires an unavoidable use of written words (telephone book or business directory, writing an application letter, finding out about corporations that might offer a position and so forth). For the individual who is looking for a place in an enterprise, this dealing with writing makes sense since it is based on "real writing" that the person needs to do and read and not on artificial exercises.

A positive response, after several stages of looking for work, gives meaning to the necessary use of reading and writing, much more surely than any theoretical training lecture.

The periods in a commercial enterprise are also useful because of the many kinds of writing the individual faces: use of machines, work instructions, orders, internal regulations, training reports and so on.

Orders from society at large

Through a network of partners within pilot groups (librarians, employees of socio-cultural associations, social workers, representatives from corporations), we are trying to encourage demand for the trainees' work. Their contribution does not have to be badly needed to be valid, but on the other hand it should arise from real need.

When an institution or organization is in this kind of partnership with groups in training whose objective is to produce something, it is because they recognize their ability to be productive, to work. This recognition sets up a favourable climate for learning that then avoids the drift into production for pedagogical reasons, where simulation predominates.

These orders from society, with their clear constraints of time and expected performance that must be defined through the technical aids that they require (workshops for reading, writing, investigation, oral expression), and because everyone has to be included, give meaning, in the short term during the training period, to a real work project.

We have only recently begun to accept orders from the public. Here are two examples:

- a request for articles about the content of their training for a magazine (MEDIATEC) was sent to a group of reading trainees. These articles were intended to sensitize a larger public to training;

- an association that planned to open a documentary resource centre asked trainees to draw up a list of documents that they, non-readers, would like to find in such a place.

Conclusion

Since its creation and the setting-up of the APP, the AFER association, owing to its growth and the recognized area of intervention that it has been able to ensure, has started to become institutionalized.

Specialists in institutional analysis have shown that institutionalization means the end of looking to the future, that is to say the abandonment of the movement's initial "revolutionary" project, even if this abandonment is not always obvious and is accompanied by a simulation of achievement intended to make it acceptable to participants. (It is symptomatic that there are so many discussions on the meaning of the association today. When such a need is felt to reflect on meaning, it is because there is no longer much left!)

There is a great danger today that we will conform to institutional training frameworks in the name of recognized technological approaches, to the detriment, even abandonment, of innovation and our original ideology.

Our action in combating illiteracy cannot make an abstraction of an ideological and political choice. The problem of illiteracy goes far beyond the context of "pedagogism" and mere technical responses:

A society only produces the number of readers it requires. It is only by changing itself that it creates conditions for new ways of sharing. An action to promote reading begins with changes in social interactions to make people responsible in their work, their leisure and their social life. A living group is a reading group, not the reverse.[4]

Our society has changed and developed over the last fifteen years. The alternative projects of the 1970s and the ideologies they derived from, no longer meet the need. Political organizations and the union movement are disintegrating, new forms of solidarity are being created, and new forms of exclusion as well ....

How, at a time when in France the question of exclusion is appearing in an ever more crucial - and more insidious - way than it was fifteen years ago (the discussions at the time centred on opening the psychiatric hospitals, today there are growing "ghettos" of long-term unemployed), can we remain consistent with the founding purpose of our association: "to offer training choices that are an alternative to exclusion"?

The answers that we can provide to this question are vital for us today, because institutional analysis has shown that in the long run, in a process of institutionalization, the only way to avoid the inherent contradiction in this process is for the organization to dissolve itself.

We have tried to respond by "restructuring" our association, but realize that this may at most bring about a better structural organization.

It is no longer possible for us to rely only on the technical skills and equipment we possess today and on the good management of our association. We must ask why we exist, and take part in the "political debates" that are shaking up our society, and in this way try to rediscover the dynamic we had throughout our history and which we believe allowed us to develop responses in the field of training adapted to combating all forms of exclusion.

We believe that the struggle against illiteracy and all forms of exclusion is not a rearguard action, quite the contrary, and we intend to be able to continue to play a part. We will provide ourselves with the means.

Notes

1. Foucambert, Jean. 1986. Les sept propositions [Seven proposals]. Mimeo.

2. Pineau, Gaston 1978. Les possibilités de l'autoformation [Possibilities in self-training]. *Revue Education Permanente* 44, October.

3. Foudi and Stankiewiez. 1987. La lutte contre le chômage de longue durée ou l'émergence d'une politique autonome [Combating long-term unemployment and the emergence of a policy of autonomy] *Revue française des affaires sociales* 3.

4. Foucambert, Jean. 1987. Pouvoir, savoir et promotion collective [Power, knowledge and collective advancement]. *Les actes de lecture* 20, December.

BASIC EDUCATION IN FLANDERS: STRENGTHS AND WEAKNESSES

Gunter Gehre
Catholic University
Leuven, Belgium

1. Introduction

For the Flemish literacy movements, the year 1990 marked a high point in two respects. First, the United Nations proclaimed International Literacy Year, and a temporary office was set up in Flanders for the occasion to co-ordinate the many activities. The commission of International Literacy Year experts also entrusted the office with publishing a White Paper. The White Paper[1] contains various opinions concerning the approaches that should be adopted to combat illiteracy effectively in Flanders.

At the same time, there was a quickening of the pace in the political arena. After a process spanning several years, the *Vlaamse Raad* (Flemish Council) issued a decree[2] "concerning the organization of basic education for adults with little schooling." The decree profoundly changed the landscape in which the structures for educating adults with little schooling were to operate. Literacy activities were also caught up in this movement. These activities (in this case collective teaching of reading and writing skills) found themselves incorporated into larger structures.

This paper was written in the context of this evolution. First, we sketch a brief history of literacy activities to date. Given the substantial changes on this part of the education map, we must seriously rethink the literacy activities themselves. We try to situate these activities (which are part of basic education) within the whole set of social and educational structures. On the basis of several specific examples of co-operation, we try to define the relationship between "literacy training" and assistance to underprivileged groups.

While acknowledging that this new constellation offers many different ways of approaching the campaign against illiteracy in a more integrated manner, we will point out the dangers and shortcomings of the current regulations.

The following paper was written from two viewpoints. To begin with, I was for several years closely associated with various aspects of literacy promotion activities. During this period, I involved myself in the specific activities of teaching reading and writing skills collectively, but I also had to deal with various questions of a political nature that antedated the regulation of basic education. Subsequently, I have continued to follow the whole evolution, although from a certain distance. This allows me to observe and comment dispassionately on the processes at work.

2. Literacy Training and Basic Education

Origins[3]

Literacy movements did not spring up in Flanders until the late 1970s. Until that time (even after that time in the case of some people), it was thought that compulsory education, which dates back to 1914, was a sufficient guarantee against illiteracy. So illiteracy was an unsuspected phenomenon in Flanders in 1978, and it was thought that every citizen was naturally capable of reading and writing. But the situation in the Belgian Army, where reading and writing lessons had been introduced in the 1950s, and in the social assistance sector, showed that "being able to read and write" was for many Flemings not nearly so foregone a conclusion as public opinion assumed it was. The result was an enormous taboo concerning this shortcoming in a person's abilities.

Literacy initiatives sprang up throughout Flanders, beginning in 1978. In most cases, these initiatives developed out of existing assistance and training structures that from the beginning could provide the material and logistic support which these initiatives required. It is striking to note that these initiatives also involved social assistance structures, although this is not so surprising when one considers that the need for this kind of activity often makes itself felt by these institutions first. From the beginning, definite efforts were made to combine training and assistance.

The *centra voor maatschappelijk werk* (social work centres), *centra voor geestelijke gezondheidszorg* (mental health care centres) and others thus formed the foundation on which the various centres developed. Most of the centres consequently gained greater autonomy over the years without ever completely abandoning the idea of combining training and assistance.

Literacy promotion activities grew by leaps and bounds in Flanders between 1978 and 1988. By 1986, Flanders had 46 literacy projects with 377 reading and writing groups and a total of almost 2,000 course participants. The association called *Alfabetisering Vlaanderen* (Flanders Literacy Promotion) co-ordinated these various initiatives, providing support, doing preparatory work, and defending their interests. The number of people working in these movements also grew very quickly, as well as the subsidies which the Flemish public authorities provided to the movements. But the public authorities' contribution remained insufficient, and it took a decree in 1990 before the assistance they provided grew to any appreciable size.

Parallel to these developments in literacy promotion activities, the early 1980s saw the appearance of numerous other initiatives aimed at people with little schooling. The *Opniew Gaan Leren* (Learning Again) initiative, for example, was designed to brush up basic knowledge picked up at school. There was also *Tweedekansonderwijs* (Second Chance Education) for adults who wanted to gain a lower or upper secondary education diploma. Problems with integrating immigrants gave rise to a wide range of language courses among the associations active in this area. Toward the late 1980s at least, these courses also received strong encouragement from the public authorities. Finally, special funds for assisting underprivileged groups also made it possible to set up numerous training projects for people with little schooling.

It is a fact that the services available for adults with little schooling were scattered and poorly co-ordinated at the end of 1989. This resulted in a lack of uniformity and numerous problems concerning pathways, orientation, correspondence between programs, and so on.

The idea of better co-ordinating the range of initiatives aimed at adults with little schooling and of developing an integrated, consistent offer of services dates back before 1990. As early as 1985, the initial outline had been drawn of a concept that was subsequently to serve as a model for the Basic Education Centres. In the early 1980s, a *Platformoverleg Basiseducatie* (Basic Education Platform) was introduced, and it gave rise to five independent projects called *Experimenten Basiseducatie* (Basic Education

Experiments) in five different locations in Flanders. These experiments were organized and supported by the *Vlaams Centrum voor Volksontwikkeling* (Flemish Popular Education Centre). For five years, there were experiments with contents, methods, management structures and co-operation agreements. But these five experiments had no monopoly on innovation or development in the field of literacy promotion activities. Other initiatives, including *Alfabetisering Vlaanderen* (Flanders Literacy Promotion), made constant efforts to innovate, especially in the areas of methodological evolution and skills development.

The experimentation phase ended at the beginning of 1990, and work began on a decree. As an analysis of the major thrusts of this document indicates, the decree ultimately reflected the model that emerged from the Flemish Popular Education Centre's experiments.

A decree for basic education

On June 28, 1990, the *Vlaamse Raad* (Flemish Council) adopted the decree concerning basic education. The decree covers three aspects of literacy promotion:

- organization of local activities at Basic Education Centres,
- creation of a support structure in the form of the Flemish Basic Education Assistance Centre, and
- creation of an advisory body called the Basic Education Council.

We will discuss these three aspects without describing them in too much detail.

The Basic Education Centres

There are currently 28 centres operating in the Flemish region. Each of these centres is responsible for organizing a coherent menu of educational activities for adults with little schooling (meaning people who have reached the age of majority without obtaining a recognized lower secondary education certificate). These activities are centred on teaching basic Dutch and basic mathematics, improving social skills, and promoting social orientation and integration. The centres can also develop guidance and organizational activities, which are supposed to encourage participants to take part in other kinds of activities by making them aware of learning and training issues.

Basic education has also become professionalized, in both its educational duties and administrative activities. The size of the staff at the centres ranges from a single employee to teams of 33 educational workers in a city like Antwerp.

A centre is eligible for official recognition if it offers at least 6,000 participant hours, calculated by multiplying the number of participants by the number of hours of training they have received. Under this arrangement, the centre gets a minimum staff allowance of one educational worker post and half an administrative worker post, and the staff allowance increases with every additional block of 4,000 participant hours.

The decree therefore regulates financial assistance. But it also calls for contributions from the communes in which the centres operate. The communes are expected, for example, to supply premises for the centres. And there are, of course, other funding possibilities.

Each centre is a non-profit association with a governing body made up of people from varied backgrounds. Both the general assembly and the board of governors contain representatives of various sectors: socio-cultural work, social promotion education, *Vlaamse Dienst voor Arbeidsbemiddeling* (Flemish Employment Office) vocational training, the commune, the Public Social Assistance Centre, and socio-educational work.

The Flemish Basic Education Assistance Centre

An assistance centre has been set up to support basic education in the Flemish Community. This centre is responsible for supervising the planning of the centres, developing material, improving the qualifications of the teaching staff and directors, ensuring the quality of the services offered, providing information, and conducting research. The centre receives all its funding from the Education Minister and, like the local centres, is a private, non-profit agency with a governing body constituted in accordance with rules laid down in the decree.

The Basic Education Council

The council provides advice to the Flemish Executive concerning official recognition of centres and the withdrawal of official recognition. It is also responsible for providing advice on desirable developments in the sector and on any preventive steps that should be taken. The council is made up of representatives of various sectors who are appointed by the Ministers of Education, Social Assistance and the Family, Culture, and Employment. A prime requirement of the council is that it should have close contacts with the basic education sector.

Some observations
Although the decree was met with enthusiasm, and the reactions from various quarters were highly positive, observers also pointed out a few negative aspects. We list some of them here without going into too much detail.

Is literacy training really possible at the Basic Education Centres? Some critics say that basic education as it is currently designed is a one-sided activity. They therefore ask whether it is really possible to promote literacy effectively at the centres. The centres in effect treat literacy training as a purely educational strategy, whereas illiteracy is actually a much more complicated problem. By restricting the problem to its educational aspect, we lose sight of the fact that lack of education is only one of the problems that under-privileged groups experience.

The creation of a legal framework provides social recognition for this kind of activity. This social recognition has been growing stronger and stronger over the past few years, but the decree gave it formal status. Basic education will from now on be better able to justify itself as a special kind of activity in relation to other agencies and structures. Of course, this last point is not unrelated to the fact that these activities have seen the cachet of "professional work" requiring "competence" replace the old "voluntary work" label.

The decree makes basic education in Flanders the ultimate responsibility of the Minister of Education. Although this decision was deliberate - basic education as a component of adult education - it can be considered a considerable change in orientation. The reason is that basic education's entire "prehistory" was situated within the Department of Culture, in the popular education sector. One wonders whether this change in direction will entail major shifts in objectives (social emancipation), methods (consideration for the specific characteristics of participants) and autonomy. Seen in this light, basic education as a teaching structure is distinct from literacy training as a strategy for remedying a lack of education.

The transition from the "forerunners" to the Basic Education Centres was a very rapid one. In less than half a year, the entire sector underwent in-depth restructuring that involved negotiations, compromises, and so on. Locally, a great deal of what already existed could be used, and the growing pains that necessarily accompany such changes will no doubt pass quickly enough. But we started practically from scratch when it came to co-ordination, and little effort has been made to incorporate what already existed into the new methods of operation. In fact, the exercise at times looks like an attempt to settle accounts with the past. In other words, one wonders whether, in launching this new kind of activity, we will be able to use the experience accumulated over the years in the effective manner it deserves.

3. Basic Education and the Network of Social Structures

As a structure designed for people with little schooling, the Basic Education Centre is one of several structures for training and social assistance. These structures could develop into a network of agreements for co-operation. And experience seems to indicate that things are in fact moving in this direction. But we must make an important observation here. The present decree on basic education explicitly calls for co-operation only at the administrative level of an institution. Of course, the decree does tend implicitly to promote co-operation in the form of initiating joint projects. But it does not really attach much value to these except in very limited circumstances, since they are not considered eligible for subsidies. The educational aspect of a problem situation must always be isolated and translated into a centrally organized educational program of limited duration. The people who implement the program must always be educators belonging to the centre or recruited for this purpose, and the program must correspond to one of the five streams of basic education. Other forms of co-operation, such as forms of education incorporated into other problem sectors, at the moment have little chance of seeing the light of day.

We would like to examine the current possibilities for co-operation in the light of a specific example. I myself am currently a member of a board of directors involved in running a Basic Education Centre in the region of Rupel-Vaartland-Klein-Brabant. I would like to use this example to introduce a set of possible avenues of co-operation, adding a few examples from other centres which I believe illustrate my point.

Co-operation at the administrative level

The decree spells out in detail how a Basic Education Centre's board of governors is to be composed. The decree is based not only on ideological considerations, but also and above all on some basic premises. The first premise is that basic education must be placed in the context of adult and continuing education. The second premise is that basic education has clear affinities and links with the structures of social assistance, and these it must maintain.

In practical terms, the first premise refers to socio-cultural work, social promotion education, and vocational training organized by the *Vlaamse Dienst voor Arbeidsbemiddeling en Beroepsopleiding* (Flemish Employment and Vocational Training Office) either in the form of middle class training or in the agricultural sector. The partners to which the second premise refers are the Public Social Assistance Centre and local socio-educational work initiatives (see Table 1). The commune is also involved. Activities aimed at immigrants are not specifically mentioned, perhaps because the situation with immigrants can differ greatly from one location to another.

The preceding deals with the forms of co-operation called for by the decree on basic education. In Section 4, we will attempt to make a few observations in this regard.

Co-operation in practice

The legislators' goal was to create, through the introduction of structural co-operation, possibilities for developing effective co-operation projects. Contacts had in many cases already been made, but many centres saw new doors open. It is difficult to say after one year what the ultimate effect of these contacts will be, but we can make out a number of positive trends. Here are a few examples.

Table 1. Composition of the Board of Directors of the Basic Education Centre (BEC) in the Rupel-Flanders Region[4]

Sector represented	BEC	Flanders
Commune	3	39
Public Social Assistance Centre	3	34
Socio-educational work	1	25
Socio-cultural work	7	164
Social promotion education	2	46
Flemish Employment and Vocational Training Office:		
vocational training	2	33
Middle Class training	0	5
Others	0	34
Total	18	380

Co-operation with the Flemish Employment and Vocational Training Office

As part of its training programs and placement work, the Flemish Employment and Vocational Training Office is regularly called upon to help people with few qualifications, especially people who lack a number of basic skills.

This makes it possible to develop co-operation with the Basic Education Centre. At the Basic Education Centre in the Rupel region, co-operation is envisaged in the following areas:

1) The *Weerwerk* (Re-employment) program, especially orientation. After all, one of the duties of the *Weerwerk* program consultants is to get people who have been unemployed for a long time working again, through appropriate training if necessary.

2) The *Schakelprojekten* (Linkage Projects) for unemployed people with little schooling who need to be retrained. The Flemish Employment and Vocational Training Office organizes these courses itself, but perhaps pays insufficient attention to basic

skills. These could be a job for the Basic Education Centre, as preparation for "linkage" training.

3) *Impulsgebieden* (Impulse Areas) are regions in Flanders with pronounced socio-economic problems to which the public authorities allocate financial assistance for implementing certain projects. A number of these projects have an educational impact as well.

Co-operation with the social assistance sector and the socio-educational sector.

Most of the problems facing clients of the social assistance sector have an educational side to them. Socio-economic problems and a lack of education very often go hand in hand. Many projects implemented in this area try to address several aspects of the problems specific to these disadvantages in an integrated manner. But the indirect message of the legislation is that certain divisions (both artificial and otherwise) should be maintained between the various strategies likely to solve this problem.

1) Co-operation with the Public Social Assistance Centres

In a number of cases, the Public Social Assistance Centre makes an award of financial assistance contingent on participation in some form of employment project (under an arrangement called "social hiring") that gets beneficiaries working again. Many of these beneficiaries lack such basic skills as reading, writing and mathematics related to various sectors (employment, for example). Co-operation with a Basic Education Centre can in this case represent an effective form of assistance.

2) Co-operation with the socio-educational work sector

As the socio-educational work sector tries to help underprivileged groups, it must address this problem while keeping in mind its various aspects. The assistance in this case consists of training projects for young, unemployed people with little schooling which are designed to produce tangible results (building a boat, for example). Vocational training and basic education go hand in hand in this area as well. General training and social training play an important role, as does the acquisition of basic skills and social skills.

3) Co-operation with the underprivileged groups

As part of their efforts to help underprivileged groups, the public authorities have made a fund available for specific projects put forward by the communes or the Public Social Assistance Centres. In this case as well, basic education can cover the educational aspect if the projects chosen are ones that make it possible to work effectively with underprivileged people. Most of these projects are still just getting off the ground.

4) Co-operation agreements

There are also a number of co-operation agreements concerning the reintegration into society of specific groups, such as former psychiatric patients, former detainees, people living on the margins of society, and so on. The need for basic and social skills is urgent in this area as well.

5) Co-operation with immigrant associations

Finally, co-operation with immigrant associations is expanding as well. In most cases, the accent is on Dutch courses. These courses result in a ever larger number of people in the basic education sector as a whole and could in the long run edge out the other kinds of activities.

Co-operation with Social Promotion Education

Co-operation with Social Promotion Education and Second Chance Education is still in its infancy, mainly because of the complete absence of any tradition in this area. The limited contacts established to date have been concentrated in the area of orientation, although the effectiveness of this (bilateral) orientation policy is subject to doubt. In addition, basic education in Flanders must develop its own identity in the context of general education and emphasize its distinctive characteristics. The prospect of basic education being "swallowed up" by the complex structures of general education and thus reduced to a marginal role is not unthinkable. We have yet to fully explore the avenues for effective co-operation with the general education sector.

Co-operation with the socio-cultural work sector

Co-operation is still in its infancy in this area as well, at least as far as everyday practices are concerned. Socio-cultural work appears to be an important partner, at least in terms of numbers.

I have the impression that up until now this numerical importance has not really translated into specific co-operation initiatives. Possible avenues of co-operation are concentrated in the area of guidance, which involves encouraging participants in one kind of activity to branch out into other activities by making them aware of learning and training issues.

Orientation as a form of co-operation

The most obvious form of co-operation is orientation. Depending on the nature of an individual's needs, a variety of institutions and structures can be called upon. The important thing is to direct individuals grappling with a given problem toward the right institution, toward the institution that can solve the problem. To do this, the Basic Education Centres will have to familiarize themselves with the other services that are available and make themselves known in their turn. The other services will have to be educated and encouraged to be on the look-out for (underlying) educational needs. The Basic Education Centre will have to respond to this need by providing target-specific information and agreeing on orientation procedures with the many services that are active in the social assistance field.

A few more examples of co-operation projects

In addition to these examples of co-operation agreements involving the Basic Education Centre in the Rupel region, we would like to mention two more examples: the first because of its importance and the second as an illustration.

Co-operation with the Fourth World movement

The "generational" poor in Flanders constitute a major group of underprivileged people. Basic Education Centres offering specially tailored educational activities cannot solve their problems. But the staff at these centres must realize that the generational poor must also be involved in efforts to address the problems caused by a lack of education and in activities aimed at helping underprivileged groups. To do this, we must think of projects that closely involve the Fourth World movement in order to develop suitable services for this category of people as well.

Projects for nomads

Several groups in our society have no fixed places of residence. It may be difficult to provide services to them in a single location for any length of time. Many education projects must necessarily be adjusted to the distinctive conditions and characteristics of the target group. The centre must show a certain degree of flexibility in continually seeking approaches that are appropriate to these groups.

The place of the literacy training process in this network

In the light of all these considerations, we believe literacy training is a component of the policy for helping underprivileged groups. The problems which these groups face are complex, and the shortcomings from which they suffer take many forms.

Although training is often considered an important tool for solving these problems, the obstacles that prevent people from becoming involved in training and taking part in courses are generally not related to education. The obstacles are very often psycho-dynamic (involving motivation), material, financial or psycho-social (involving family situations). It is precisely in these areas that most of the structures of the social assistance sector operate. But they too often encounter problems involving education, such as a lack of basic skills. This is the point where social assistance and education overlap. It is also a point that offers a chance to co-operate more intensively in helping underprivileged groups.

The relationship between social assistance and assistance for underprivileged groups is necessarily one of reciprocity, in that the two partners have their own responsibilities and make their own particular contributions. According to De Riek[5], a good method of helping people is one that emancipates them, especially if the goal is to help them in the long term. In concrete terms, this means that those who provide assistance must not limit themselves to the specific assistance that was requested, but must look for the problems that prompted the request. This search may turn up latent or manifest problems involving education. It is important that those who provide assistance should be able to recognize and express these problems if they are to orient the client effectively.

But it can also be helpful to develop a program together, resulting in what is called "integrated training". In this situation, it is essential to tailor the educational process to the need if a lasting solution is to be found. It is also important to ensure that the individuals themselves see a connection with the original need. Using this method, many satisfactory projects could be developed with the other institutions providing assistance. The educational aspect of a problem could be addressed more effectively in its educational context. To this end, basic education can offer its experience in the fields of methodology and instruction, while social assistance creates the conditions for finding a permanent solution and providing effective support. We wish to point out once again here that much remains to be done if we are to improve guidance and attract the potential participants in basic educational activities.

4. Literacy Training in Basic Education: Strengths and Weaknesses

Having described the situation as it exists, we wish to make a number of observations. The new decree held out great promise, and the creation of the centres raised enormous expectations. But we must keep our eyes open and maintain a critical attitude. By issuing a decree to govern this sector and by precisely describing how the sector is to organize itself, we have set in motion a process of institutionalization to which many organizations and institutions fall victim. There has been regular criticism to this effect in other countries, notably the Netherlands. The Netherlands also structured its basic education a few years ago, and it is important to compare what is happening in that country to the way in which this sector is developing in Flanders. Above all, we must avoid making the same mistakes.

Let us examine the following observations one by one.

- The structures which have been put in place guarantee the sector's social integration (see above). But its integration into the whole social assistance network and the educational system has yet to be carried out in practice. Much will depend in this process on the abilities of the individuals concerned and their affinity for this kind of work, since the management structures are not always manned by field workers. Most of the managers are administrative types, and this does not always make for sufficiently dynamic programming development. In some cases, it would perhaps be a good idea to separate central management from programming (by setting up a kind of advisory working group).

- The construction of Basic Education Centres has made it possible to bring all the forces together and end the chronic dispersal of training services for adults with little schooling. But there are reasons to wonder whether this streamlining has not led us to throw the baby out with the bath water. Can we learn from the experiences of experts who have "gone down this road" before? Is it always possible to promote the development of innovations and abilities at the grassroots level? The demands on teaching staff are considerable and could stand in the way.

- Co-operation with other social sectors is possible, but is certainly not being encouraged, nor is much value being attached to it. Projects involving co-operation are vehicles for innovation, and could have dynamic effects on activities of this kind. But these projects consume a great deal of energy and time. Unless considerable value is attached to these initiatives, we believe they will not last long. The reason is that pragmatic minds will very quickly opt for consolidating the services offered (to ensure their survival), and this will result in a loss of dynamic energy.

- The decree calls for a very broad approach to the concept of "insufficient schooling" in order to offer maximum opportunities to a target group that in Flanders includes a large number of individuals, despite the increase in school attendance rates. Precisely because of this very broad approach, there is a danger of officials adopting a system that is centred solely on target groups who are easy to reach with courses that can be offered over and over again. The immigrant population has also begun to learn about the Basic Education Centres and now quite understandably makes use of the Dutch courses which these centres offer.

We must therefore ask ourselves whether we might not ultimately lose sight of native Belgians who are illiterate and whether they will still make use of the educational services which we offer.

- The integration of basic education into the general education system raises questions about the distinctive nature of this sector and its place in the larger framework of education for adults. We will have to find points of correlation with the general education system while avoiding being absorbed by it. The risk of "assimilation into the school sector" is real, and one might wonder whether it will still be possible to organize training programs that are centred on the participants. From this viewpoint, basic education will have continually to strive to legitimize itself and prove its autonomy. The pressure from "related fields" will only increase. The employment sector will stress its need for qualified personnel, and the general education sector will try to incorporate basic education into a curriculum structure that makes it as easy as possible to transfer into the continuing education system. The social assistance sector will continue to emphasize assistance to underprivileged groups. Basic education will have to find a place of its own in this mosaic and take care to preserve its distinctiveness.

- Finally, there is the larger social project of helping underprivileged groups. To this end, basic education adds another structure, enabling us better to address this problem from several different directions. But this line of reasoning is very dangerous. There is a danger that illiteracy will be reduced in this framework to a simple educational problem that can be dealt with through appropriate courses and programs. But illiteracy's links with socio-economic problems were stressed several times during International Literacy Year. An even better way to put it would be to say that illiteracy is one aspect of the problems that underprivileged groups experience. We can therefore mount a reasonable defence of the idea of intensive co-operation with the social assistance sector that makes it possible to develop pluralistic strategies and solutions in a co-operative framework.

5. Conclusion

The issue of the role of the community associations movement in Flanders is approached differently today. It could be said that the associations have opted for a more comfortable system with better subsidies, and that their work falls totally within the framework of the Basic Education Centres.

For the moment, the associations really exist only on paper (as registered non-profit organizations). They have effectively incorporated themselves into the centres. It is quite possible that the next step will be to give them official status as institutions.

In my view, basic education in Flanders needs, at the very least, an associations movement that addresses illiteracy in its whole social, political and economic context. We need a movement that takes up a position alongside the education system and can provide criticism.

To do this, the associations movement must treat illiteracy as a cultural and political problem. This presupposes a reorganization and a redefinition of its goals, as concerns new social movements, for example.

After the "prehistory" of basic education, the struggle against illiteracy has entered a new phase, with very different orientations. History begins with the year zero: International Literacy Year.

Notes

1. Adriaensens, E. ed. et al. 1991. *Internationaal Jaar van de Alfabetisering: Witboek* (International Literacy Year: White Paper). Brussels: Stuurgroep IJA (International Literacy Year Steering Committee).

2. Decree Concerning the Organization of Basic Education for Adults With Little Schooling, June 28, 1990.

3. We draw in this section on Goffinet, S.A. and Van Damme, D. 1990. *Functional Illiteracy in Belgium.* Brussels: King Baudouin Foundation; Hamburg: Unesco Institute for Education.

4. De Jong, L. et al. 1991. *Het eerste leer-jaar. Rapport over de ontwikkeling van de basiseducatie 1990-1991.* (The First Year, A Year of Learning. 1990-1991. Report on the Development of Basic Education). Mechelen: *VOCB.*

5. De Riek, A. 1991. *Kansarmoede en alfabetisering* (Poverty of Opportunities and Literacy Training). Leuven: LUCAS.

LITERACY TACTICS IN THE
COMMUNITY ORGANIZATIONS MOVEMENT

Jean-Paul Hautecoeur
Unesco Institute for Education
Hamburg, Germany

In the course of a few days in October, 1991, almost all the authors of the preceding studies met at Namur, Belgium, in a seminar conducted in almost closed retreat.[1] The immediate aim of the meeting was to finish the book together.

But the event was too much of a unique occasion to be summarized in a conclusion and to transform it into a jubilee celebration. Other individuals and associations participated in it. And the "authors" had not come only to add their piece to the table of contents. There was something else to be done: namely try to go beyond the particular characteristics of local and national organizations in order to give an international identity to this movemeent, to find a common ground upon which to cooperate in order to consolidate local action and initiate work at the multi-national level.[2]

Is it possible to speak of a single community organizations movement within the domain of literacy education? What can be done, as an informal international association, to strengthen this movement?

It is the research done on this issue which will be the subject of this final chapter. The first part deals simultaneously with the introduction and conclusion of the meeting: the participants, the expectations that had been formulated, and the projects that were finally decided upon. The second part is devoted to contrasting assessments of the various associations and to an analysis of the national situations within which their work is carried out. The third part goes into greater detail into the various portrayals of literacy education.

In the speeches, a number of key words can be identified which come together into clusters of meaning, attracting or repelling each other along certain directions so as to yield an overall picture of the collective action being undertaken. The whole picture, of course, is imaginary, but it does reflect experiences, real history, and a will to new action. The cross-sectional study of the strong meanings being conveyed will be the subject of the book's conclusion.

During the seminar, Gunter Gehre pointed out the important ideological function of the community organizations movement, in contrast to government organizations. In fact, it might be that the main strategy of this movement is its search for a highly ideological position. In the meantime, its position in time and space is mainly characterized by transitoriness and movement, mobility rather than by the appropriation of the terrain, by tactical pragmatism in less charted areas rather than by full-scale offensive strategies for the universal eradication of illiteracy.

Therefore, *Alpha 92* did not offer strategies for actions to be undertaken by the community organizations movement for combating illiteracy, at least according to the authorized presentations. Rather, what was revealed consisted of local experiences, experimental efforts at association in uncharted terrain, research activities rather than programs and national "mechanisms", some good parting shots but also a good deal of self-criticism. The only common strategy of this movement seems to be its discursive, ideological, and utopian quest: to read and talk about everything in order to change everything, or to put it more modestly, to create open spaces in which words, knowledge, and symbols (i.e. writings) can be exchanged.

All, or nearly all of the authors made reference to Paulo Freire. With great power of conviction, he named the force behind this struggle the "possible dream", to be realized through cultural action in uncharted territory. José Luis Corzo also refers to Lorenzo Milani, whose pedagogy began with an inversion (subversion) of values: acknowledging the existence of illiteracy precisely where it is said not to exist, among the "uncultivated" dominant classes, particularly in the schools. Then begin with what is most urgent: the literacy education of the educators.

This is where we are at: joint, experimental cultural action, taken in partnership, in the game of the inversion of values in which a radical inversion has already taken place, namely exclusivism. The participants in the seminar left in search of a new language and other social, material and mental conditions in order to better "hear" the words and knowledge of the excluded. This conclusion of the book will, I hope, reflect the spirit and the letter of the meeting.

1. A Seminar: Beginning and End

A variety of associations

Who came to the Namur Seminar? What was the profile of the associations? Without trying to construct a scientific classification, one can for practical purposes distinguish the various associations according to their functions, their clienteles, their partners, their localities, their organization in relation to the national or regional public authorities, their messages, etc. The diversity and the marked differences among the associations will keep us from trying to reconstruct a unidimensional account and from trying to offer a uniform description of a movement made up of distinct positions and obeying no one comprehensive directive.

- There are some de facto associations that are destined for a very short, or not a very long life; all the others are registered or incorporated, and are destined to last. The "pool" of governmental and non-governmental organizations of S. Gregorio in Portugal, as well as the European network coordinated by the Centre universitaire de formation continue (CUFCO) of Angers in France, whose participating members change each year on the occasion of their meetings, are of the first type.

- While the two Portuguese associations are mostly composed of representatives from government organizations, they cannot be said to simply constitute a body which coordinates public services in which local organizations simply happen to "appear". The autonomy of the field teams is imperative, as is the case with an association which has local, individual and organizational partners. But the above two projects were created as a result of a planned decision. Once the three-year and the five-year programs are over, the budgets essentially come to an end and the associations are dissolved.

- The degree of autonomy vis-à-vis the State varies considerably. In Flanders, a network of associations which are registered as non-profit-making is entirely under the direction of a ministry. Their organization was the subject of a decree. In Belgium's French community, the network of community organizations practically covers the whole field of literacy education, but the work status of the participants and their training come under government policy. In Ireland, as is the case with Whitfield Adult Basic Education Trust (WABET) in Scotland, autonomy is almost complete, except for some very modest subsidies. In France, Action-Formation-Etude-Recherche (AFER) is quite autonomous, even self-managed, but a large portion of its funding is derived from national "mechanisms" which are of a constraining nature. The three present Quebec associations (2 local and one provincial) are relatively autonomous like their Francophone Belgian, Irish and Scottish counterparts, but feel the pressure of a uniform national program and of extensive local and provincial educational authorities.

- To a great extent the economy of the organizations depends on the situations described above. Some of them, it seems, are comfortable, stable, "super equipped" and do not keep track of the length of international telephone communications. Others are forced to ask that calls be postponed and live below the poverty level: two examples being the Irish National Adult Literacy Agency (NALA) network and La Jarnigoine in Montreal.

- There are regional or national associations which coordinate a network of local organizations, namely of local associations which offer front-line services, and which may also be associations of associations (as is the case with WABET).

- Not all the associations come under the label of literacy education, except in Portugal, where they are part of integrated development projects. None of them really do so in Scotland and Flanders, where the issue is basic education. Some of them do so to a very slight extent, as is the case with AFER where personalized training is provided. Some are a little more involved in literacy education, for example the Unité de formation Cannes-Méditerrannée (UFCM), a small training unit for everyone at all levels.

- Finally, the associations differ from each other according to the places where they intervene and their public. Their activities unfold within the communities where they work, in their own premises or, lacking these, within public facilities made available to them by the municipalities, educational organizations, etc. Their public can be unique or varied, voluntarily heterogeneous or homogeneous, living in a "ghetto" or dispersed. But in the great majority of cases, the associations devote themselves and belong to a specific space, a neighbourhood, a unit of low rental housing, or in a social, cultural community of varying composition (women, immigrants, or young people on the one hand, a community of gypsies, a village, a segregated neighbourhood on the other).

The picture that emerges contains many contrasts, but it is far from representing all organizations which are involved in literacy education. Many original or innovative types of association were not represented at this seminar, one of its characteristics being that it was mainly Francophone, either as a language of origin of the participants or as a second language.

How were the participants selected? Mainly on the basis of two criteria: the known quality of their work and of the persons who perform it - the association's trade mark, with an emphasis on applied research and innovation - and intervention beside/outside the educational field, which also presupposes experimental activities outside the "mainstream" in the struggle against illiteracy. In addition, the participants included ideologists who are firmly engaged in the community organizations movement, and coordinators of national and international networks.

Among the thirty or so persons who were present, about fifteen of them had agreed to write, with or without my collaboration, a monograph on their field work or an article based on a research activity in which they were involved.

Expectations

Some barely visible tendencies were identifiable at the beginning even before participants had had time to introduce themselves, to come to know each other, to exchange views, to begin to draw or move away from each other, to isolate themselves and to confront each other.

- One of those tendencies has to do with the search for an "integral approach", or how an association can succeed when dealing with powerful sectors, such as the public and private sectors, while at the same time preserving its identity. The two key terms are strength and partnership. They attract each other, but what is at stake is the association's identity and autonomy. It is clear that one cannot act effectively and extend one's scope of action in isolation and with precarious means. Government spokesmen are no longer the only possible or preferred partners. When concentrating on the local and regional level, one must widen the partnership and be able to associate with powerful sectors: the economic and financial sectors, the political sector, elected municipal officials, public services, the community organizations sector, the university, etc. If what is collectively at stake is the fight against exclusivism, then one must acquire the means that are needed in order to succeed. It is of concern to the whole of society. It must do more.

- From the above two key words, strength and partnership, another set of expectations is discernible which can be expressed with the words liberty, alternative, counterbalance, specificity, and autonomy. The search for effective action, presence, and a more solid association with the various partners implies an autonomous position vis-à-vis the public authorities and the "stong powers". The question was phrased as follows: "How does one associate oneself with the public authorities and at the same time gain in autonomy"? Or: "How far can one go and still be innovative and preserve one's identity"?

- Another view is also that of a movement that is at its last gasp, and which will soon have no other choice than to integrate with the public sector or give up an overly exhausting fight. How does one resolve this dilemma? Must one continue to fight simply in order to preserve a hardly recognized association status, to defend what has been gained, and to win a political support which only assures survival? Must one do this for a cause whose results are hardly visible, when the means continue to diminish, partners cannot be found, and the fighting spirit is at its lowest ebb? Or, to put it differently, how does one win acknowledgement for the important role played by an association movement committed to socio-cultural activities aimed at fighting poverty when these activities have been institutionalized and public investments in them have already been judged as too burdensome?

- Expectations, on the other hand, are high with respect to the practical work done in the area of literacy education. What are the means available to render students more independent and more responsible for their own learning? How does one evaluate the work done so as to be able to communicate the results in a more convincing manner? What else can be done to stimulate the mobilization and commitment of new partners? How does one link literacy education to an integrated development program? How does one break down the division between the work done on behalf of literacy and the more specific problem of education?

- For many, it is unusual to participate in an international seminar on the theme of experiments in literacy education within the community organizations movement. The event occurred at a time when many variables were shared within the international community: the growth of exclusivism, the search for strategies for intervention other than "targeted literacy education" (alpha-bétisation ponctuelle), the tendency towards the institutionalization of associations within the context of new legislation on basic education. Therefore, it is an opportune time to learn to discover, exchange, make known, and reflect on local experiences through a multinational and inter-personal exchange.

- A book is now in progress, actually the present group's only joint international project. How can it be used, made known, and disseminated better? But that comes later... What research activity should one undertake to further this cooperation begun within an international network of community oganizations? How can an organization such as the Unesco Institute for Education help stimulate innovation and the search for greater effectiveness in our actions?

These were the expectations of the group at the beginning of the seminar. One must realize that the agenda for the meeting was not a smorgasbord of unprecedented questions, or that the participants did not have the spare time to organize the exchange of ideas as they wished. A great portion of the seminar was structured on the basis of the sketch contained in the table of contents: reports, comments, and questions. It was difficult to maintain a flow in the series of questions and direct answers due to the time taken up by translation. It was only at the end of the proceedings, and always on borrowed time, that it was possible to exchange more freely and to collectively seek what should be done next.

Consequences

The aim of the closing exercise was not to avoid ending the seminar with ideological discussions, but to arrive at detailed plans of action which were realistic and applicable at the local level.

We were finally able to speak of the community organizations movement as a whole if only to inquire into its unity, its consensus and the priority of joint action at the international level. Positions are varied. For some, local action should come first. Another international event is conceivable only after local work has been done to justify it. For others, this movement contains too many contradictions. On the one hand, the associations are often in competition with each other. On the other hand, they do not use the same language. And how is it to acquire greater credibility when there is a tendency to indulge in self-deprecation, thus projecting a very negative picture of literacy education?

Two minimum "undertakings" are proposed to the associations so that they may become more coherent and "improve their credit" in their transactions with public and private authorities:

- recognize that literacy education can be an end in itself, as a legitimate democratic demand of society;

- project a positive image of the work involved in literacy education and of the people one works with.

The political value of the issue is sufficiently powerful for it to be made part of local development strategies which can then be strengthened by international support: i.e., a political value derived from positive action at the local or regional level. To these possibilities for a constructive association movement one can add the proposal for joint research for an association charter which would serve as a means of liaison between a local association, a regional or national network fighting against exclusivism, and a commitment at the international level.

Another possible initiative is the establishment of an international link between two local organizations, i.e. twinning or the association of two literacy education networks on the model of twinning between municipalities. The aim of this would be to create the conditions for inter-cultural exchanges between learners, between trainers, and between organizations which share the same willingness to escape from a condition of marginality. Two literacy education associations are now working along these lines. This project can be extended. It is expensive. How can it be financed?

As for the usefulness of creating a new and more formal network of associations, it was pointed out that several networks exist and that the exchanges between networks of community organizations could benefit from the use of existing channels. The publication *Alpha 92*, as well as the Namur seminar are an initiative of the Unesco Institute for Education, which already coordinates an international exchange network. This network overlaps the European Network for Training, Action and Research in Literacy Education as well as an international bulletin published by UNESCO (*Adult Education Information Notes*).

The group that was present consisted mainly of authors gathered around the same publishing project, and not of official representatives of national groups. This gathering represented the end of the book. It was still necessary to ensure an efficient distribution and to render it useful to associations at the local level.

It was suggested that a reading guide be prepared, based on the questions dealt with during the siminar, to ensure a more practical use of the texts within the training and learning groups. It was suggested that summaries be prepared and published in local bulletins, to facilitate distribution. It was recommended that the comments on the texts also be published in local bulletins, in order to facilitate their distribution. It was recomended that the comments on the texts also be published;[2] that this publication be made better known in Anglophone countries (published in English since 1990, it is also published in Spanish in 1992) and that possibilities for its publication in Portuguese be explored.

If promoted vigorously, the book may also serve as a powerful medium for the mobilization of the social and political partners. Excerpts could be circulated at municipal council meetings. To make profitable use of its international value at the local level, it is suggested that one of the authors be invited at organizational or training sessions.

One theme has been put forward for the next publication of *Alpha*: participatory research. How are learners to be made to participate in research?

Usually, an assembly of this type tries to adopt at least a minimum amount of organization so that it can be set up again at another place; it sets aside some time for its organization; it sets a rhythm, routines; it gets people involved. There was no follow-up to the idea of a charter for the community organizations movement, for twinning, for affirmative action, nor any other follow-up to the *Alpha* publication, except at the local level. The focus for action is mainly local.

But much was said about another book, written by "the excluded". The animators working in literacy education have passed the ball to those who were not there. In addition, it was proposed that the ideas and projects launched during the seminar be presented to the students in the associations. It is for them to decide what follow-up there should be. They already constitute an international community: one must find the means for facilitating the circulation of their writings, to create opportunities for exchanges in foreign languages, both among individuals and groups.

This is the main theme of this conclusion of the seminar. If one must still speak of strategies for the community organizations movement, one must look for them in the *conditions that must be created so that the excluded can produce real writings of their own*: creating a place where individual and collective writings can be published; making local initiatives and productions known; circulating newspapers written by students; opening a writing competition between several countries and several languages; having a bookmobile travel on an international circuit; organizing writing, speaking, visual, and musical events such as a book fair, a poetry/video/theatre festival, etc.

To stimulate expression, communication, the exchange of ideas through genuine writing which is rooted in life and not in pedagogical simulation, also presupposes that the trainers or animators are "converted" and "sensitized". However, they can also block expression because they have the power to decide who is capable, who is authorized to write. Sessions on literacy education must be addressed to the animators-educators, as recommended by Milani. That can be done also in seminars, colloquia, through newspapers, etc.

There were, however, some dissenting voices with respect to this writing project. The "learners" are not there, we cannot decide for them. The experience of the International Literacy Year Book, put together by the "professionals", will have been a negative experience as an opportunity for "learners" to express themselves. A writing competition runs the danger of promoting its organizers rather than the unheard voices. Also, this mobilization by means of writings by the participants supposes that a lot of groundwork has been laid for all protagonists. A message which merely says that "you can write" will not do.

An *itinerary for the circulation of the writings,* for the book collection, has been arranged between Brussels, Lille, Lyon, Madrid, Québec and Edinburgh, which overlaps with the twinning between Cannes and Namur and a popular culture event.

An *applied research project on the theme of the writings produced by the "excluded"* was considered, to be supported by the Unesco Institute for Education (UIE). The coordinators of the Collectif d'alphabétisation de Bruxelles, of the Comité de liaison pour l'alphabétisation et la promotion (CLAP, Lyon) and UIE will meet to develop this research plan and seek the means for implementing it.

2. A Mixed Balance Sheet on Literacy Education

The national contexts of the work performed by the associations determine to a great extent the analysis that they produce regarding the difficulties that are encountered and the results that are obtained. Also determining are their ideologies, the ways in which they view their work and the aims of literacy education, which in turn are also linked to the history of each movement within its own particular national or regional context.

The difficulties facing the associations

In Francophone Belgium, as in Quebec, the associations reflect the condition of their own public: poverty. The evaluation made of the difficulties and limits of the work done in the area of literacy education to a great extent reflects the precarious means available for this work: personnel which is under-qualified, inexperienced, unstable, voluntary; permanent staff members who are overworked, exhausted, discouraged; the loss of the more competent people to positions that have better status and are better paid. Poverty causes not only the instability and de-activation of the personnel, but also instability in the planning of activities, forecasts, and investments. In the Namur region, an intensive mobilization campaign in the fight against illiteracy ended with the disturbing realization that it was impossible to meet the growing demand. The means were simply not there.

The difficult working conditions that are common to Quebec and Wallonia, to which one might add Ireland and the UK at the present liberal-ultra conservative political juncture, are due to different circumstances. The Walloon associations occupy almost the whole field of literacy education; they rest on a great social partnership; they are recognized by the public authorities and by the municipalities; they are part of a network of very active community organizations in the fight against poverty. Their ties to the cultural and social affairs sector serves, according to the coordinators, as a guarantee of their autonomy and the broad range of their involvement in education for the disadvantaged.

By comparison, the Quebec associations try to survive in a more adverse environment. They constitute only a small portion of the literacy education sector, often on a sub-contracting basis. Their obligatory partner is the educational system, which has the legitimate mandate for literacy education, absorbing most of the public resources allocated to it. Although recognized as adult education organizations, their autonomy in the area of education for the disadvantaged is quite limited within the framework of a single national program. They can no longer rely on a multi-purpose network of independent organizations which have not survived ten years of budgetary restrictions and general impoverishment. With some exceptions, they now have no other choice but to work for the educational system, with the advantages and negative consequences that that entails, consequences which resemble those noted in Dutch-speaking Belgium.

In Flanders, basic education has been semi-nationalized. The associations come under a provision administered by the Education sector. The difficulties described by G. Gehre are dreadful, but the comparison with the Quebec situation renders them very similar. The inter-sectorial cooperation of local centres exists only in their boards of directors. The work on literacy education tends to be subjected to educational administration: "a problematic situation must always be isolated and be translated into an educational program of a specific duration...This danger of formalized schooling is real". This means centralized programming, distancing of "learners" (also known as "clients", as in Quebec), standardized recruitment of educators and standardization of their tasks, above all the search for profitability calculated in terms of the rate of growth of the clientele ("consolidation of supply"), and consequently the marginalization if not the abandonment of a "social" approach to literacy education, and courses that are in demand are favoured, such as second-language courses.

In the two Portuguese experiences, the main difficulties encountered by the field teams were similar due to the inter-institutional nature of the associations. Local activity is dependent on the traditions and institutions to which it is attached, traditions and ideologies which can come into conflict with each other. The local team is subjected to the hierarchical structure of the bureaucratic mechanisms, as opposed to the search for dialogic relationships in the field. But the two experiments have also demonstrated that the institutional nature of the interventions was not incompatible with local activity that was self-directed, open to a partnership with local organizations; also, that a social service can be better equipped to perform this type of intervention than adult education.

The experiment at S. Gregorio involving a gypsy community revealed some of the major cultural difficulties inherent in an intervention which cannot be isolated from the incompatible relationships between the majority and a minority which exist in society. The field team's determination and methodology were not enough to overcome this fact. The literacy education which is imposed (by all evidence) for the purpose of integration and development is seen by the gypsies as an acculturation which threatens the survival of their group. The process of change directed from the outside has the effect of strengthening the group's solidarity, as evidenced by attitudes of "resistance to change", which are also expressions of cultural assertiveness.

This fundamentally conflictual inter-cultural parameter noted at S. Gregorio can be transposed to the inter-class relationship which separates - without always opposing - the animators and the participants in literacy-related activities. Participation cannot be forced, particularly in an educational project which generally is not a priority for the target population. The value of this participation, central in the ideology of many organizations, is not shared "naturally" by the "participants". Strategies for the channelling of the learning objectives, or even for the substitution of educational objectives by social services or actions are necesary to attract this participation. Even in this case, "the difficulty," said Omer Arrijs, "is to go beyond the stage of selling a social service or form of social assistance, in order to initiate a process of education or training for the disadvantaged".

The relationships between animators-trainers and participants-learners can be antagonistic. Francesco Azzimonti sees the role of literacy workers as a possible obstacle to the initiation and exchange of written communication. Describing their partners as incompetent, handicapped or oppressed, the trainers have declared them unfit for any written contribution which is not part of a pedagogical exercise. One gets the impression that such an environment is not considered attractive by the new pariahs! It is to be expected, therefore, that one of the main difficulties identified a bit everywhere by the literacy workers can be defined as a "problem of motivation". As in the case of gypsies or any other proletarianized minority, absence may indeed be understood as a refusal to attend for a reason, and the diagnosis made by the educators may be viewed as a denial based on a knowledge and identity of the targeted victims. "Those who are excluded do not want to come!" This is undoubtedly the main difficulty in the recent history of literacy education, a difficulty which many associations have been unable to resolve, regardless of the national context.[3]

In contrast with the Walloon and Quebec associations is the case of associations which provide a public service on the model of a private enterprise; i.e. possessing means deemed sufficient thanks to a favorable national situation (a crisis, unemployment!), thanks to a partnership with many regional organizations and, undoubtedly, thanks to a "recognized professional expertise". The animators from AFER point to institutionalization as the special difficulty of this situation where one has put "too much water in one's wine". The contradiction between the organization's explicit objectives - autonomy, self-management, self-directed learning - and those of the partner organizations - socio-professional rehabilitation, technical training - which have determined the "specifications" turns the action in question into a sham. If the aims of the association do not change, then the appearance of the contradiction is clearly viewed as "self-dissolution". F. Gosset and D. Andreau verbally added the following sub-title to their text: "How much should we restrain our desire to develop!"

Finally, one major difficulty for many associations which intervene in an international situation characterized by the breakdown of dualistic societies and the swelling of the ranks of the excluded, is the impossibility of sustaining the objective of literacy education when the real demand is for aid or for resistance to the exasperation caused by the conditions of daily life. Olivia Oliveira concluded with the need for an active commitment within the Portuguese society in order to ensure the respect and application of the rights of man, and therefore a role of political "mediator" beyond the shantytown. At WABET, in spite of all the optimism and the priority given to the objective of community education, it was realized that a major difficulty was the dissociation of the pedagogical objective from the social objectives of the commitment to the community. At La Jarnigoine, there was reference to the strategy of giving a full expression to the voice of women. At Alpha Mons-Borinage, multiple activities in order to provide services and the political organization of the association networks involved in the fight against exclusivism was deemed inevitable. At AFER, one found it untenable to offer technical services and individualized teaching to trainers whose function (barely recognized) is on the verge of hindering collectivization and the organization of the resistance - the construction of an alternative, according to the authors - within "ghettos for people seeking long-term employment". It also happens that these questions are not raised, due to the old-fashioned militancy in the "fight against illiteracy" or to a clearly territorial professionalization of literacy education.

Thus, the national context, the position in the training market, the type of association and public, the international economic situation (in fact a structural crisis of world capitalism) are some of the factors which reflect the range of difficulties faced by associations working in literacy education. These difficulties are part of the still encouraging list of "results" achieved by associations, albeit results which are not always those that were expected.

The results

It is a shared view that the evaluation of the results achieved in community literacy education cannot be confused with a measure of individual learning, in technical, linguistic or educational terms. Even in the Portuguese context, where complete illiteracy is very widespread and where literacy education also has this objective of educational learning (certificates are issued), "the evaluation must be made within a more comprehensive context where the scope of the results goes beyond the amount of school learning" (O. Oliveira).

Excluded from the theme of this seminar were questions pertaining to individualized learning. Most of the participants conceived their work as a search for the real conditions - in real life - conducive to communication, expression, exchange, production of meaning, identity, culture, and accepted knowledge, worthy of being shared and transmitted. Here, among many others, are two clear expressions of this:

> Without a strategy for intervention, literacy education remains an empty shell without substance, an academic task devoted to failure on all fronts. (Sylvie Roy)

> Learning is about creating knowledge (reading the world), strengthening voices that have been silenced (writing who you are) and telling others what you have discovered (reaching an audience). (Barton, Hamilton and Ivanic)[4]

The individual results sought are to be found less in the process of written expression and more in the change of attitudes, in the view of the world and the involvement in concrete action for development. One loves to quote Paulo Freire: "Knowledge cannot be transfered, it is created within and through action which affects reality." The results to be looked for range from changes which are imperceptible, ordinary, and "anecdotal" regarding daily life to political organization on a much larger scale ("to theory" - Elise de

Coster) in the fight against exclusivism, in the reclaiming of democratic rights or even in the implementation of other collective models of development, thus breaking with the dominant practices (see P. Georis). Here, within these *anti-literacy education* practices operating in solidarity with the marginalized populations, one cannot apply the individualized evaluation criteria of the "dominant" model of literacy which is "functional" and which aims at "socio-vocational integration". Here is an example drawn from the conclusion of two years of field work with the Portuguese gypsies:

- make the inter-cultural relationship more solid,

- give a constructive meaning to the gypsies'demands,

- try to meet survival requirements under the best conditions,

- fight the feeling of powerlessness,

- arrange better learning conditions for the young, while aiming for greater independence,

- ensure that human rights are respected,

- work towards endogenous cultural development rather than towards integration, etc.

In this as in many other cases, writing is not listed in the priorities for action (except for the teaching of children). The objectives of intervention were redefined during the activity, by correcting the initial "errors" which were due to ethnocentrism and misunderstanding on the part of the participants. These have redefined their roles by transforming their research activity into a process of intercultural dialogue. What have been the results of two years of intensive intervention? They have been immense, even if one must start all over again!

The animators' self-evaluations apparently contain a number of discouraging observations that might be described as "culs de sac" or as an "acute awareness of dead-ends". Those who are most excluded do not attend. For those who do come and who stay, the services provided do not at all change the exclusion relationship and even strengthen it: "Literacy education delimits and widens the gap it claims to bridge" (O. Arrijs). But in view of these generally negative results, as insurmountable as the difficulties and as unrealizable as the objectives striven for may be, given the short time available for action, many of the evaluations are still positive. A very small sign of change can have exponential effects. As conveyed in this observation by Madalena Dias:

> A large portion of the population remained passive, but it began to understand the movement...The number of those who joined exceeded the expectations of all participants. The existence of an unthought-of movement became visible. It involved other activities...It began to generate its own model of participation.

Similar observations are made by Blair Denwette in Scotland, where the strategy for implementation in the community yielded the results anticipated with respect to the involvement of individuals and local associations - "with the community" - and even in the commitment of some individuals in basic educational work - "by the community". All the associations experienced some changes which were significant, visible, observable and analyzed, which allow the objectivization of activities, the critique of prior premises, experimentation with new tactics, liaison and exchange with outside groups, the organization of larger networks of solidatry and education for the disadvantaged.

Among the conditions required for successful action, in addition to the essential principle of community participaion, many participants emphasize the importance of the time factor. The strategy of small steps at a time does not produce significant results over the short term. "Change is very slow". The work in the areas of culture, the development of language, material, geographical, symbolic exchanges in a community and the transformation of relations between a community and the outside partners supposes planning over a three, five or six-year period, as well as a permanent field team and the flexible development of the sequence of activities. For example, at S. Gregorio the field study goes on throughout the duration of the intervention. It changes with time. Its traditional pre-literacy function tends to encompass even literacy education. Observation through participation turns into a gradual beginning of a real dialogue with the community, a rare liaison, and a vehicle for joint projects. It takes years for this approach to reverse an exclusivist relationship that took root precisely where its existence is denied: between the participants and their assistants. The desired result is to be sought in this very process of the transformation of the rules which govern the exchange.

Often, the activity is evaluated on the basis of the extent to which initial objectives are achieved. Here, the value of the activity is assessed in relation to changing objectives. The desired quality does not lie in the technique used in applying the rules of method: it lies in the degree of flexibility and malleability, in the degree to which action is adapted to circumstances (O. Oliveira). At S. Gregorio, it is surprising that the direction of change was reversed. For a long time, it was the gypsies who had to change. Faced with the so-called "resistance to change" on the part of the gypsies, the interveners changed. Beginning with a position where the desired aim was progress, they ended up with the "recognition of their human dignity", of "acceptance" and "respect" for differences, the "meeting of cultures, "bilateral information", "dialectical interrelation", and "dialogue". This radical reversal of values and of the meaning of literacy education germinated for three years. This has led to a new realization of what cultural intervention really involves: "Unless some relationships between the two cultures are changed and counteracted, they risk becoming a form of 'cultural genocide'".

Hence the force behind the argument made by Milani which was shared by many participants at the seminar: literacy education needs first to be directed at the literacy workers, otherwise they risk foisting on others their own views regarding illiteracy since their actions have the effect of reinforcing their own scornful conviction rather than changing the condition of their victims.

A final evaluation of the work done on behalf of literacy education in an organization which claims to be an alternative school for the young while integrating community action, should assess the shift that has taken place from emphasis on the nature of the results to be attained to the self-criticism that is necessary for literacy education to occur:

> The young always have urgent needs to be met in addition to literacy education. If we must identify results in our work, it must be precisely the degree to which affective and social needs have been met...The two

most important needs continue to be work and social and loving relations, as is the case with all of us...Reading and writing continues to be the vaguest and most difficult expectation to realize. (S. Roy)

3. Literacy in the Plural

There are some associations which shamelessly label their "clientele" as illiterate or uneducated. It is made up of individuals who are handicapped and in need of assistance of a psychosocial, pedagogical, and therapeutic nature. Literacy education should be a special kind of intervention, in a location identified as such, conducted by personnel ranging from volunteers to re-educators and up to professional psychologists. The service provided for the development of language abilities seeks to meet the practical demands of written communication or recycling within a training program, while at the same time rehabilitating the individuals with respect to their self-image and their relationship with their immediate surroundings. One could call this type of intervention psychopedagogical.

Other associations have a more social approach. The "illiterates" are above all people who have been excluded, not handicapped but normal people who have been marginalized from the ordinary channels of social interaction. They make up the growing class of "losers" in the dual society. There, literacy is understood as an attempt at re-integration into the interaction networks at the community and socio-linguistic level as well as an attempt at multifaceted assistance in solving some of the daily problems connected with poverty. The basic or supplemental language training is not always a front-line service. It may be combined with a whole series of "transversal" services or community activities. The typical profile of the intervener is that of a social animator possessing a different training, or even an inter-disciplinary team which also provides education for the disadvantaged.

There are some associations of a third kind, whose relationship to literacy education is more cultural than social. For these, illiteracy is mainly the ethnocentric attribute applied by the dominant institutions to the minorities and to certain proletarianized cultural groups. To rectify the proclaimed linguistic, educational and cultural "deficit", they offer experiences based on different linguistic and cultural heritages. Their actions are part of a desire to advance minority individuals and groups rather than of a unified, often nationalistic, offensive to "fight illiteracy". These associations which work within someone else's culture tend to define their interventions as an antidote, or as a different sort of literacy education. This consists mainly in a better arrangement of the conditions for endogenous cultural expression, finding opportunities for inter-cultural communication, and for validating differences.

This triad of associations has simplified reality considerably. The associations tend, in varying degrees, to share a combination of these conceptions and practices which are also objectively based on the type(s) of public with whom they work. However, the scheme does help to identify the various positions with respect to aims, limits, and strategies of literacy education as well as with respect to their evaluation.

Within the group as a whole, the first position which views literacy education as a "specific" educational service aimed at adults who do not know how to read and write, or not very well, represents a minority of organizations. Literacy education can be viewed as an end in itself from the theoretical or legal point of view that everyone has the right to a minimum education. Its reduction to a technical intervention, however, is generally associated with the public adult education services whose vocation is to ensure this specialized and universal function, or with networks of community organizations under the control of public organizations responsible for national basic training programs.

For some, literacy education as such refers to a by-gone age. It has not yielded the expected results. It was based on an unrealistic vision of its potential and on an illusion with respect to how necessary it was, other than from the point of view of the literacy workers. The aggressive approach to the "fight against illiteracy" could only result in the consolidation of the new professional clan of literacy workers, while better sorting out the desired clientele. Moreover, in view of the doubtful results of this "primitive" mobilization (here we are speaking of the "prehistory of literacy education"), the offerings of basic education have expanded in terms of course material and learning, and it has been considerably extended to the public at numerous levels, profiles and projects. It has also lost its initial designation as literacy education by adopting a rather wide range of labels (for which a census should be taken!).

For others, work focused on writing and reading is in no way excluded, but it cannot be conducted by itself. It must be part of life as a whole and integrated into the social calendar of local communities. While literacy education is not an independent or priority need, all others needs nevertheless are related to it. The regeneration of the social space, as the identity of the individuals who live within it (poorly), is accomplished by means of this "transversal process of basic education", as described at WABET. In a comprehensive development project, linguistic training is integrated within a "broader process of social rehabilitation".

The "decompartmentalizing" of adult literacy education is particularly applicable to generations. In a community approach, prority goes to the literacy education and schooling of the young. Literacy education among mothers, after-school daycare, Saturday workshops, work with teachers, literacy work with the young "to heal injury caused by school", community activities integrating children, liaison and joint activities with youth organizations, these are just some of the examples cited which seek to link adult literacy education with that of the young generations as well as with educators in the educational system. Such contacts, contrary to professional and institutional territoriality, can sometimes generate conflict and close other doors, as seen in the example from Portugal.

For many, literacy education as part of a more comprehensive cultural, social or community action has moved from the classroom to the street, to the neighbourhood, to other associations, to places where real production takes place: it has been emancipated from the specialized educational space so as to operate "in real life". Where it is still identified with a specific place, it is called shop, home, centre, local, etc. There, it no longer exists independently, it is explicitly tied to its social context. It is open, it operates as a network, it acts in interaction with other community partners, it delegates much of its work to other local organizations. The picture that emerges is that of an exploded centre whose varied activities involving "communication" and "global expression" can in fact only develop within this multifaceted interaction and exchange.

This breaking down of barriers also affects the distinction between the tutor or trainer on the one hand, and the learner or participant on the other. They can be confused because of their social origin: they must come from the same environment, and speak the same language. One may attempt to trace the educational distance which separates them: the interveners will be recruited on the basis of social commitment and community experience and not on the basis of "recognized competence". Some also want to view the role of learner as autonomous by acknowledging his power to self-manage his projects or the role of self-trainer, the latter being justifiable only as the facilitator of the transfer. Where these statutory distinctions are clearly rejected, the people involved in the various collective projects will be represented as actors performing multiple roles, having the same democratic rights and the same demands. Thus, one has gone from a univalent "learner" to a "participant" wearing several hats, the main difference remaining being that between permanent employee or salaried employee versus volunteer or participant who lives in a "precarious state".

This tendency to view the two sides as the same or as similiar, however, in place of the traditional dual relationship, is criticized for several reasons. It can camouflage manipulation on a massive scale; it creates an egalitarian mythology which hinders the development of needed services; it deprives professionals of their identity, of their very own language and of suitable techniques for intervention. These limits apply particularly to the purposes of literacy education in the narrow sense (learning how to write), which must be distinguished from socialization activities, as well as to the places where these activities occur which should not be confused with a "drop-in" centre. Finally, the tendency to expand literacy education is not carried to its logical conclusion.

It should be pointed out that there are many illiterate people who justify "technical" work and that the role of teachers of reading and writing is central to an integrated team. For Omer Arrijs for example, even if "the solution for us is not the same as it is in society", courses have not been given up in the literacy education centre, rather they are being developed.

One subject which generates broad consensus, in spite of the differences of contexts and tendencies evoked, is the concept of literacy education within the social process associated with education for the disadvantaged. This type of education is part of a real social space, "in real life". Therefore, it creeps into the language, into the values, in the exchanges within a local community in order to render explicit or create meaning and value, to develop the force of expression and of demands, to find new partners and attempt to open the closed spaces of those who are in seclusion. One no

468

longer believes in the sublime aims of "the liberation of the oppressed", not even through their imminent rehabilitation under the impetus of human rights and dignity. Experience has shown that intervention leads less to the breaking down, and more to the management of the spheres of exclusion which in fact are becoming more extensive. We all know that desired results are mitigated and deferred to the distant future. Nevertheless, action in literacy education implies the commitment of participants beyond an immediate individual interest, as is the case when professional technical services are provided. Work in the areas of language, meaning and communication opens up new possibilities for exchange and dialogue that until now were closed.

The aim of this work common to most of the actors involved in this research[5] is not integration, nor admission, nor any other social recompense promised at the end of the activity. Rather, it lies in changing the course of events or in the opening of avenues other than submission to what appears to be beyond remedy. Everyone believes that language conceals this subtle force, and that is what they are trying to develop through what is still known as literacy education.

Conclusion

The conclusions of the seminar have been presented. In this synthesis, I have attempted to describe the various types of presentation, while being careful not to ignore the differences and seeking to place the various positions within their local and national contexts. In closing, I will try to highlight once again the main tendencies of the proceedings of the associations, so that they will not be confused with strategies. These tendencies point to diachronous and synchronous changes in meaning, of movement within various groups which must be differentiated from intentional change motivated by any one strategy or line of thinking.

The initial title of the seminar has not been changed: Literacy Strategies in Community Organizations ("Stratégies d'alphabétisation dans le mouvement associatif"). It should have been changed. Community organizations are not unified, they do not have a strategy. Groups of community organizations do not seek to win the battle in the fight against illiteracy. They do not present a common front against an imaginary enemy or against a perceived danger. They constitute small units whose main quality is undoubtedly their adaptability to local conditions, precisely where it is hardest. Their main aim is to generate solidarity, which in turn achieves its ends through the learning of a language, through dialogue, through exchange, and the development of a stronger voice.

Thus, one of the main characteristics of these heterogeneous associations is to operate differently, independently and beyond the limited territories of strong organizations. The most common distancing that is taking place is vis-à-vis the school: "It is not enough to perfect the educational model and to attach it to the extra-curricular sector: they must be transformed together on the basis of social strategies and practices" (M. Dias).

The second type of mobility consists of the transfer of special-ized professional facilities towards ordinary social mechanisms in daily life. The place where the action occurs tends to be confused with "real life", with its familiar routines, and is integrated into the community calendar.

The shift implies a change in the rules of the game. The actors are polyvalent and constitute a motley group; if possible they have emerged from the "milieu", from the "ordinary world" as they say in Quebec. The principle of autonomy means that one is forced to find one's own means and discipline for self-management.

A local association overlaps with the texture of solidarity whose common locus is precisely what is marginal - i.e. a local, precarious, and repressed element which exists outside the confines of conven-tional social space. It gains by becoming part of a larger integrated organization, a federation, a "network". But the local action also supposes that one works in conjunction with the legitimate powers and certain strong organizations: these tactical combinations are known as "partnerships". This is something which is being eagerly sought at this time.

One does not avoid politicians, but one no longer confronts them as in the past through slogans, in close ranks or as a party. One invites them to the site, to the locale, in order to reach a pact or sign a charter (of non-aggression, of solidarity, on respect for human rights, on the right to dignity, etc.). Politicians have been displaced. In zones where exclusion exists, one looks for the means of survival, for legitimacy, for an alternative to illusory inclusion, which is sometimes intentionally refused. This is valuable both for the economy and for culture: it is a search for other values, ranging from an attempt to make room for those suffering from repression to the establishment of toleration, indeed to be accepting in spite of everything.

Is this a new ideology? Recent history has rendered the idea of crisis commonplace, it has widened its effects, enormously widened the manpower affected, and linked things universally, things which until recently were viewed on a continental or national scale. The proletariat will not come to power, thank you! The positive values which today animate action within these associations are: solidarity for the respect and application of human rights, alternative organization for self-centered development, creation of networks for exchange in everyday life, liaison between the local and the global through the regular telephone, for want of other electronic means.

And what about literacy education? There are still many traces left of past "mechanisms", of campaigns for the eradication of illiteracy or utopias for development. Many associations also work in the pay of strong institutions which have planned continuing education as a substitute for work and for delinquency. Others have created many compartments and experimented with numerous communication tactics, speech, and exchange of knowledge, etc.

The pedagogical ideology of literacy education is no longer an area trodden by many associations or, if it is, spitefully. The "specifications" assure the "perennial" nature of these organizations, but they are too burdensome. In the area of language, as elsewhere, resistance is being organized against exclusion since these organizations have by now established for themselves a long-term presence: intercultural partnerships, "joint investigations", traveling exhibitions, theatrical occupations, radio broadcasts, concerts, writing competitions...even involving people who would never have written. The Namur Seminar ended with this call for a search for the means, the conditions, and the places for broadcasting these messages or things that need to be said more freely and in different ways.

While literacy education, the word (or its regional equivalents such as basic education, learning how to read and write etc.), has not been replaced, its techniques have been employed differently and transformed into other places and circumstances, into other actions that one would like to call open rather than the closed space of pedagogy and programs associated with basic education. Experiments are being conducted with new approaches that are less technical and more tactical, allowing an appreciation of all the meanings associated with the tricky task of writing. There is also an attempt to reverse the usual direction of literacy education by focusing it on those who belong to the "included", particularly those doing the "including", the trainers and other employment officials.

"Can one still speak of literacy education?" asks F. Azzimonti.[6] The other sort of pedagogy practised among the excluded "but who are rich in knowledge, in experience, and history...will undoubtedly no longer be literacy education"; this is the conclusion, reached in a questioning sort of way, by O. Arrijs. "And what if literacy were to be the opposite of an isolated school?" asks tentatively S. Roy by way of conclusion, implying that a utopian sort of community organization is already being experimented with everywhere. As for J. L. Corzo, he ended by calling for more celebration in order to better reverse the austere moral atmosphere which characterizes the educational ethos at the lower levels. The research now under way in the field of culture and ordinary language is also infused with this spirit of enjoyment which animates all these current experiments in literacy education.

Notes

1. Ute Jaehn was absent. Elise de Coster was replaced by Maryse Perreault.

2. A report on the Namur Seminar, entitled *Stratégies d'alphabétisation dans le mouvement associatif*, is distributed free of charge by the Unesco Institute for Education. It is in French, with a summary in English.

3. Hautecoeur, Jean-Paul. 1990. Generous Offer, Flagging Demand: The Current Paradox of Literacy. In J.P. Hautecoeur, ed. *Alpha 90* (113-132). Hamburg: Unesco Institue for Education/ Montreal: Quebec Ministry of Education.

4. "Acquiring literacy means acquiring the means of knowing ("read to understand the world", to use Freire's words), to raise one's voice after one has always kept silent (write what one is) and communicate to others what one has learned (reach a public)," M. Hamilton, R. Ivanic and D. Barton.

472

5. Hautecoeur, Jean-Paul. 1991. *Action Research in Literacy*. Ottawa: National Literacy Secretariat. (Bilingual edition, French/English).

6. Azzimonti, Francesco. 1989. L'alphabétisation éclatée. *Hommes et migrations* 1119 (Feb.): 27-32.